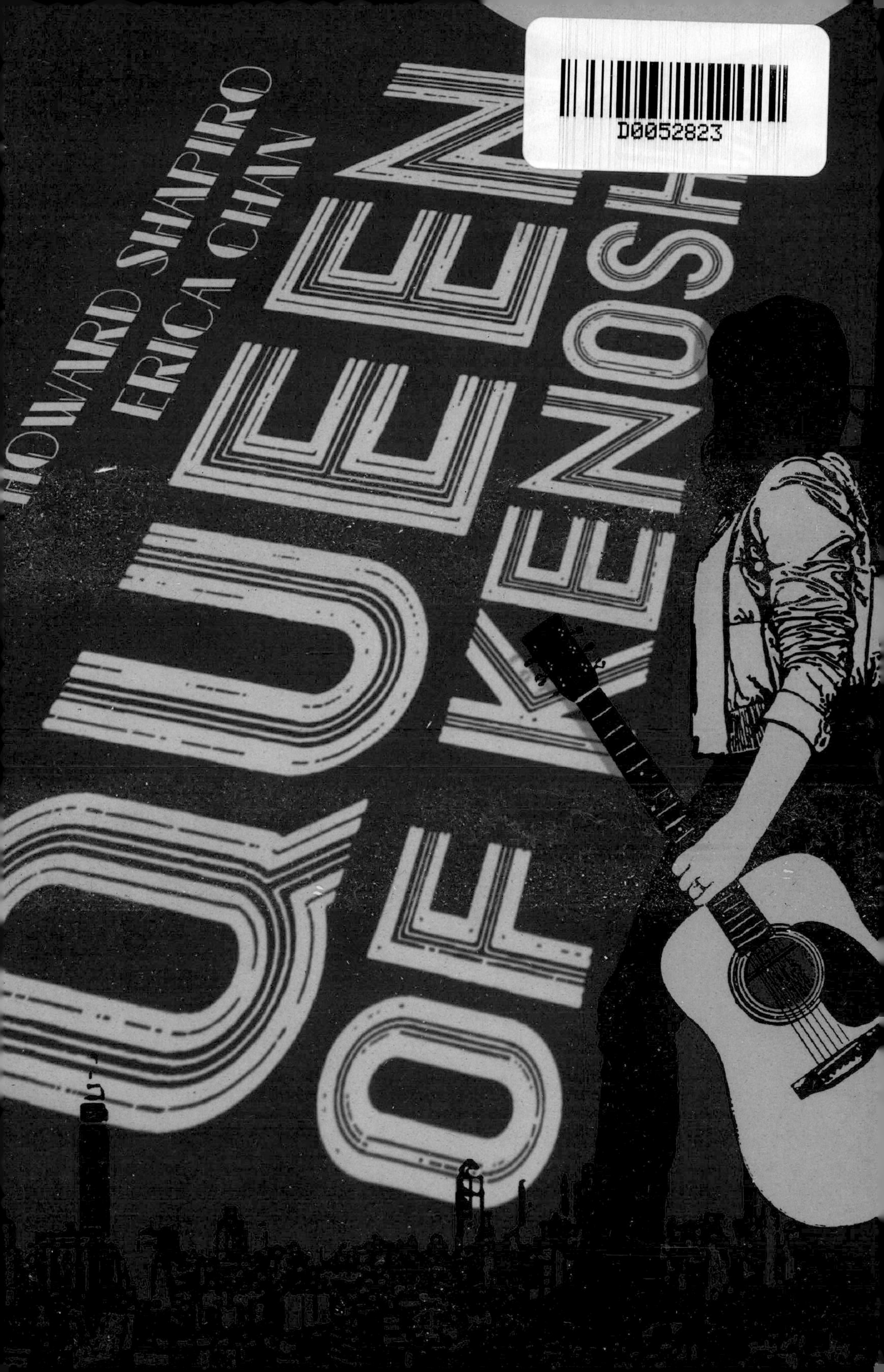
QUEEN OF KENOSHA
HOWARD SHAPIRO
ERICA CHAN

QUEEN OF KENOSHA

Howard Shapiro

Animal Media Group, LLC
Pittsburgh

Queen Of Kenosha
Copyright 2018 by Howard Shapiro

Animal Media Group books may be ordered through booksellers or by contacting:

Animal Media Group
100 1st Ave suite 1100
Pittsburgh, PA 15222
www.animalmediagroup.com

412-566-5656

Animal Media Group is distributed by Consortium Book Sales & Distribution Co

ISBN: 978-0-9974315-2-0 (pblc)
ISBN: 978-0-9974315-3-7 (eblc)

Acknowledgements:

Thanks to all of my friends at Animal Inc. and Animal Media Group LLC you guys made this all possible and for that I will always be grateful and appreciative! Bruce Springsteen, Big Country, Rush, U2, Pete Townshend, The Who, Bob Dylan, The Rolling Stones, The Clash, Green Day, Eric Clapton, Tom Petty, Stan Lee, Bob Kane, Jeff Jones, Davide DiRenzo, Kenny Greer, (the great) Jimmy Holmstrom, Scott Morrison, Joel Bloom (along with Clarence), the Catanzarite Family, Jean Vallesteros, Bryant & Barbra Dillon, Andrew Cosby, Katharine Kan, Calvin Reid, John Maher the YA and Graphic Novel book blogging communities (too many to name but thank you for all you do!)

Very special thanks to my all-star team of the great, great, great Erica Chan, Saida Temofonte, Michael Killen, Kris Boban and Shara Zaval for their creativity, vision and hard work bringing this story to life. It was a long haul my friends, but I wouldn't have wanted to make the journey without you guys by my side. Thanks to our group of beta readers whose input was invaluable – Peter Diggins, Thomas Maluck, Isaiah Roby and Jill Jemmett. Also, special thanks to Brianne Halverson for her work on the publicity and marketing fronts. I also wanted to single out and say thanks to my good friend Christina Hickey. If it wasn't for you, Christina, this book would not exist. You are a great friend and collaborator and thank you for all that you have done for me and my writing! A huge shout out to Tom Cochrane for his friendship, inspiration and the kindness extended to me over the years… you're the best, my friend! To my sister Jody Shapiro and my mom Alice Shapiro whose strength and character are second to none. I love you so much.

Extra special thanks to Gina, Sasha and Nikita, for putting up with me on a daily basis.

This book is dedicated to the loving and everlasting memory of my dad, Arnold Shapiro (7/21/31 – 11/11/05),

"Mi manchi ogni giorno e io ti amo mio caro amico"

Queen of Kenosha, A Supersonic Storybook and Animal Media Group LLC Production was filmed on location in Pittsburgh, PA, St. Louis, MO, Brooklyn, NY, Los Angeles, CA, Minneapolis, MN, Chicago, IL, Toronto, ON and of course, Kenosha, WI!

For more information please log onto *www.animalmediagroup.com* or www.howardshapiro.net. Please send your comments, questions or feedback to info@animalmediagroup.com or *hockeyplayer4life@gmail.com* Please check out my pages on Facebook *http://www.facebook.com/hockeyplayer4life* and *http://www.facebook.com/pages/Howard-Shapiro/296610707017204?ref=ts* Please also look for me on Goodreads, Instagram and on Twitter (*@hockeyplayer*)

Note From The Author:

First off, thank you for giving me and the entire team who worked on "Queen of Kenosha" the chance to share our book with you. With so many entertainment options running up against a dearth of free time for people these days, it's tremendously appreciated that you would take the time and make the effort to read our book. That is something we do not take lightly and again, we truly, truly appreciate the chance to share our story with you.

This book is completely fictional but it was greatly inspired by real life events and people. I had a great time doing research for the book in trying to make seem possible or realistic, although it is not. Along those lines I'd like to note (and thank the writers) the following articles and books were a great help to me:

"Hitler in Los Angeles: How Jews and Their Spies Foiled Nazi Plots Against Hollywood and America" book by Steven J. Ross (Bloomsbury, October 2017)

"MI5 Files: Nazis Planned 'Fourth Reich' In Post-War Europe" article by Duncan Gardham from April 2011

"Operation Pastorious" Wikipedia page

"The Truth Behind The ODESSA File" article by Guy Walters published on The Telegraph (*http://www.telegraph.co.uk*) on October 20, 2011

"20 Extraordinary Facts About CIA Extraordinary Rendition and Secret Detention" article by Jonathan Horowitz and Stacy Cammarano. Posted on February 5, 2013 in the Open Society Foundations website.

"All Female Bands of the 1960's – Happy Women's History Month" posted by Eric Brightwell on March 3, 2014 from the Amoeba Music – Amoeblog

Over the years many readers have commented positively on the "Recommended Listening" songs I put at the chapter fronts. What started out as a fun thing to do when I did "The Stereotypical Freaks" took on a whole life of its own. So, for "Queen of Kenosha" we have again listed the songs but with a wrinkle this time. As you'll notice there is one song listed on each chapter front from Nina Overstreet. Being that Nina is a fictional character these songs in real life, do not exist. But in the fictional world that we've created, they do exist and the songs listed would have been on Nina's first album in 1963. We went one step further and include at the end of the book what the cover of Nina's debut album looks like as well as the liner note/lyric sheet.

We hope you enjoy the story and hope to see you again soon as the great Nina Overstreet will return! On behalf of the entire team, thank you again for your support and see you soon!

Howard Shapiro
May 2018

RECOMMENDED LISTENING:

I FALL TO PIECES
BY PATSY CLINE

YOU'RE A BIG GIRL NOW
BY BOB DYLAN

LOVE MAKES NO SENSE
BY NINA OVERSTREET

CHAPTER
ONE

You're
a Big Girl
Now

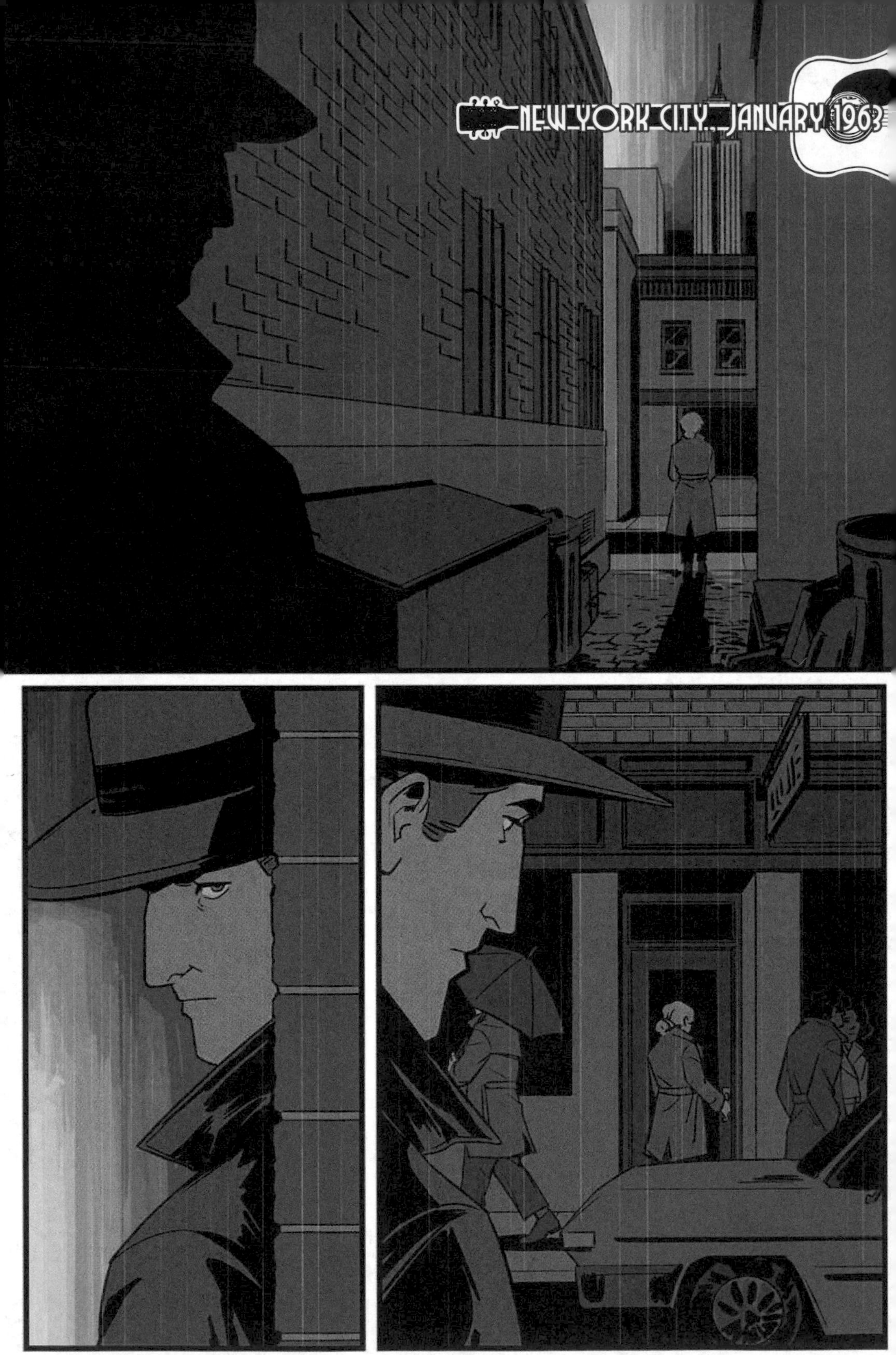
NEW YORK CITY... JANUARY 1963

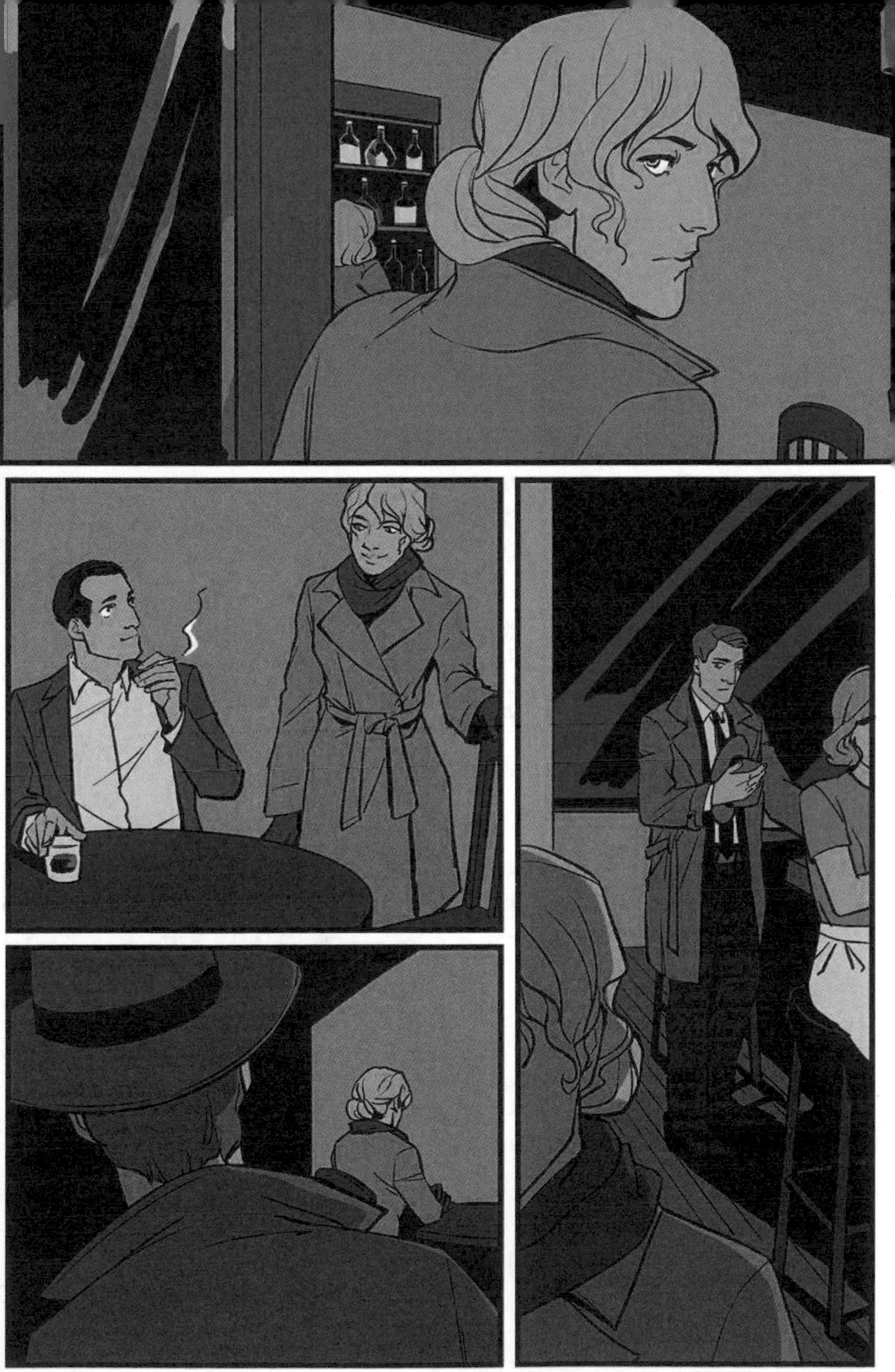

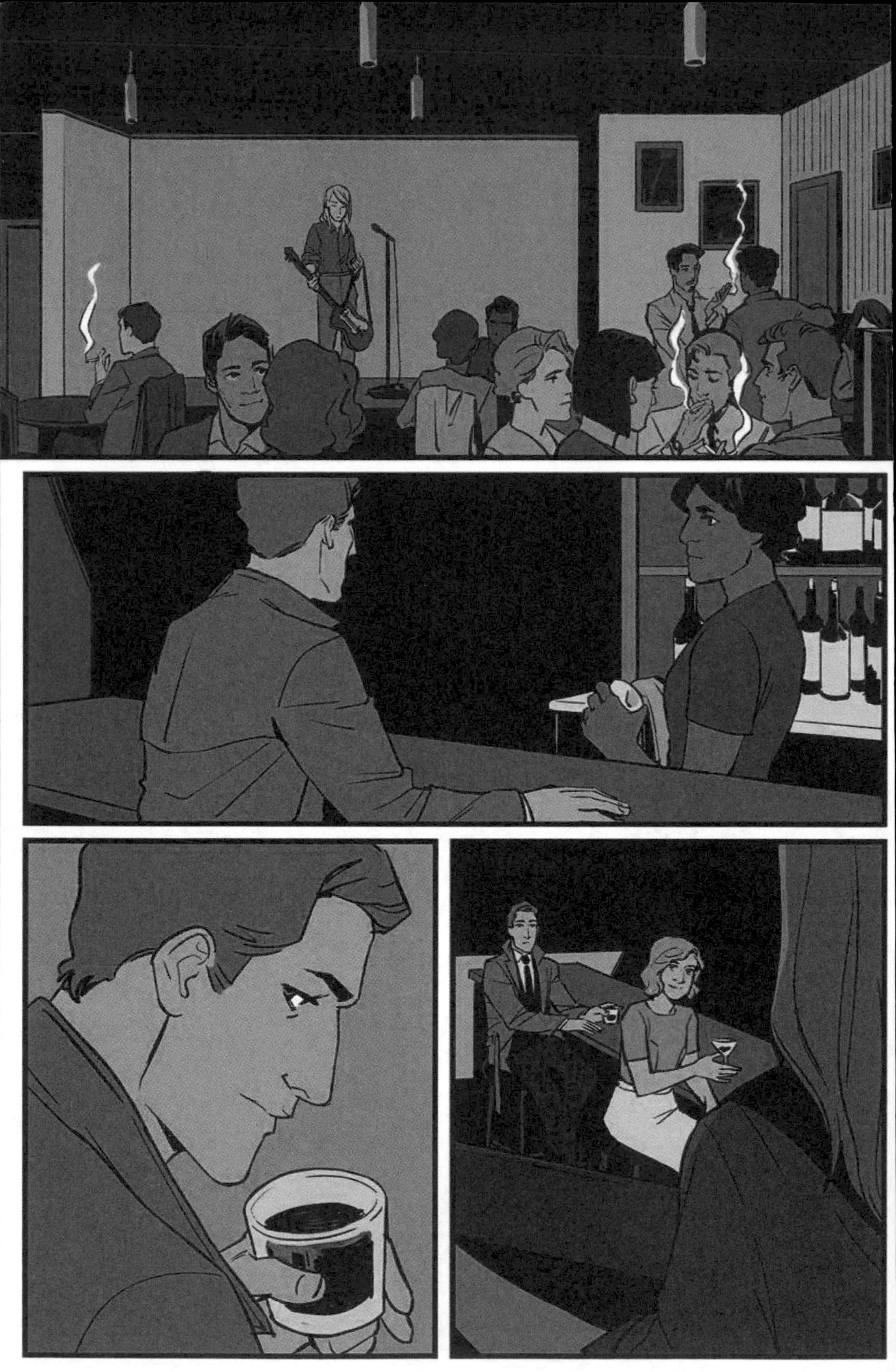

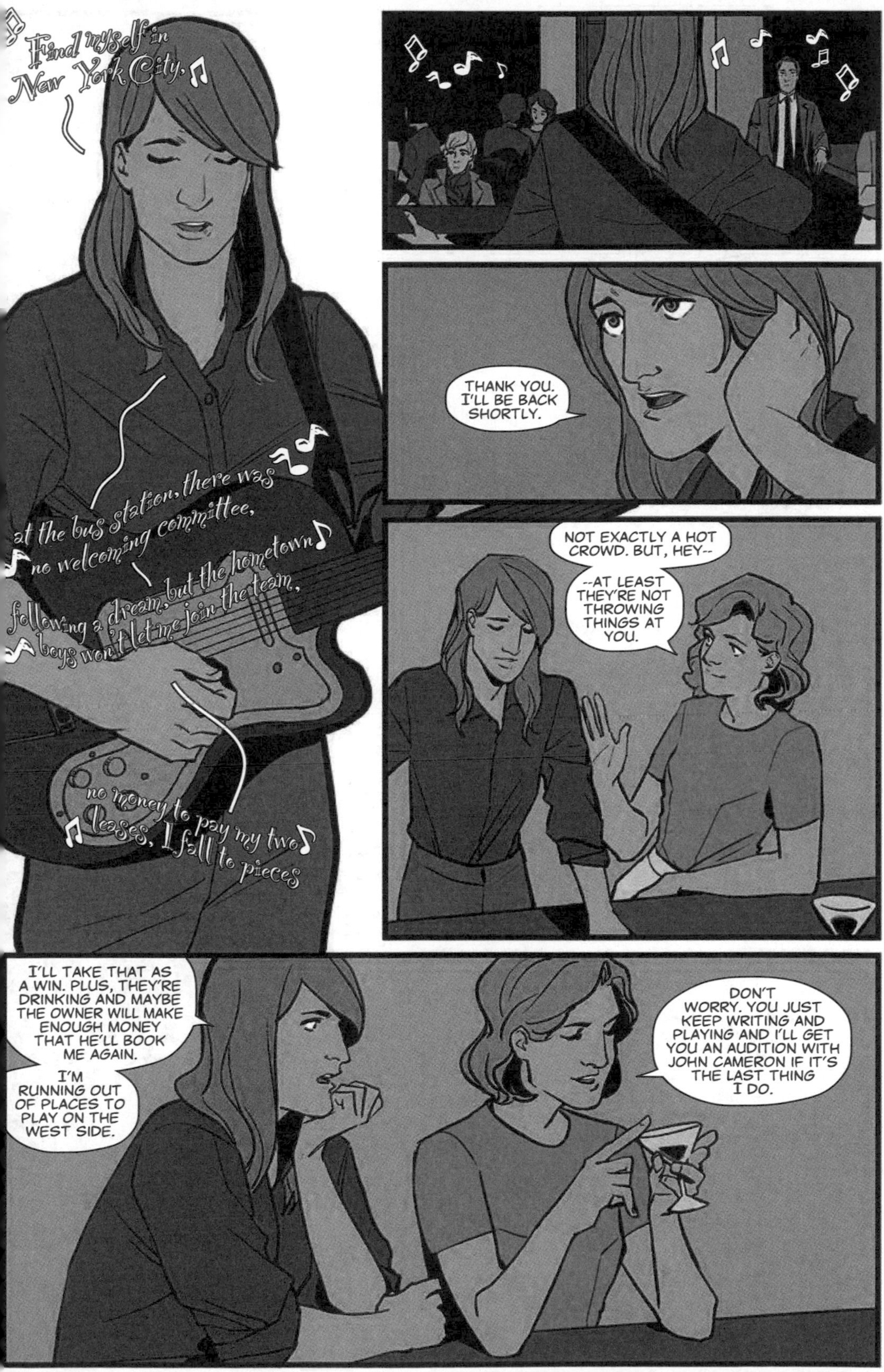
Find myself in New York City,
at the bus station, there was no welcoming committee,
following a dream, but the hometown boys won't let me join the team,
no money to pay my two leases, I fall to pieces
THANK YOU. I'LL BE BACK SHORTLY.
NOT EXACTLY A HOT CROWD. BUT, HEY--
--AT LEAST THEY'RE NOT THROWING THINGS AT YOU.
I'LL TAKE THAT AS A WIN. PLUS, THEY'RE DRINKING AND MAYBE THE OWNER WILL MAKE ENOUGH MONEY THAT HE'LL BOOK ME AGAIN.
I'M RUNNING OUT OF PLACES TO PLAY ON THE WEST SIDE.
DON'T WORRY. YOU JUST KEEP WRITING AND PLAYING AND I'LL GET YOU AN AUDITION WITH JOHN CAMERON IF IT'S THE LAST THING I DO.

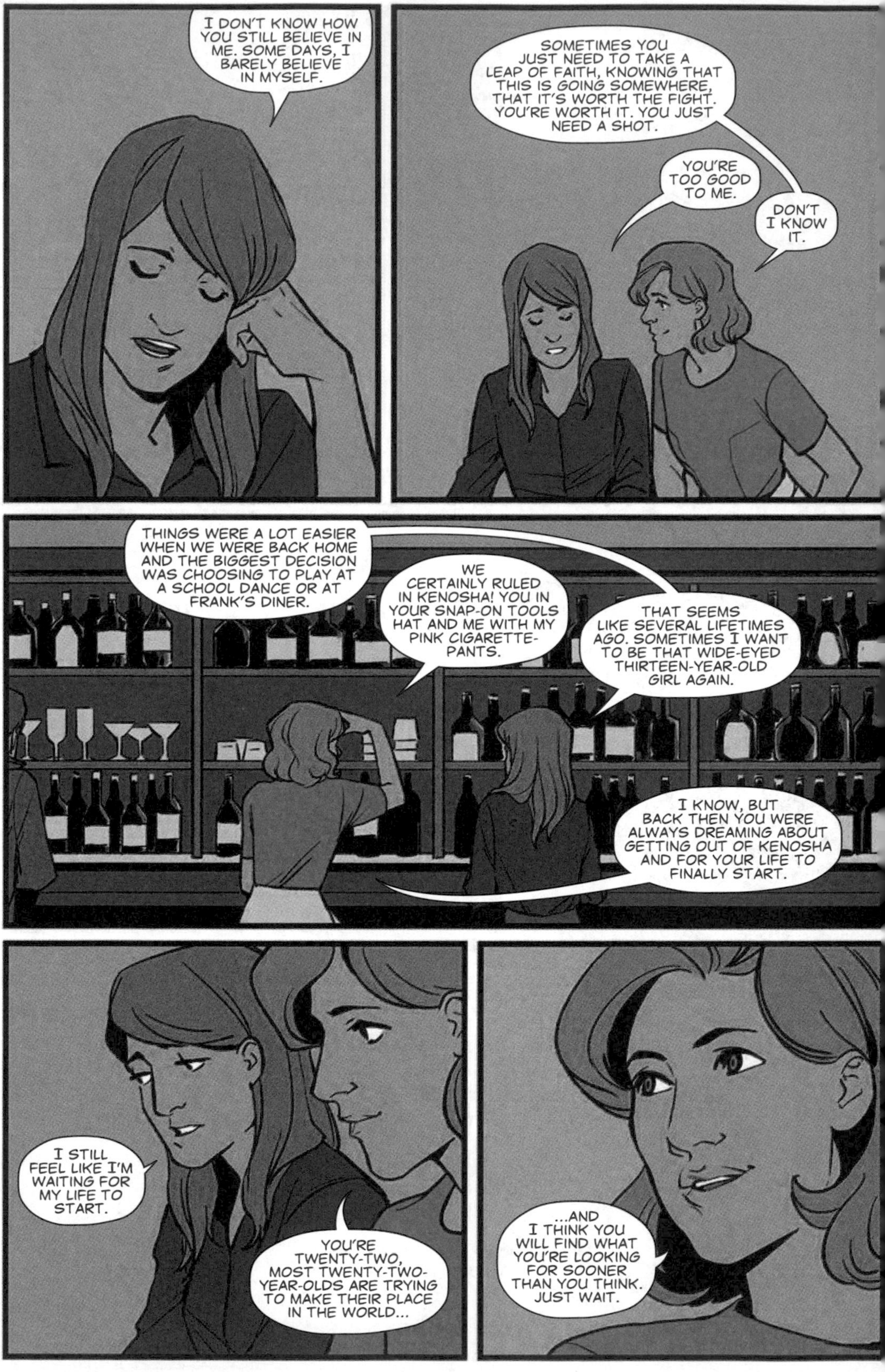
I DON'T KNOW HOW YOU STILL BELIEVE IN ME. SOME DAYS, I BARELY BELIEVE IN MYSELF.
SOMETIMES YOU JUST NEED TO TAKE A LEAP OF FAITH, KNOWING THAT THIS IS GOING SOMEWHERE, THAT IT'S WORTH THE FIGHT. YOU'RE WORTH IT. YOU JUST NEED A SHOT.
YOU'RE TOO GOOD TO ME.
DON'T I KNOW IT.
THINGS WERE A LOT EASIER WHEN WE WERE BACK HOME AND THE BIGGEST DECISION WAS CHOOSING TO PLAY AT A SCHOOL DANCE OR AT FRANK'S DINER.
WE CERTAINLY RULED IN KENOSHA! YOU IN YOUR SNAP-ON TOOLS HAT AND ME WITH MY PINK CIGARETTE-PANTS.
THAT SEEMS LIKE SEVERAL LIFETIMES AGO. SOMETIMES I WANT TO BE THAT WIDE-EYED THIRTEEN-YEAR-OLD GIRL AGAIN.
I KNOW, BUT BACK THEN YOU WERE ALWAYS DREAMING ABOUT GETTING OUT OF KENOSHA AND FOR YOUR LIFE TO FINALLY START.
I STILL FEEL LIKE I'M WAITING FOR MY LIFE TO START.
YOU'RE TWENTY-TWO, MOST TWENTY-TWO-YEAR-OLDS ARE TRYING TO MAKE THEIR PLACE IN THE WORLD...
...AND I THINK YOU WILL FIND WHAT YOU'RE LOOKING FOR SOONER THAN YOU THINK. JUST WAIT.

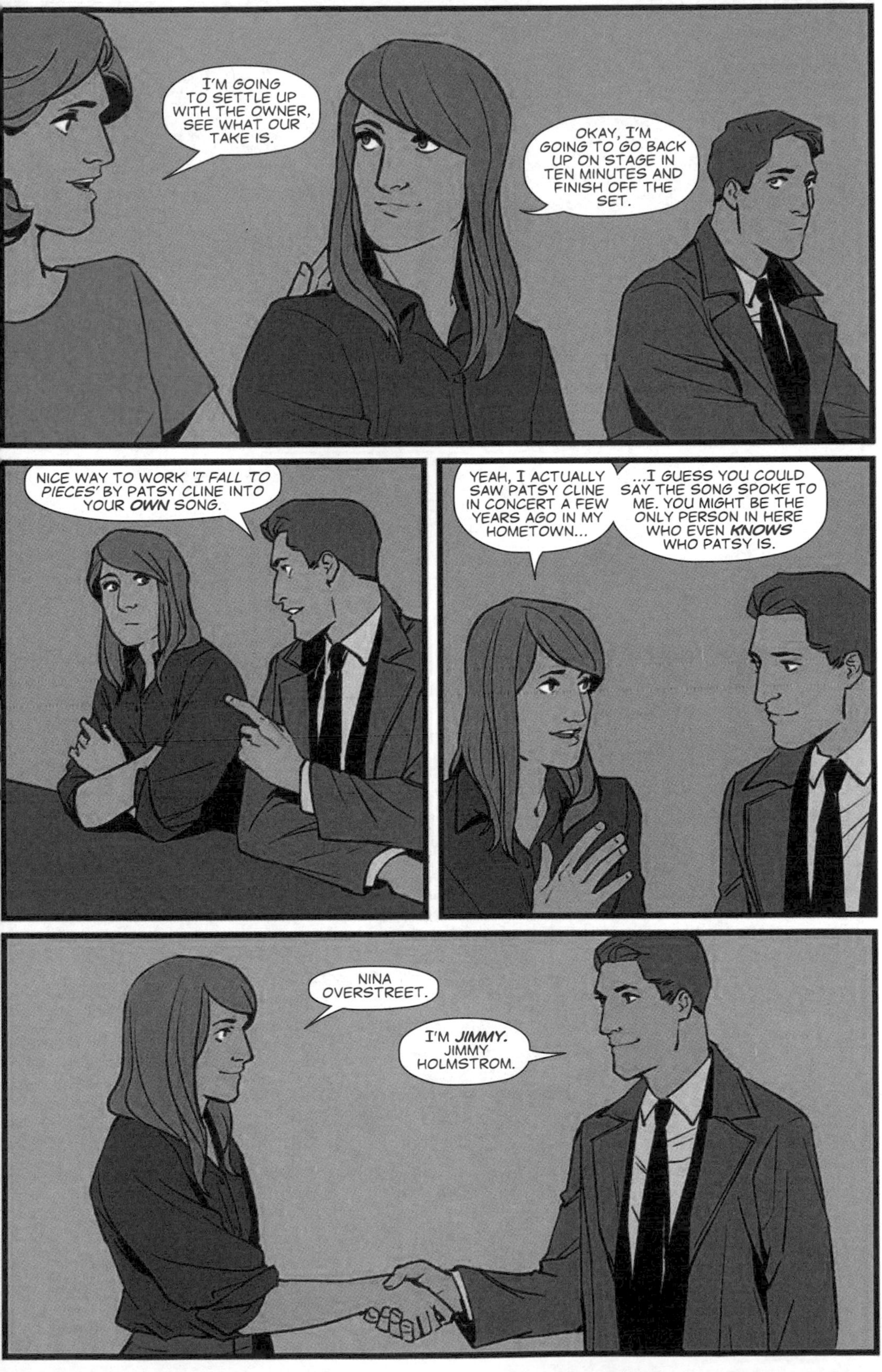
I'M GOING TO SETTLE UP WITH THE OWNER, SEE WHAT OUR TAKE IS.
OKAY, I'M GOING TO GO BACK UP ON STAGE IN TEN MINUTES AND FINISH OFF THE SET.
NICE WAY TO WORK *'I FALL TO PIECES'* BY PATSY CLINE INTO YOUR ***OWN*** SONG.
YEAH, I ACTUALLY SAW PATSY CLINE IN CONCERT A FEW YEARS AGO IN MY HOMETOWN...
...I GUESS YOU COULD SAY THE SONG SPOKE TO ME. YOU MIGHT BE THE ONLY PERSON IN HERE WHO EVEN ***KNOWS*** WHO PATSY IS.
NINA OVERSTREET.
I'M ***JIMMY.*** JIMMY HOLMSTROM.

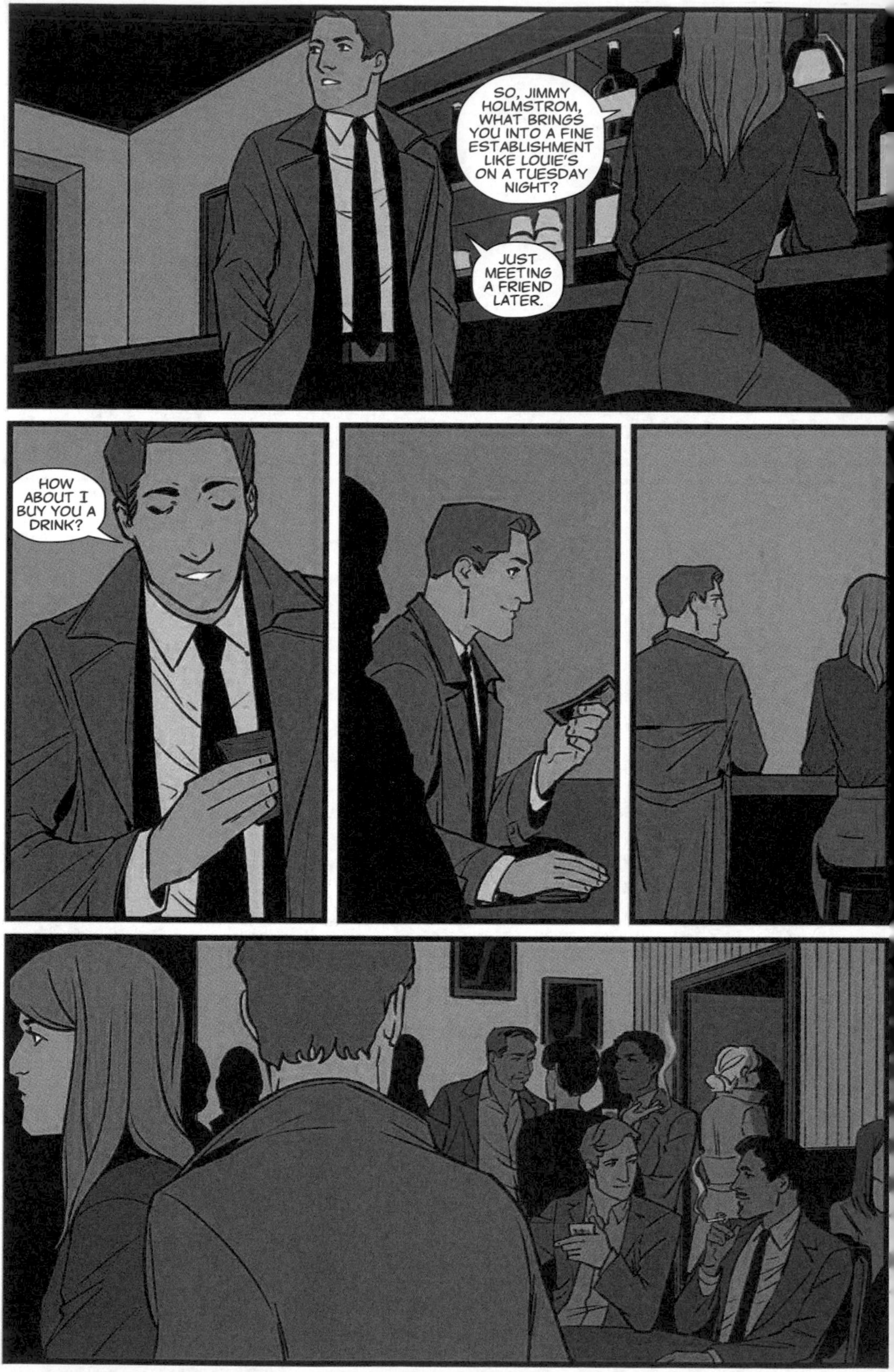
SO, JIMMY HOLMSTROM, WHAT BRINGS YOU INTO A FINE ESTABLISHMENT LIKE LOUIE'S ON A TUESDAY NIGHT?
JUST MEETING A FRIEND LATER.
HOW ABOUT I BUY YOU A DRINK?

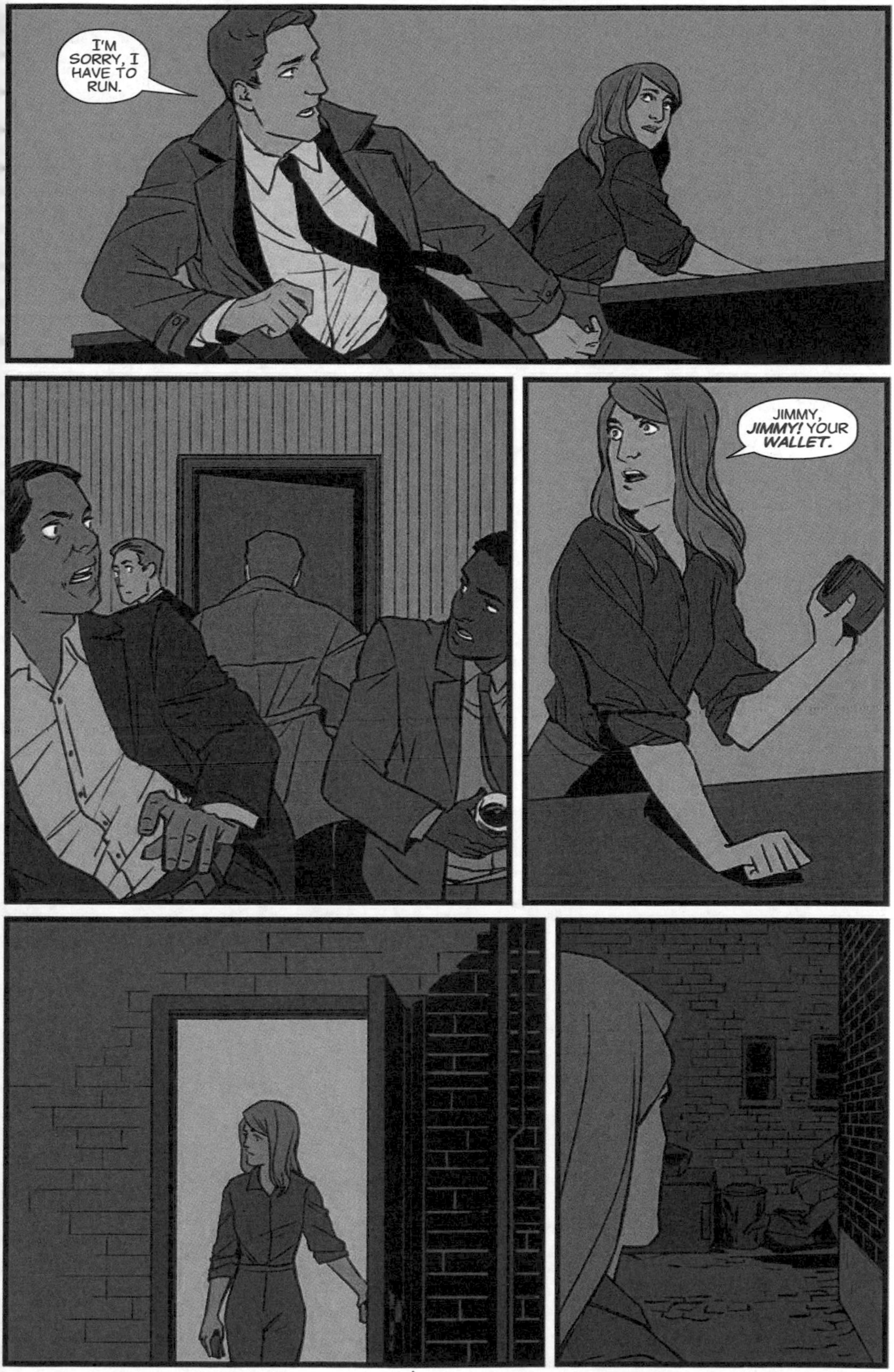
I'M SORRY, I HAVE TO RUN.
JIMMY, *JIMMY!* YOUR *WALLET.*

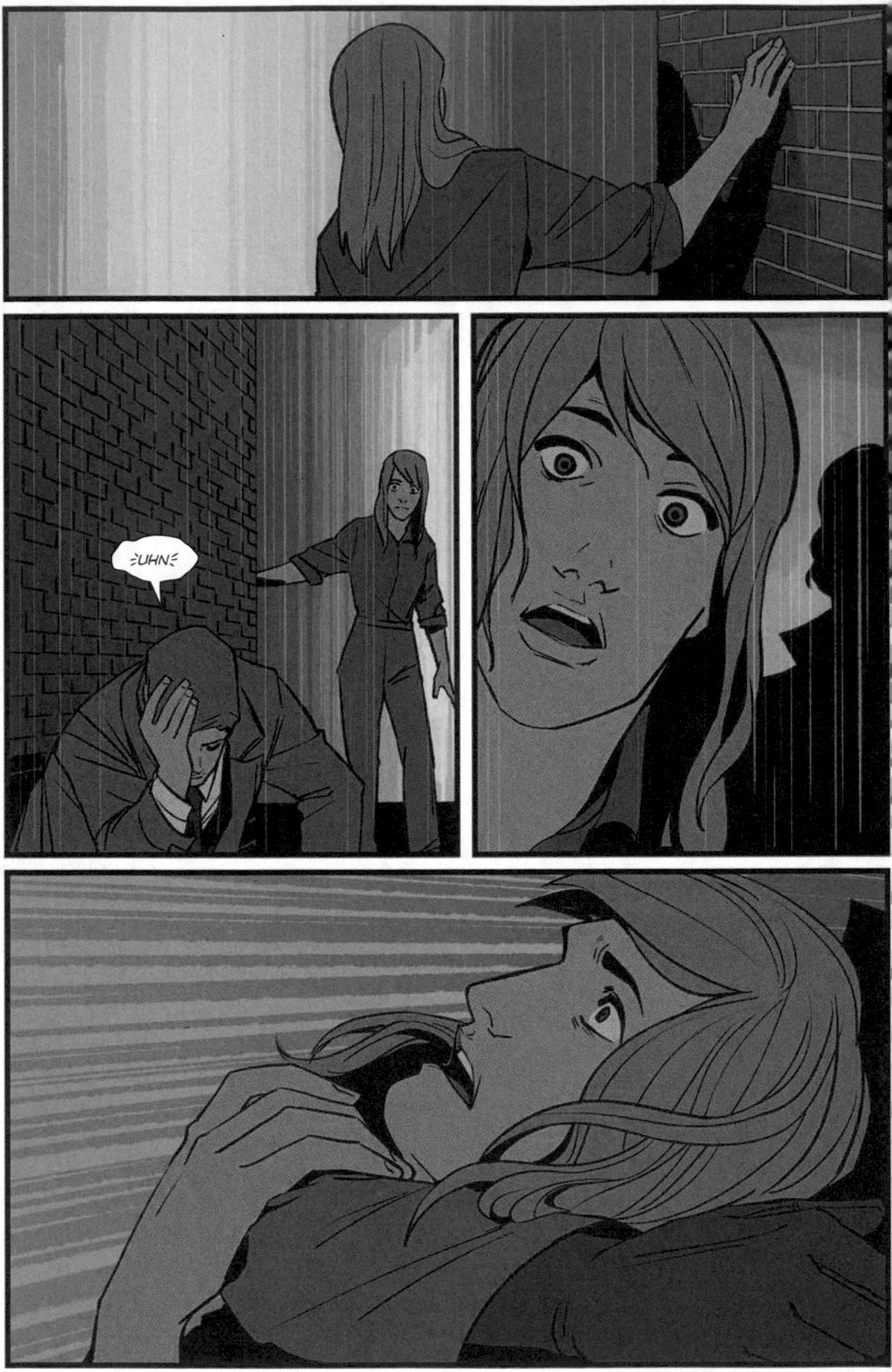
UHN

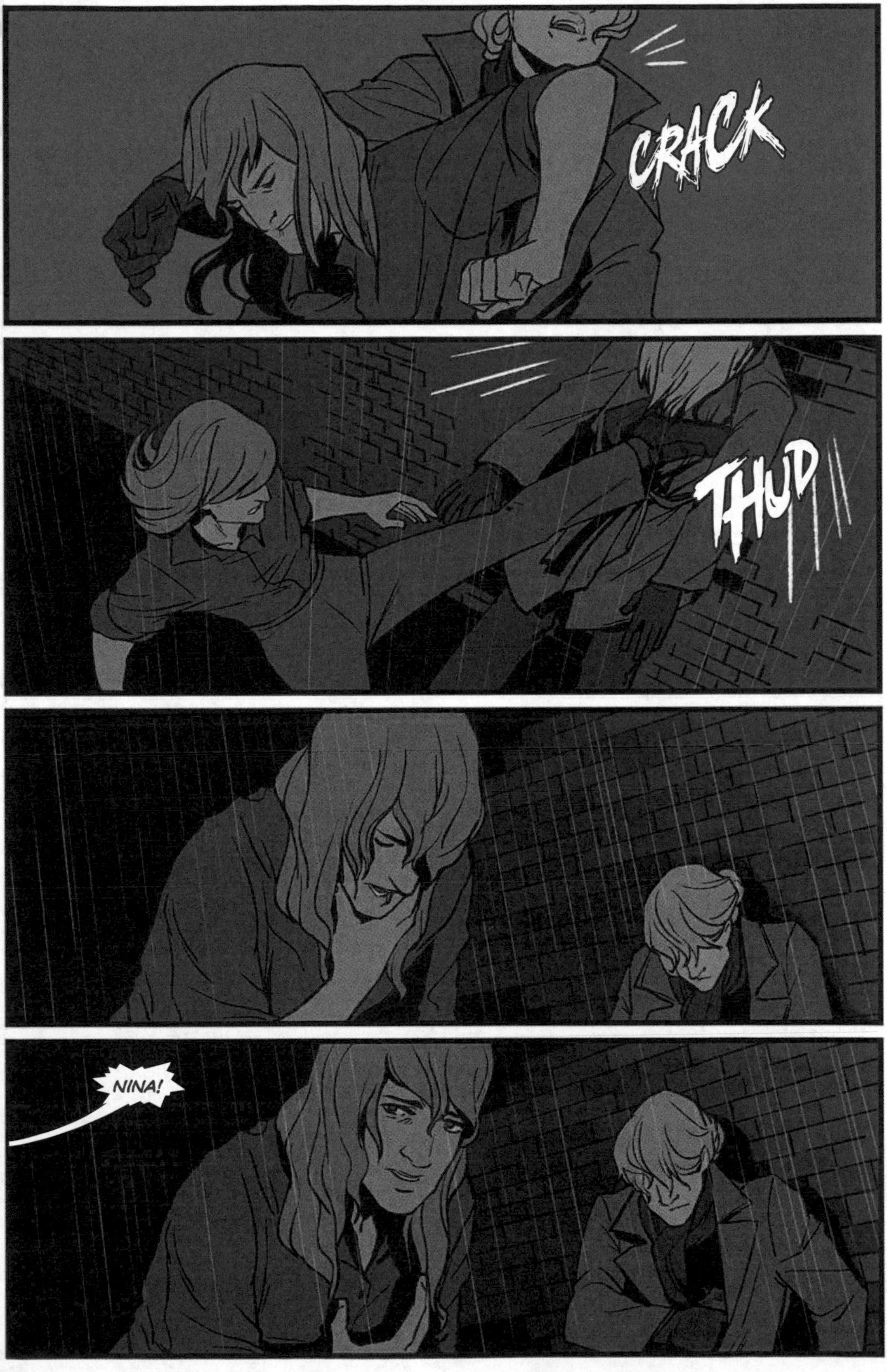
CRACK
THUD
NINA!

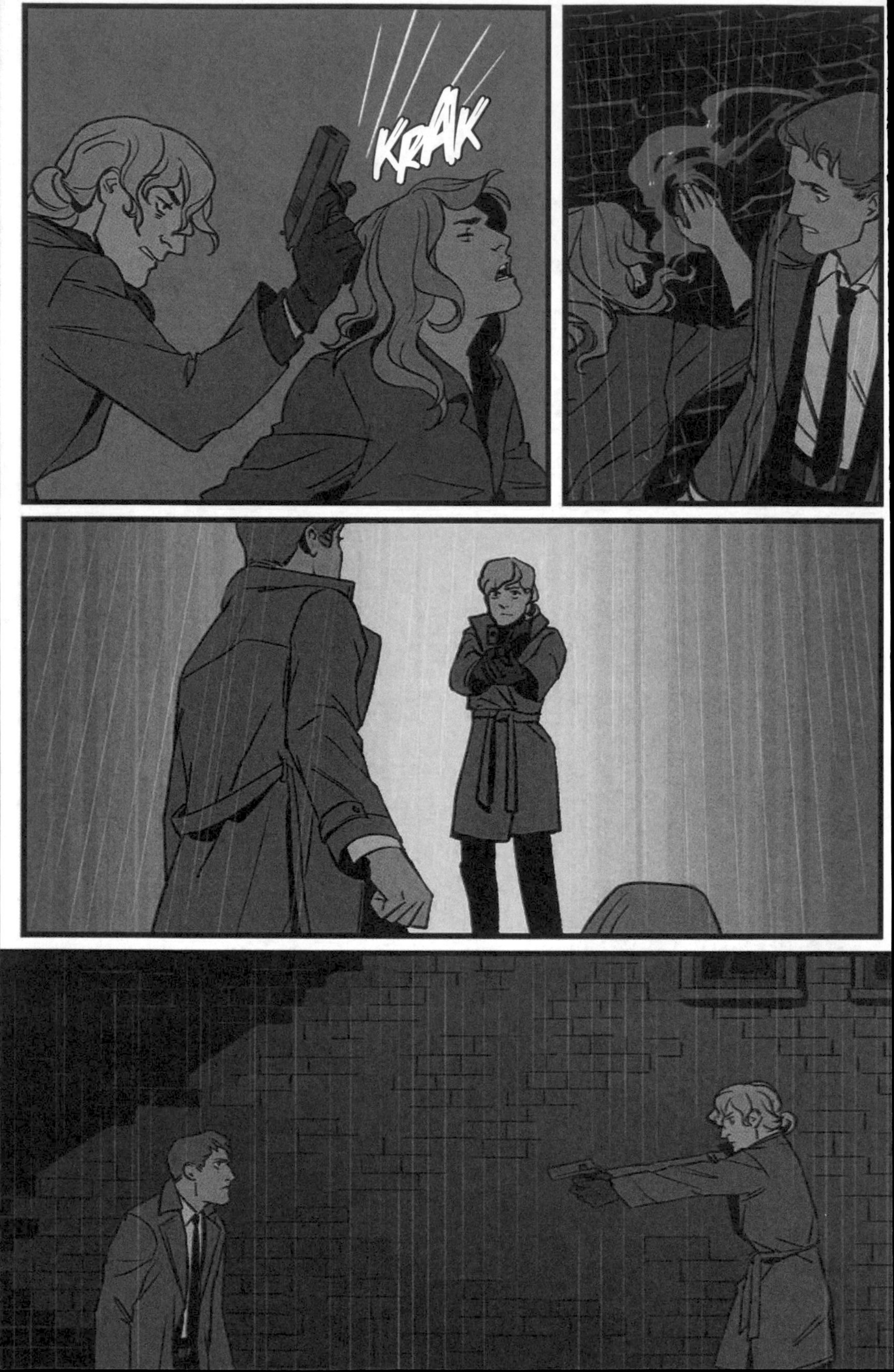
KRAK

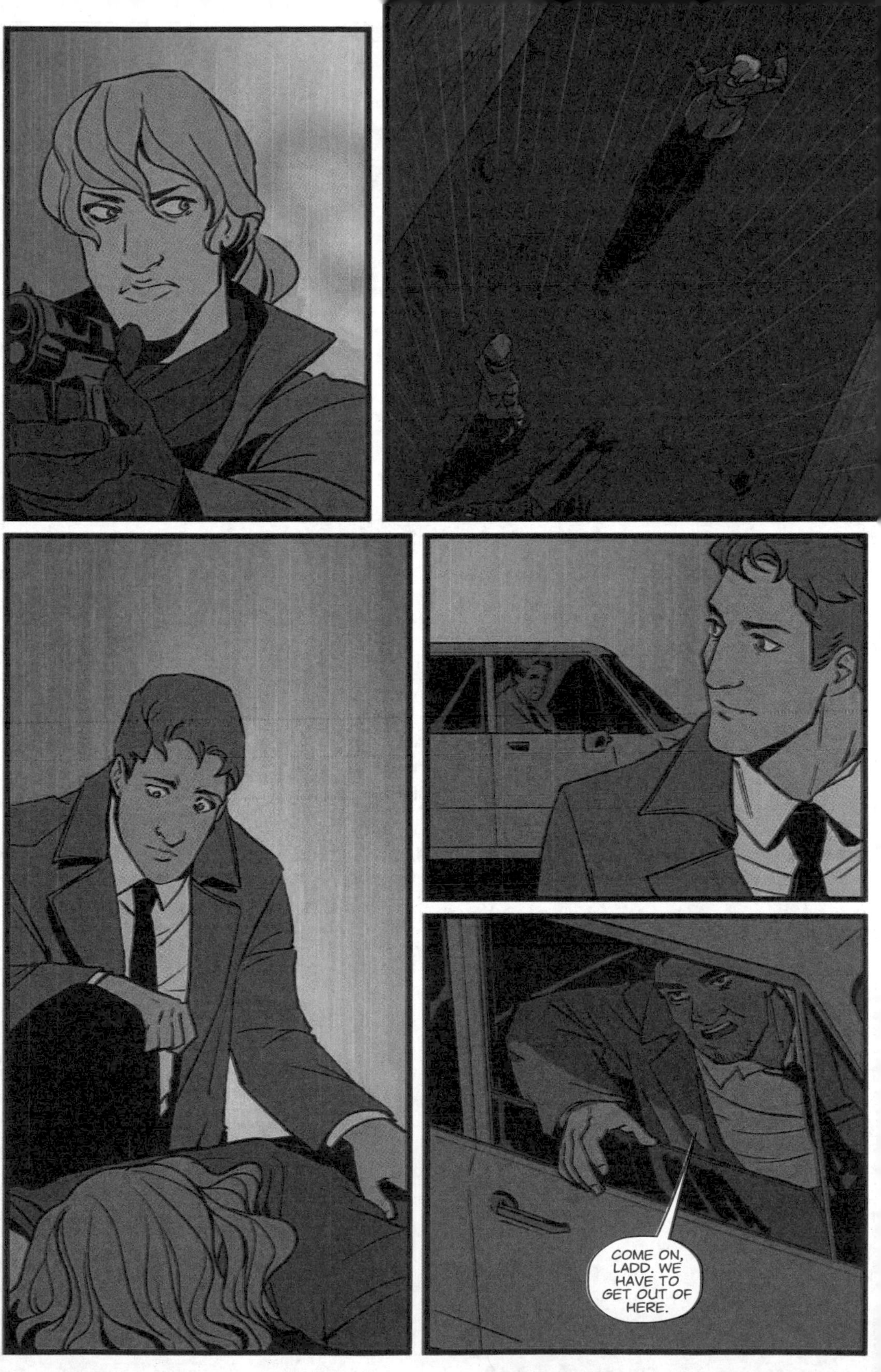
COME ON, LADD. WE HAVE TO GET OUT OF HERE.

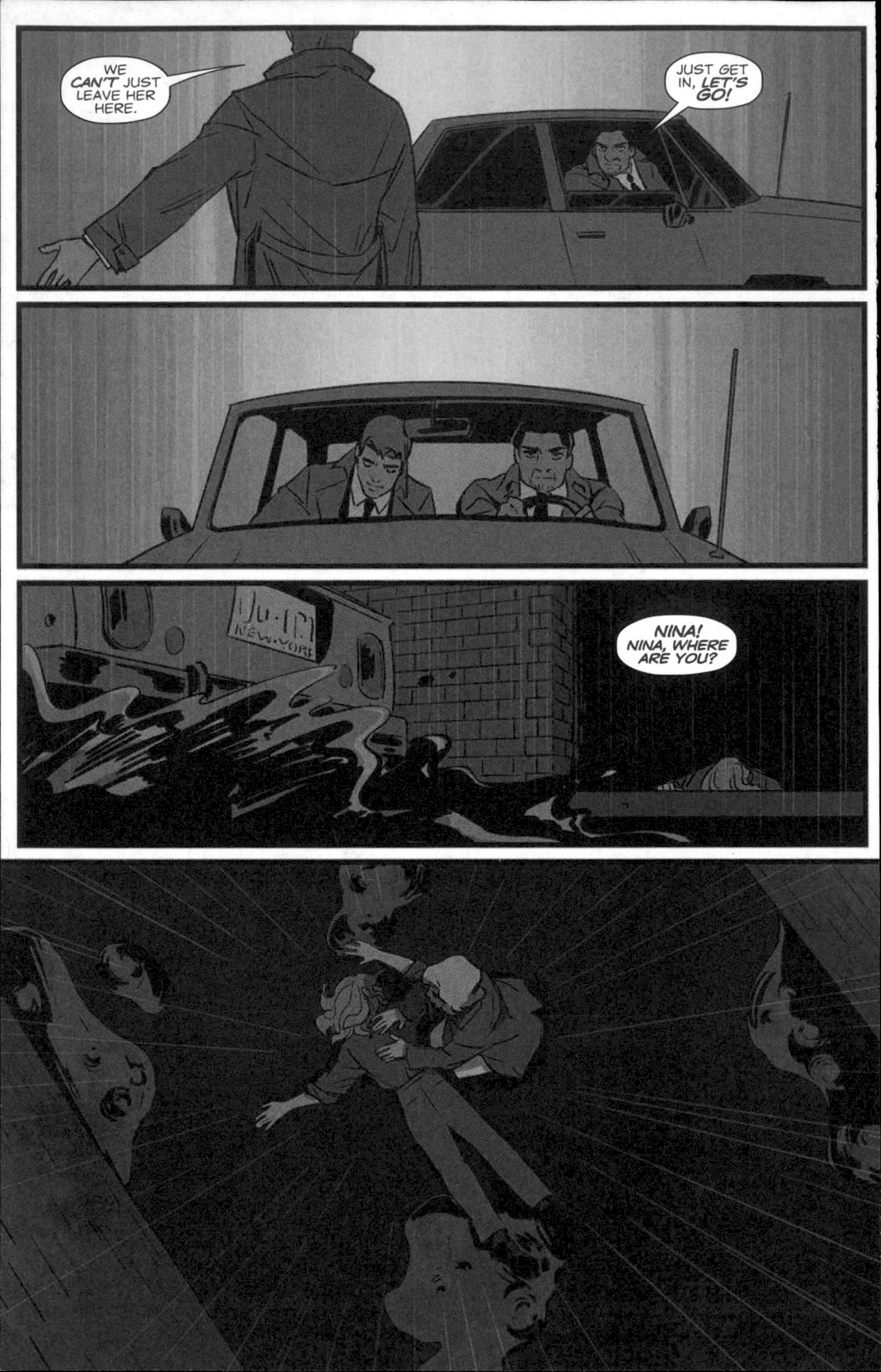
WE CAN'T JUST LEAVE HER HERE.
JUST GET IN, LET'S GO!
NEW.YORK
NINA! NINA, WHERE ARE YOU?

RECOMMENDED LISTENING:

BOTH SIDES, NOW
BY JONI MITCHELL

STATE OF LOVE AND TRUST
BY PEARL JAM

HELP ME FROM MYSELF
BY NINA OVERSTREET

CHAPTER TWO

Myself

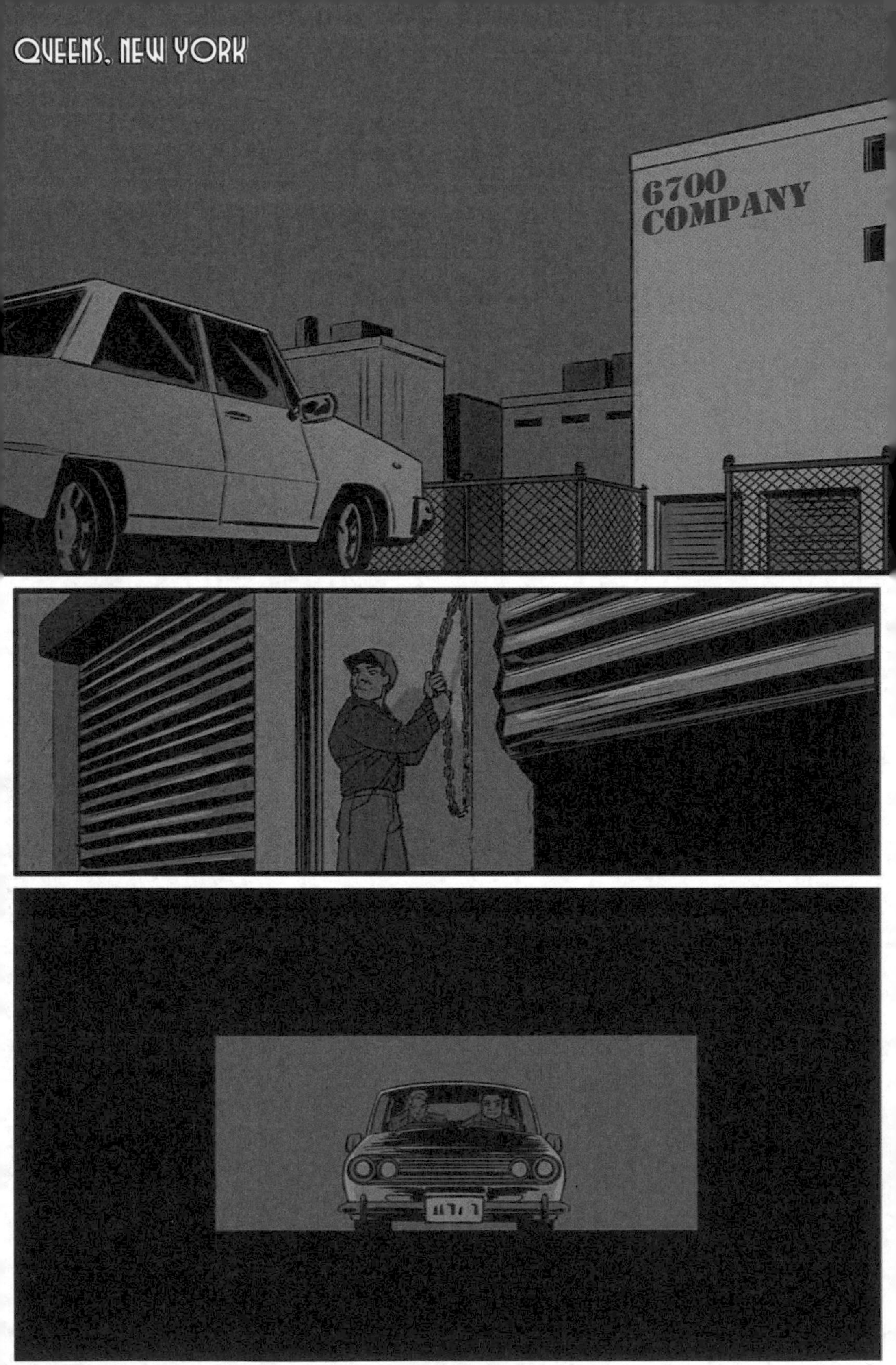
QUEENS, NEW YORK
6700
COMPANY

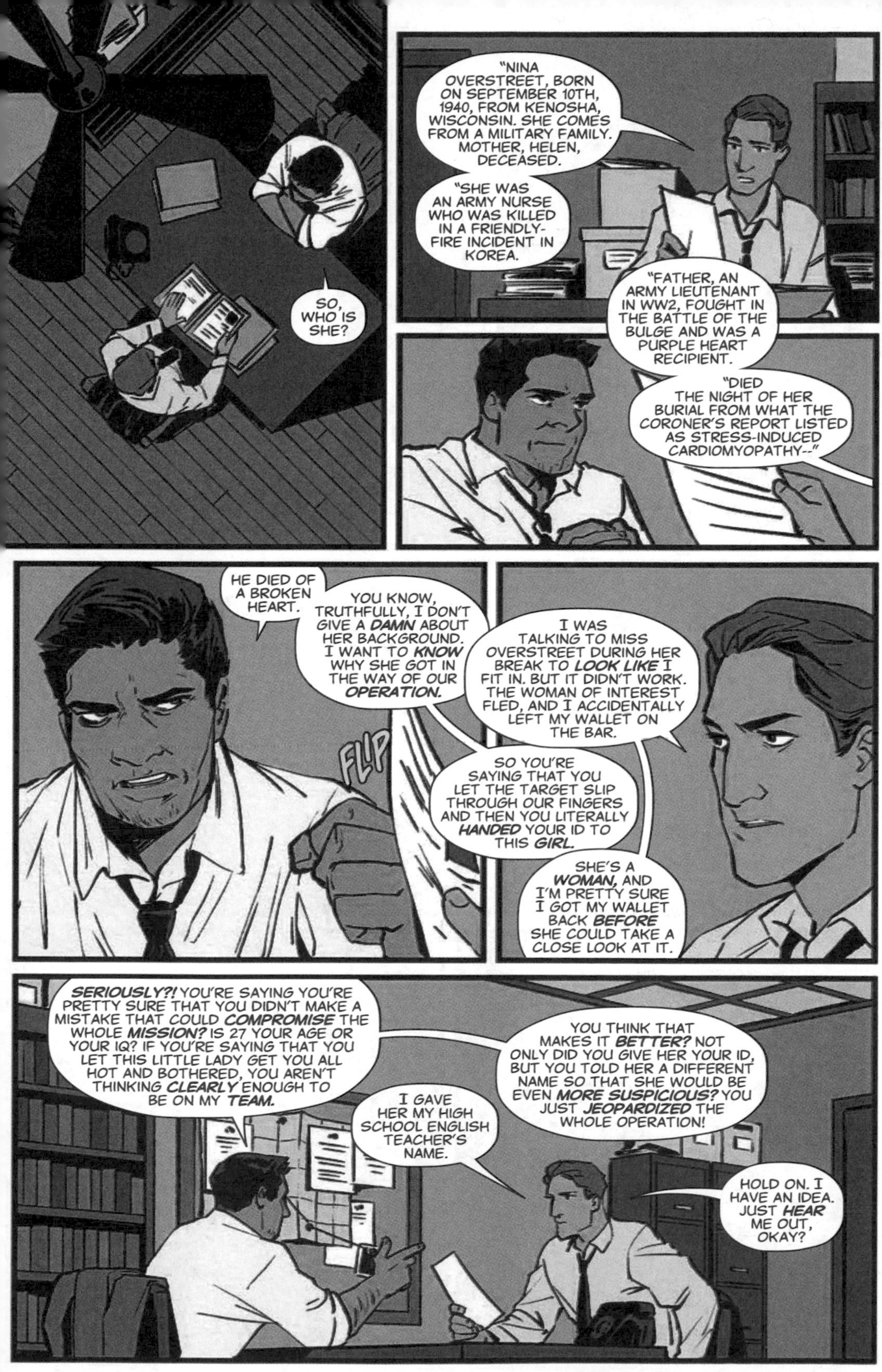
SO, WHO IS SHE?
"NINA OVERSTREET, BORN ON SEPTEMBER 10TH, 1940, FROM KENOSHA, WISCONSIN. SHE COMES FROM A MILITARY FAMILY. MOTHER, HELEN, DECEASED.
"SHE WAS AN ARMY NURSE WHO WAS KILLED IN A FRIENDLY-FIRE INCIDENT IN KOREA.
"FATHER, AN ARMY LIEUTENANT IN WW2, FOUGHT IN THE BATTLE OF THE BULGE AND WAS A PURPLE HEART RECIPIENT.
"DIED THE NIGHT OF HER BURIAL FROM WHAT THE CORONER'S REPORT LISTED AS STRESS-INDUCED CARDIOMYOPATHY--"
HE DIED OF A BROKEN HEART.
YOU KNOW, TRUTHFULLY, I DON'T GIVE A DAMN ABOUT HER BACKGROUND. I WANT TO KNOW WHY SHE GOT IN THE WAY OF OUR OPERATION.
FLIP
I WAS TALKING TO MISS OVERSTREET DURING HER BREAK TO LOOK LIKE I FIT IN. BUT IT DIDN'T WORK. THE WOMAN OF INTEREST FLED, AND I ACCIDENTALLY LEFT MY WALLET ON THE BAR.
SO YOU'RE SAYING THAT YOU LET THE TARGET SLIP THROUGH OUR FINGERS AND THEN YOU LITERALLY HANDED YOUR ID TO THIS GIRL.
SHE'S A WOMAN, AND I'M PRETTY SURE I GOT MY WALLET BACK BEFORE SHE COULD TAKE A CLOSE LOOK AT IT.
SERIOUSLY?! YOU'RE SAYING YOU'RE PRETTY SURE THAT YOU DIDN'T MAKE A MISTAKE THAT COULD COMPROMISE THE WHOLE MISSION? IS 27 YOUR AGE OR YOUR IQ? IF YOU'RE SAYING THAT YOU LET THIS LITTLE LADY GET YOU ALL HOT AND BOTHERED, YOU AREN'T THINKING CLEARLY ENOUGH TO BE ON MY TEAM.
I GAVE HER MY HIGH SCHOOL ENGLISH TEACHER'S NAME.
YOU THINK THAT MAKES IT BETTER? NOT ONLY DID YOU GIVE HER YOUR ID, BUT YOU TOLD HER A DIFFERENT NAME SO THAT SHE WOULD BE EVEN MORE SUSPICIOUS? YOU JUST JEOPARDIZED THE WHOLE OPERATION!
HOLD ON. I HAVE AN IDEA. JUST HEAR ME OUT, OKAY?

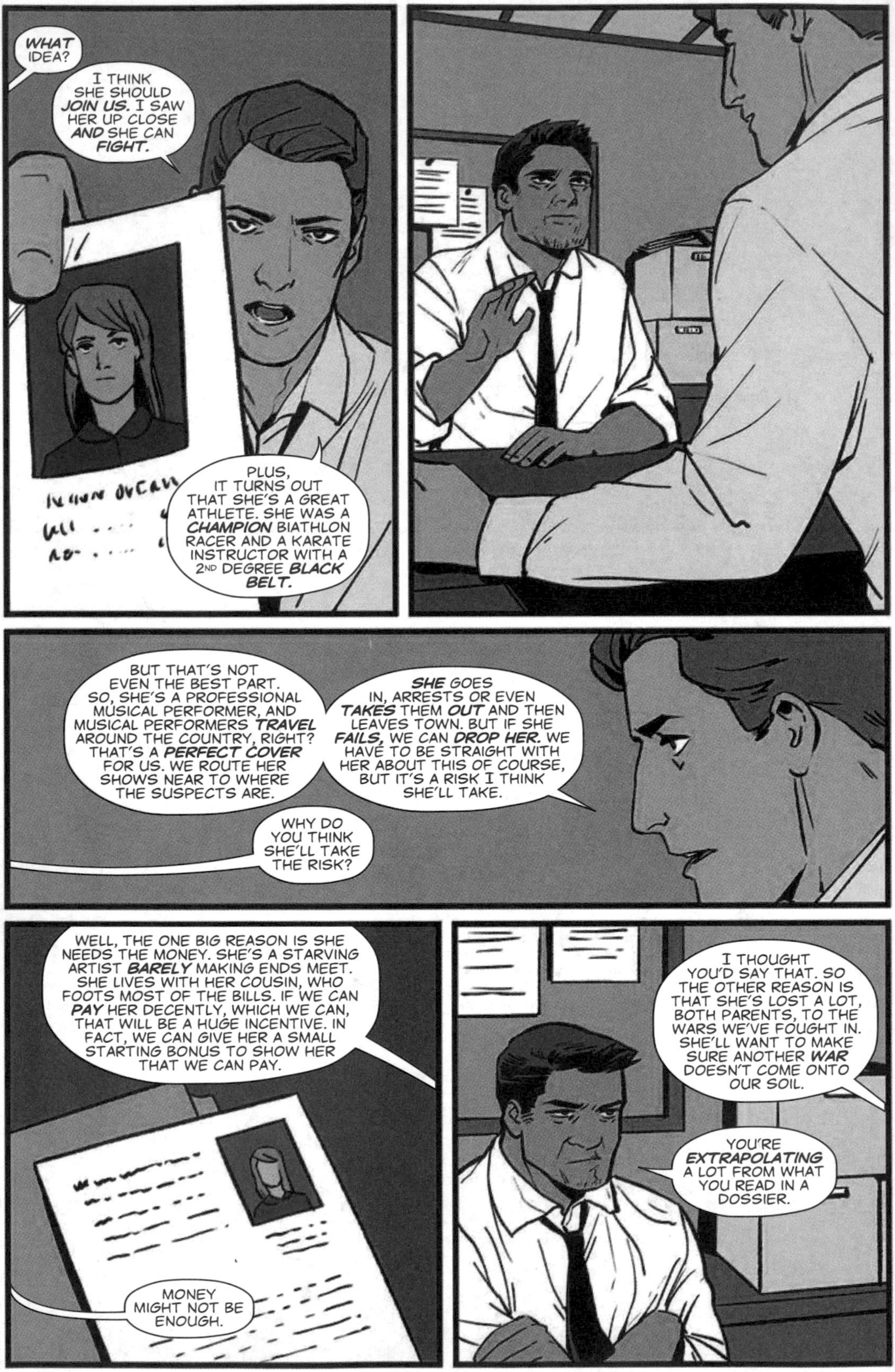

WHAT IDEA?
I THINK SHE SHOULD JOIN US. I SAW HER UP CLOSE AND SHE CAN FIGHT.
PLUS, IT TURNS OUT THAT SHE'S A GREAT ATHLETE. SHE WAS A CHAMPION BIATHLON RACER AND A KARATE INSTRUCTOR WITH A 2ND DEGREE BLACK BELT.
BUT THAT'S NOT EVEN THE BEST PART. SO, SHE'S A PROFESSIONAL MUSICAL PERFORMER, AND MUSICAL PERFORMERS TRAVEL AROUND THE COUNTRY, RIGHT? THAT'S A PERFECT COVER FOR US. WE ROUTE HER SHOWS NEAR TO WHERE THE SUSPECTS ARE.
SHE GOES IN, ARRESTS OR EVEN TAKES THEM OUT AND THEN LEAVES TOWN. BUT IF SHE FAILS, WE CAN DROP HER. WE HAVE TO BE STRAIGHT WITH HER ABOUT THIS OF COURSE, BUT IT'S A RISK I THINK SHE'LL TAKE.
WHY DO YOU THINK SHE'LL TAKE THE RISK?
WELL, THE ONE BIG REASON IS SHE NEEDS THE MONEY. SHE'S A STARVING ARTIST BARELY MAKING ENDS MEET. SHE LIVES WITH HER COUSIN, WHO FOOTS MOST OF THE BILLS. IF WE CAN PAY HER DECENTLY, WHICH WE CAN, THAT WILL BE A HUGE INCENTIVE. IN FACT, WE CAN GIVE HER A SMALL STARTING BONUS TO SHOW HER THAT WE CAN PAY.
MONEY MIGHT NOT BE ENOUGH.
I THOUGHT YOU'D SAY THAT. SO THE OTHER REASON IS THAT SHE'S LOST A LOT, BOTH PARENTS, TO THE WARS WE'VE FOUGHT IN. SHE'LL WANT TO MAKE SURE ANOTHER WAR DOESN'T COME ONTO OUR SOIL.
YOU'RE EXTRAPOLATING A LOT FROM WHAT YOU READ IN A DOSSIER.

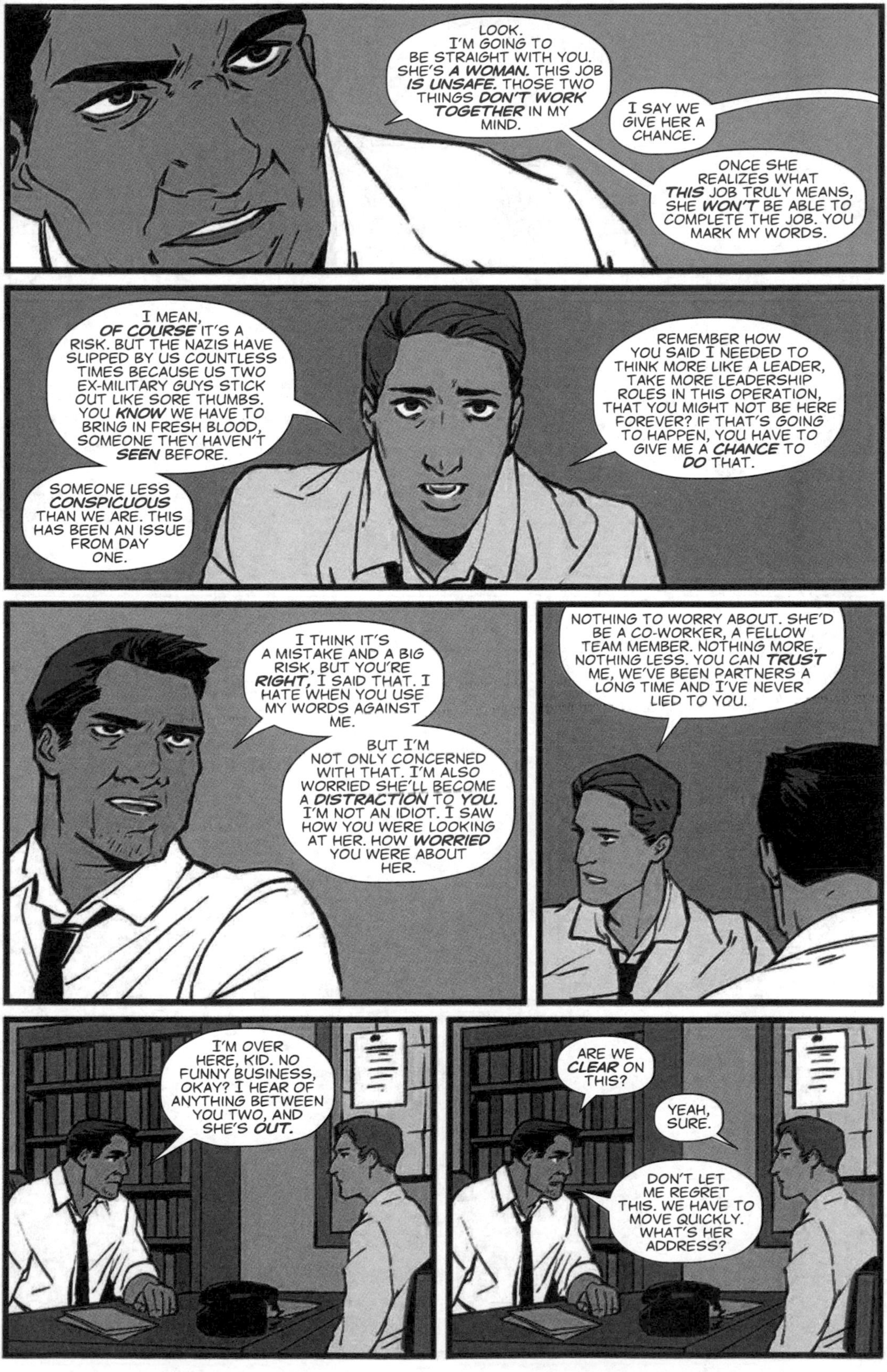
LOOK. I'M GOING TO BE STRAIGHT WITH YOU. SHE'S A WOMAN. THIS JOB IS UNSAFE. THOSE TWO THINGS DON'T WORK TOGETHER IN MY MIND.
I SAY WE GIVE HER A CHANCE.
ONCE SHE REALIZES WHAT THIS JOB TRULY MEANS, SHE WON'T BE ABLE TO COMPLETE THE JOB. YOU MARK MY WORDS.
I MEAN, OF COURSE IT'S A RISK. BUT THE NAZIS HAVE SLIPPED BY US COUNTLESS TIMES BECAUSE US TWO EX-MILITARY GUYS STICK OUT LIKE SORE THUMBS. YOU KNOW WE HAVE TO BRING IN FRESH BLOOD, SOMEONE THEY HAVEN'T SEEN BEFORE.
SOMEONE LESS CONSPICUOUS THAN WE ARE. THIS HAS BEEN AN ISSUE FROM DAY ONE.
REMEMBER HOW YOU SAID I NEEDED TO THINK MORE LIKE A LEADER, TAKE MORE LEADERSHIP ROLES IN THIS OPERATION, THAT YOU MIGHT NOT BE HERE FOREVER? IF THAT'S GOING TO HAPPEN, YOU HAVE TO GIVE ME A CHANCE TO DO THAT.
I THINK IT'S A MISTAKE AND A BIG RISK, BUT YOU'RE RIGHT, I SAID THAT. I HATE WHEN YOU USE MY WORDS AGAINST ME.
BUT I'M NOT ONLY CONCERNED WITH THAT. I'M ALSO WORRIED SHE'LL BECOME A DISTRACTION TO YOU. I'M NOT AN IDIOT. I SAW HOW YOU WERE LOOKING AT HER. HOW WORRIED YOU WERE ABOUT HER.
NOTHING TO WORRY ABOUT. SHE'D BE A CO-WORKER, A FELLOW TEAM MEMBER. NOTHING MORE, NOTHING LESS. YOU CAN TRUST ME, WE'VE BEEN PARTNERS A LONG TIME AND I'VE NEVER LIED TO YOU.
I'M OVER HERE, KID. NO FUNNY BUSINESS, OKAY? I HEAR OF ANYTHING BETWEEN YOU TWO, AND SHE'S OUT.
ARE WE CLEAR ON THIS?
YEAH, SURE.
DON'T LET ME REGRET THIS. WE HAVE TO MOVE QUICKLY. WHAT'S HER ADDRESS?

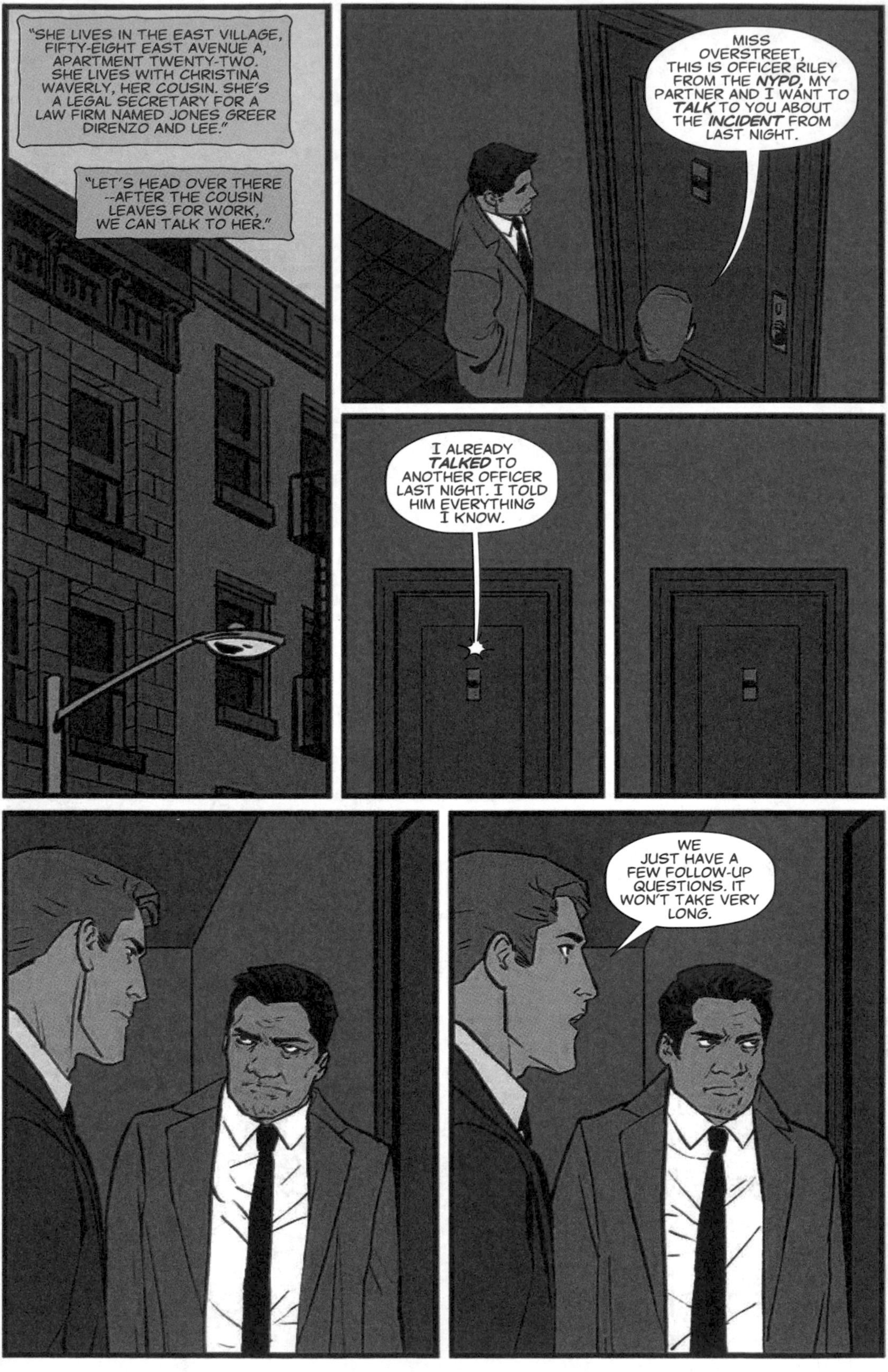
"SHE LIVES IN THE EAST VILLAGE, FIFTY-EIGHT EAST AVENUE A, APARTMENT TWENTY-TWO. SHE LIVES WITH CHRISTINA WAVERLY, HER COUSIN. SHE'S A LEGAL SECRETARY FOR A LAW FIRM NAMED JONES GREER DIRENZO AND LEE."
"LET'S HEAD OVER THERE --AFTER THE COUSIN LEAVES FOR WORK, WE CAN TALK TO HER."
MISS OVERSTREET, THIS IS OFFICER RILEY FROM THE NYPD, MY PARTNER AND I WANT TO TALK TO YOU ABOUT THE INCIDENT FROM LAST NIGHT.
I ALREADY TALKED TO ANOTHER OFFICER LAST NIGHT. I TOLD HIM EVERYTHING I KNOW.
WE JUST HAVE A FEW FOLLOW-UP QUESTIONS. IT WON'T TAKE VERY LONG.

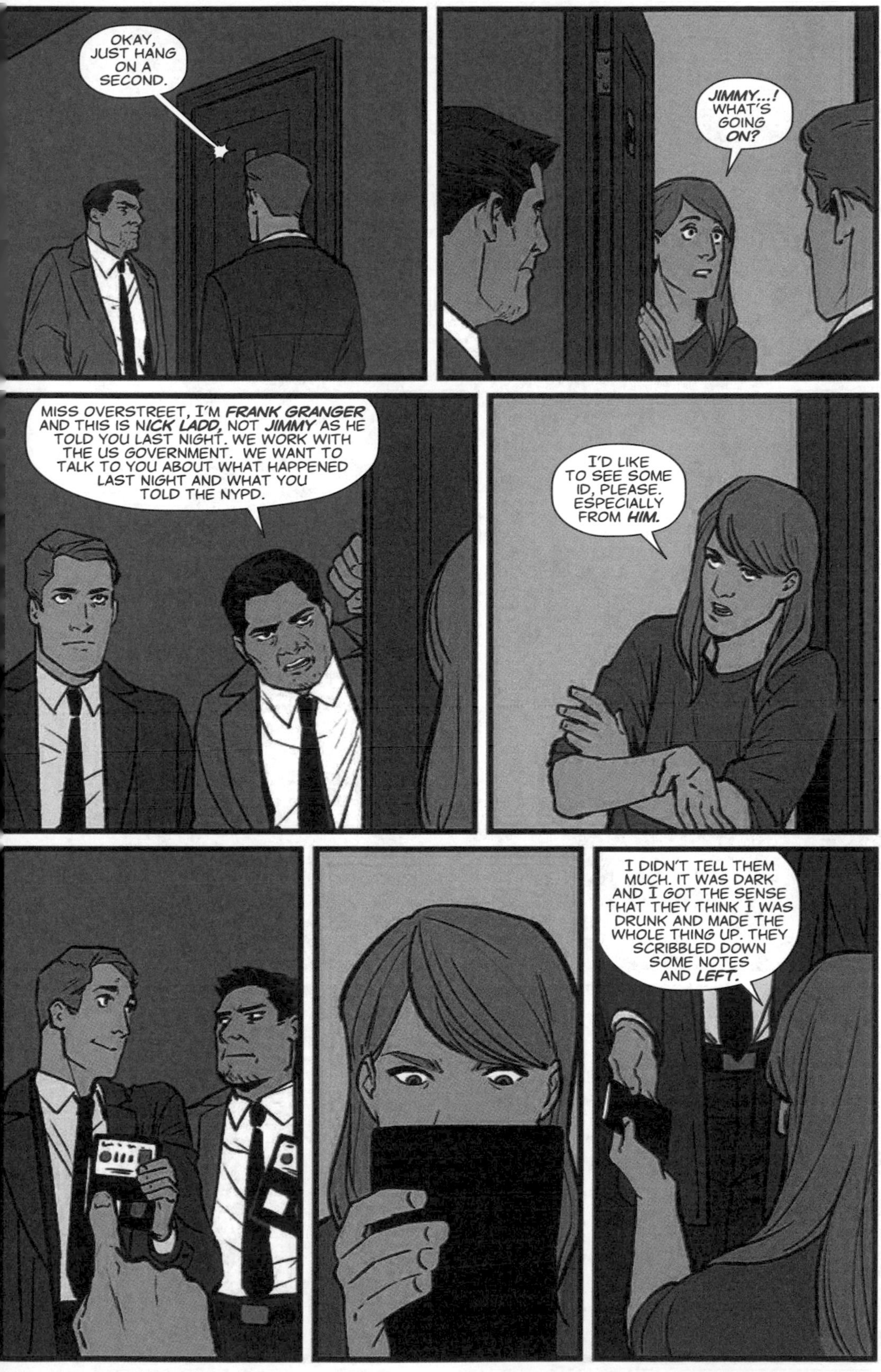
OKAY, JUST HANG ON A SECOND.
JIMMY...! WHAT'S GOING ON?
MISS OVERSTREET, I'M FRANK GRANGER AND THIS IS NICK LADD, NOT JIMMY AS HE TOLD YOU LAST NIGHT. WE WORK WITH THE US GOVERNMENT. WE WANT TO TALK TO YOU ABOUT WHAT HAPPENED LAST NIGHT AND WHAT YOU TOLD THE NYPD.
I'D LIKE TO SEE SOME ID, PLEASE. ESPECIALLY FROM HIM.
I DIDN'T TELL THEM MUCH. IT WAS DARK AND I GOT THE SENSE THAT THEY THINK I WAS DRUNK AND MADE THE WHOLE THING UP. THEY SCRIBBLED DOWN SOME NOTES AND LEFT.

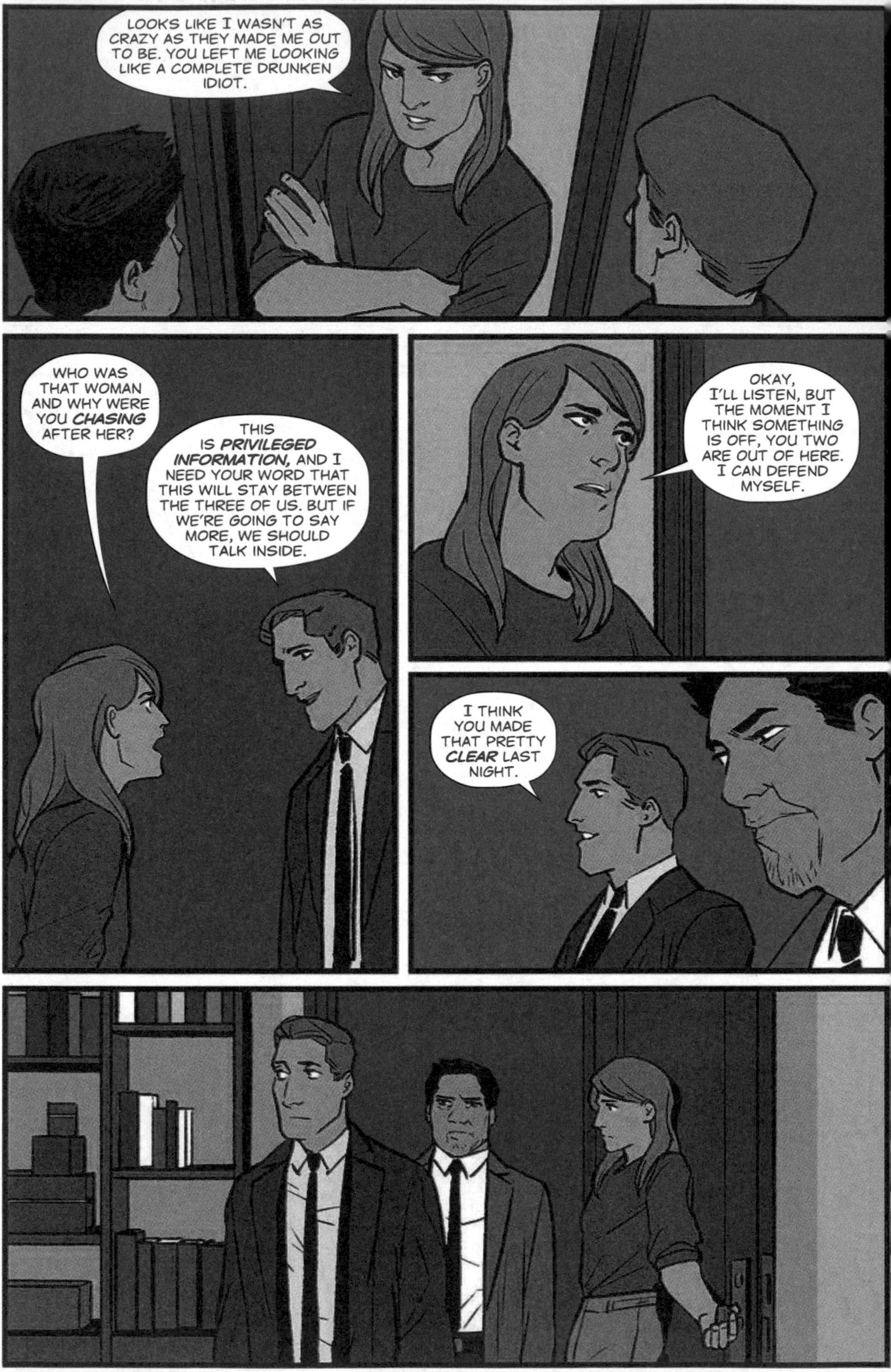
LOOKS LIKE I WASN'T AS CRAZY AS THEY MADE ME OUT TO BE. YOU LEFT ME LOOKING LIKE A COMPLETE DRUNKEN IDIOT.
WHO WAS THAT WOMAN AND WHY WERE YOU *CHASING* AFTER HER?
THIS IS ***PRIVILEGED INFORMATION,*** AND I NEED YOUR WORD THAT THIS WILL STAY BETWEEN THE THREE OF US. BUT IF WE'RE GOING TO SAY MORE, WE SHOULD TALK INSIDE.
OKAY, I'LL LISTEN, BUT THE MOMENT I THINK SOMETHING IS OFF, YOU TWO ARE OUT OF HERE. I CAN DEFEND MYSELF.
I THINK YOU MADE THAT PRETTY ***CLEAR*** LAST NIGHT.

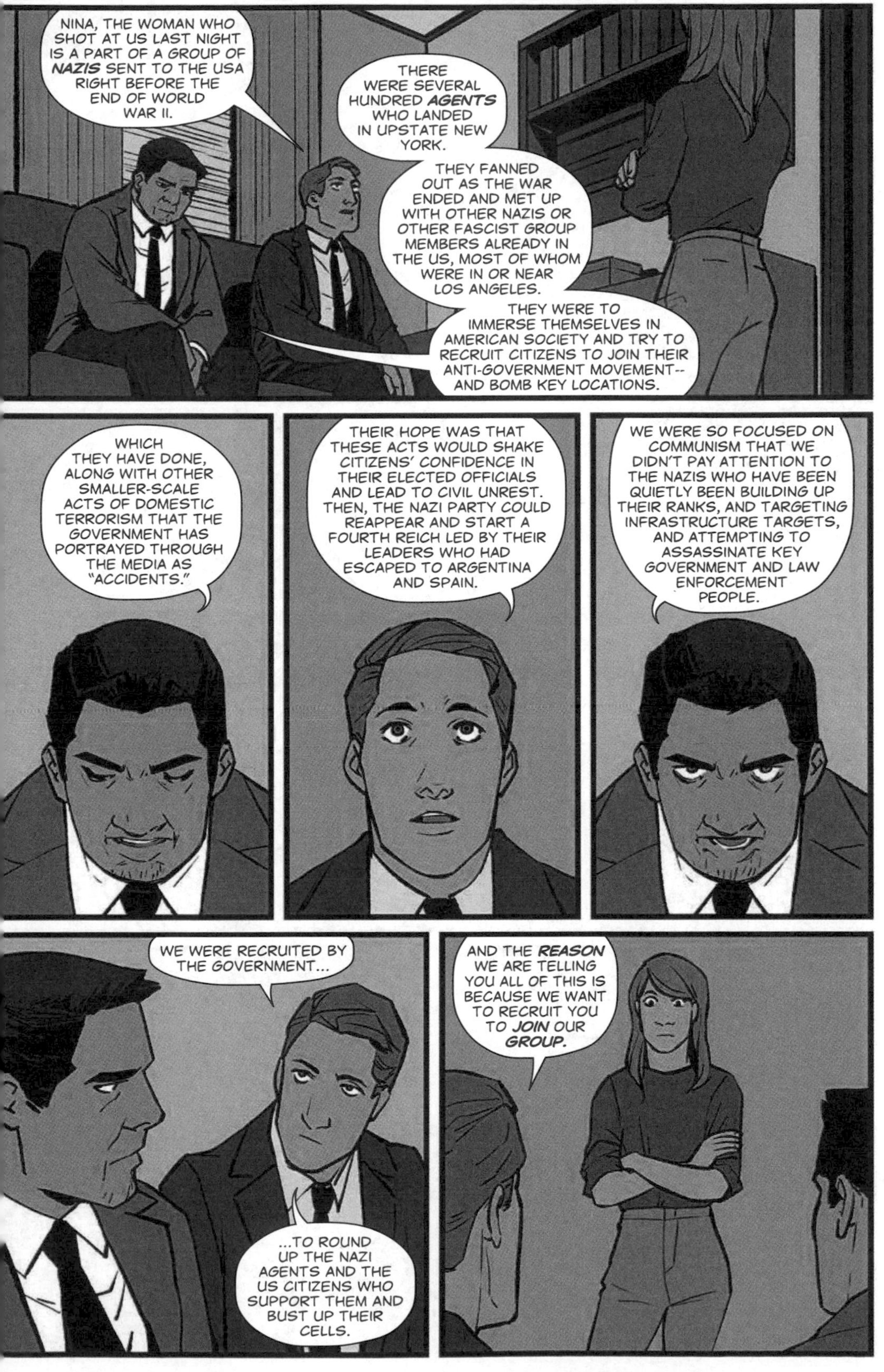
NINA, THE WOMAN WHO SHOT AT US LAST NIGHT IS A PART OF A GROUP OF *NAZIS* SENT TO THE USA RIGHT BEFORE THE END OF WORLD WAR II.
THERE WERE SEVERAL HUNDRED *AGENTS* WHO LANDED IN UPSTATE NEW YORK.
THEY FANNED OUT AS THE WAR ENDED AND MET UP WITH OTHER NAZIS OR OTHER FASCIST GROUP MEMBERS ALREADY IN THE US, MOST OF WHOM WERE IN OR NEAR LOS ANGELES.
THEY WERE TO IMMERSE THEMSELVES IN AMERICAN SOCIETY AND TRY TO RECRUIT CITIZENS TO JOIN THEIR ANTI-GOVERNMENT MOVEMENT-- AND BOMB KEY LOCATIONS.
WHICH THEY HAVE DONE, ALONG WITH OTHER SMALLER-SCALE ACTS OF DOMESTIC TERRORISM THAT THE GOVERNMENT HAS PORTRAYED THROUGH THE MEDIA AS "ACCIDENTS."
THEIR HOPE WAS THAT THESE ACTS WOULD SHAKE CITIZENS' CONFIDENCE IN THEIR ELECTED OFFICIALS AND LEAD TO CIVIL UNREST. THEN, THE NAZI PARTY COULD REAPPEAR AND START A FOURTH REICH LED BY THEIR LEADERS WHO HAD ESCAPED TO ARGENTINA AND SPAIN.
WE WERE SO FOCUSED ON COMMUNISM THAT WE DIDN'T PAY ATTENTION TO THE NAZIS WHO HAVE BEEN QUIETLY BEEN BUILDING UP THEIR RANKS, AND TARGETING INFRASTRUCTURE TARGETS, AND ATTEMPTING TO ASSASSINATE KEY GOVERNMENT AND LAW ENFORCEMENT PEOPLE.
WE WERE RECRUITED BY THE GOVERNMENT...
...TO ROUND UP THE NAZI AGENTS AND THE US CITIZENS WHO SUPPORT THEM AND BUST UP THEIR CELLS.
AND THE *REASON* WE ARE TELLING YOU ALL OF THIS IS BECAUSE WE WANT TO RECRUIT YOU TO *JOIN* OUR *GROUP.*

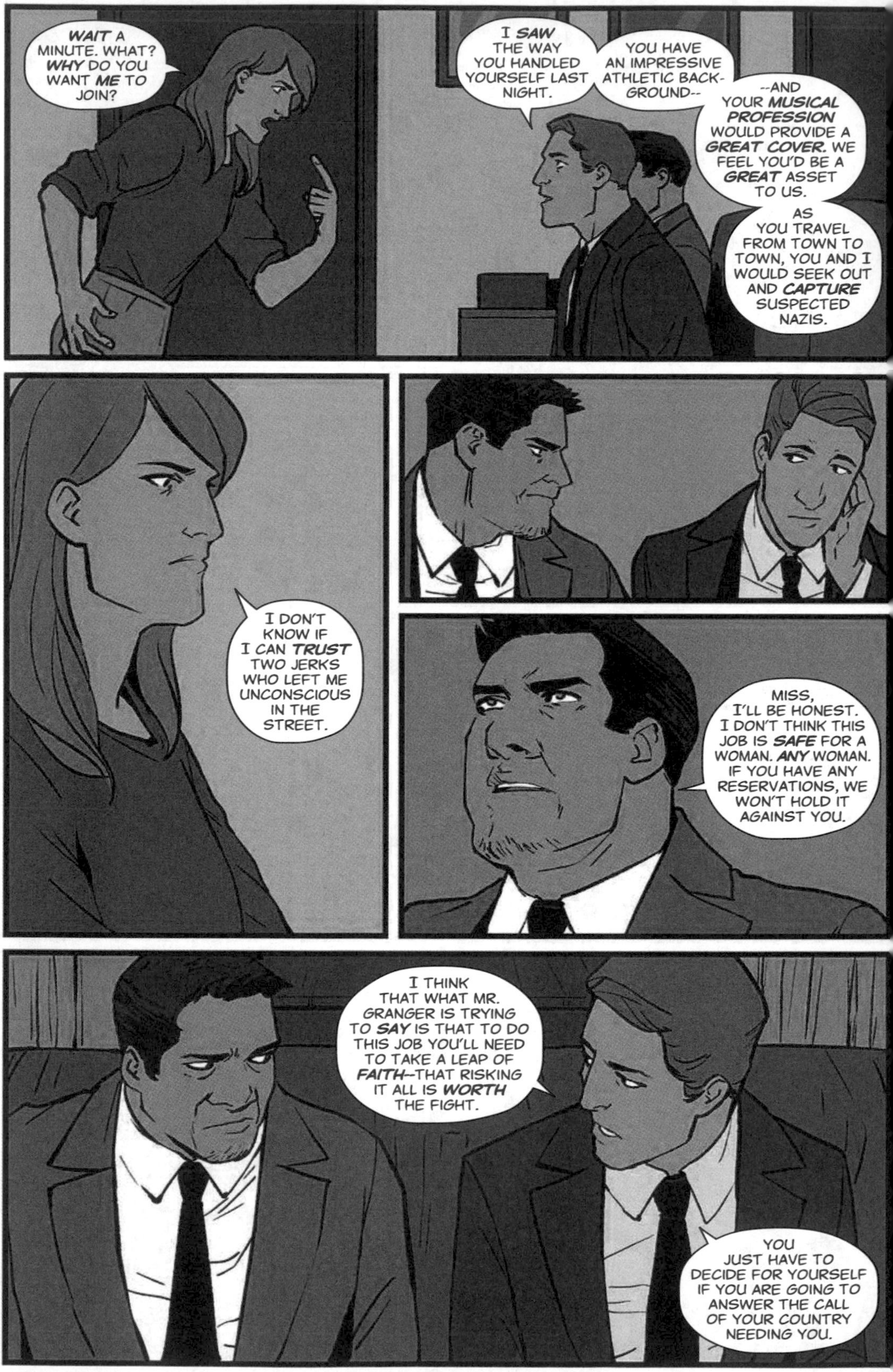
WAIT A MINUTE. WHAT? WHY DO YOU WANT ME TO JOIN?
I SAW THE WAY YOU HANDLED YOURSELF LAST NIGHT.
YOU HAVE AN IMPRESSIVE ATHLETIC BACK-GROUND--
--AND YOUR MUSICAL PROFESSION WOULD PROVIDE A GREAT COVER. WE FEEL YOU'D BE A GREAT ASSET TO US.
AS YOU TRAVEL FROM TOWN TO TOWN, YOU AND I WOULD SEEK OUT AND CAPTURE SUSPECTED NAZIS.
I DON'T KNOW IF I CAN TRUST TWO JERKS WHO LEFT ME UNCONSCIOUS IN THE STREET.
MISS, I'LL BE HONEST. I DON'T THINK THIS JOB IS SAFE FOR A WOMAN. ANY WOMAN. IF YOU HAVE ANY RESERVATIONS, WE WON'T HOLD IT AGAINST YOU.
I THINK THAT WHAT MR. GRANGER IS TRYING TO SAY IS THAT TO DO THIS JOB YOU'LL NEED TO TAKE A LEAP OF FAITH--THAT RISKING IT ALL IS WORTH THE FIGHT.
YOU JUST HAVE TO DECIDE FOR YOURSELF IF YOU ARE GOING TO ANSWER THE CALL OF YOUR COUNTRY NEEDING YOU.

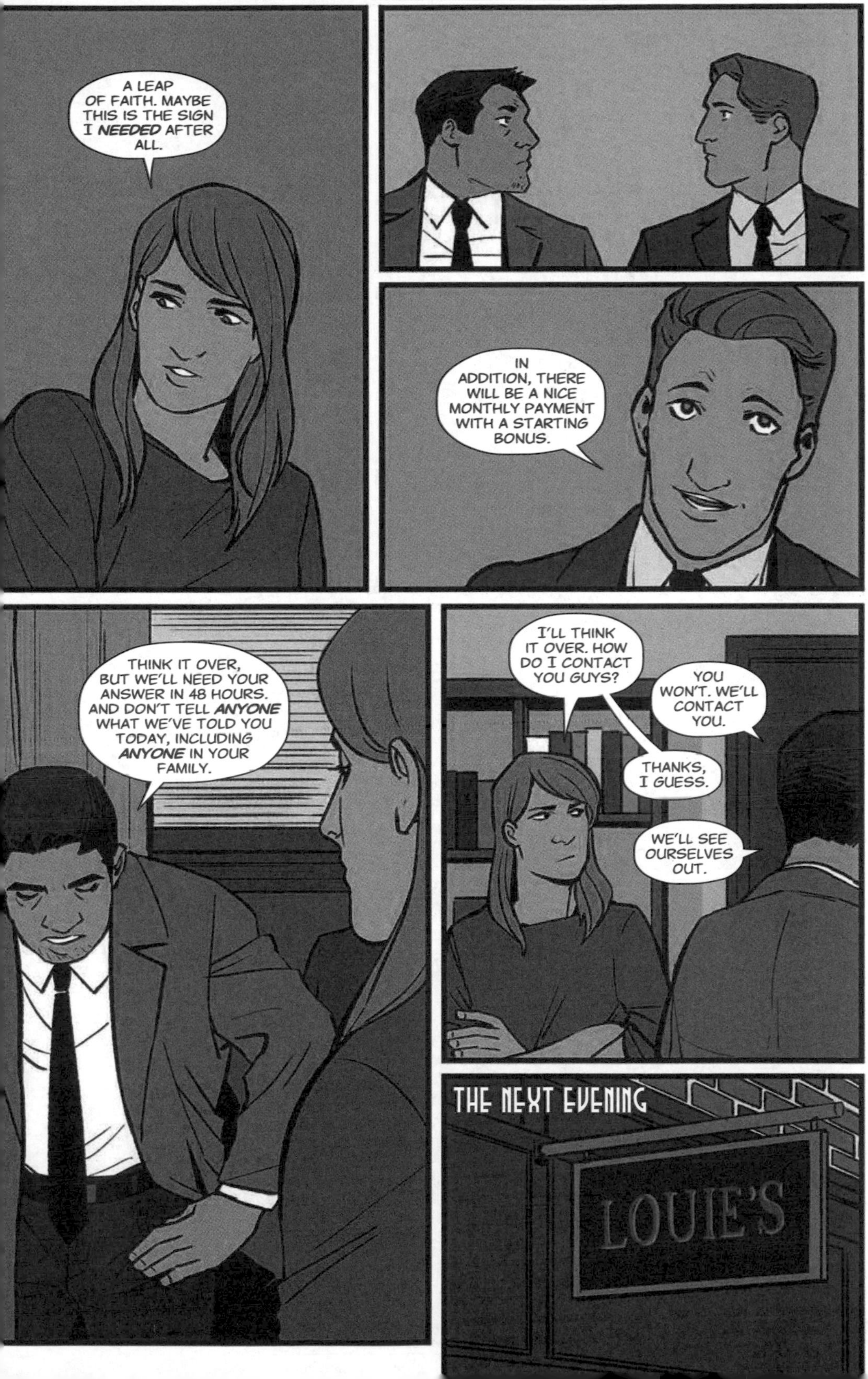
A LEAP OF FAITH. MAYBE THIS IS THE SIGN I NEEDED AFTER ALL.
IN ADDITION, THERE WILL BE A NICE MONTHLY PAYMENT WITH A STARTING BONUS.
THINK IT OVER, BUT WE'LL NEED YOUR ANSWER IN 48 HOURS. AND DON'T TELL ANYONE WHAT WE'VE TOLD YOU TODAY, INCLUDING ANYONE IN YOUR FAMILY.
I'LL THINK IT OVER. HOW DO I CONTACT YOU GUYS?
YOU WON'T. WE'LL CONTACT YOU.
THANKS, I GUESS.
WE'LL SEE OURSELVES OUT.
THE NEXT EVENING
LOUIE'S

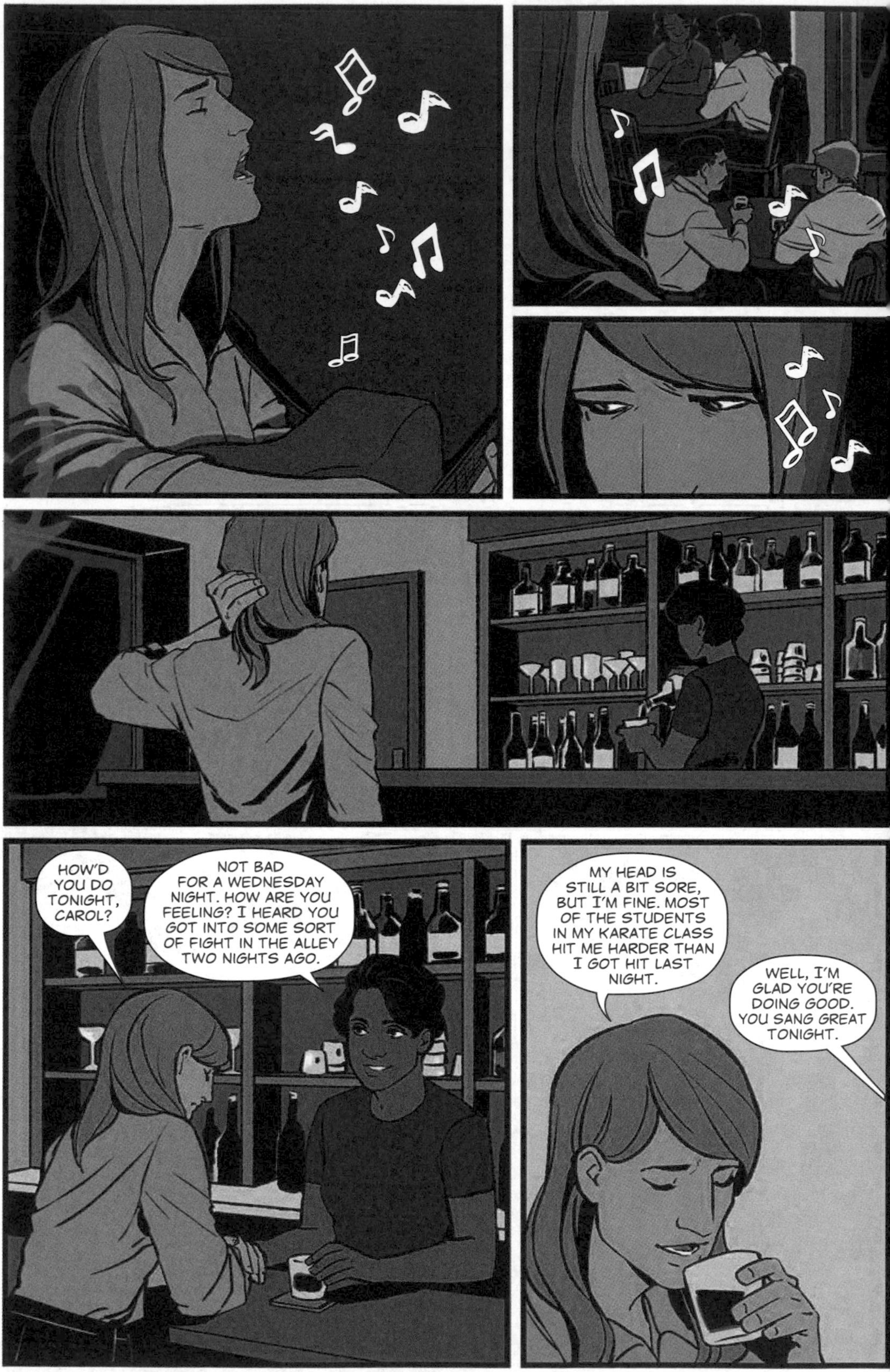
HOW'D YOU DO TONIGHT, CAROL?
NOT BAD FOR A WEDNESDAY NIGHT. HOW ARE YOU FEELING? I HEARD YOU GOT INTO SOME SORT OF FIGHT IN THE ALLEY TWO NIGHTS AGO.
MY HEAD IS STILL A BIT SORE, BUT I'M FINE. MOST OF THE STUDENTS IN MY KARATE CLASS HIT ME HARDER THAN I GOT HIT LAST NIGHT.
WELL, I'M GLAD YOU'RE DOING GOOD. YOU SANG GREAT TONIGHT.

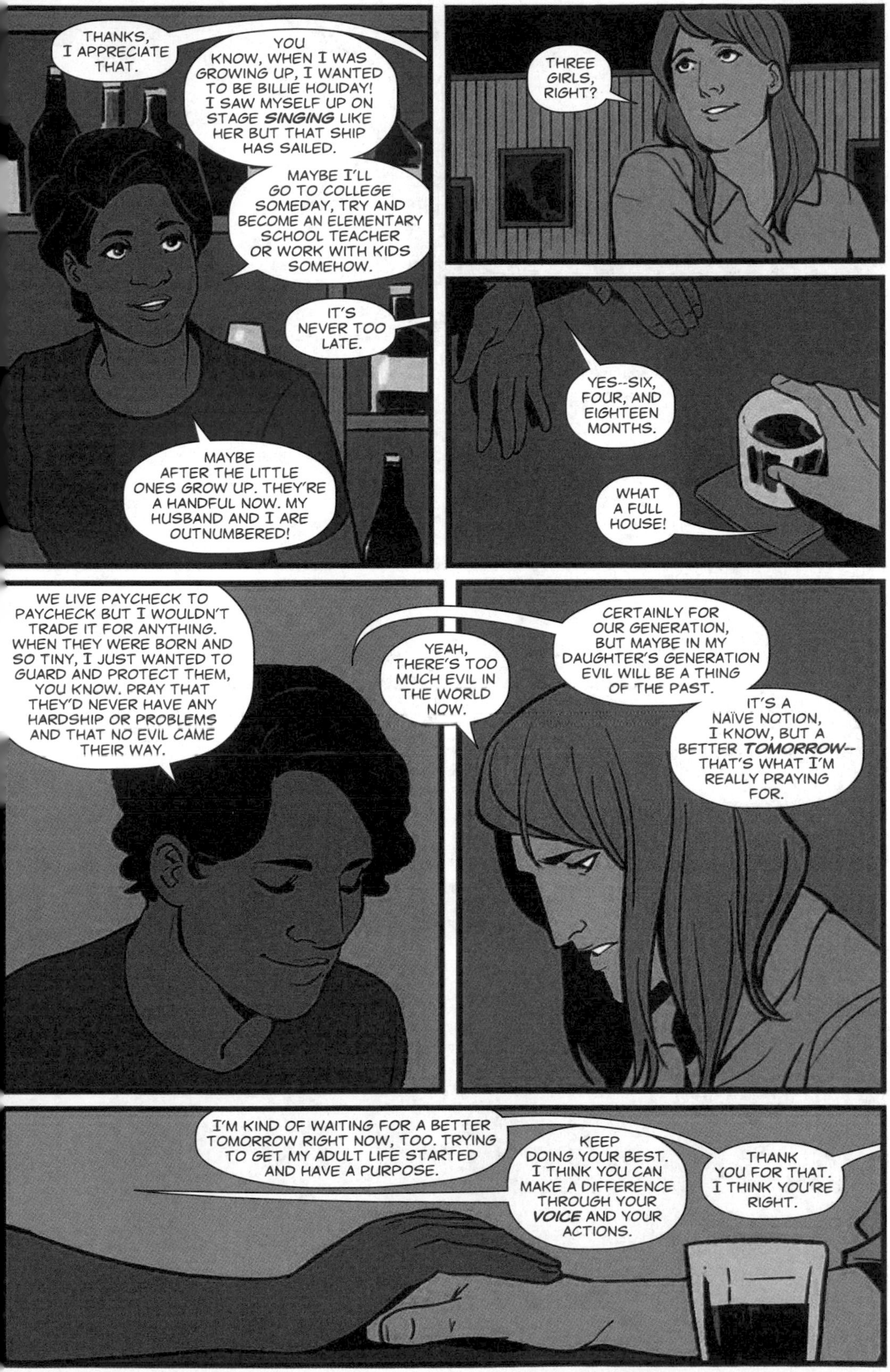
THANKS, I APPRECIATE THAT.
YOU KNOW, WHEN I WAS GROWING UP, I WANTED TO BE BILLIE HOLIDAY! I SAW MYSELF UP ON STAGE *SINGING* LIKE HER BUT THAT SHIP HAS SAILED.
MAYBE I'LL GO TO COLLEGE SOMEDAY, TRY AND BECOME AN ELEMENTARY SCHOOL TEACHER OR WORK WITH KIDS SOMEHOW.
IT'S NEVER TOO LATE.
MAYBE AFTER THE LITTLE ONES GROW UP. THEY'RE A HANDFUL NOW. MY HUSBAND AND I ARE OUTNUMBERED!
THREE GIRLS, RIGHT?
YES--SIX, FOUR, AND EIGHTEEN MONTHS.
WHAT A FULL HOUSE!
WE LIVE PAYCHECK TO PAYCHECK BUT I WOULDN'T TRADE IT FOR ANYTHING. WHEN THEY WERE BORN AND SO TINY, I JUST WANTED TO GUARD AND PROTECT THEM, YOU KNOW. PRAY THAT THEY'D NEVER HAVE ANY HARDSHIP OR PROBLEMS AND THAT NO EVIL CAME THEIR WAY.
YEAH, THERE'S TOO MUCH EVIL IN THE WORLD NOW.
CERTAINLY FOR OUR GENERATION, BUT MAYBE IN MY DAUGHTER'S GENERATION EVIL WILL BE A THING OF THE PAST.
IT'S A NAÏVE NOTION, I KNOW, BUT A BETTER *TOMORROW*-- THAT'S WHAT I'M REALLY PRAYING FOR.
I'M KIND OF WAITING FOR A BETTER TOMORROW RIGHT NOW, TOO. TRYING TO GET MY ADULT LIFE STARTED AND HAVE A PURPOSE.
KEEP DOING YOUR BEST. I THINK YOU CAN MAKE A DIFFERENCE THROUGH YOUR *VOICE* AND YOUR ACTIONS.
THANK YOU FOR THAT. I THINK YOU'RE RIGHT.

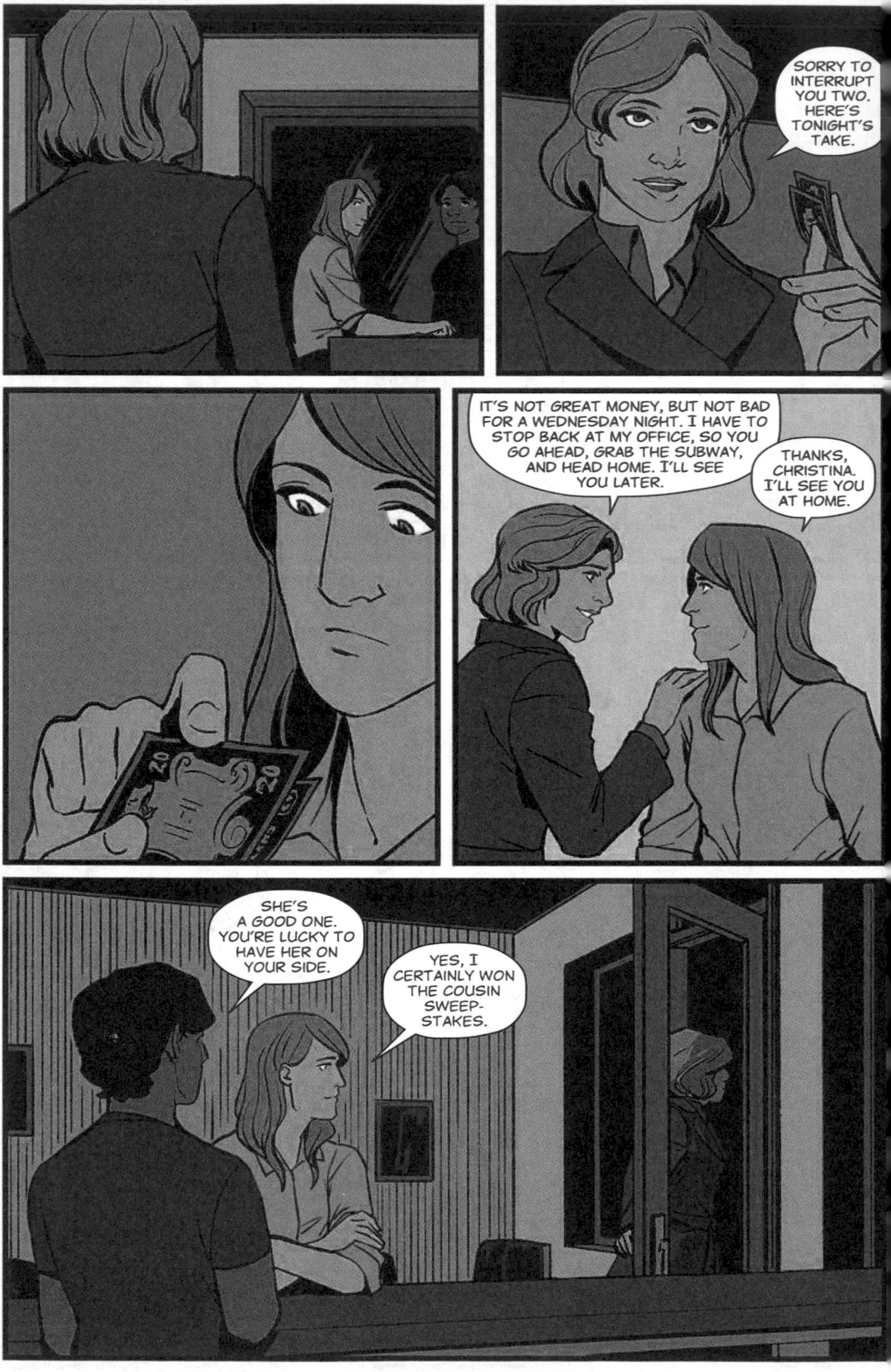
SORRY TO INTERRUPT YOU TWO. HERE'S TONIGHT'S TAKE.
IT'S NOT GREAT MONEY, BUT NOT BAD FOR A WEDNESDAY NIGHT. I HAVE TO STOP BACK AT MY OFFICE, SO YOU GO AHEAD, GRAB THE SUBWAY, AND HEAD HOME. I'LL SEE YOU LATER.
THANKS, CHRISTINA. I'LL SEE YOU AT HOME.
SHE'S A GOOD ONE. YOU'RE LUCKY TO HAVE HER ON YOUR SIDE.
YES, I CERTAINLY WON THE COUSIN SWEEP-STAKES.

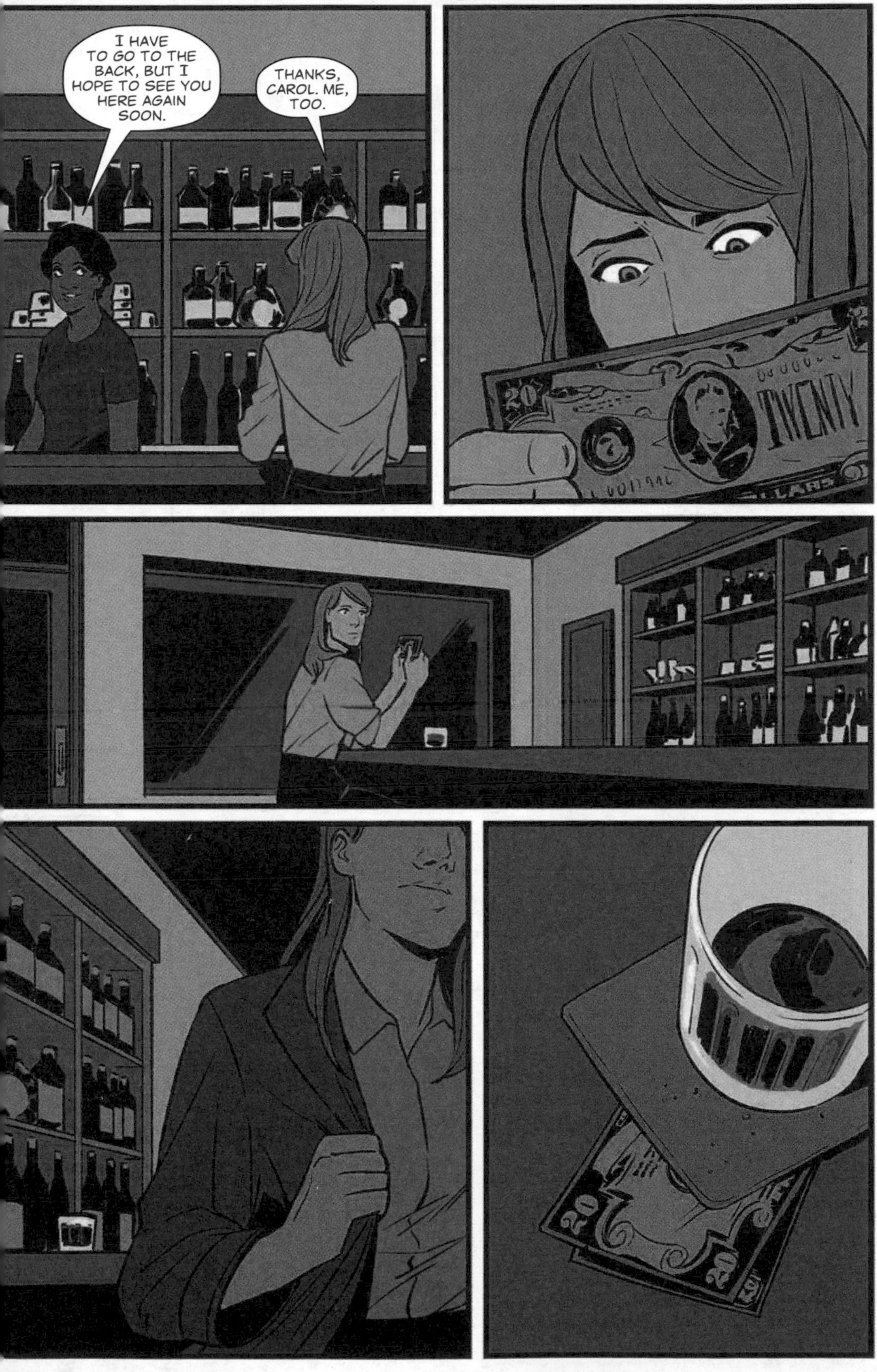
I HAVE TO GO TO THE BACK, BUT I HOPE TO SEE YOU HERE AGAIN SOON.
THANKS, CAROL. ME, TOO.
TWENTY

RECOMMENDED LISTENING:

DIAMONDS AND RUST
BY JOAN BAEZ

HONEY BEE
BY TOM PETTY AND THE HEARTBREAKERS

STARDOM IN ACTON
BY PETE TOWNSHEND

[I'M THE] QUEEN OF KENOSHA
BY NINA OVERSTREET

CHAPTER THREE

The Queen of Kenosha

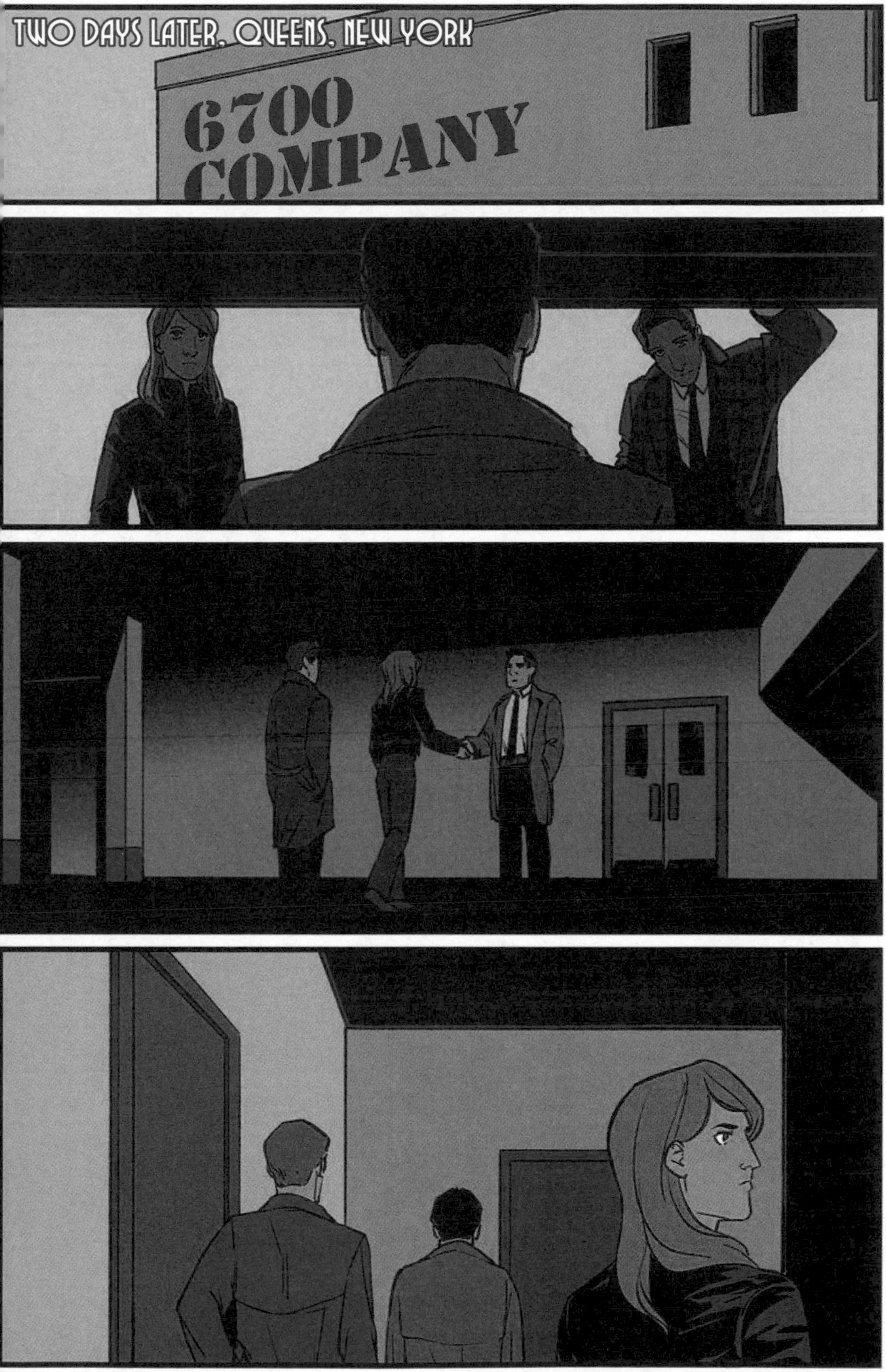
TWO DAYS LATER, QUEENS, NEW YORK
6700
COMPANY

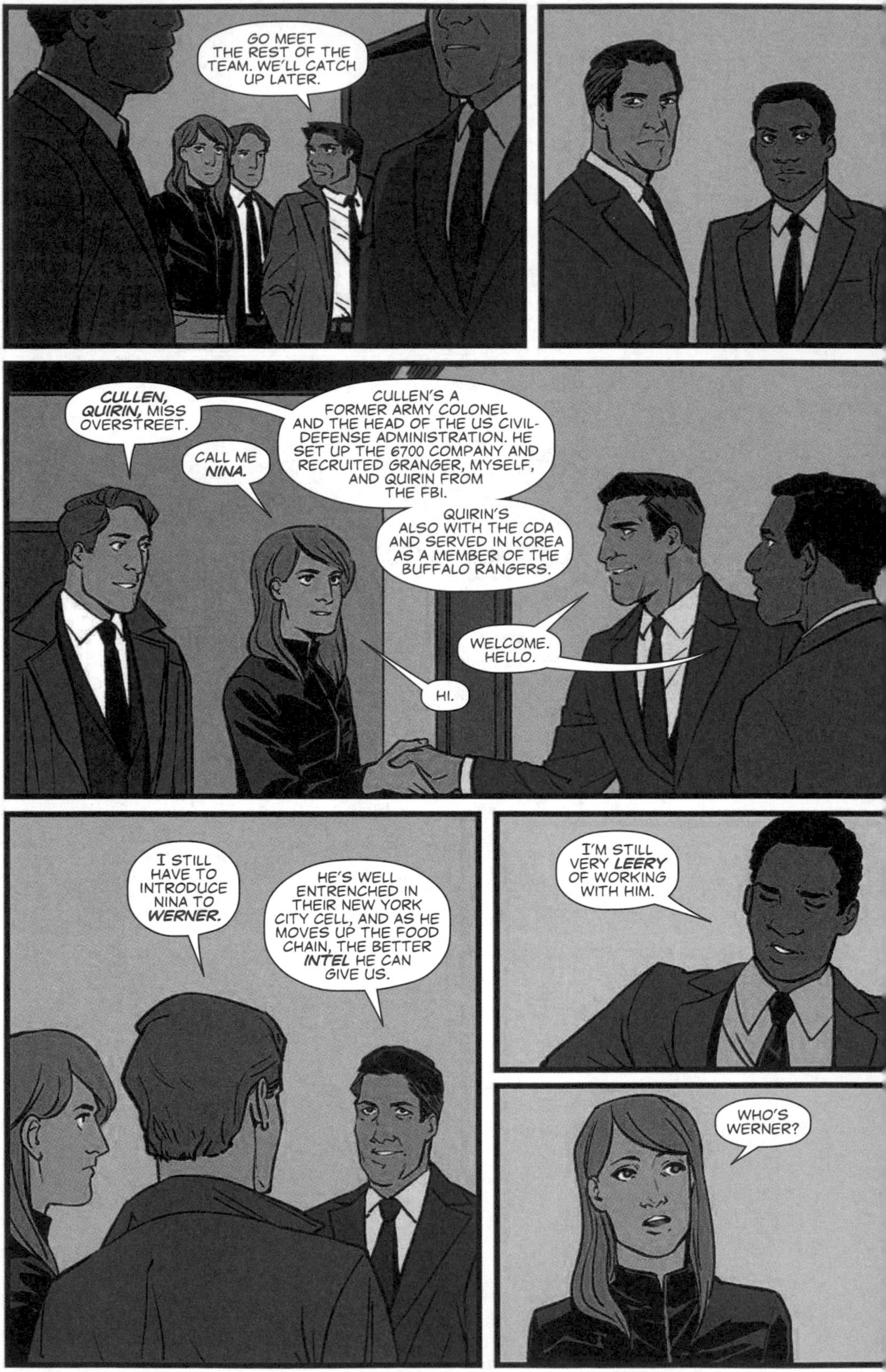
GO MEET THE REST OF THE TEAM. WE'LL CATCH UP LATER.
CULLEN, QUIRIN, MISS OVERSTREET.
CALL ME NINA.
CULLEN'S A FORMER ARMY COLONEL AND THE HEAD OF THE US CIVIL-DEFENSE ADMINISTRATION. HE SET UP THE 6700 COMPANY AND RECRUITED GRANGER, MYSELF, AND QUIRIN FROM THE FBI.
QUIRIN'S ALSO WITH THE CDA AND SERVED IN KOREA AS A MEMBER OF THE BUFFALO RANGERS.
WELCOME. HELLO.
HI.
I STILL HAVE TO INTRODUCE NINA TO WERNER.
HE'S WELL ENTRENCHED IN THEIR NEW YORK CITY CELL, AND AS HE MOVES UP THE FOOD CHAIN, THE BETTER INTEL HE CAN GIVE US.
I'M STILL VERY LEERY OF WORKING WITH HIM.
WHO'S WERNER?

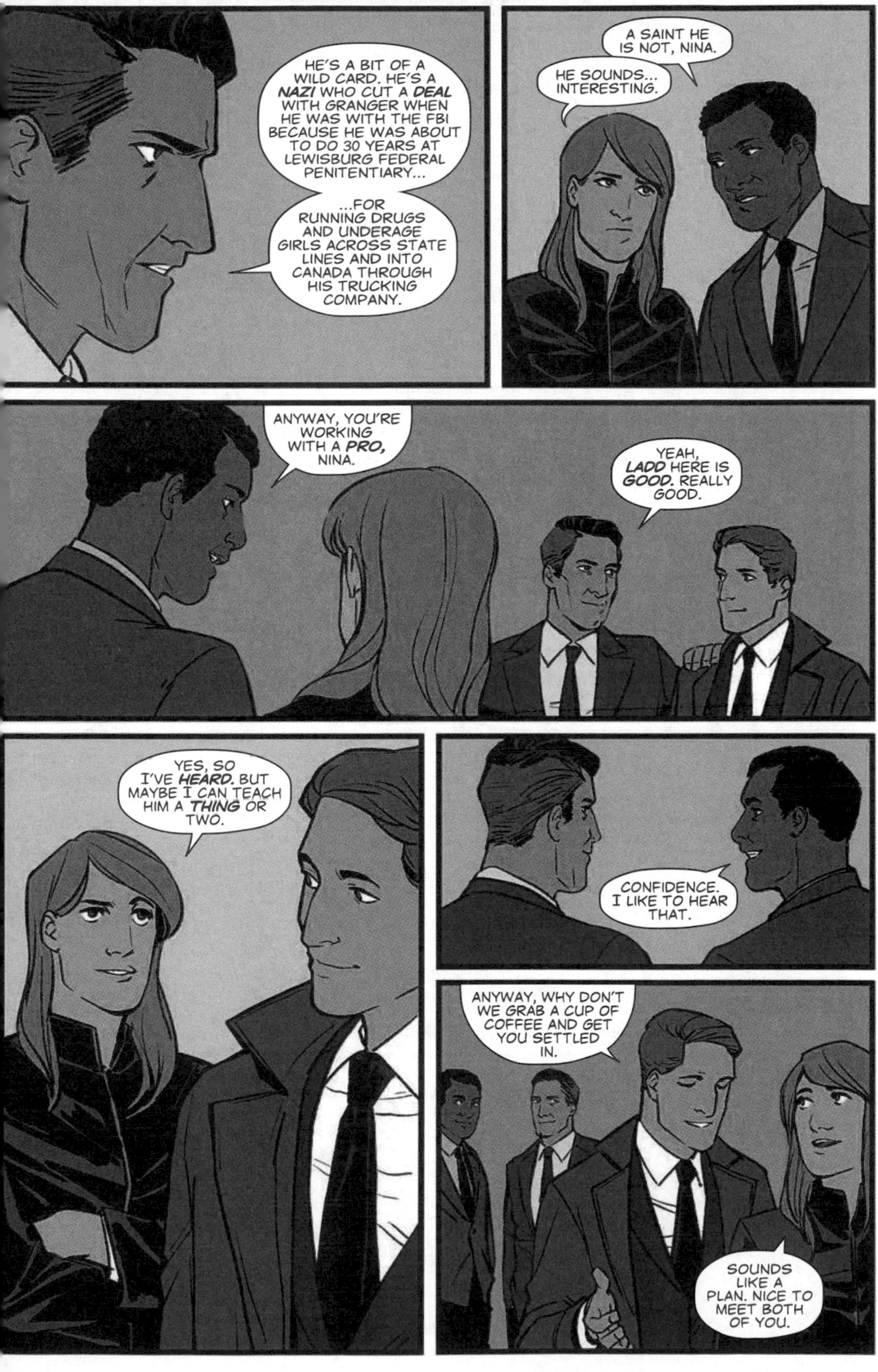
HE'S A BIT OF A WILD CARD. HE'S A NAZI WHO CUT A DEAL WITH GRANGER WHEN HE WAS WITH THE FBI BECAUSE HE WAS ABOUT TO DO 30 YEARS AT LEWISBURG FEDERAL PENITENTIARY...
...FOR RUNNING DRUGS AND UNDERAGE GIRLS ACROSS STATE LINES AND INTO CANADA THROUGH HIS TRUCKING COMPANY.
A SAINT HE IS NOT, NINA.
HE SOUNDS... INTERESTING.
ANYWAY, YOU'RE WORKING WITH A PRO, NINA.
YEAH, LADD HERE IS GOOD. REALLY GOOD.
YES, SO I'VE HEARD. BUT MAYBE I CAN TEACH HIM A THING OR TWO.
CONFIDENCE. I LIKE TO HEAR THAT.
ANYWAY, WHY DON'T WE GRAB A CUP OF COFFEE AND GET YOU SETTLED IN.
SOUNDS LIKE A PLAN. NICE TO MEET BOTH OF YOU.

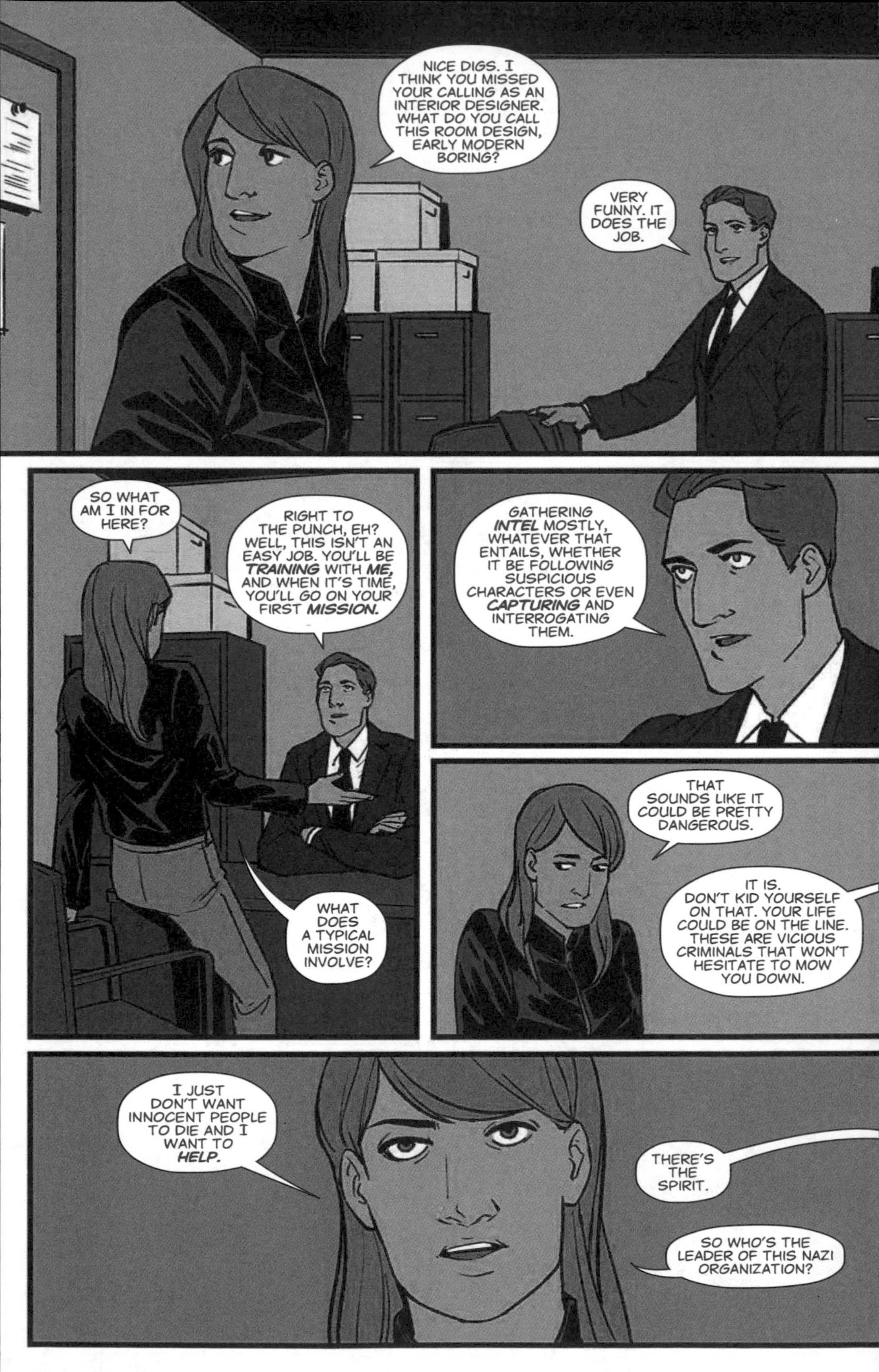
NICE DIGS. I THINK YOU MISSED YOUR CALLING AS AN INTERIOR DESIGNER. WHAT DO YOU CALL THIS ROOM DESIGN, EARLY MODERN BORING?
VERY FUNNY. IT DOES THE JOB.
SO WHAT AM I IN FOR HERE?
RIGHT TO THE PUNCH, EH? WELL, THIS ISN'T AN EASY JOB. YOU'LL BE TRAINING WITH ME, AND WHEN IT'S TIME, YOU'LL GO ON YOUR FIRST MISSION.
WHAT DOES A TYPICAL MISSION INVOLVE?
GATHERING INTEL MOSTLY, WHATEVER THAT ENTAILS, WHETHER IT BE FOLLOWING SUSPICIOUS CHARACTERS OR EVEN CAPTURING AND INTERROGATING THEM.
THAT SOUNDS LIKE IT COULD BE PRETTY DANGEROUS.
IT IS. DON'T KID YOURSELF ON THAT. YOUR LIFE COULD BE ON THE LINE. THESE ARE VICIOUS CRIMINALS THAT WON'T HESITATE TO MOW YOU DOWN.
I JUST DON'T WANT INNOCENT PEOPLE TO DIE AND I WANT TO HELP.
THERE'S THE SPIRIT.
SO WHO'S THE LEADER OF THIS NAZI ORGANIZATION?

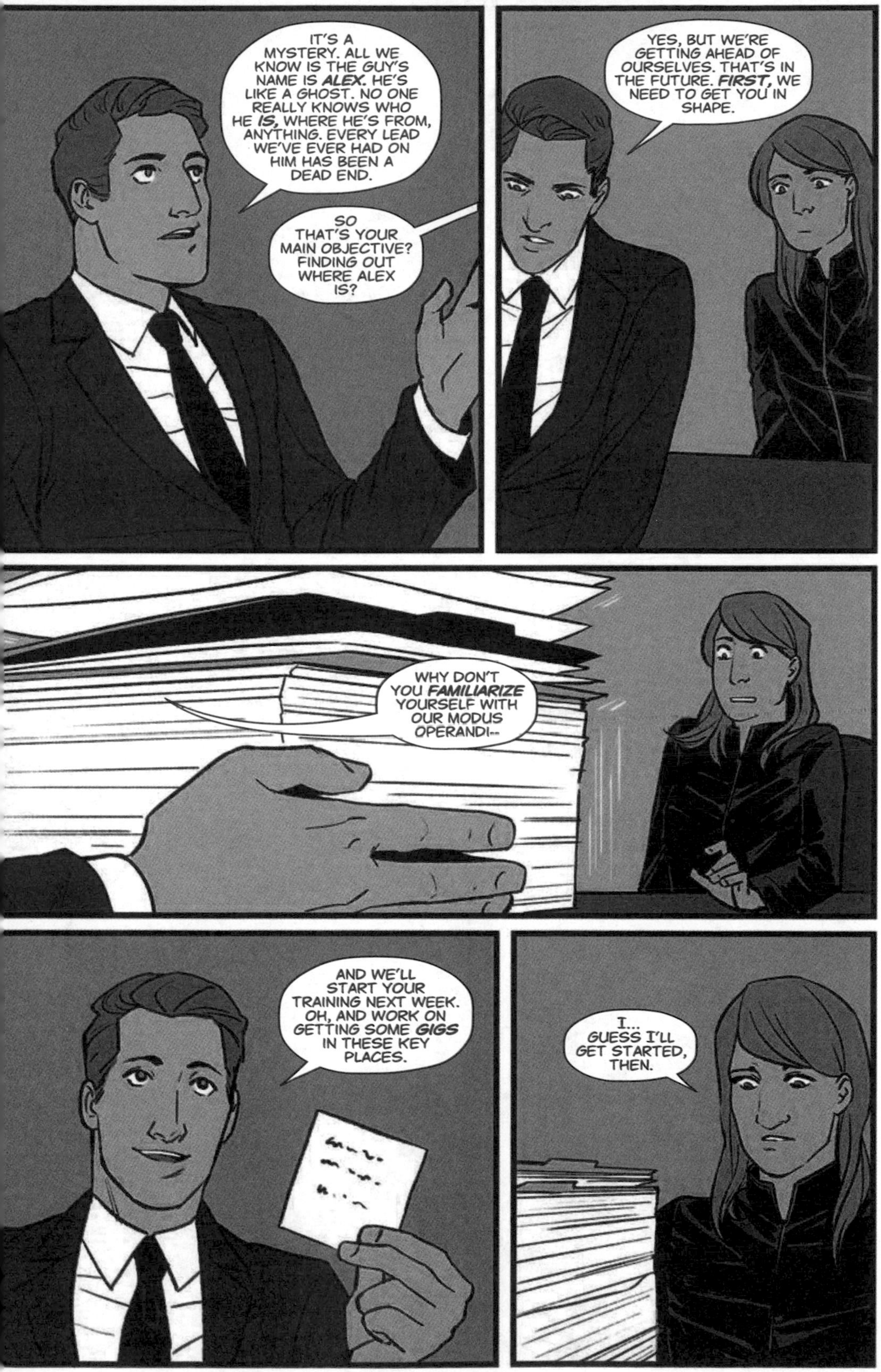
IT'S A MYSTERY. ALL WE KNOW IS THE GUY'S NAME IS ALEX. HE'S LIKE A GHOST. NO ONE REALLY KNOWS WHO HE IS, WHERE HE'S FROM, ANYTHING. EVERY LEAD WE'VE EVER HAD ON HIM HAS BEEN A DEAD END.
SO THAT'S YOUR MAIN OBJECTIVE? FINDING OUT WHERE ALEX IS?
YES, BUT WE'RE GETTING AHEAD OF OURSELVES. THAT'S IN THE FUTURE. FIRST, WE NEED TO GET YOU IN SHAPE.
WHY DON'T YOU FAMILIARIZE YOURSELF WITH OUR MODUS OPERANDI--
AND WE'LL START YOUR TRAINING NEXT WEEK. OH, AND WORK ON GETTING SOME GIGS IN THESE KEY PLACES.
I... GUESS I'LL GET STARTED, THEN.

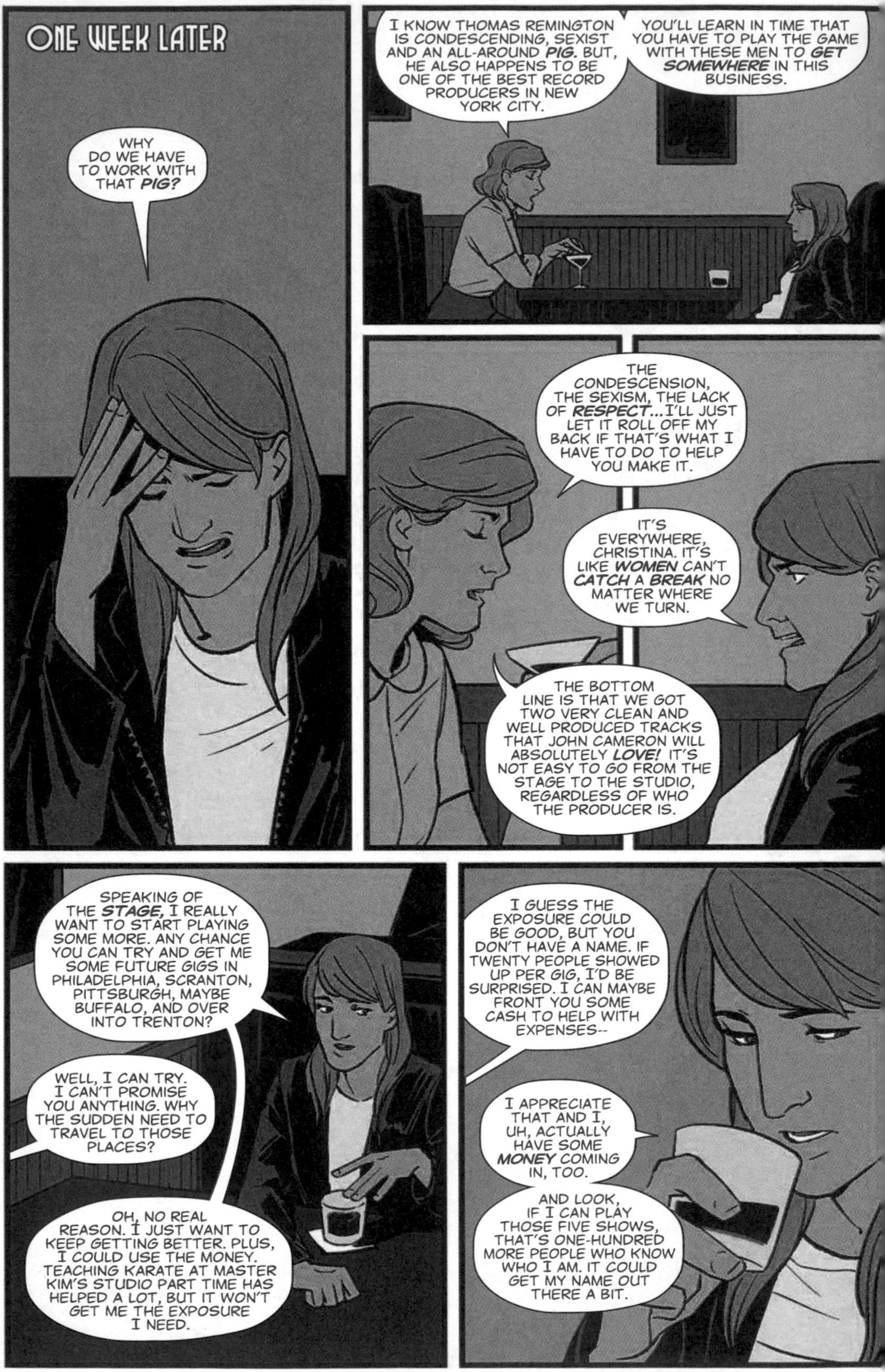
ONE WEEK LATER
WHY DO WE HAVE TO WORK WITH THAT PIG?
I KNOW THOMAS REMINGTON IS CONDESCENDING, SEXIST AND AN ALL-AROUND PIG. BUT, HE ALSO HAPPENS TO BE ONE OF THE BEST RECORD PRODUCERS IN NEW YORK CITY.
YOU'LL LEARN IN TIME THAT YOU HAVE TO PLAY THE GAME WITH THESE MEN TO GET SOMEWHERE IN THIS BUSINESS.
THE CONDESCENSION, THE SEXISM, THE LACK OF RESPECT...I'LL JUST LET IT ROLL OFF MY BACK IF THAT'S WHAT I HAVE TO DO TO HELP YOU MAKE IT.
IT'S EVERYWHERE, CHRISTINA. IT'S LIKE WOMEN CAN'T CATCH A BREAK NO MATTER WHERE WE TURN.
THE BOTTOM LINE IS THAT WE GOT TWO VERY CLEAN AND WELL PRODUCED TRACKS THAT JOHN CAMERON WILL ABSOLUTELY LOVE! IT'S NOT EASY TO GO FROM THE STAGE TO THE STUDIO, REGARDLESS OF WHO THE PRODUCER IS.
SPEAKING OF THE STAGE, I REALLY WANT TO START PLAYING SOME MORE. ANY CHANCE YOU CAN TRY AND GET ME SOME FUTURE GIGS IN PHILADELPHIA, SCRANTON, PITTSBURGH, MAYBE BUFFALO, AND OVER INTO TRENTON?
WELL, I CAN TRY. I CAN'T PROMISE YOU ANYTHING. WHY THE SUDDEN NEED TO TRAVEL TO THOSE PLACES?
OH, NO REAL REASON. I JUST WANT TO KEEP GETTING BETTER. PLUS, I COULD USE THE MONEY. TEACHING KARATE AT MASTER KIM'S STUDIO PART TIME HAS HELPED A LOT, BUT IT WON'T GET ME THE EXPOSURE I NEED.
I GUESS THE EXPOSURE COULD BE GOOD, BUT YOU DON'T HAVE A NAME. IF TWENTY PEOPLE SHOWED UP PER GIG, I'D BE SURPRISED. I CAN MAYBE FRONT YOU SOME CASH TO HELP WITH EXPENSES--
I APPRECIATE THAT AND I, UH, ACTUALLY HAVE SOME MONEY COMING IN, TOO.
AND LOOK, IF I CAN PLAY THOSE FIVE SHOWS, THAT'S ONE-HUNDRED MORE PEOPLE WHO KNOW WHO I AM. IT COULD GET MY NAME OUT THERE A BIT.

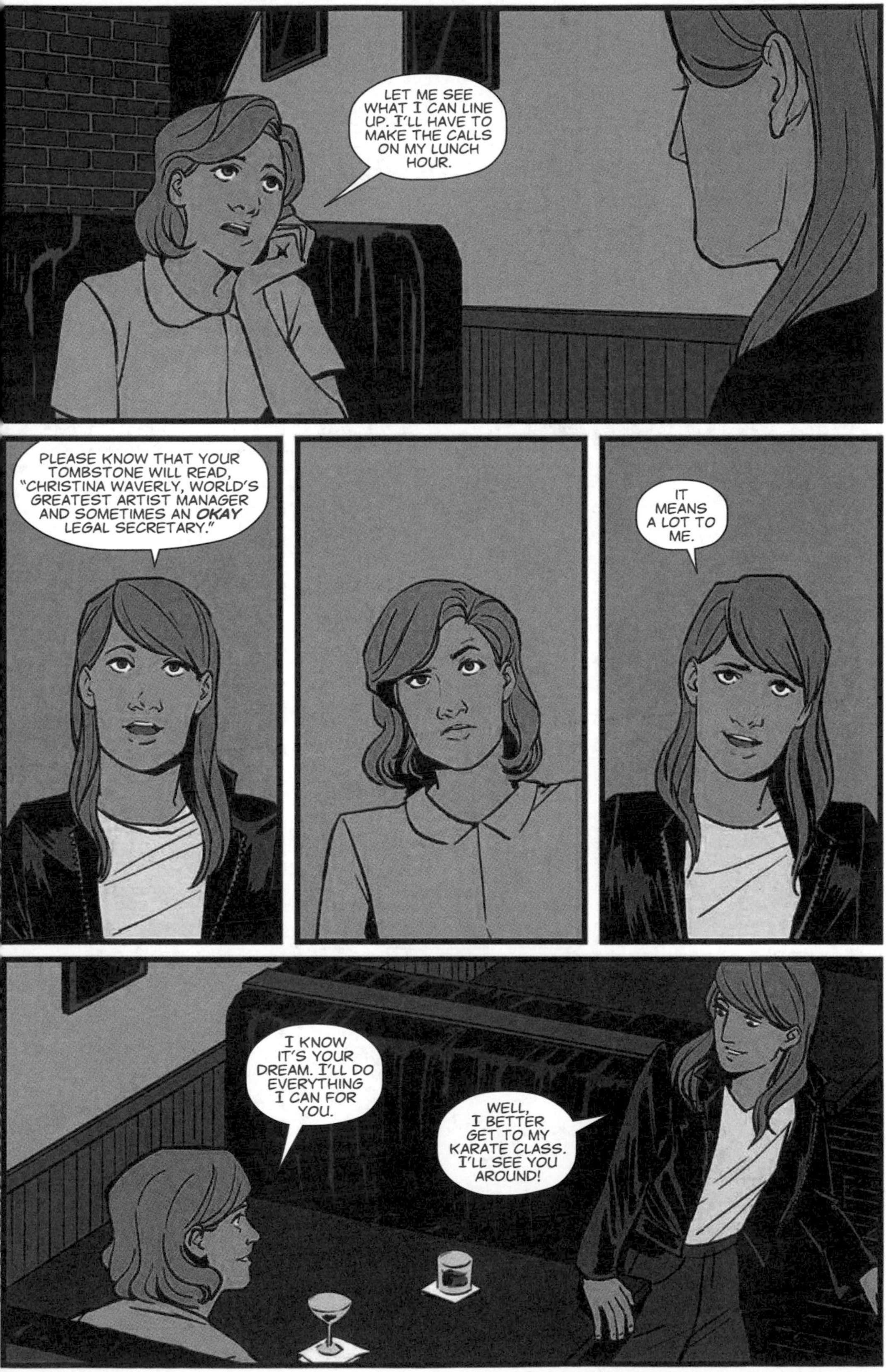
LET ME SEE WHAT I CAN LINE UP. I'LL HAVE TO MAKE THE CALLS ON MY LUNCH HOUR.
PLEASE KNOW THAT YOUR TOMBSTONE WILL READ, "CHRISTINA WAVERLY, WORLD'S GREATEST ARTIST MANAGER AND SOMETIMES AN *OKAY* LEGAL SECRETARY."
IT MEANS A LOT TO ME.
I KNOW IT'S YOUR DREAM. I'LL DO EVERYTHING I CAN FOR YOU.
WELL, I BETTER GET TO MY KARATE CLASS. I'LL SEE YOU AROUND!

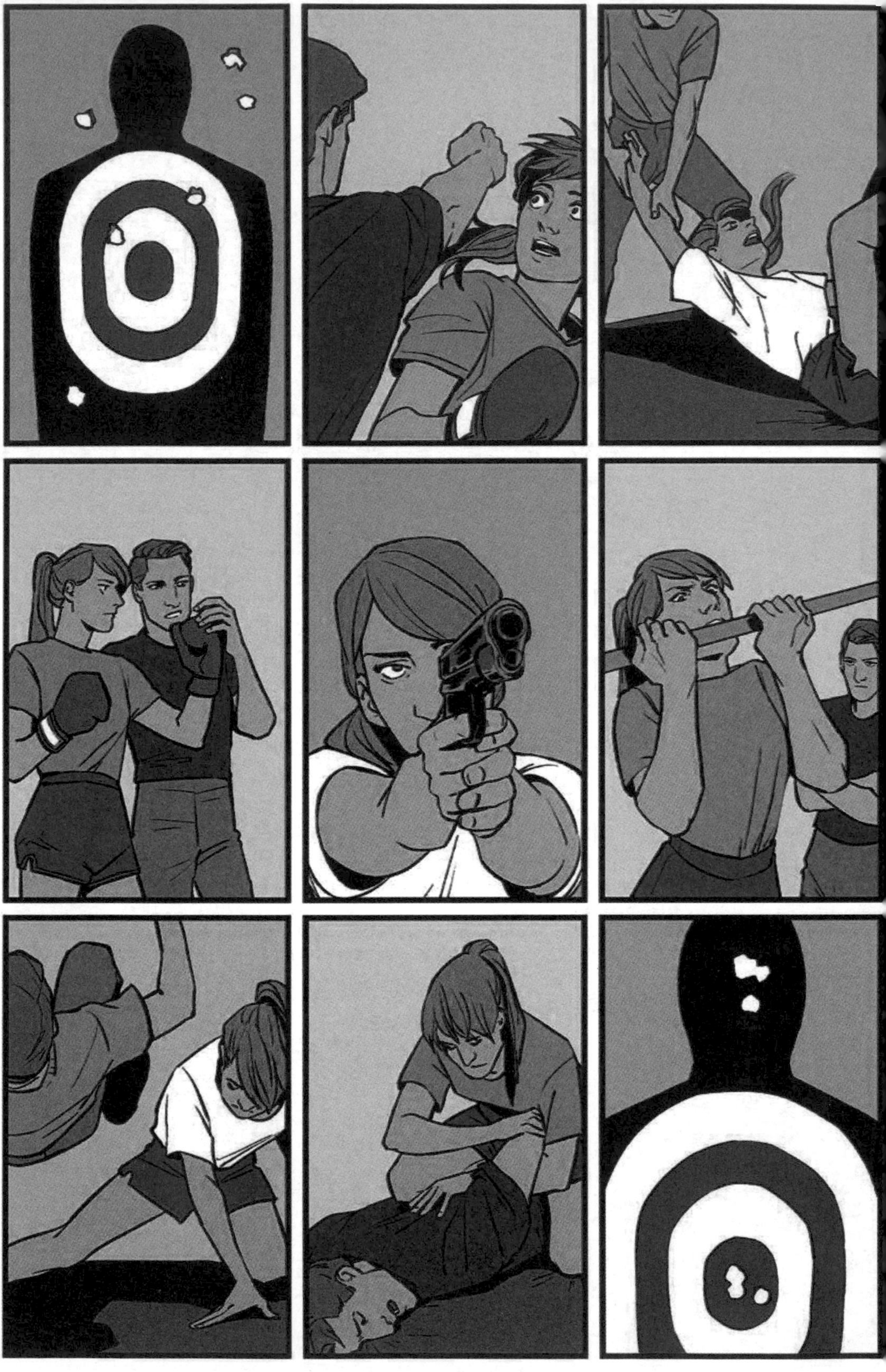

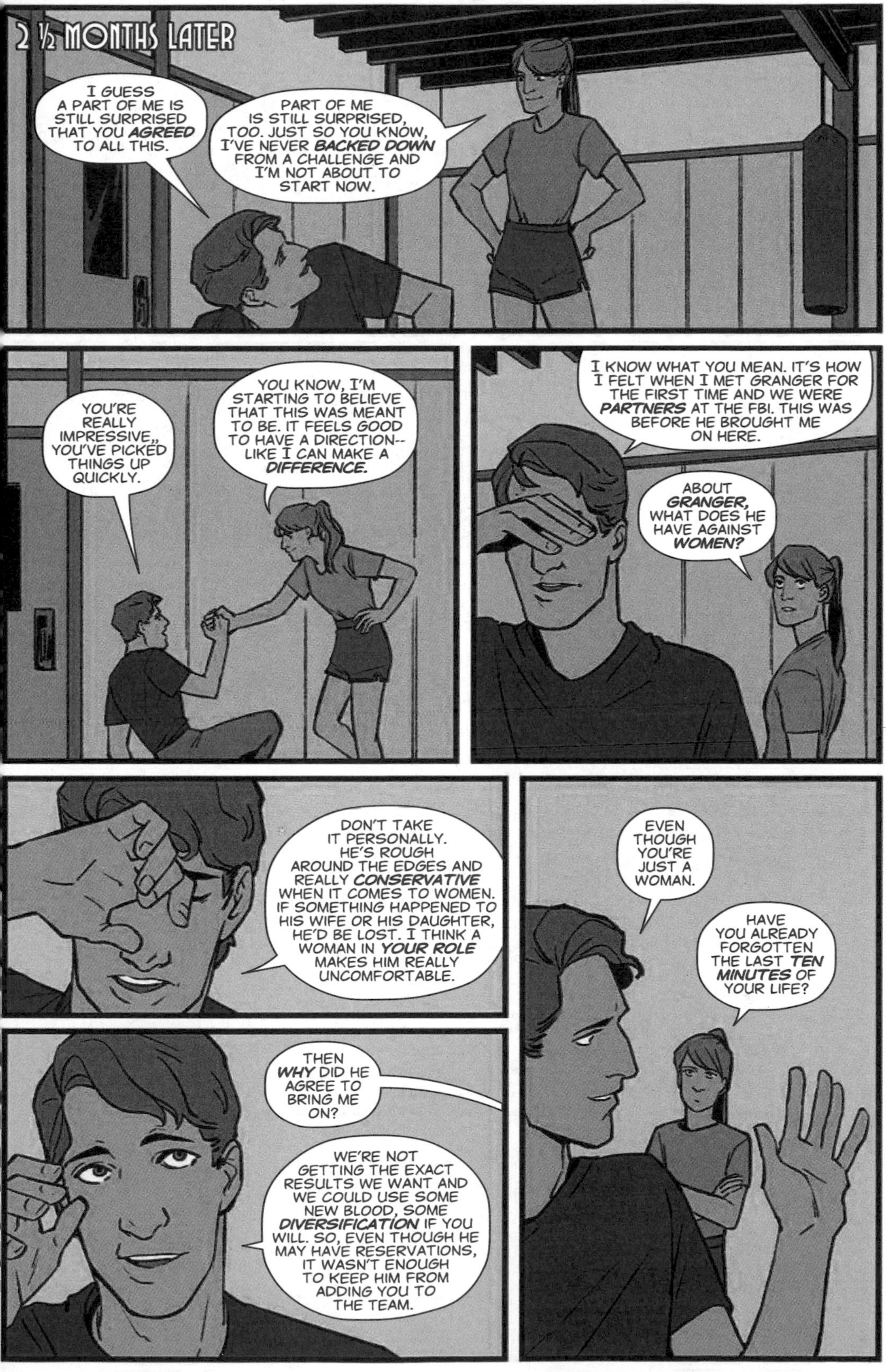
2 ½ MONTHS LATER
I GUESS A PART OF ME IS STILL SURPRISED THAT YOU AGREED TO ALL THIS.
PART OF ME IS STILL SURPRISED, TOO. JUST SO YOU KNOW, I'VE NEVER BACKED DOWN FROM A CHALLENGE AND I'M NOT ABOUT TO START NOW.
YOU'RE REALLY IMPRESSIVE,, YOU'VE PICKED THINGS UP QUICKLY.
YOU KNOW, I'M STARTING TO BELIEVE THAT THIS WAS MEANT TO BE. IT FEELS GOOD TO HAVE A DIRECTION-- LIKE I CAN MAKE A DIFFERENCE.
I KNOW WHAT YOU MEAN. IT'S HOW I FELT WHEN I MET GRANGER FOR THE FIRST TIME AND WE WERE PARTNERS AT THE FBI. THIS WAS BEFORE HE BROUGHT ME ON HERE.
ABOUT GRANGER, WHAT DOES HE HAVE AGAINST WOMEN?
DON'T TAKE IT PERSONALLY. HE'S ROUGH AROUND THE EDGES AND REALLY CONSERVATIVE WHEN IT COMES TO WOMEN. IF SOMETHING HAPPENED TO HIS WIFE OR HIS DAUGHTER, HE'D BE LOST. I THINK A WOMAN IN YOUR ROLE MAKES HIM REALLY UNCOMFORTABLE.
THEN WHY DID HE AGREE TO BRING ME ON?
WE'RE NOT GETTING THE EXACT RESULTS WE WANT AND WE COULD USE SOME NEW BLOOD, SOME DIVERSIFICATION IF YOU WILL. SO, EVEN THOUGH HE MAY HAVE RESERVATIONS, IT WASN'T ENOUGH TO KEEP HIM FROM ADDING YOU TO THE TEAM.
EVEN THOUGH YOU'RE JUST A WOMAN.
HAVE YOU ALREADY FORGOTTEN THE LAST TEN MINUTES OF YOUR LIFE?

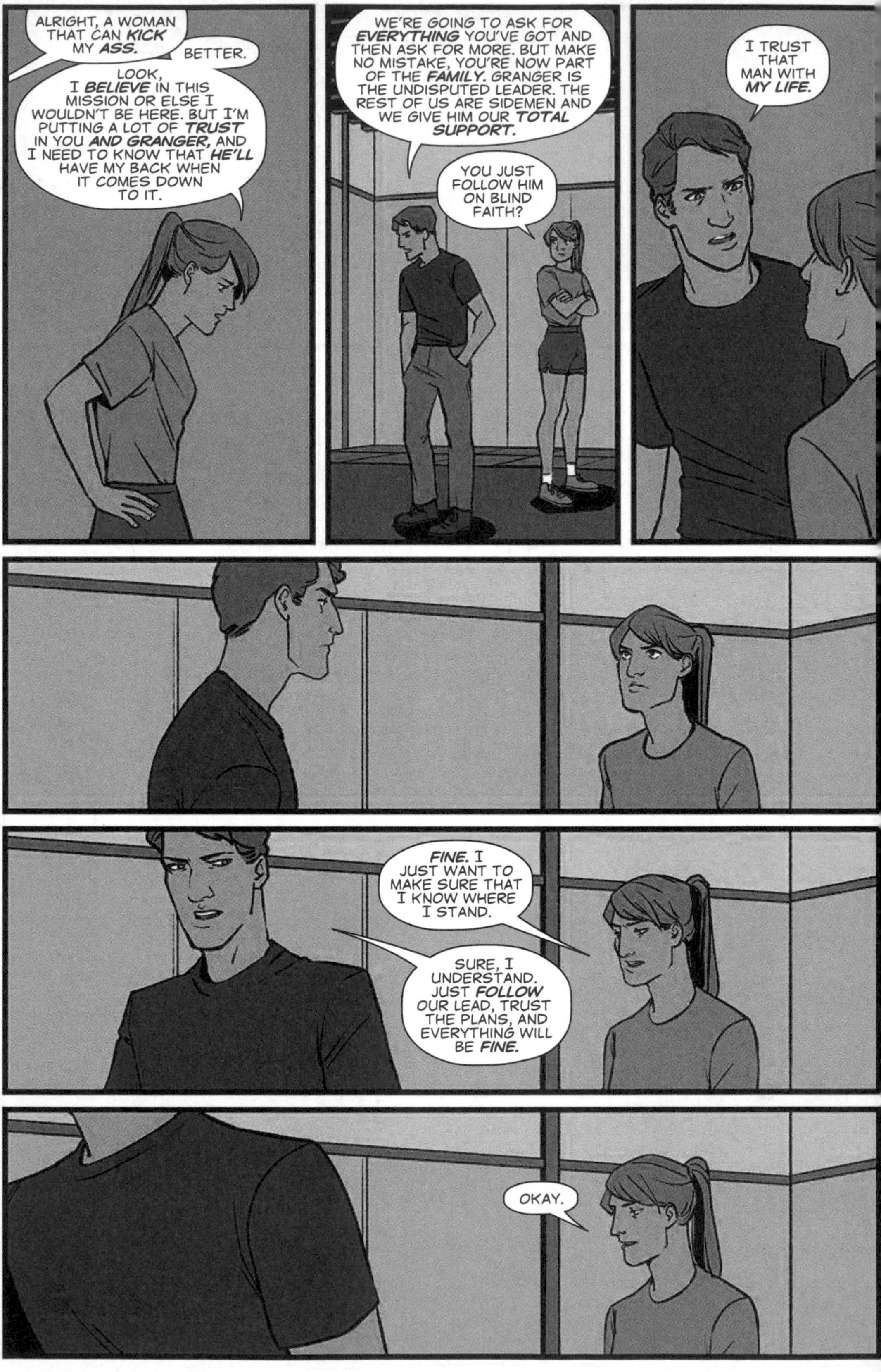
ALRIGHT, A WOMAN THAT CAN KICK MY ASS.
BETTER.
LOOK, I BELIEVE IN THIS MISSION OR ELSE I WOULDN'T BE HERE. BUT I'M PUTTING A LOT OF TRUST IN YOU AND GRANGER, AND I NEED TO KNOW THAT HE'LL HAVE MY BACK WHEN IT COMES DOWN TO IT.
WE'RE GOING TO ASK FOR EVERYTHING YOU'VE GOT AND THEN ASK FOR MORE. BUT MAKE NO MISTAKE, YOU'RE NOW PART OF THE FAMILY. GRANGER IS THE UNDISPUTED LEADER. THE REST OF US ARE SIDEMEN AND WE GIVE HIM OUR TOTAL SUPPORT.
YOU JUST FOLLOW HIM ON BLIND FAITH?
I TRUST THAT MAN WITH MY LIFE.
FINE. I JUST WANT TO MAKE SURE THAT I KNOW WHERE I STAND.
SURE, I UNDERSTAND. JUST FOLLOW OUR LEAD, TRUST THE PLANS, AND EVERYTHING WILL BE FINE.
OKAY.

RECOMMENDED LISTENING:

I'LL NEVER NEED MORE THAN THIS
BY ELLIE GREENWICH

AMERICAN EULOGY
BY GREEN DAY

A HOSTAGE OF THE SOUL
BY NINA OVERSTREET

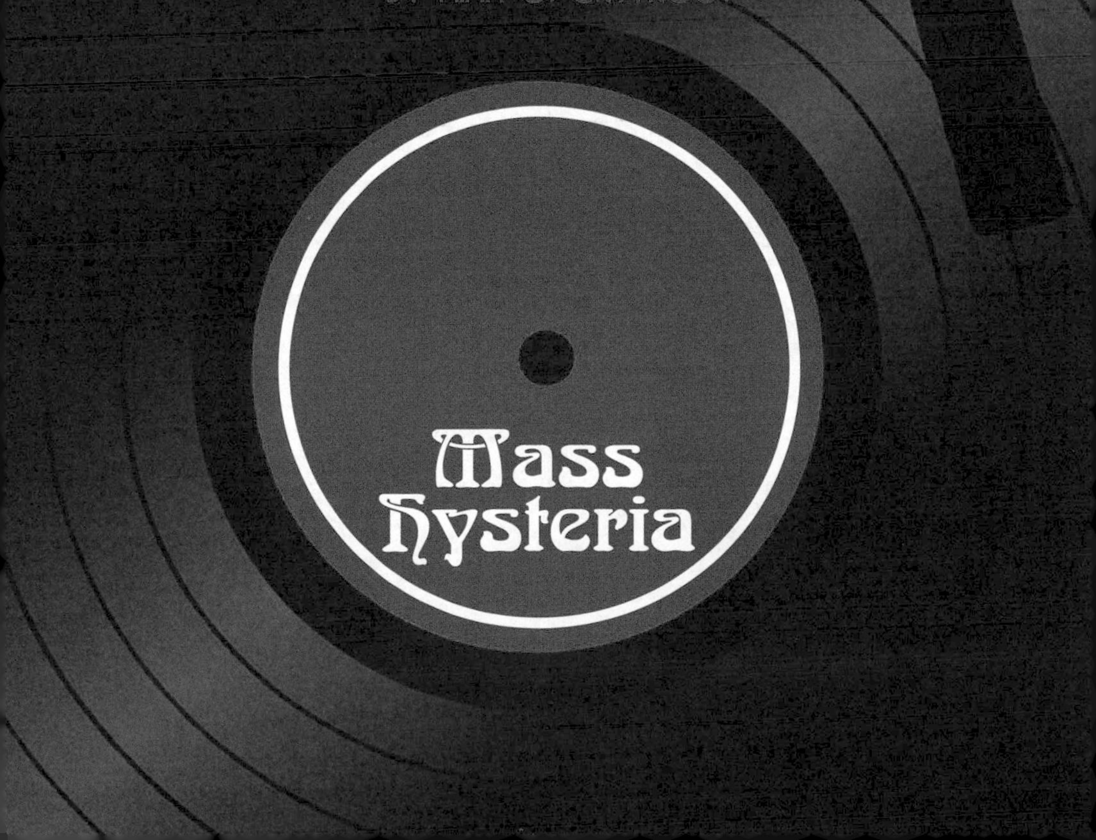
Mass
Hysteria

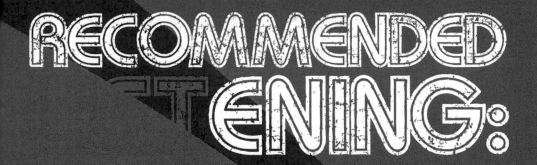

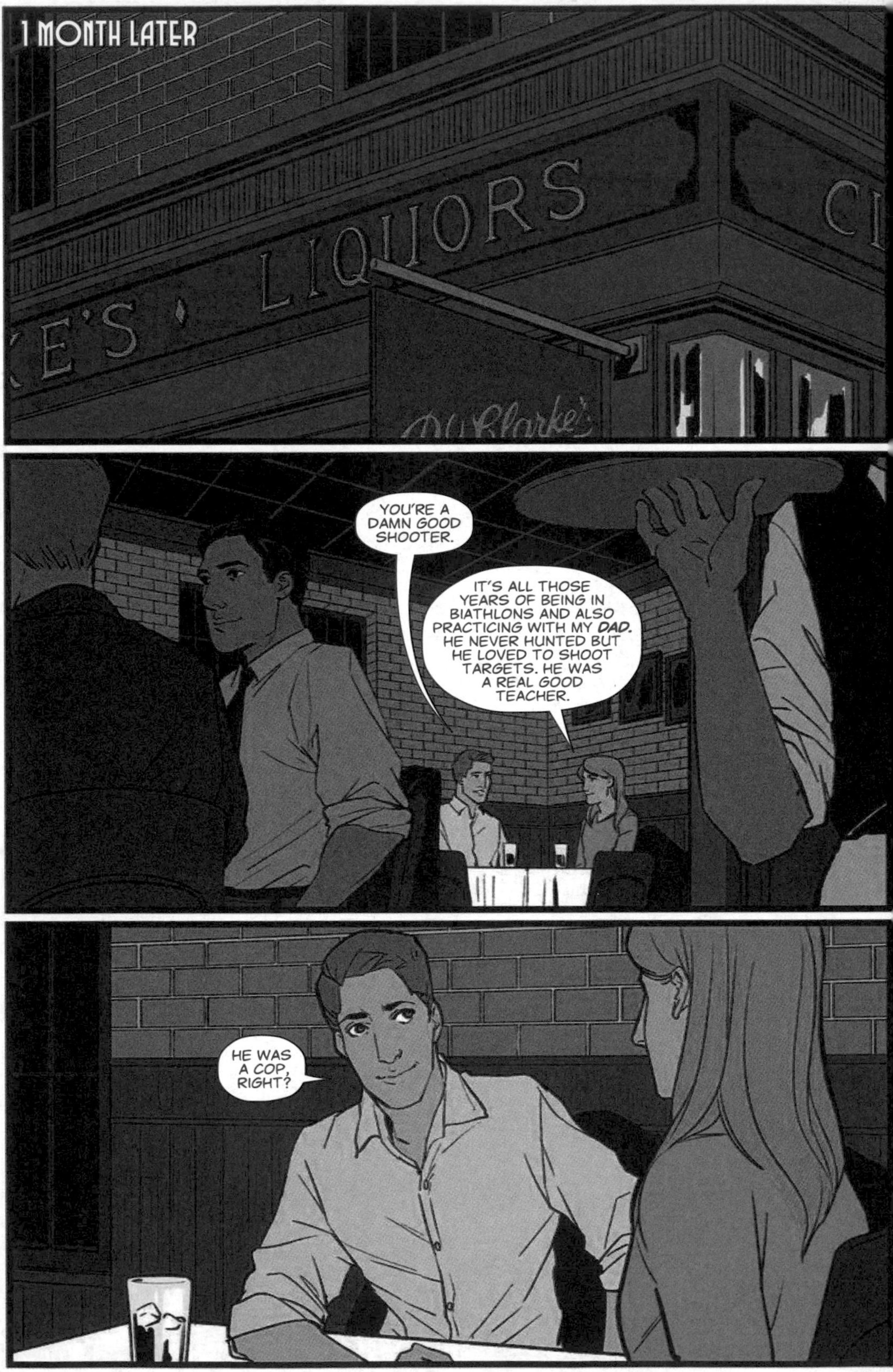
1 MONTH LATER
LIQUORS
YOU'RE A DAMN GOOD SHOOTER.
IT'S ALL THOSE YEARS OF BEING IN BIATHLONS AND ALSO PRACTICING WITH MY *DAD*. HE NEVER HUNTED BUT HE LOVED TO SHOOT TARGETS. HE WAS A REAL GOOD TEACHER.
HE WAS A COP, RIGHT?

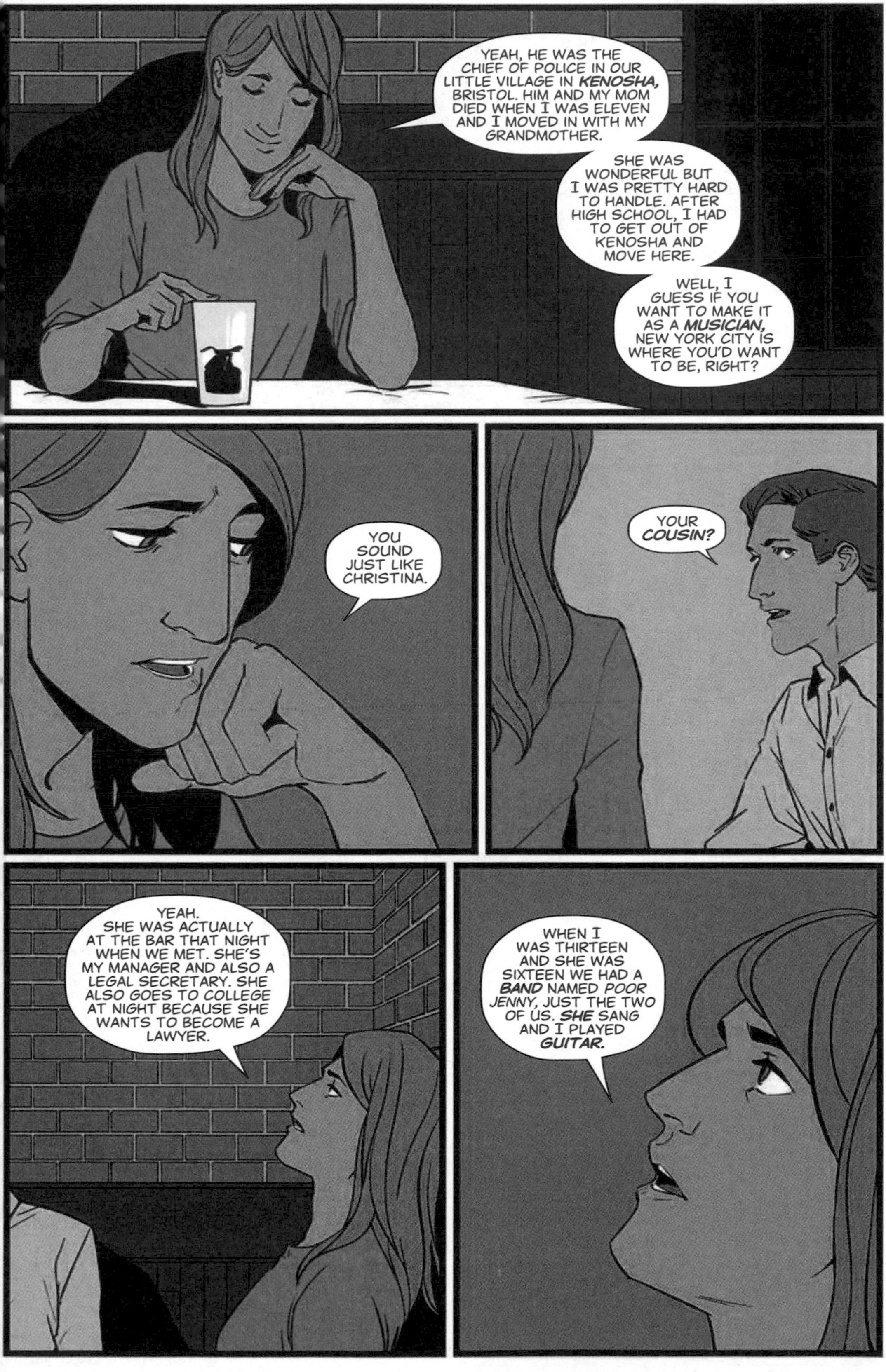

YEAH, HE WAS THE CHIEF OF POLICE IN OUR LITTLE VILLAGE IN **KENOSHA,** BRISTOL. HIM AND MY MOM DIED WHEN I WAS ELEVEN AND I MOVED IN WITH MY GRANDMOTHER.
SHE WAS WONDERFUL BUT I WAS PRETTY HARD TO HANDLE. AFTER HIGH SCHOOL, I HAD TO GET OUT OF KENOSHA AND MOVE HERE.
WELL, I GUESS IF YOU WANT TO MAKE IT AS A **MUSICIAN,** NEW YORK CITY IS WHERE YOU'D WANT TO BE, RIGHT?
YOU SOUND JUST LIKE CHRISTINA.
YOUR **COUSIN?**
YEAH. SHE WAS ACTUALLY AT THE BAR THAT NIGHT WHEN WE MET. SHE'S MY MANAGER AND ALSO A LEGAL SECRETARY. SHE ALSO *GOES* TO COLLEGE AT NIGHT BECAUSE SHE WANTS TO BECOME A LAWYER.
WHEN I WAS THIRTEEN AND SHE WAS SIXTEEN WE HAD A **BAND** NAMED *POOR JENNY*, JUST THE TWO OF US. ***SHE*** SANG AND I PLAYED **GUITAR.**

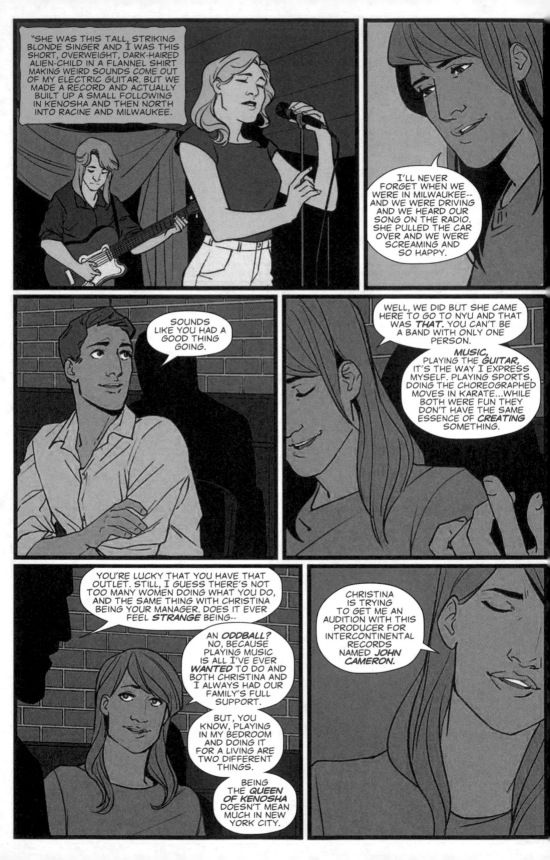

"SHE WAS THIS TALL, STRIKING BLONDE SINGER AND I WAS THIS SHORT, OVERWEIGHT, DARK-HAIRED ALIEN-CHILD IN A FLANNEL SHIRT MAKING WEIRD SOUNDS COME OUT OF MY ELECTRIC GUITAR. BUT WE MADE A RECORD AND ACTUALLY BUILT UP A SMALL FOLLOWING IN KENOSHA AND THEN NORTH INTO RACINE AND MILWAUKEE.

I'LL NEVER FORGET WHEN WE WERE IN MILWAUKEE-- AND WE WERE DRIVING AND WE HEARD OUR SONG ON THE RADIO. SHE PULLED THE CAR OVER AND WE WERE SCREAMING AND SO HAPPY.

SOUNDS LIKE YOU HAD A GOOD THING GOING.

WELL, WE DID BUT SHE CAME HERE TO GO TO NYU AND THAT WAS *THAT.* YOU CAN'T BE A BAND WITH ONLY ONE PERSON.

MUSIC, PLAYING THE *GUITAR,* IT'S THE WAY I EXPRESS MYSELF. PLAYING SPORTS, DOING THE CHOREOGRAPHED MOVES IN KARATE...WHILE BOTH WERE FUN THEY DON'T HAVE THE SAME ESSENCE OF *CREATING* SOMETHING.

YOU'RE LUCKY THAT YOU HAVE THAT OUTLET. STILL, I GUESS THERE'S NOT TOO MANY WOMEN DOING WHAT YOU DO, AND THE SAME THING WITH CHRISTINA BEING YOUR MANAGER. DOES IT EVER FEEL *STRANGE* BEING--

AN *ODDBALL?* NO, BECAUSE PLAYING MUSIC IS ALL I'VE EVER *WANTED* TO DO AND BOTH CHRISTINA AND I ALWAYS HAD OUR FAMILY'S FULL SUPPORT.

BUT, YOU KNOW, PLAYING IN MY BEDROOM AND DOING IT FOR A LIVING ARE TWO DIFFERENT THINGS.

BEING THE *QUEEN OF KENOSHA* DOESN'T MEAN MUCH IN NEW YORK CITY.

CHRISTINA IS TRYING TO GET ME AN AUDITION WITH THIS PRODUCER FOR INTERCONTINENTAL RECORDS NAMED *JOHN CAMERON.*

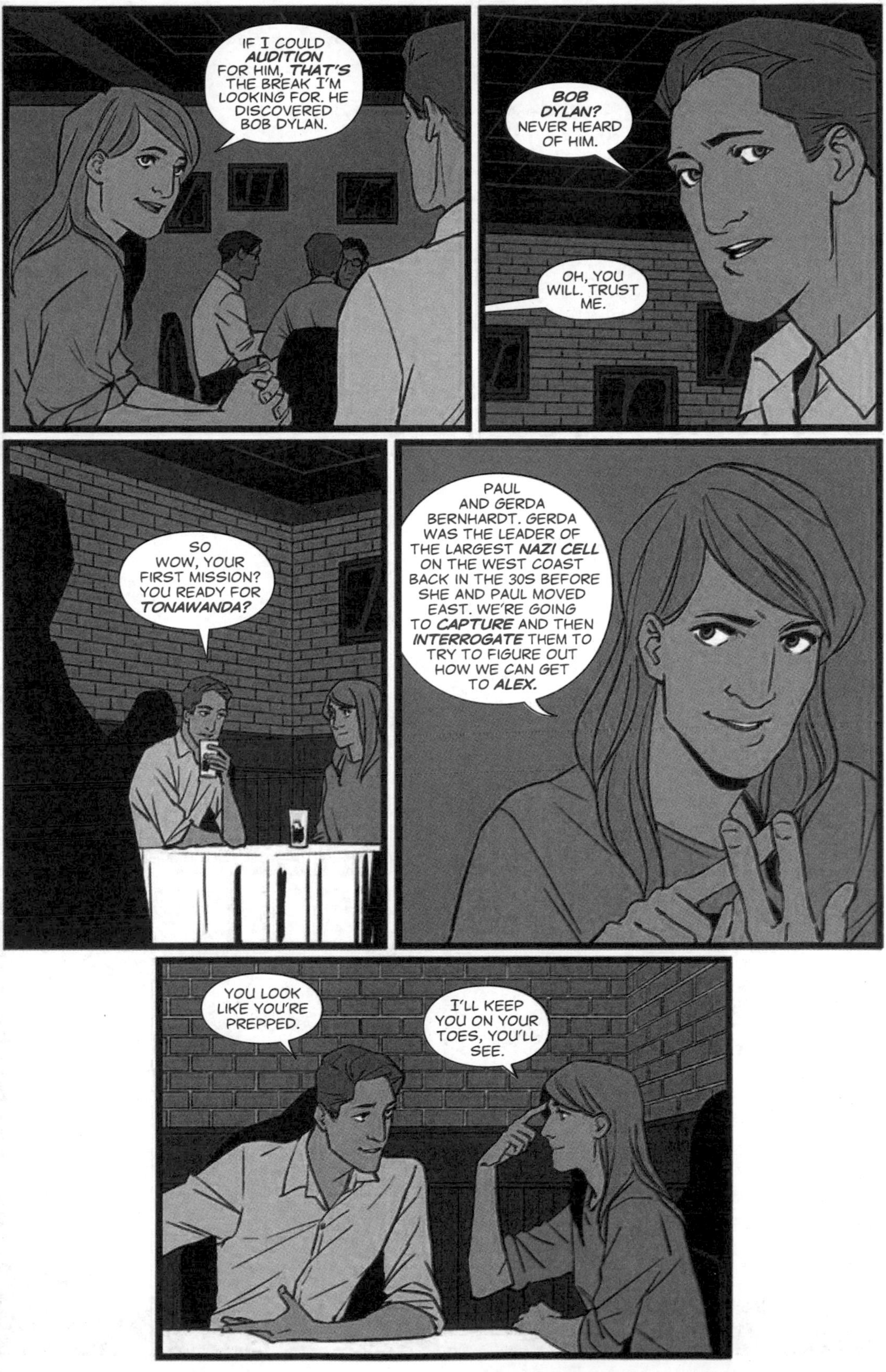
IF I COULD AUDITION FOR HIM, THAT'S THE BREAK I'M LOOKING FOR. HE DISCOVERED BOB DYLAN.
BOB DYLAN? NEVER HEARD OF HIM.
OH, YOU WILL. TRUST ME.
SO WOW, YOUR FIRST MISSION? YOU READY FOR TONAWANDA?
PAUL AND GERDA BERNHARDT. GERDA WAS THE LEADER OF THE LARGEST NAZI CELL ON THE WEST COAST BACK IN THE 30S BEFORE SHE AND PAUL MOVED EAST. WE'RE GOING TO CAPTURE AND THEN INTERROGATE THEM TO TRY TO FIGURE OUT HOW WE CAN GET TO ALEX.
YOU LOOK LIKE YOU'RE PREPPED.
I'LL KEEP YOU ON YOUR TOES, YOU'LL SEE.

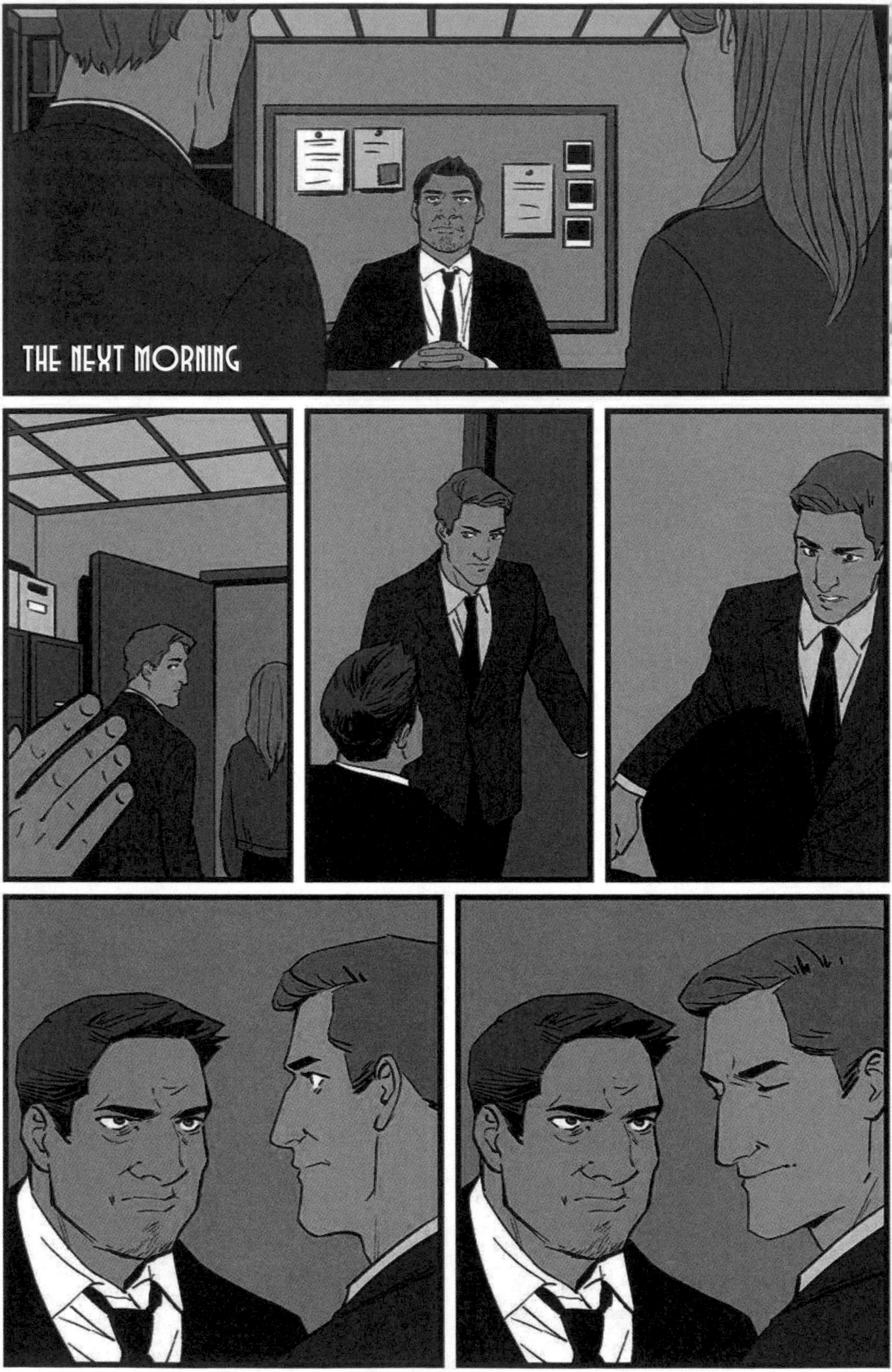
THE NEXT MORNING

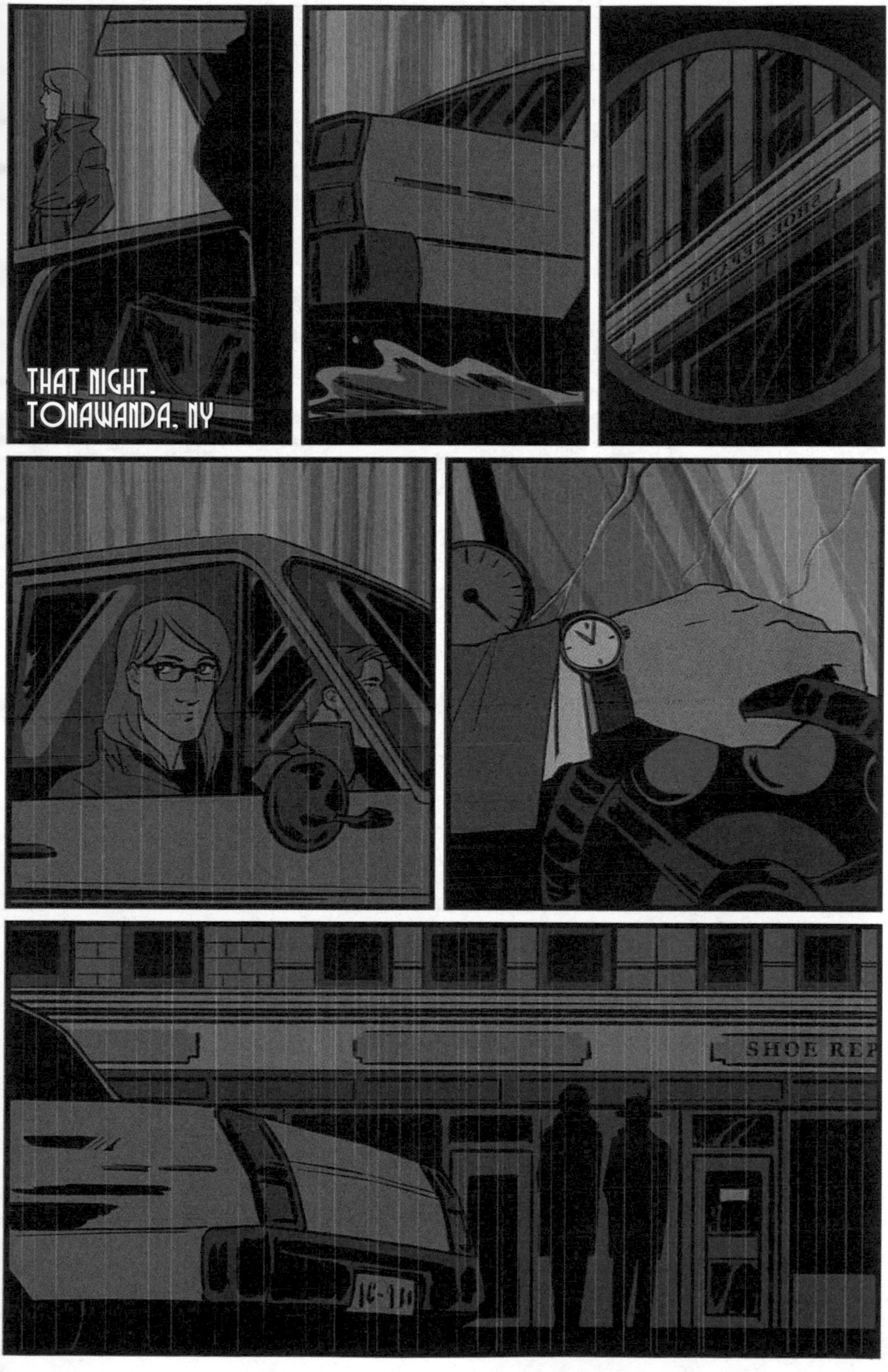
THAT NIGHT.
TONAWANDA, NY
SHOE REP

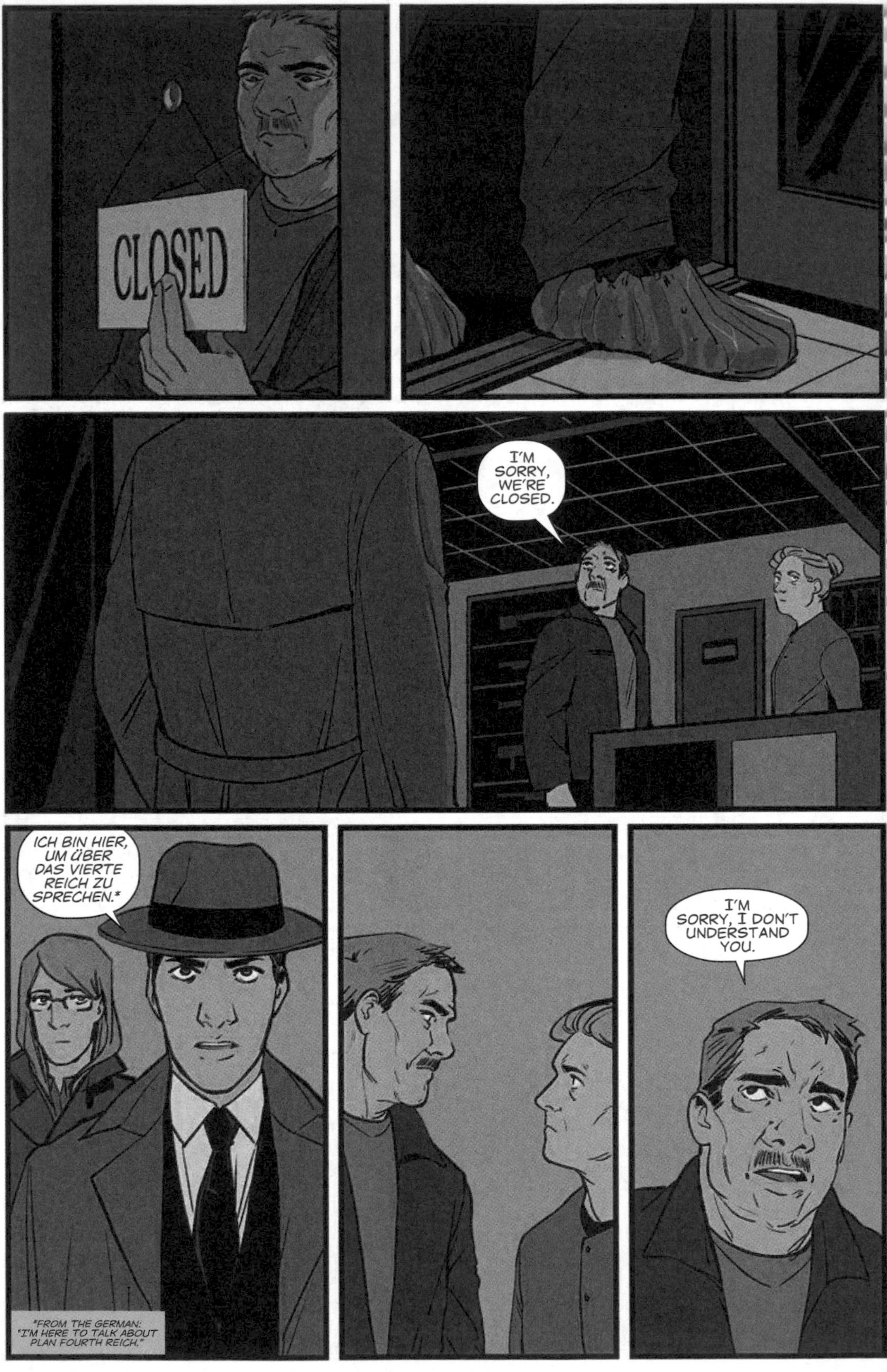
CLOSED
I'M SORRY, WE'RE CLOSED.
ICH BIN HIER, UM ÜBER DAS VIERTE REICH ZU SPRECHEN.*
*FROM THE GERMAN: "I'M HERE TO TALK ABOUT PLAN FOURTH REICH."
I'M SORRY, I DON'T UNDERSTAND YOU.

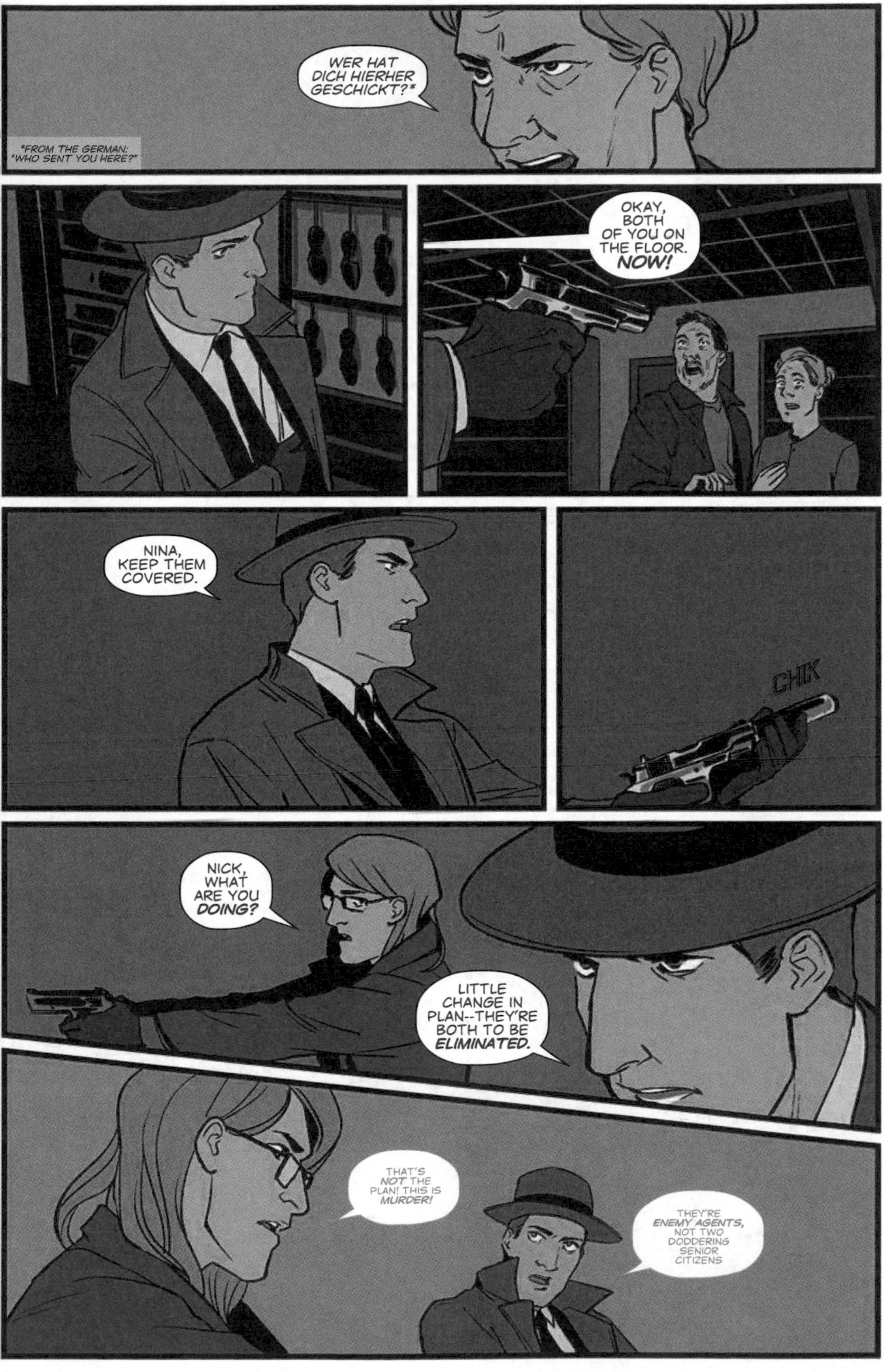
WER HAT DICH HIERHER GESCHICKT?*
*FROM THE GERMAN: "WHO SENT YOU HERE?"
OKAY, BOTH OF YOU ON THE FLOOR. NOW!
NINA, KEEP THEM COVERED.
CHIK
NICK, WHAT ARE YOU DOING?
LITTLE CHANGE IN PLAN--THEY'RE BOTH TO BE ELIMINATED.
THAT'S NOT THE PLAN! THIS IS MURDER!
THEY'RE ENEMY AGENTS, NOT TWO DODDERING SENIOR CITIZENS

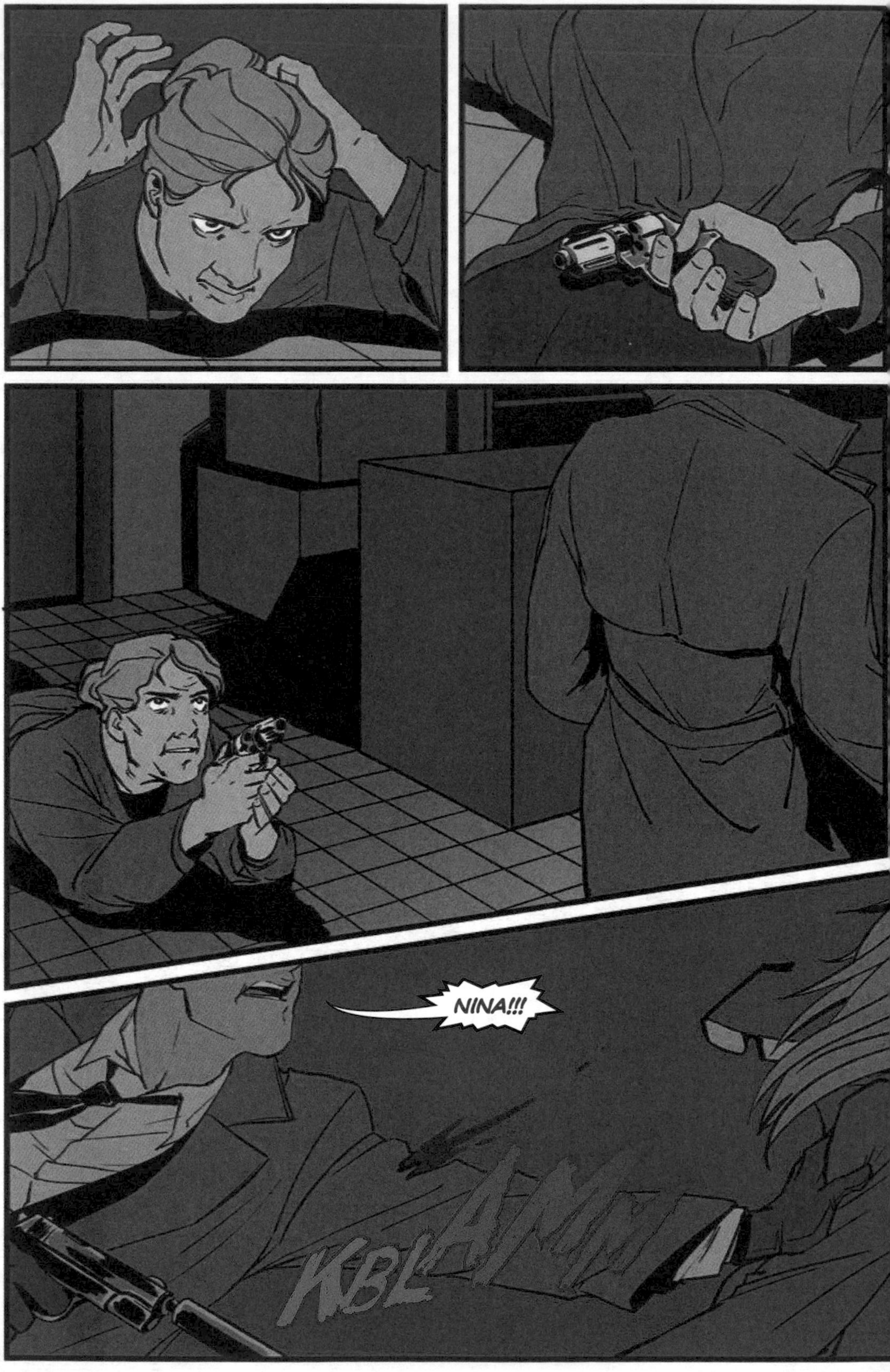
NINA!!!
KBLAMM!

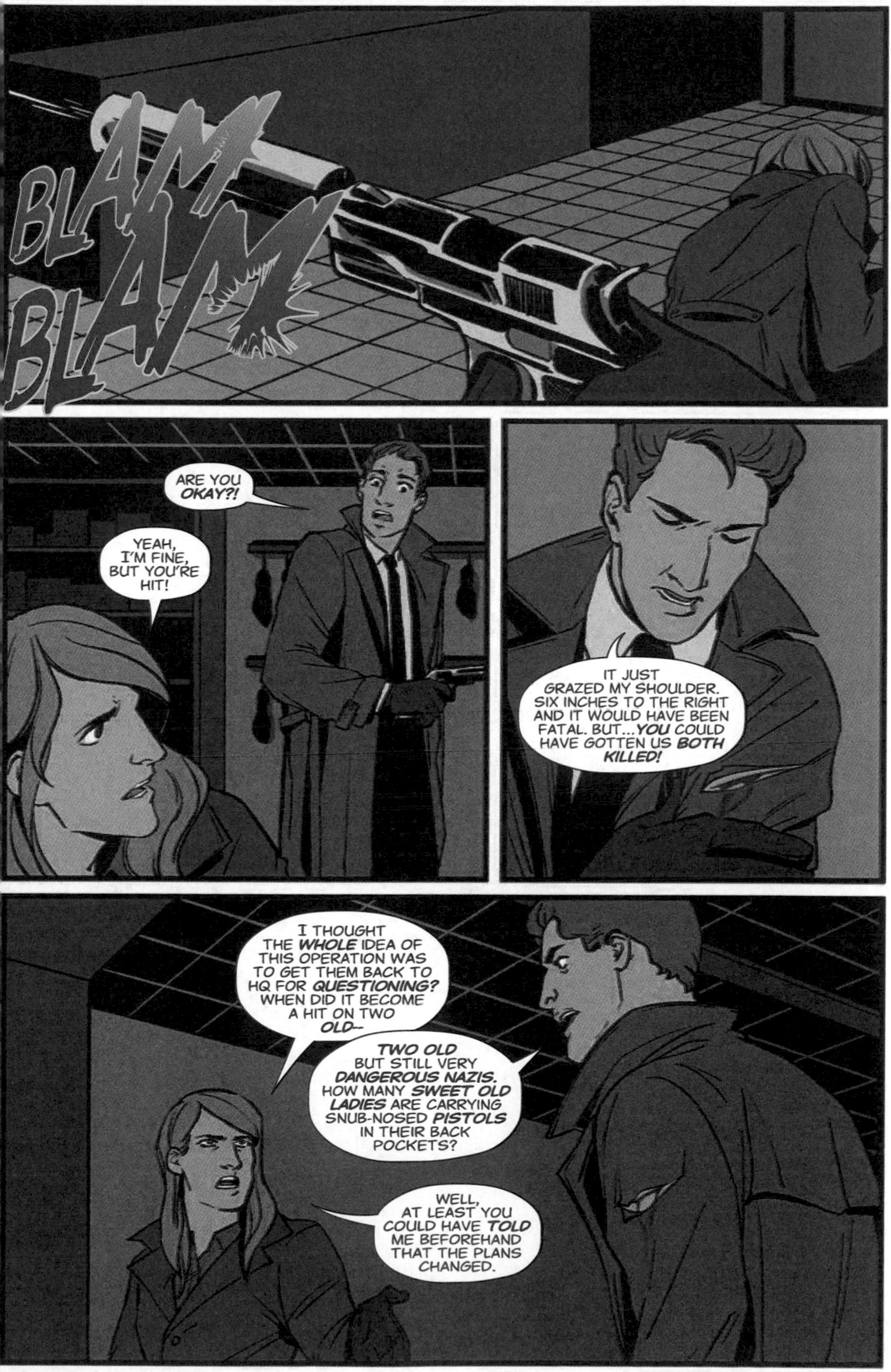
BLAM BLAM
BLAM
ARE YOU OKAY?!
YEAH, I'M FINE, BUT YOU'RE HIT!
IT JUST GRAZED MY SHOULDER. SIX INCHES TO THE RIGHT AND IT WOULD HAVE BEEN FATAL. BUT...YOU COULD HAVE GOTTEN US BOTH KILLED!
I THOUGHT THE WHOLE IDEA OF THIS OPERATION WAS TO GET THEM BACK TO HQ FOR QUESTIONING? WHEN DID IT BECOME A HIT ON TWO OLD--
TWO OLD BUT STILL VERY DANGEROUS NAZIS. HOW MANY SWEET OLD LADIES ARE CARRYING SNUB-NOSED PISTOLS IN THEIR BACK POCKETS?
WELL, AT LEAST YOU COULD HAVE TOLD ME BEFOREHAND THAT THE PLANS CHANGED.

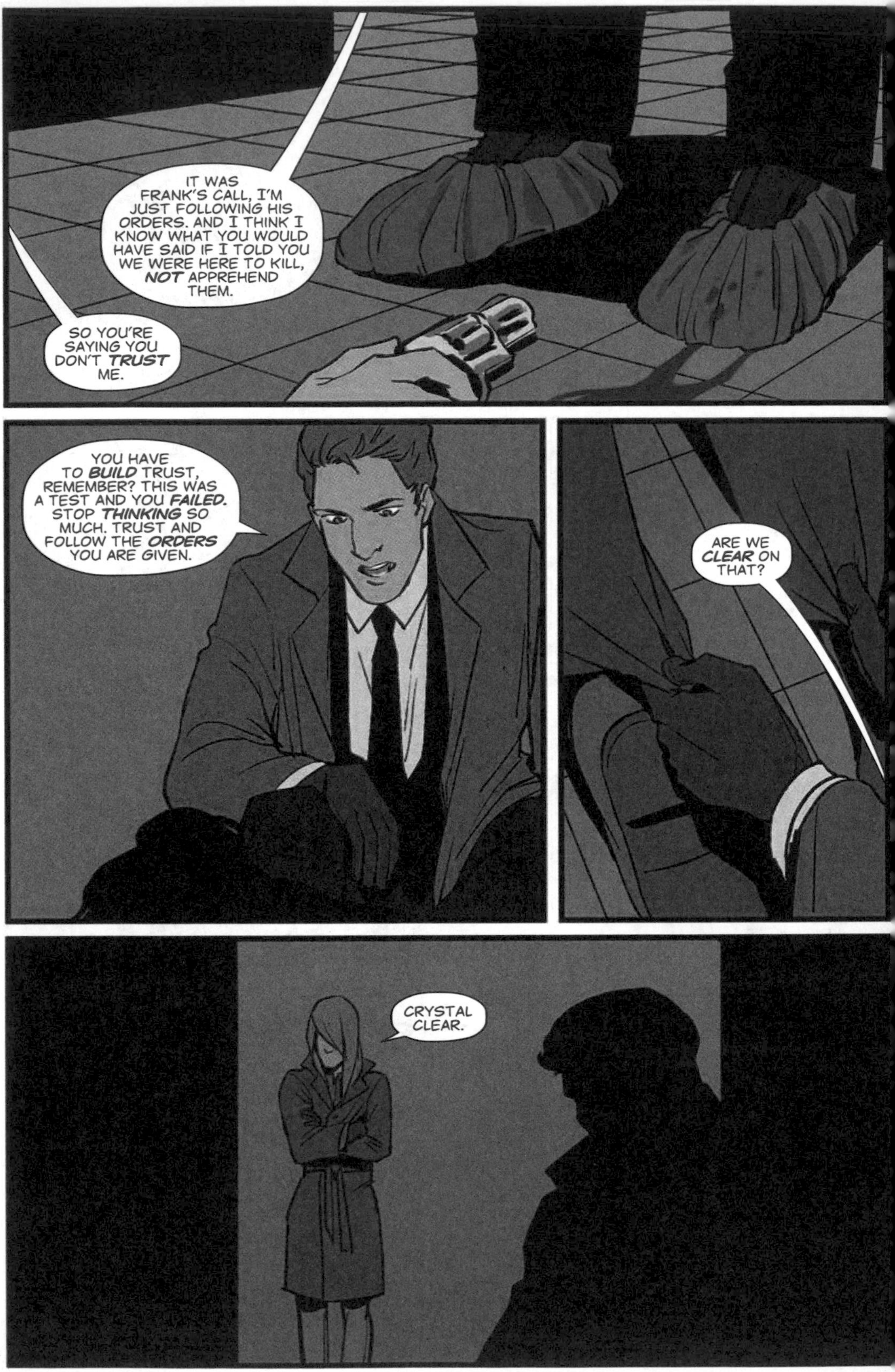
IT WAS FRANK'S CALL, I'M JUST FOLLOWING HIS ORDERS. AND I THINK I KNOW WHAT YOU WOULD HAVE SAID IF I TOLD YOU WE WERE HERE TO KILL, *NOT* APPREHEND THEM.
SO YOU'RE SAYING YOU DON'T *TRUST* ME.
YOU HAVE TO *BUILD* TRUST, REMEMBER? THIS WAS A TEST AND YOU *FAILED.* STOP *THINKING* SO MUCH. TRUST AND FOLLOW THE *ORDERS* YOU ARE GIVEN.
ARE WE *CLEAR* ON THAT?
CRYSTAL CLEAR.

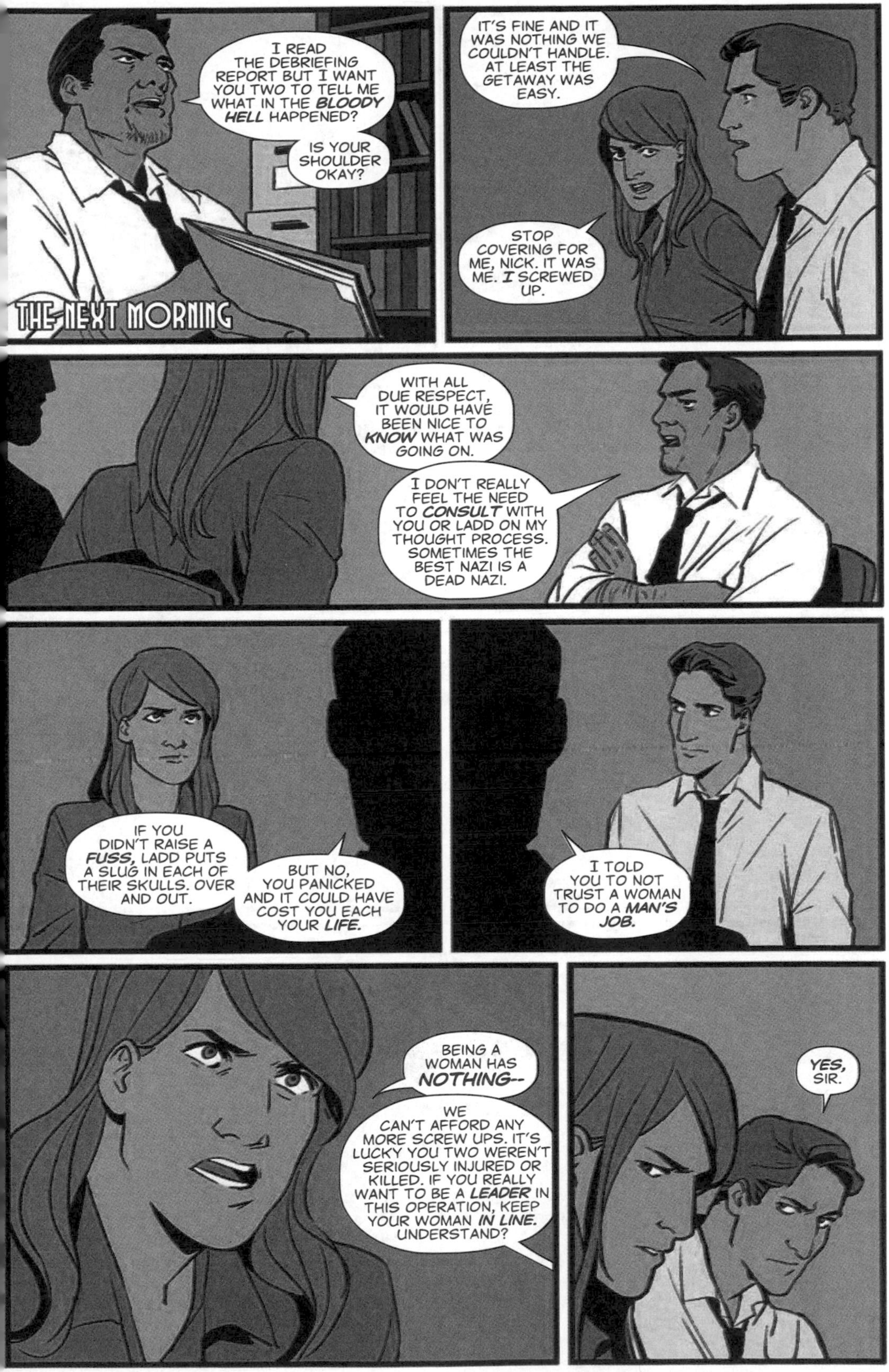
THE NEXT MORNING
I READ THE DEBRIEFING REPORT BUT I WANT YOU TWO TO TELL ME WHAT IN THE BLOODY HELL HAPPENED?
IS YOUR SHOULDER OKAY?
IT'S FINE AND IT WAS NOTHING WE COULDN'T HANDLE. AT LEAST THE GETAWAY WAS EASY.
STOP COVERING FOR ME, NICK. IT WAS ME. I SCREWED UP.
WITH ALL DUE RESPECT, IT WOULD HAVE BEEN NICE TO KNOW WHAT WAS GOING ON.
I DON'T REALLY FEEL THE NEED TO CONSULT WITH YOU OR LADD ON MY THOUGHT PROCESS. SOMETIMES THE BEST NAZI IS A DEAD NAZI.
IF YOU DIDN'T RAISE A FUSS, LADD PUTS A SLUG IN EACH OF THEIR SKULLS. OVER AND OUT.
BUT NO, YOU PANICKED AND IT COULD HAVE COST YOU EACH YOUR LIFE.
I TOLD YOU TO NOT TRUST A WOMAN TO DO A MAN'S JOB.
BEING A WOMAN HAS NOTHING--
WE CAN'T AFFORD ANY MORE SCREW UPS. IT'S LUCKY YOU TWO WEREN'T SERIOUSLY INJURED OR KILLED. IF YOU REALLY WANT TO BE A LEADER IN THIS OPERATION, KEEP YOUR WOMAN IN LINE. UNDERSTAND?
YES, SIR.

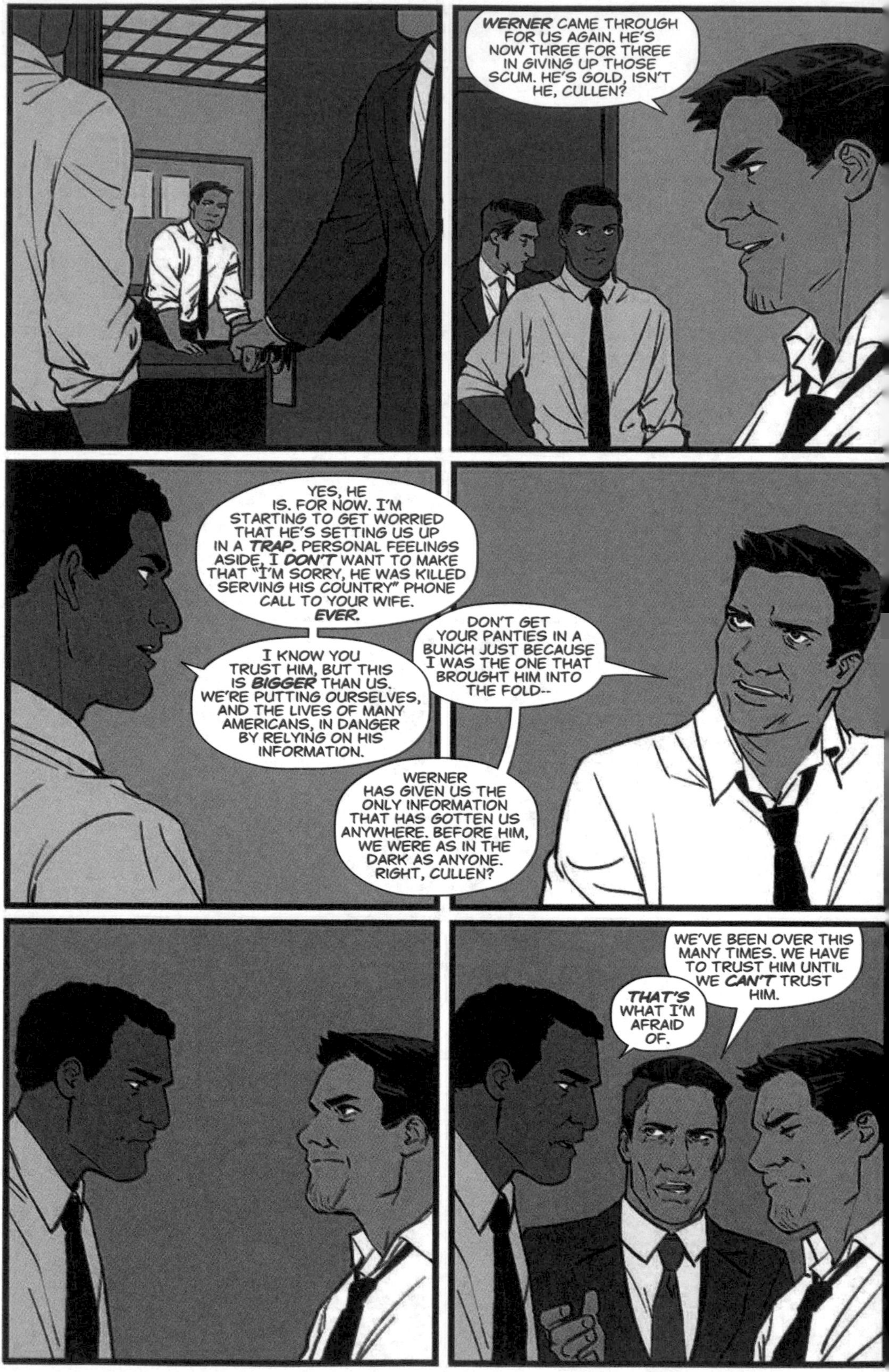
WERNER CAME THROUGH FOR US AGAIN. HE'S NOW THREE FOR THREE IN GIVING UP THOSE SCUM. HE'S GOLD, ISN'T HE, CULLEN?
YES, HE IS. FOR NOW. I'M STARTING TO GET WORRIED THAT HE'S SETTING US UP IN A TRAP. PERSONAL FEELINGS ASIDE, I DON'T WANT TO MAKE THAT "I'M SORRY, HE WAS KILLED SERVING HIS COUNTRY" PHONE CALL TO YOUR WIFE. EVER.
I KNOW YOU TRUST HIM, BUT THIS IS BIGGER THAN US. WE'RE PUTTING OURSELVES, AND THE LIVES OF MANY AMERICANS, IN DANGER BY RELYING ON HIS INFORMATION.
DON'T GET YOUR PANTIES IN A BUNCH JUST BECAUSE I WAS THE ONE THAT BROUGHT HIM INTO THE FOLD--
WERNER HAS GIVEN US THE ONLY INFORMATION THAT HAS GOTTEN US ANYWHERE. BEFORE HIM, WE WERE AS IN THE DARK AS ANYONE. RIGHT, CULLEN?
WE'VE BEEN OVER THIS MANY TIMES. WE HAVE TO TRUST HIM UNTIL WE CAN'T TRUST HIM.
THAT'S WHAT I'M AFRAID OF.

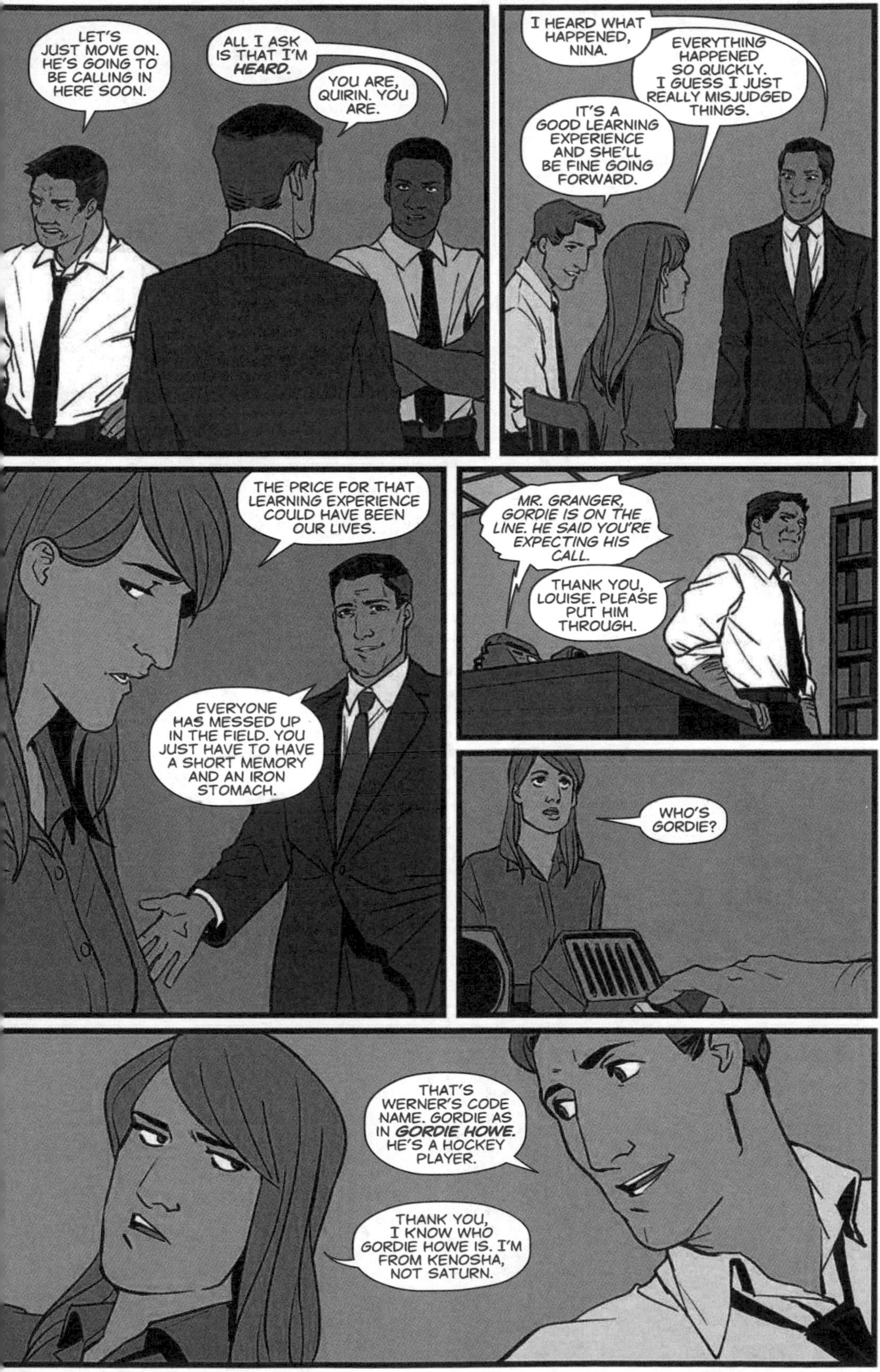
LET'S JUST MOVE ON. HE'S GOING TO BE CALLING IN HERE SOON.
ALL I ASK IS THAT I'M HEARD.
YOU ARE, QUIRIN. YOU ARE.
I HEARD WHAT HAPPENED, NINA.
EVERYTHING HAPPENED SO QUICKLY. I GUESS I JUST REALLY MISJUDGED THINGS.
IT'S A GOOD LEARNING EXPERIENCE AND SHE'LL BE FINE GOING FORWARD.
THE PRICE FOR THAT LEARNING EXPERIENCE COULD HAVE BEEN OUR LIVES.
EVERYONE HAS MESSED UP IN THE FIELD. YOU JUST HAVE TO HAVE A SHORT MEMORY AND AN IRON STOMACH.
MR. GRANGER, GORDIE IS ON THE LINE. HE SAID YOU'RE EXPECTING HIS CALL.
THANK YOU, LOUISE. PLEASE PUT HIM THROUGH.
WHO'S GORDIE?
THAT'S WERNER'S CODE NAME. GORDIE AS IN GORDIE HOWE. HE'S A HOCKEY PLAYER.
THANK YOU, I KNOW WHO GORDIE HOWE IS. I'M FROM KENOSHA, NOT SATURN.

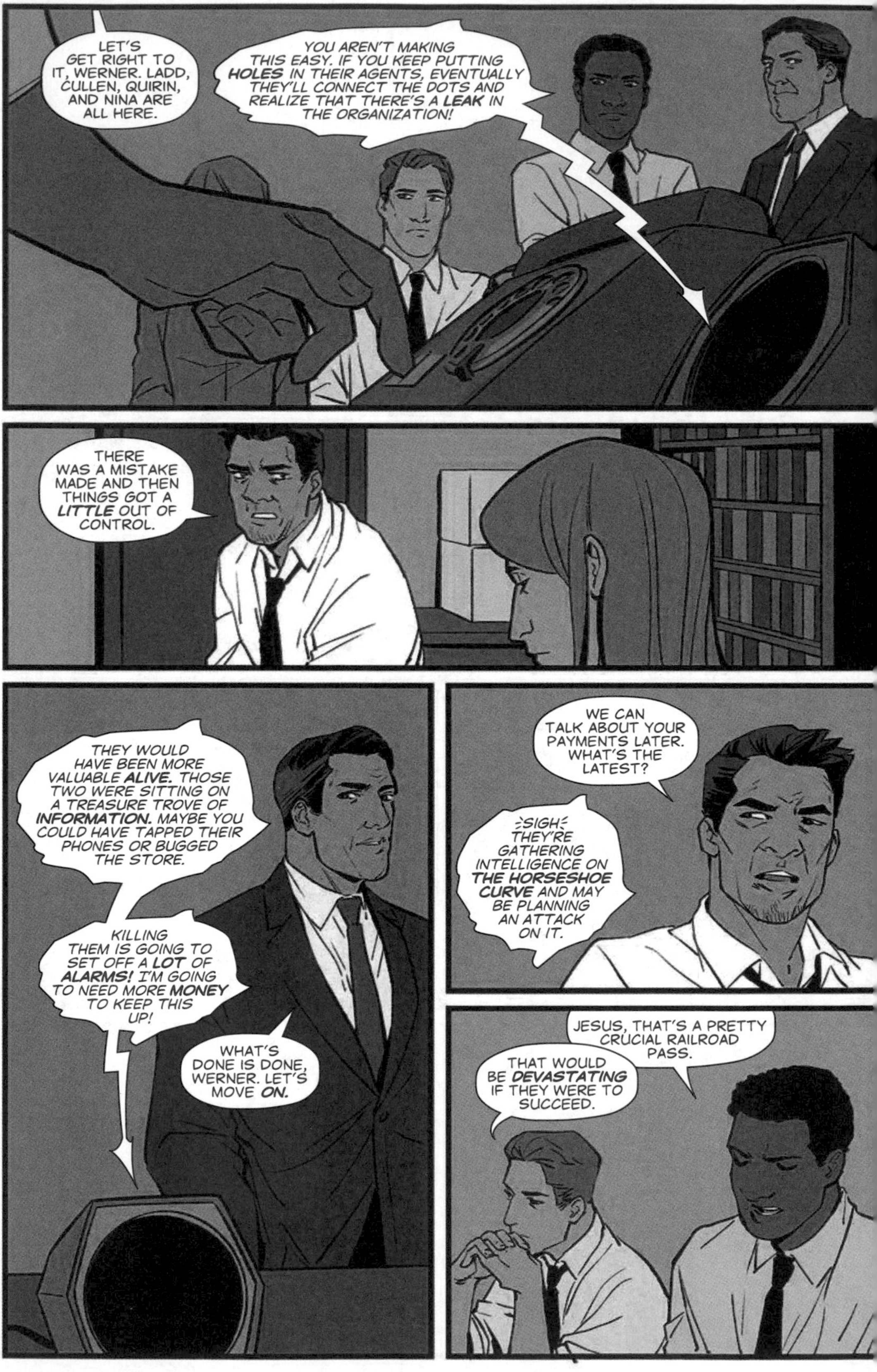
LET'S GET RIGHT TO IT, WERNER. LADD, CULLEN, QUIRIN, AND NINA ARE ALL HERE.
YOU AREN'T MAKING THIS EASY. IF YOU KEEP PUTTING HOLES IN THEIR AGENTS, EVENTUALLY THEY'LL CONNECT THE DOTS AND REALIZE THAT THERE'S A LEAK IN THE ORGANIZATION!
THERE WAS A MISTAKE MADE AND THEN THINGS GOT A LITTLE OUT OF CONTROL.
THEY WOULD HAVE BEEN MORE VALUABLE ALIVE. THOSE TWO WERE SITTING ON A TREASURE TROVE OF INFORMATION. MAYBE YOU COULD HAVE TAPPED THEIR PHONES OR BUGGED THE STORE.
KILLING THEM IS GOING TO SET OFF A LOT OF ALARMS! I'M GOING TO NEED MORE MONEY TO KEEP THIS UP!
WHAT'S DONE IS DONE, WERNER. LET'S MOVE ON.
WE CAN TALK ABOUT YOUR PAYMENTS LATER. WHAT'S THE LATEST?
SIGH
THEY'RE GATHERING INTELLIGENCE ON THE HORSESHOE CURVE AND MAY BE PLANNING AN ATTACK ON IT.
JESUS, THAT'S A PRETTY CRUCIAL RAILROAD PASS.
THAT WOULD BE DEVASTATING IF THEY WERE TO SUCCEED.

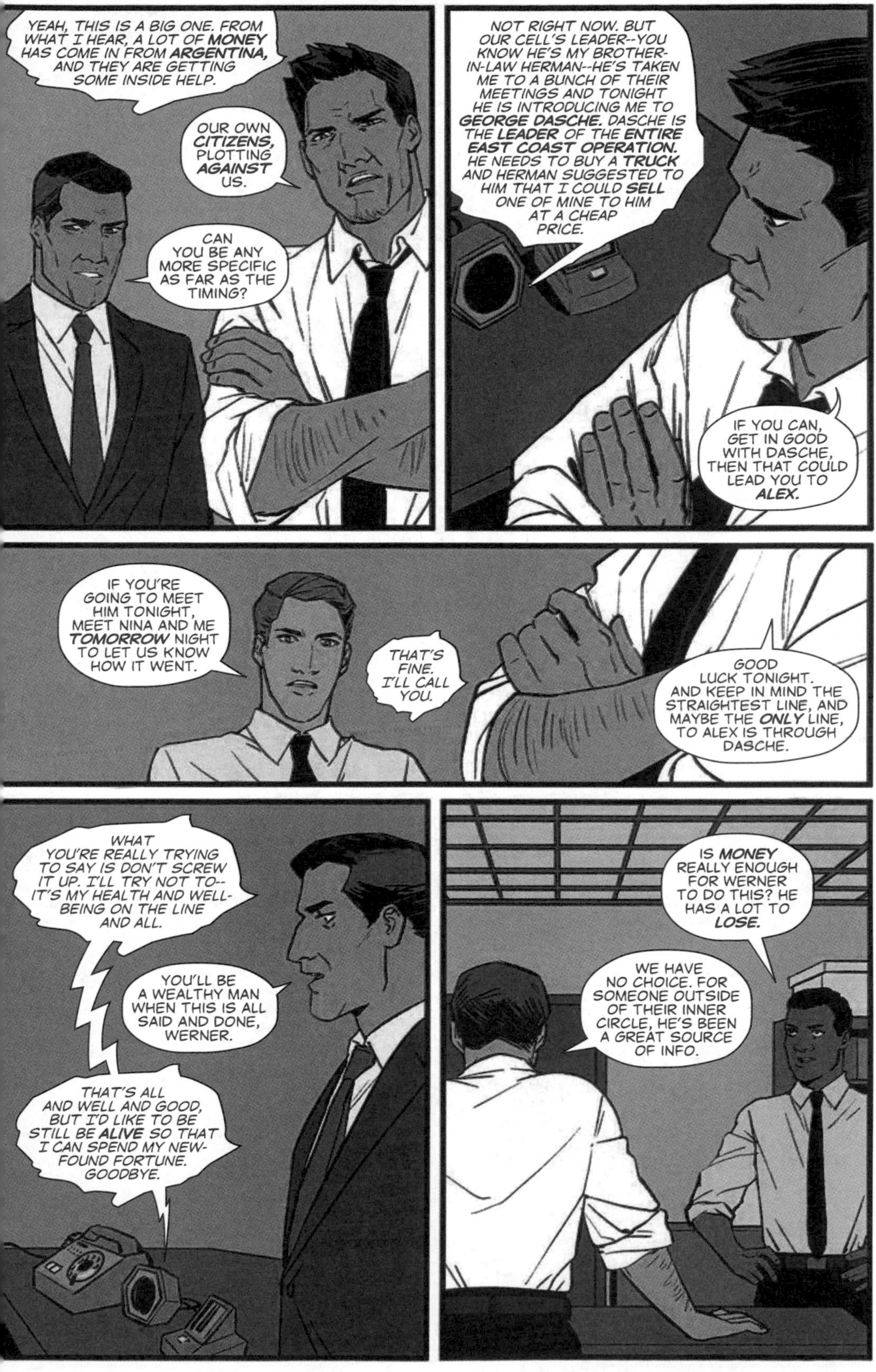
YEAH, THIS IS A BIG ONE. FROM WHAT I HEAR, A LOT OF MONEY HAS COME IN FROM ARGENTINA, AND THEY ARE GETTING SOME INSIDE HELP.
OUR OWN CITIZENS, PLOTTING AGAINST US.
CAN YOU BE ANY MORE SPECIFIC AS FAR AS THE TIMING?
NOT RIGHT NOW. BUT OUR CELL'S LEADER--YOU KNOW HE'S MY BROTHER-IN-LAW HERMAN--HE'S TAKEN ME TO A BUNCH OF THEIR MEETINGS AND TONIGHT HE IS INTRODUCING ME TO GEORGE DASCHE. DASCHE IS THE LEADER OF THE ENTIRE EAST COAST OPERATION. HE NEEDS TO BUY A TRUCK AND HERMAN SUGGESTED TO HIM THAT I COULD SELL ONE OF MINE TO HIM AT A CHEAP PRICE.
IF YOU CAN, GET IN GOOD WITH DASCHE, THEN THAT COULD LEAD YOU TO ALEX.
IF YOU'RE GOING TO MEET HIM TONIGHT, MEET NINA AND ME TOMORROW NIGHT TO LET US KNOW HOW IT WENT.
THAT'S FINE. I'LL CALL YOU.
GOOD LUCK TONIGHT. AND KEEP IN MIND THE STRAIGHTEST LINE, AND MAYBE THE ONLY LINE, TO ALEX IS THROUGH DASCHE.
WHAT YOU'RE REALLY TRYING TO SAY IS DON'T SCREW IT UP. I'LL TRY NOT TO--IT'S MY HEALTH AND WELL-BEING ON THE LINE AND ALL.
YOU'LL BE A WEALTHY MAN WHEN THIS IS ALL SAID AND DONE, WERNER.
THAT'S ALL AND WELL AND GOOD, BUT I'D LIKE TO BE STILL BE ALIVE SO THAT I CAN SPEND MY NEW-FOUND FORTUNE. GOODBYE.
IS MONEY REALLY ENOUGH FOR WERNER TO DO THIS? HE HAS A LOT TO LOSE.
WE HAVE NO CHOICE. FOR SOMEONE OUTSIDE OF THEIR INNER CIRCLE, HE'S BEEN A GREAT SOURCE OF INFO.

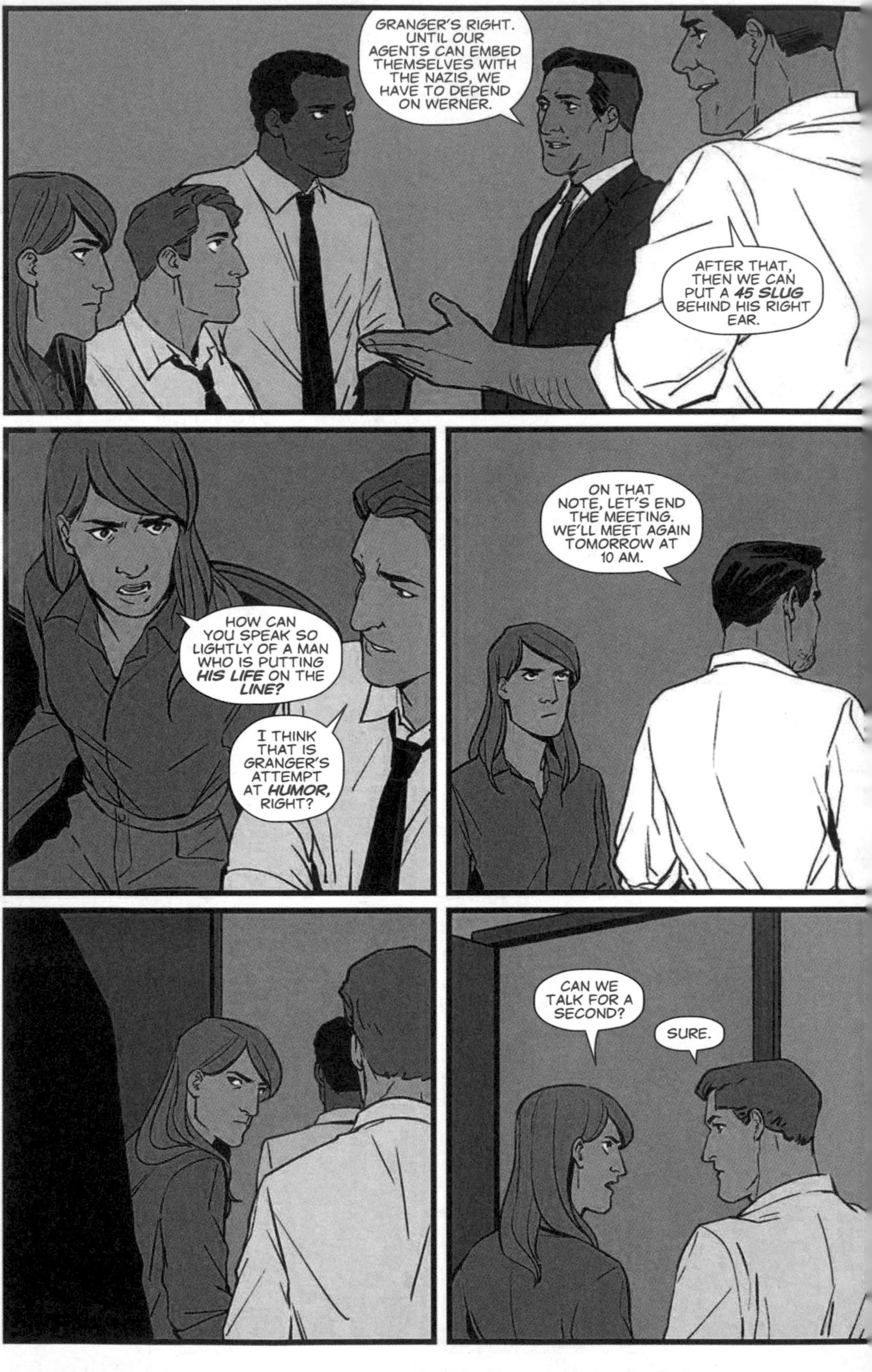
GRANGER'S RIGHT. UNTIL OUR AGENTS CAN EMBED THEMSELVES WITH THE NAZIS, WE HAVE TO DEPEND ON WERNER.
AFTER THAT, THEN WE CAN PUT A 45 SLUG BEHIND HIS RIGHT EAR.
HOW CAN YOU SPEAK SO LIGHTLY OF A MAN WHO IS PUTTING HIS LIFE ON THE LINE?
I THINK THAT IS GRANGER'S ATTEMPT AT HUMOR, RIGHT?
ON THAT NOTE, LET'S END THE MEETING. WE'LL MEET AGAIN TOMORROW AT 10 AM.
CAN WE TALK FOR A SECOND?
SURE.

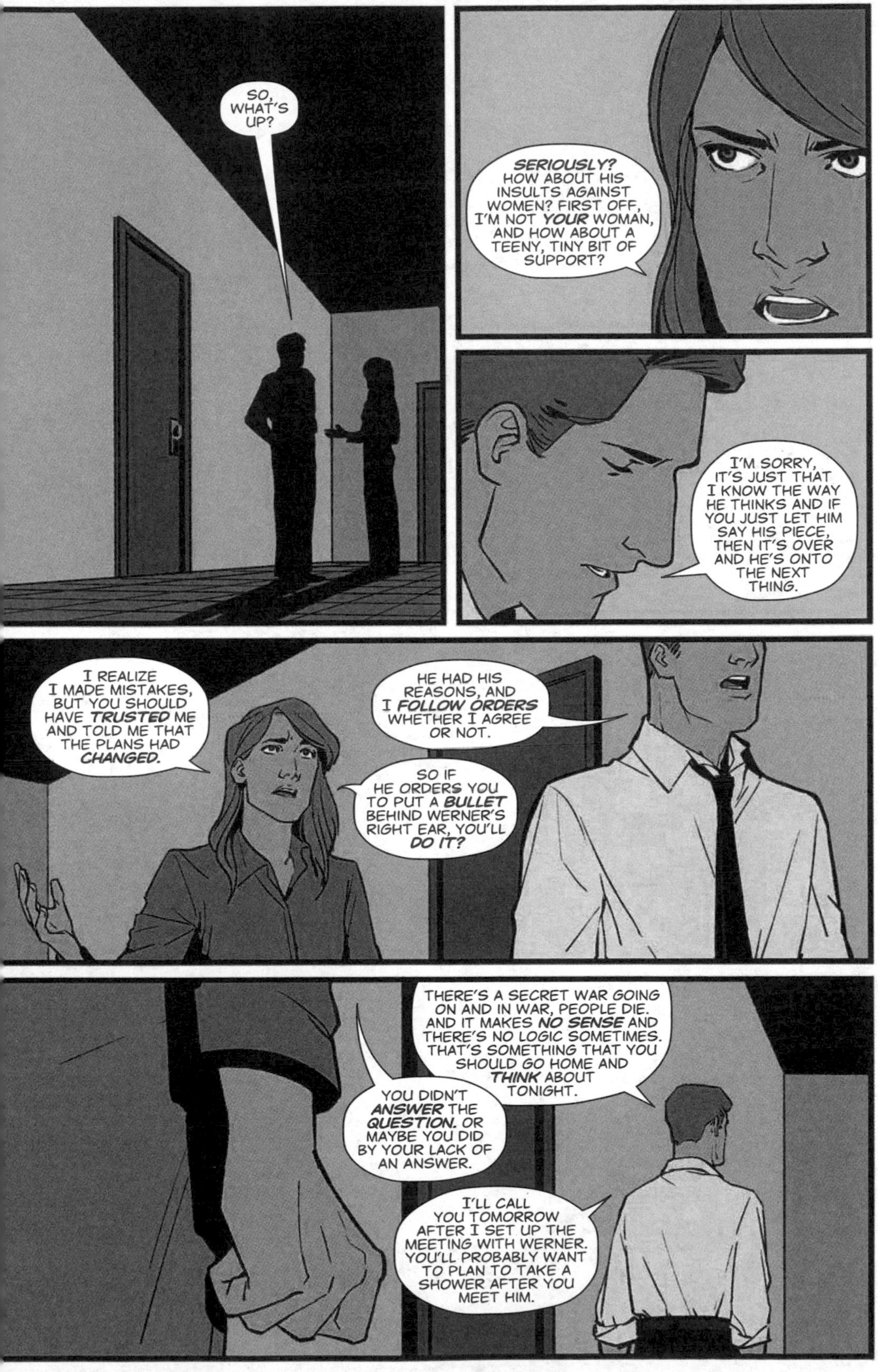
SO, WHAT'S UP?
SERIOUSLY? HOW ABOUT HIS INSULTS AGAINST WOMEN? FIRST OFF, I'M NOT YOUR WOMAN, AND HOW ABOUT A TEENY, TINY BIT OF SUPPORT?
I'M SORRY, IT'S JUST THAT I KNOW THE WAY HE THINKS AND IF YOU JUST LET HIM SAY HIS PIECE, THEN IT'S OVER AND HE'S ONTO THE NEXT THING.
I REALIZE I MADE MISTAKES, BUT YOU SHOULD HAVE TRUSTED ME AND TOLD ME THAT THE PLANS HAD CHANGED.
HE HAD HIS REASONS, AND I FOLLOW ORDERS WHETHER I AGREE OR NOT.
SO IF HE ORDERS YOU TO PUT A BULLET BEHIND WERNER'S RIGHT EAR, YOU'LL DO IT?
THERE'S A SECRET WAR GOING ON AND IN WAR, PEOPLE DIE. AND IT MAKES NO SENSE AND THERE'S NO LOGIC SOMETIMES. THAT'S SOMETHING THAT YOU SHOULD GO HOME AND THINK ABOUT TONIGHT.
YOU DIDN'T ANSWER THE QUESTION. OR MAYBE YOU DID BY YOUR LACK OF AN ANSWER.
I'LL CALL YOU TOMORROW AFTER I SET UP THE MEETING WITH WERNER. YOU'LL PROBABLY WANT TO PLAN TO TAKE A SHOWER AFTER YOU MEET HIM.

RECOMMENDED LISTENING:

WHEN A WOMAN'S HAD ENOUGH
BY SHEMIKA COPELAND

WOULD?
BY ALICE IN CHAINS

HAVE I RUN TOO FAR TO GET HOME?
BY NINA OVERSTREET

CHAPTER FIVE

Try To
See It Once
My Way

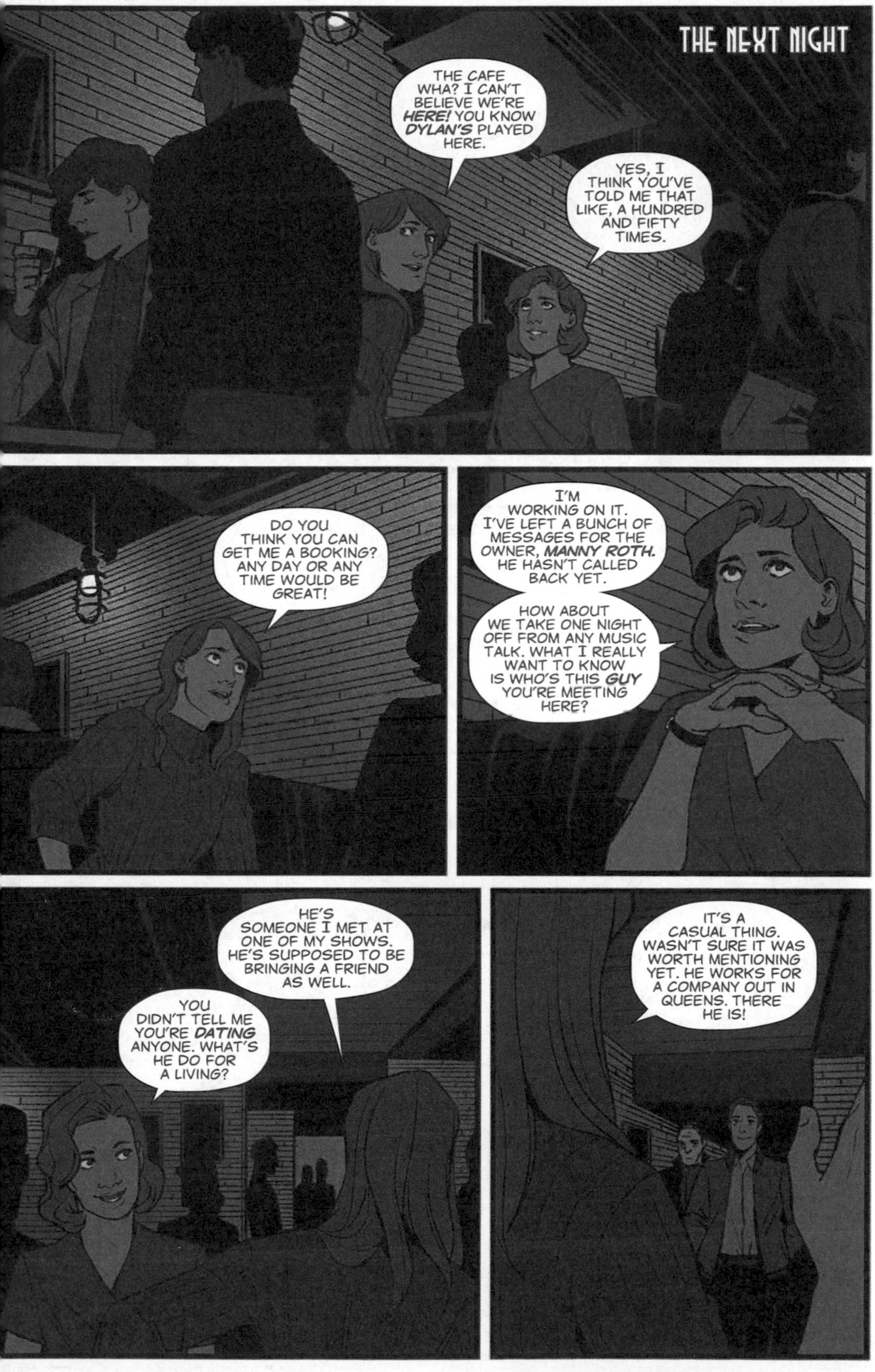
THE NEXT NIGHT
THE CAFE WHA? I CAN'T BELIEVE WE'RE HERE! YOU KNOW DYLAN'S PLAYED HERE.
YES, I THINK YOU'VE TOLD ME THAT LIKE, A HUNDRED AND FIFTY TIMES.
DO YOU THINK YOU CAN GET ME A BOOKING? ANY DAY OR ANY TIME WOULD BE GREAT!
I'M WORKING ON IT. I'VE LEFT A BUNCH OF MESSAGES FOR THE OWNER, MANNY ROTH. HE HASN'T CALLED BACK YET.
HOW ABOUT WE TAKE ONE NIGHT OFF FROM ANY MUSIC TALK. WHAT I REALLY WANT TO KNOW IS WHO'S THIS GUY YOU'RE MEETING HERE?
HE'S SOMEONE I MET AT ONE OF MY SHOWS. HE'S SUPPOSED TO BE BRINGING A FRIEND AS WELL.
YOU DIDN'T TELL ME YOU'RE DATING ANYONE. WHAT'S HE DO FOR A LIVING?
IT'S A CASUAL THING. WASN'T SURE IT WAS WORTH MENTIONING YET. HE WORKS FOR A COMPANY OUT IN QUEENS. THERE HE IS!

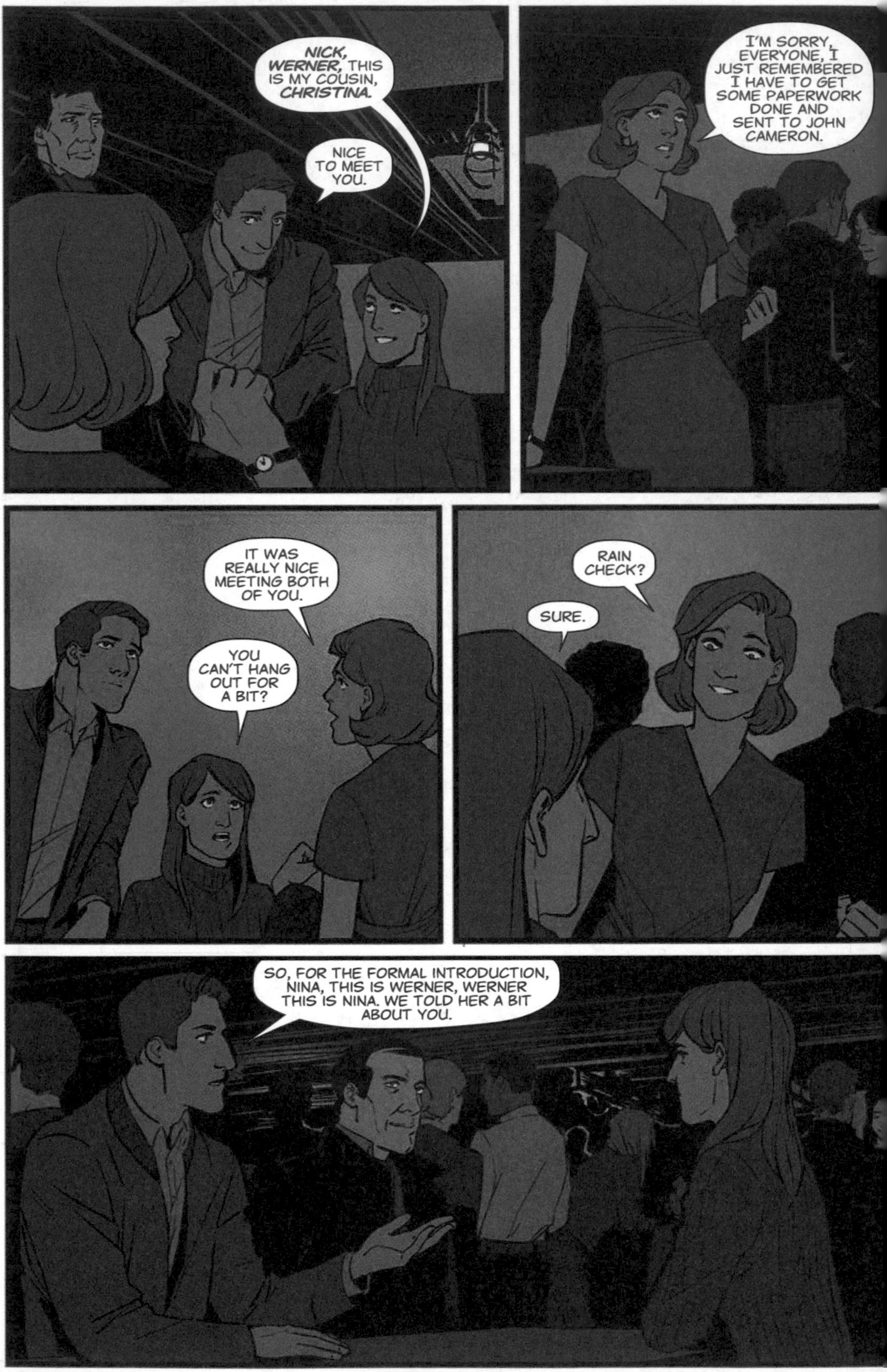
NICK, WERNER, THIS IS MY COUSIN, CHRISTINA.
NICE TO MEET YOU.
I'M SORRY, EVERYONE, I JUST REMEMBERED I HAVE TO GET SOME PAPERWORK DONE AND SENT TO JOHN CAMERON.
IT WAS REALLY NICE MEETING BOTH OF YOU.
YOU CAN'T HANG OUT FOR A BIT?
RAIN CHECK?
SURE.
SO, FOR THE FORMAL INTRODUCTION, NINA, THIS IS WERNER, WERNER THIS IS NINA. WE TOLD HER A BIT ABOUT YOU.

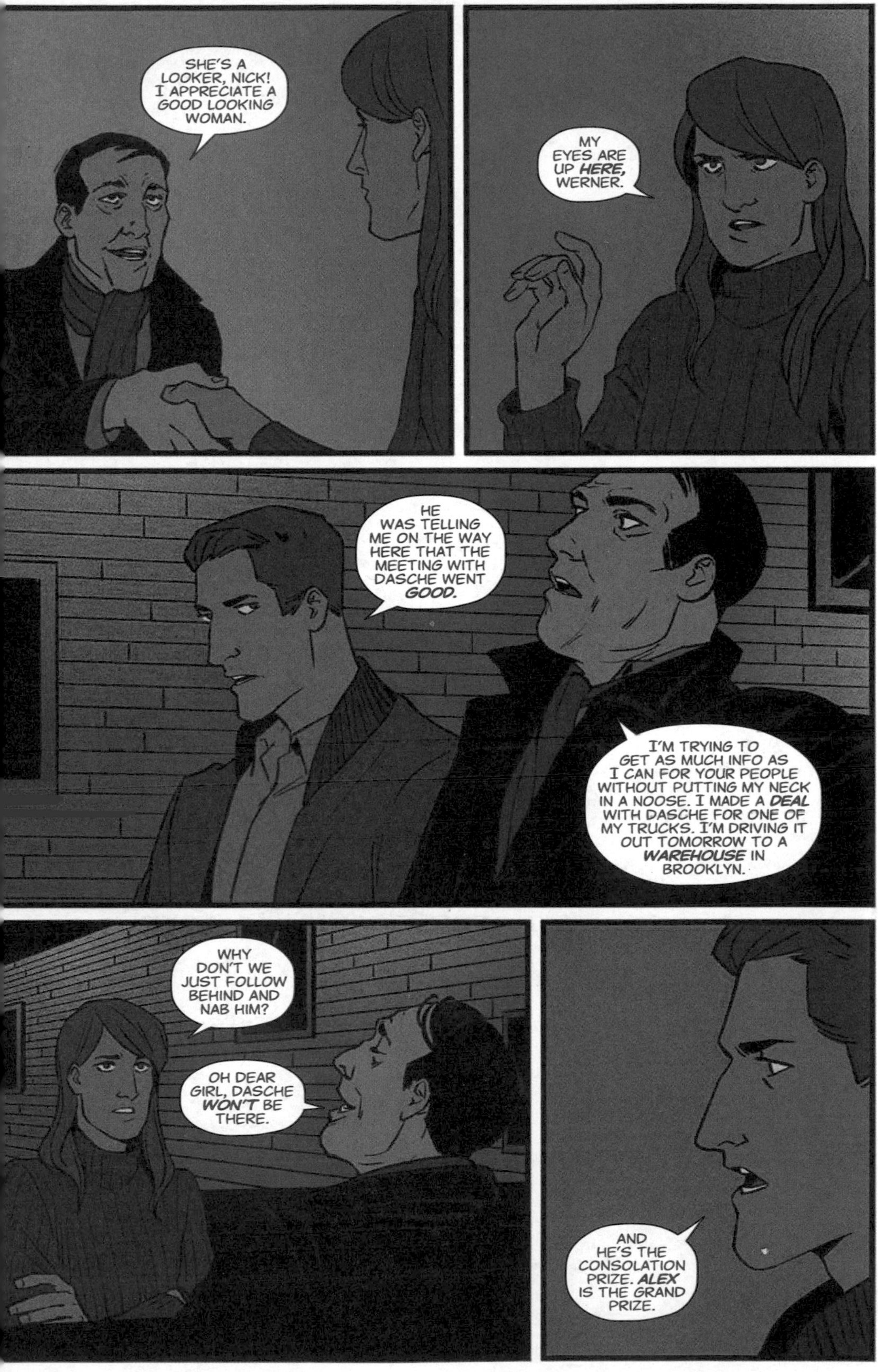
SHE'S A LOOKER, NICK! I APPRECIATE A GOOD LOOKING WOMAN.
MY EYES ARE UP HERE, WERNER.
HE WAS TELLING ME ON THE WAY HERE THAT THE MEETING WITH DASCHE WENT GOOD.
I'M TRYING TO GET AS MUCH INFO AS I CAN FOR YOUR PEOPLE WITHOUT PUTTING MY NECK IN A NOOSE. I MADE A DEAL WITH DASCHE FOR ONE OF MY TRUCKS. I'M DRIVING IT OUT TOMORROW TO A WAREHOUSE IN BROOKLYN.
WHY DON'T WE JUST FOLLOW BEHIND AND NAB HIM?
OH DEAR GIRL, DASCHE WON'T BE THERE.
AND HE'S THE CONSOLATION PRIZE. ALEX IS THE GRAND PRIZE.

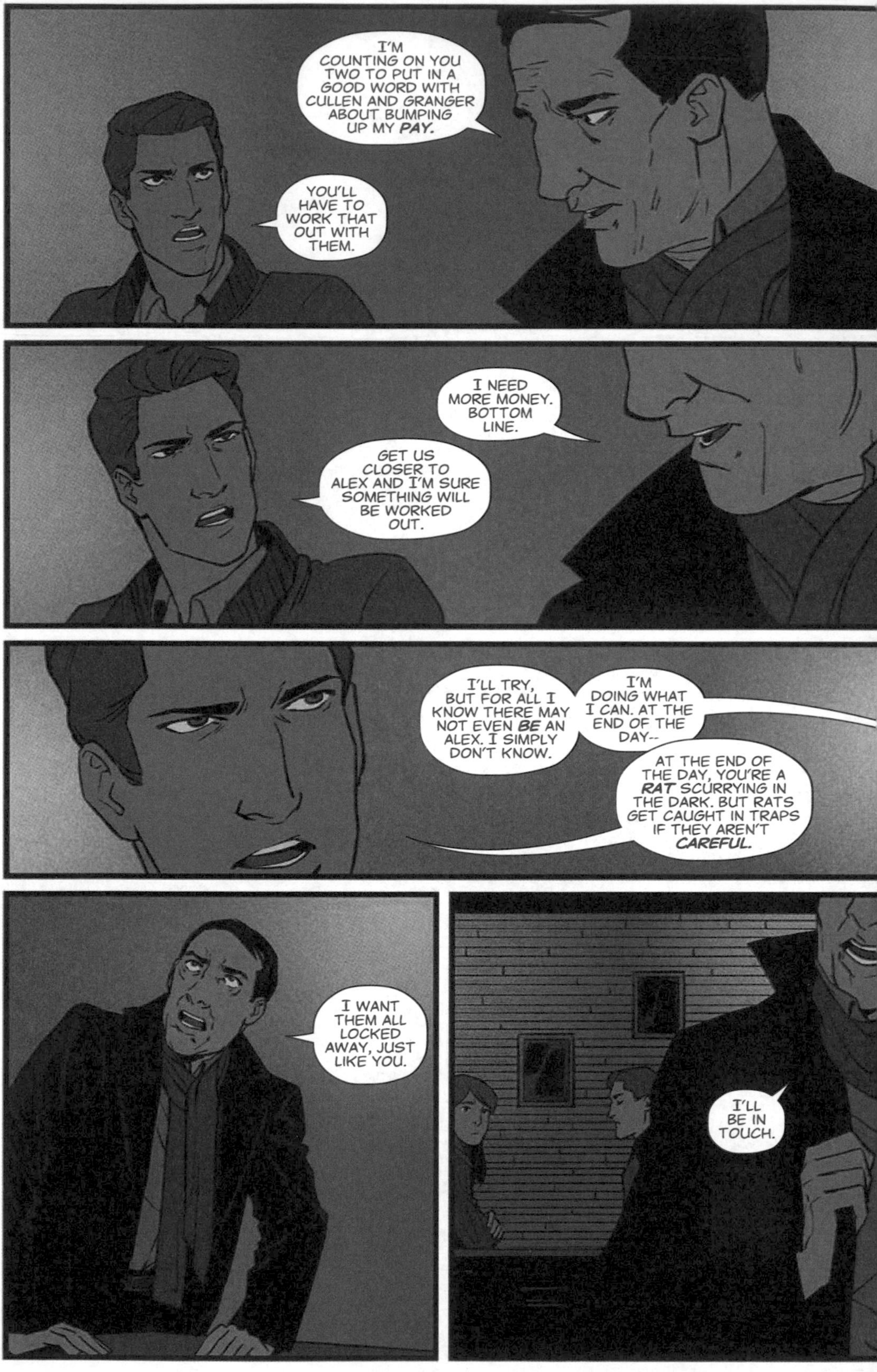
I'M COUNTING ON YOU TWO TO PUT IN A GOOD WORD WITH CULLEN AND GRANGER ABOUT BUMPING UP MY PAY.
YOU'LL HAVE TO WORK THAT OUT WITH THEM.
I NEED MORE MONEY. BOTTOM LINE.
GET US CLOSER TO ALEX AND I'M SURE SOMETHING WILL BE WORKED OUT.
I'LL TRY, BUT FOR ALL I KNOW THERE MAY NOT EVEN BE AN ALEX. I SIMPLY DON'T KNOW.
I'M DOING WHAT I CAN. AT THE END OF THE DAY--
AT THE END OF THE DAY, YOU'RE A RAT SCURRYING IN THE DARK. BUT RATS GET CAUGHT IN TRAPS IF THEY AREN'T CAREFUL.
I WANT THEM ALL LOCKED AWAY, JUST LIKE YOU.
I'LL BE IN TOUCH.

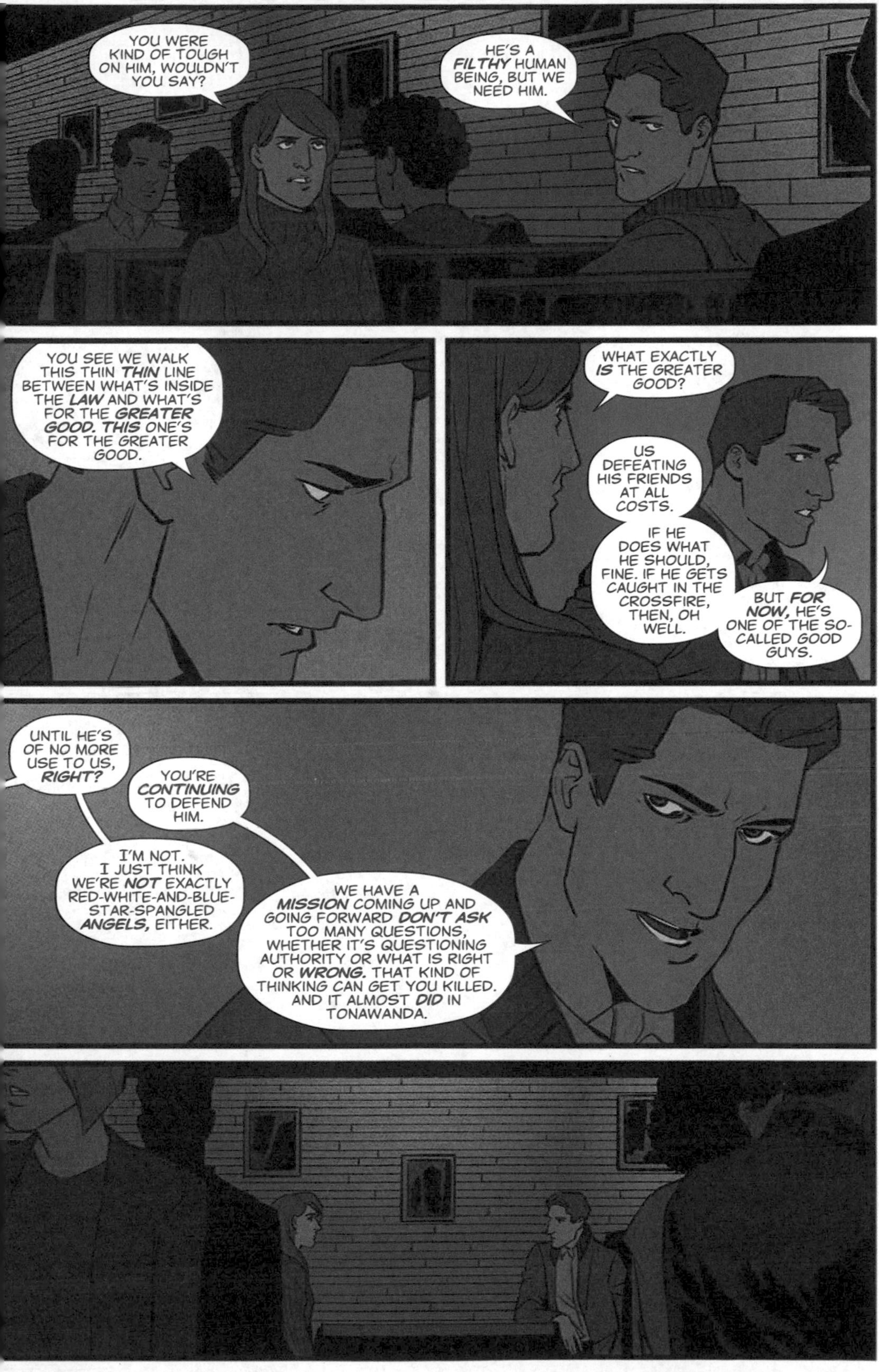

YOU WERE KIND OF TOUGH ON HIM, WOULDN'T YOU SAY?
HE'S A FILTHY HUMAN BEING, BUT WE NEED HIM.
YOU SEE WE WALK THIS THIN THIN LINE BETWEEN WHAT'S INSIDE THE LAW AND WHAT'S FOR THE GREATER GOOD. THIS ONE'S FOR THE GREATER GOOD.
WHAT EXACTLY IS THE GREATER GOOD?
US DEFEATING HIS FRIENDS AT ALL COSTS.
IF HE DOES WHAT HE SHOULD, FINE. IF HE GETS CAUGHT IN THE CROSSFIRE, THEN, OH WELL.
BUT FOR NOW, HE'S ONE OF THE SO-CALLED GOOD GUYS.
UNTIL HE'S OF NO MORE USE TO US, RIGHT?
YOU'RE CONTINUING TO DEFEND HIM.
I'M NOT. I JUST THINK WE'RE NOT EXACTLY RED-WHITE-AND-BLUE-STAR-SPANGLED ANGELS, EITHER.
WE HAVE A MISSION COMING UP AND GOING FORWARD DON'T ASK TOO MANY QUESTIONS, WHETHER IT'S QUESTIONING AUTHORITY OR WHAT IS RIGHT OR WRONG. THAT KIND OF THINKING CAN GET YOU KILLED. AND IT ALMOST DID IN TONAWANDA.

RECOMMENDED LISTENING:

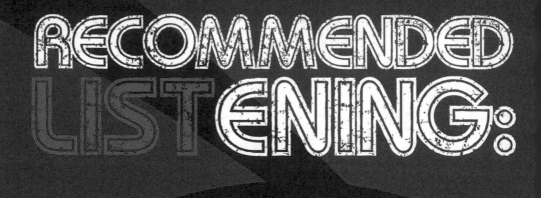

WORK ME, LORD
BY JANIS JOPLIN

STUCK IN A MOMENT YOU CAN'T GET OUT OF
BY U2

THIS TIME WILL PASS
BY NINA OVERSTREET

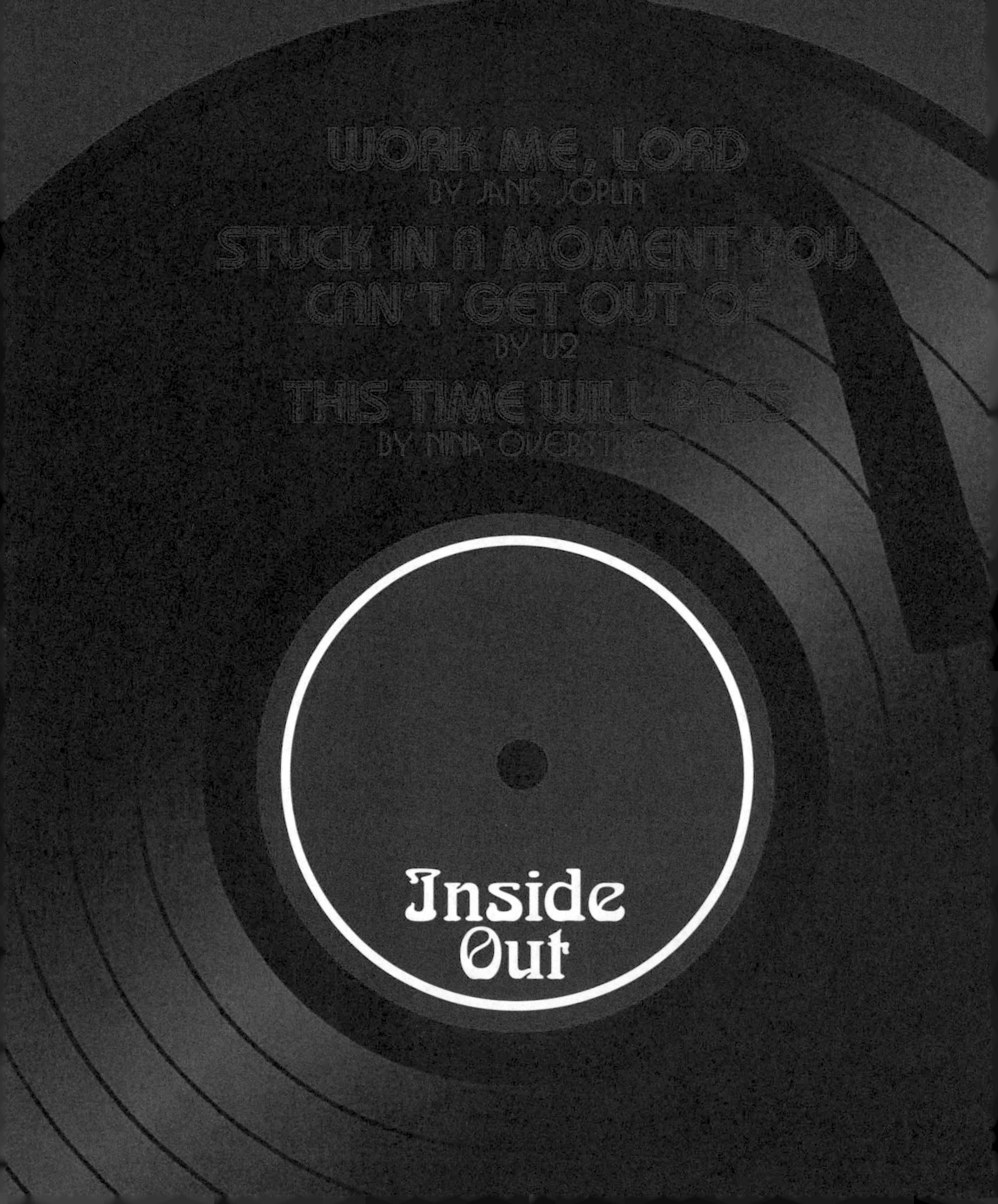
Inside
Out

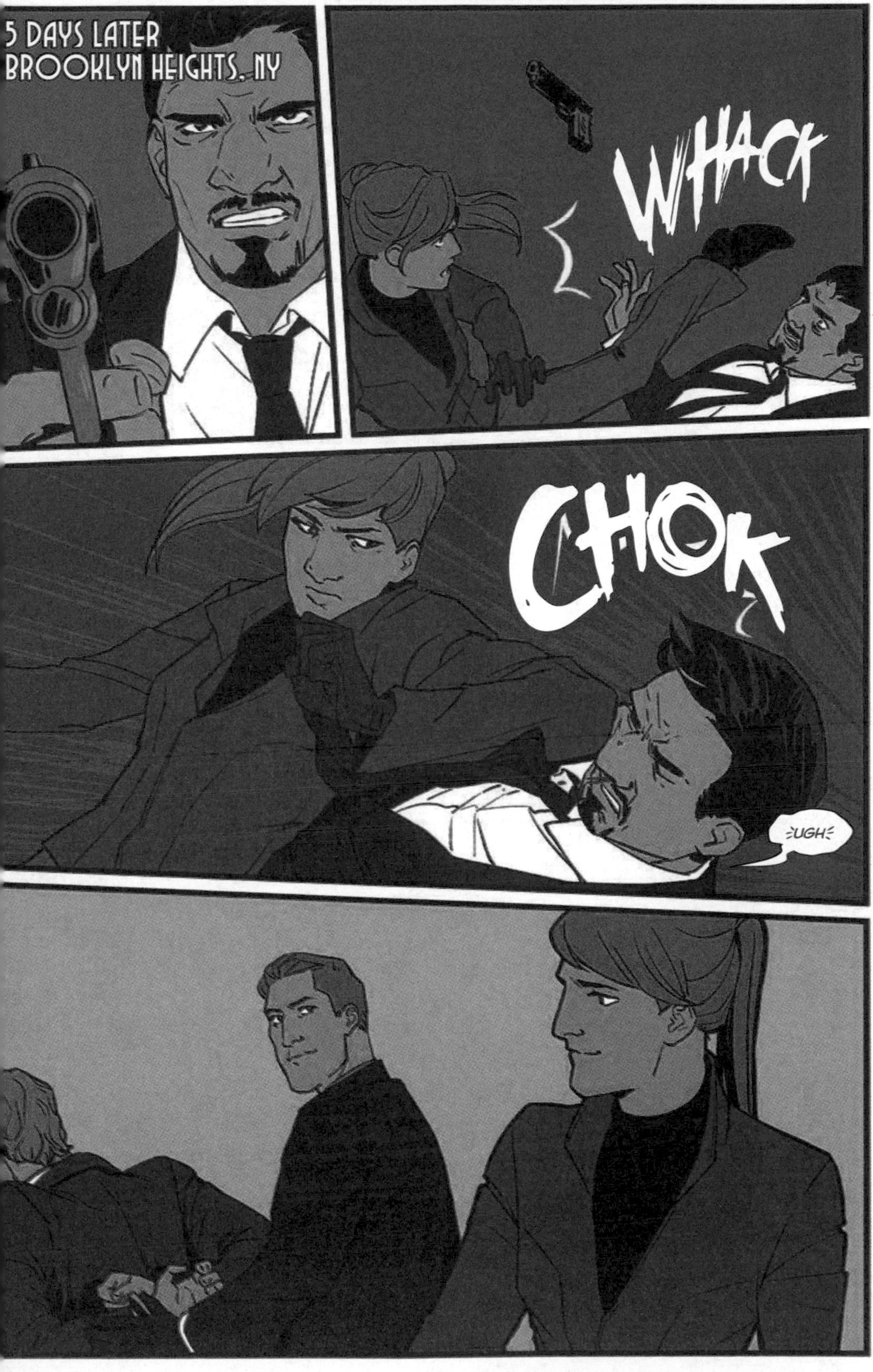
5 DAYS LATER
BROOKLYN HEIGHTS, NY
WHACK
CHOK
UGH

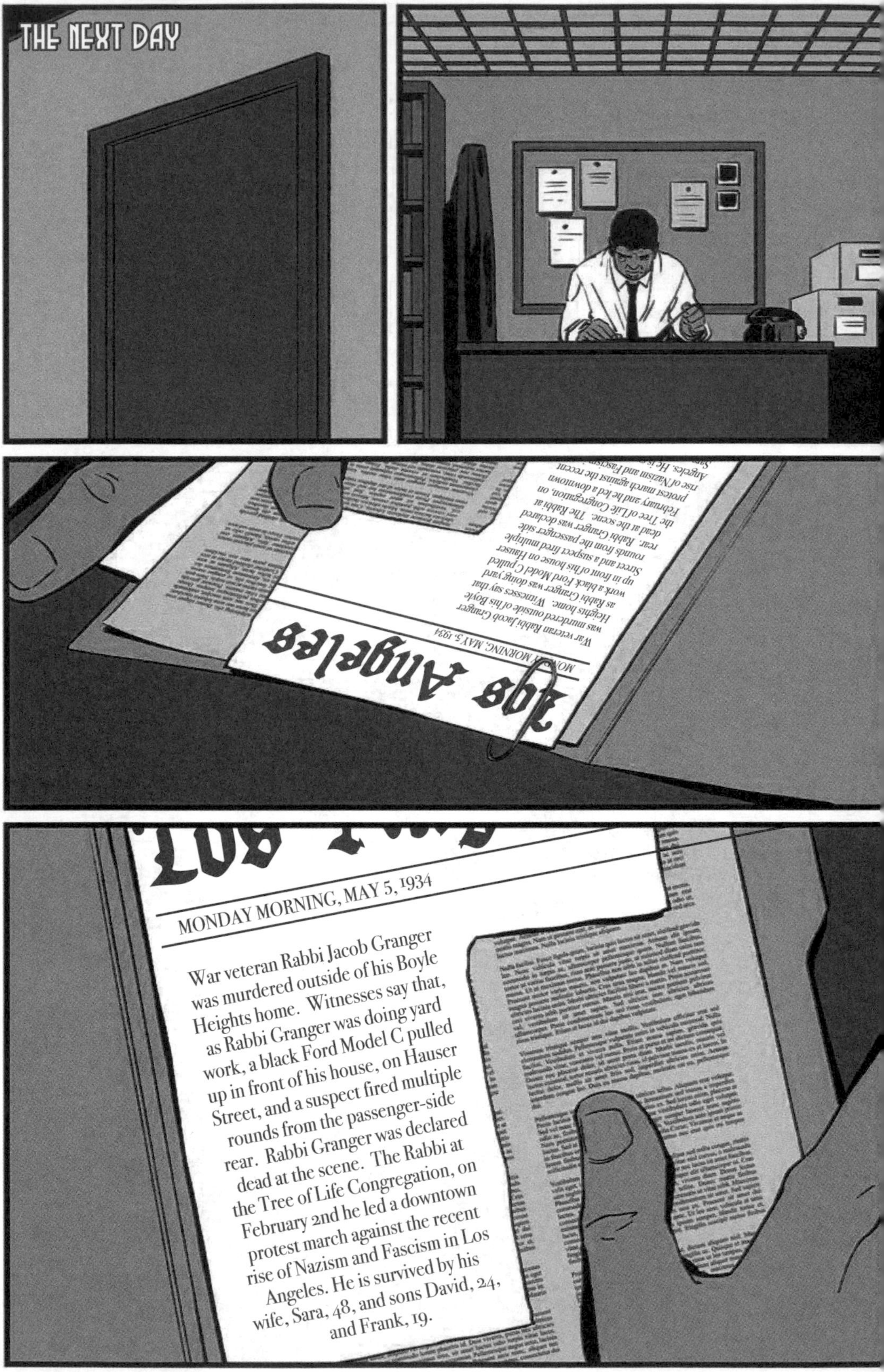
THE NEXT DAY
MONDAY MORNING, MAY 5, 1934
War veteran Rabbi Jacob Granger was murdered outside of his Boyle Heights home. Witnesses say that, as Rabbi Granger was doing yard work, a black Ford Model C pulled up in front of his house, on Hauser Street, and a suspect fired multiple rounds from the passenger-side rear. Rabbi Granger was declared dead at the scene. The Rabbi at the Tree of Life Congregation, on February 2nd he led a downtown protest march against the recent rise of Nazism and Fascism in Los Angeles. He is survived by his wife, Sara, 48, and sons David, 24, and Frank, 19.

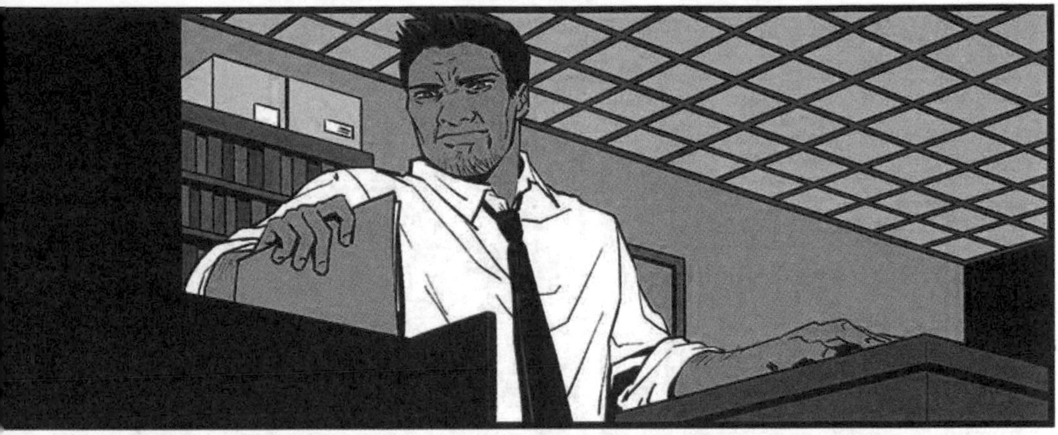

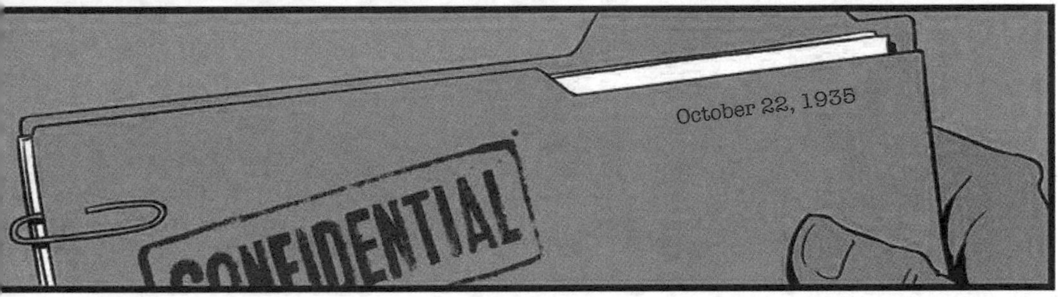
October 22, 1935
CONFIDENTIAL

BERNHARDT'S ACQUITTED ON CONSPIRACY TO COMMIT MURDER CHARGE OF RABBI JACOB GRANGER

Francis - I'm very upset that Paul and Gerda Bernhardt were set free. A legal technicality? Please. I have strong suspicions that the judge in this case, Henry Parker, is like the Bernhardts -- they are all members of the Nazi Party. I want you to undertake surveillance of him immediately.

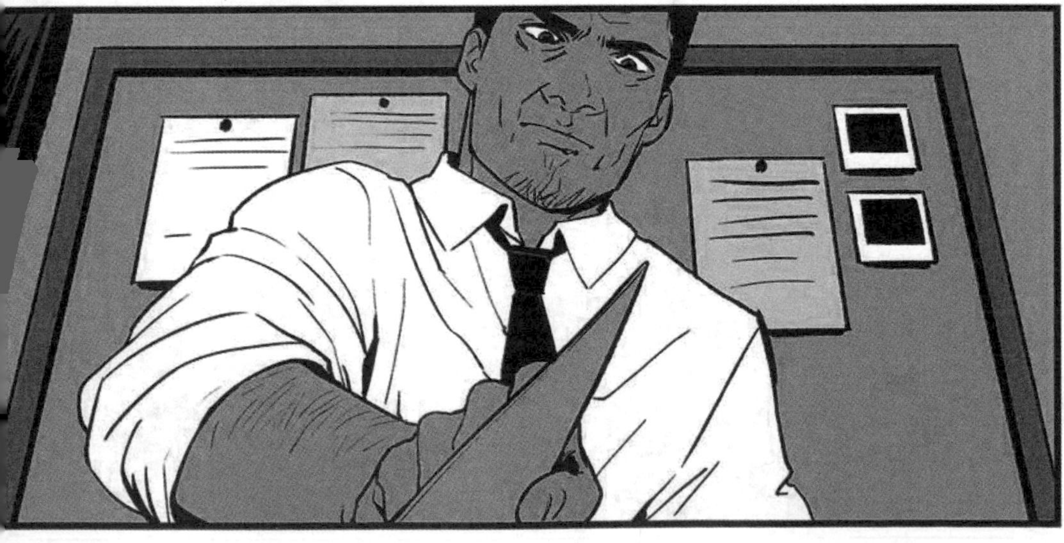

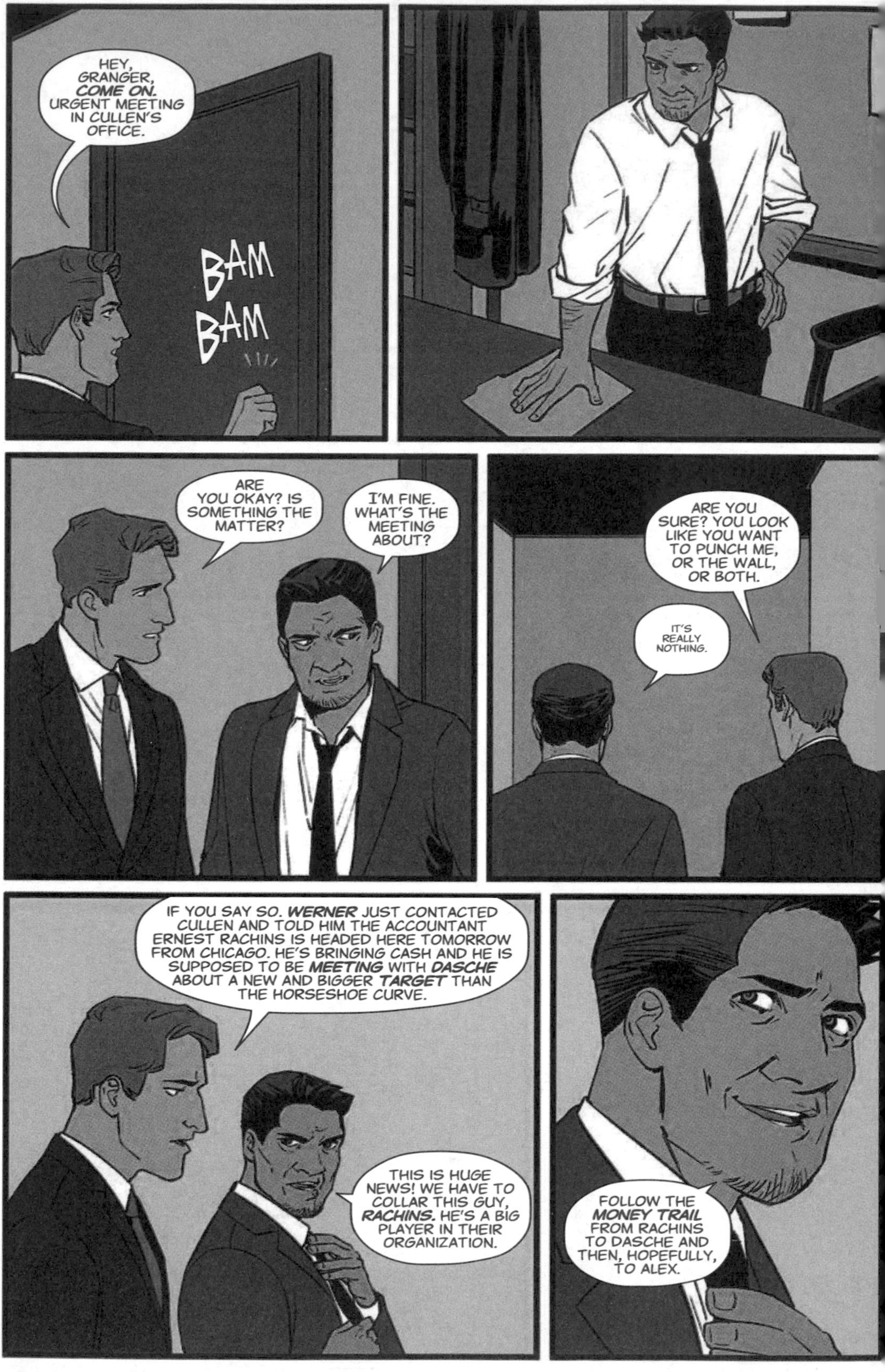
HEY, GRANGER, COME ON. URGENT MEETING IN CULLEN'S OFFICE.
BAM BAM
ARE YOU OKAY? IS SOMETHING THE MATTER?
I'M FINE. WHAT'S THE MEETING ABOUT?
ARE YOU SURE? YOU LOOK LIKE YOU WANT TO PUNCH ME, OR THE WALL, OR BOTH.
IT'S REALLY NOTHING.
IF YOU SAY SO. WERNER JUST CONTACTED CULLEN AND TOLD HIM THE ACCOUNTANT ERNEST RACHINS IS HEADED HERE TOMORROW FROM CHICAGO. HE'S BRINGING CASH AND HE IS SUPPOSED TO BE MEETING WITH DASCHE ABOUT A NEW AND BIGGER TARGET THAN THE HORSESHOE CURVE.
THIS IS HUGE NEWS! WE HAVE TO COLLAR THIS GUY, RACHINS. HE'S A BIG PLAYER IN THEIR ORGANIZATION.
FOLLOW THE MONEY TRAIL FROM RACHINS TO DASCHE AND THEN, HOPEFULLY, TO ALEX.

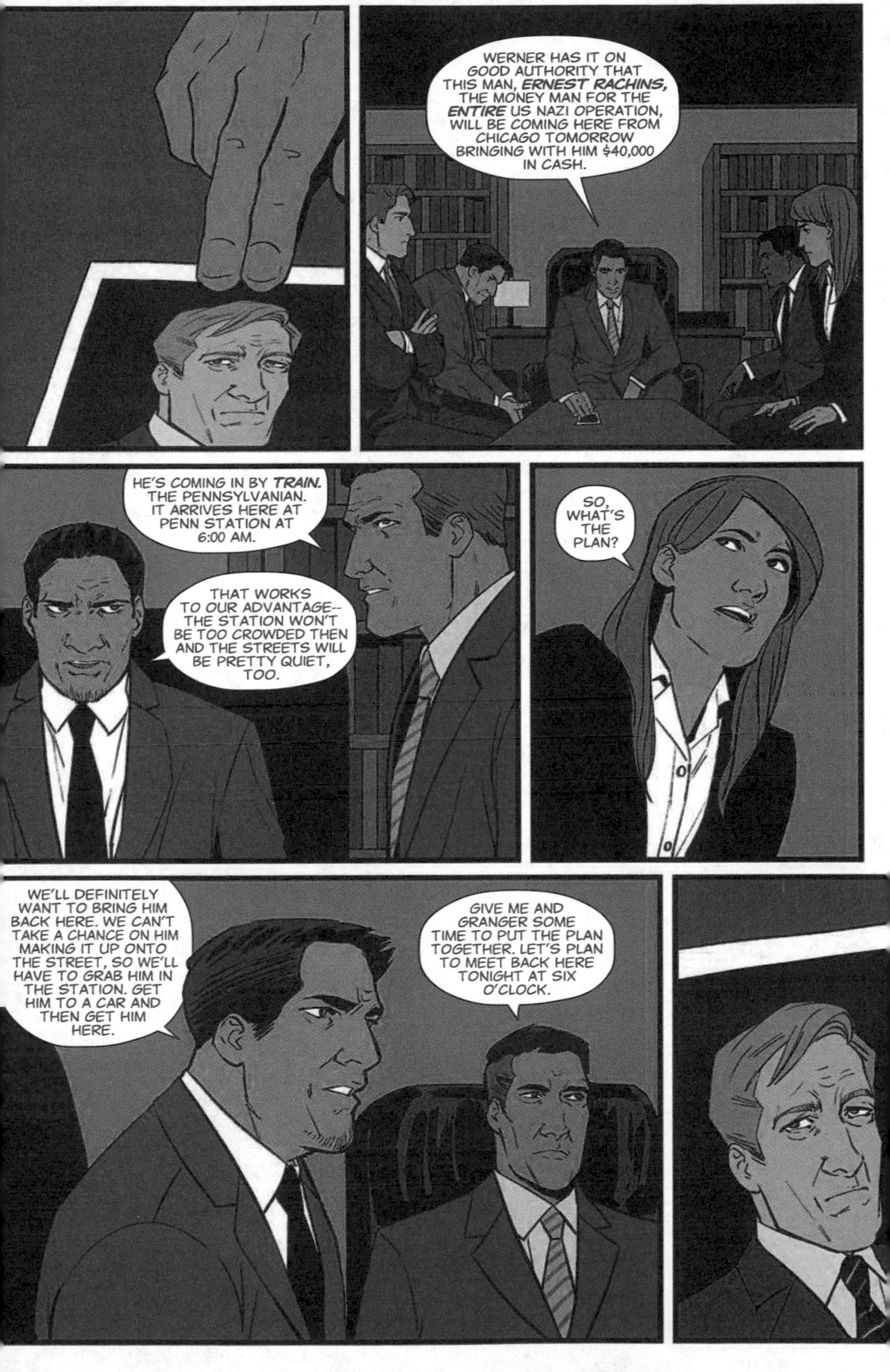
WERNER HAS IT ON GOOD AUTHORITY THAT THIS MAN, ERNEST RACHINS, THE MONEY MAN FOR THE ENTIRE US NAZI OPERATION, WILL BE COMING HERE FROM CHICAGO TOMORROW BRINGING WITH HIM $40,000 IN CASH.
HE'S COMING IN BY TRAIN. THE PENNSYLVANIAN. IT ARRIVES HERE AT PENN STATION AT 6:00 AM.
THAT WORKS TO OUR ADVANTAGE-- THE STATION WON'T BE TOO CROWDED THEN AND THE STREETS WILL BE PRETTY QUIET, TOO.
SO, WHAT'S THE PLAN?
WE'LL DEFINITELY WANT TO BRING HIM BACK HERE. WE CAN'T TAKE A CHANCE ON HIM MAKING IT UP ONTO THE STREET, SO WE'LL HAVE TO GRAB HIM IN THE STATION. GET HIM TO A CAR AND THEN GET HIM HERE.
GIVE ME AND GRANGER SOME TIME TO PUT THE PLAN TOGETHER. LET'S PLAN TO MEET BACK HERE TONIGHT AT SIX O'CLOCK.

RECOMMENDED LISTENING:

BACK ON THE CHAIN GANG
BY CHRISSIE HYNDE AND THE PRETENDERS

FLY ME COURAGEOUS
BY DRIVIN & CRYIN

CIRCLE OF DECEPTION
BY NINA OVERSTREET

CHAPTER
SEVEN

Threats
and Miscon-
ceptions

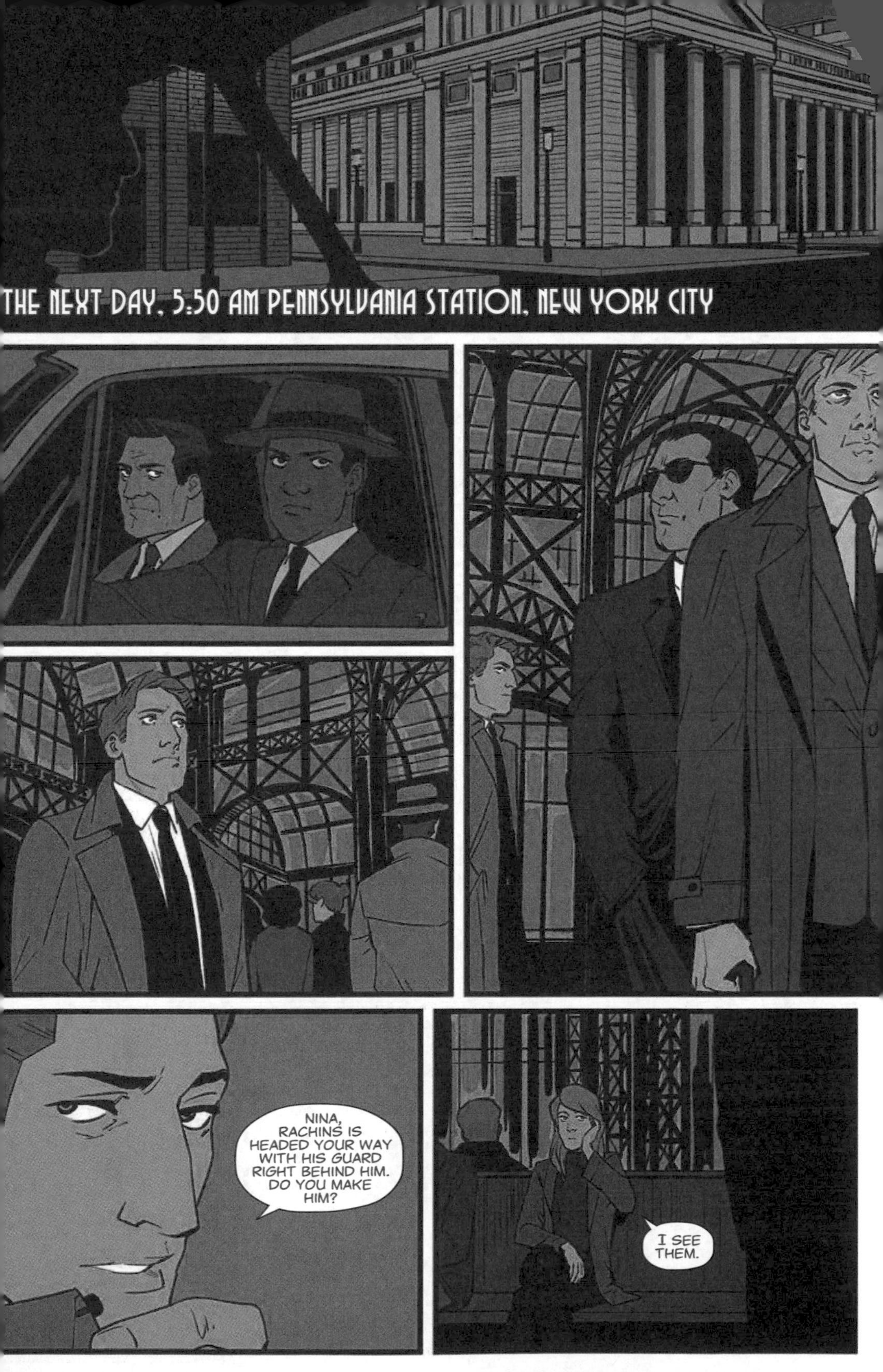
THE NEXT DAY, 5:50 AM PENNSYLVANIA STATION, NEW YORK CITY
NINA, RACHINS IS HEADED YOUR WAY WITH HIS GUARD RIGHT BEHIND HIM. DO YOU MAKE HIM?
I SEE THEM.

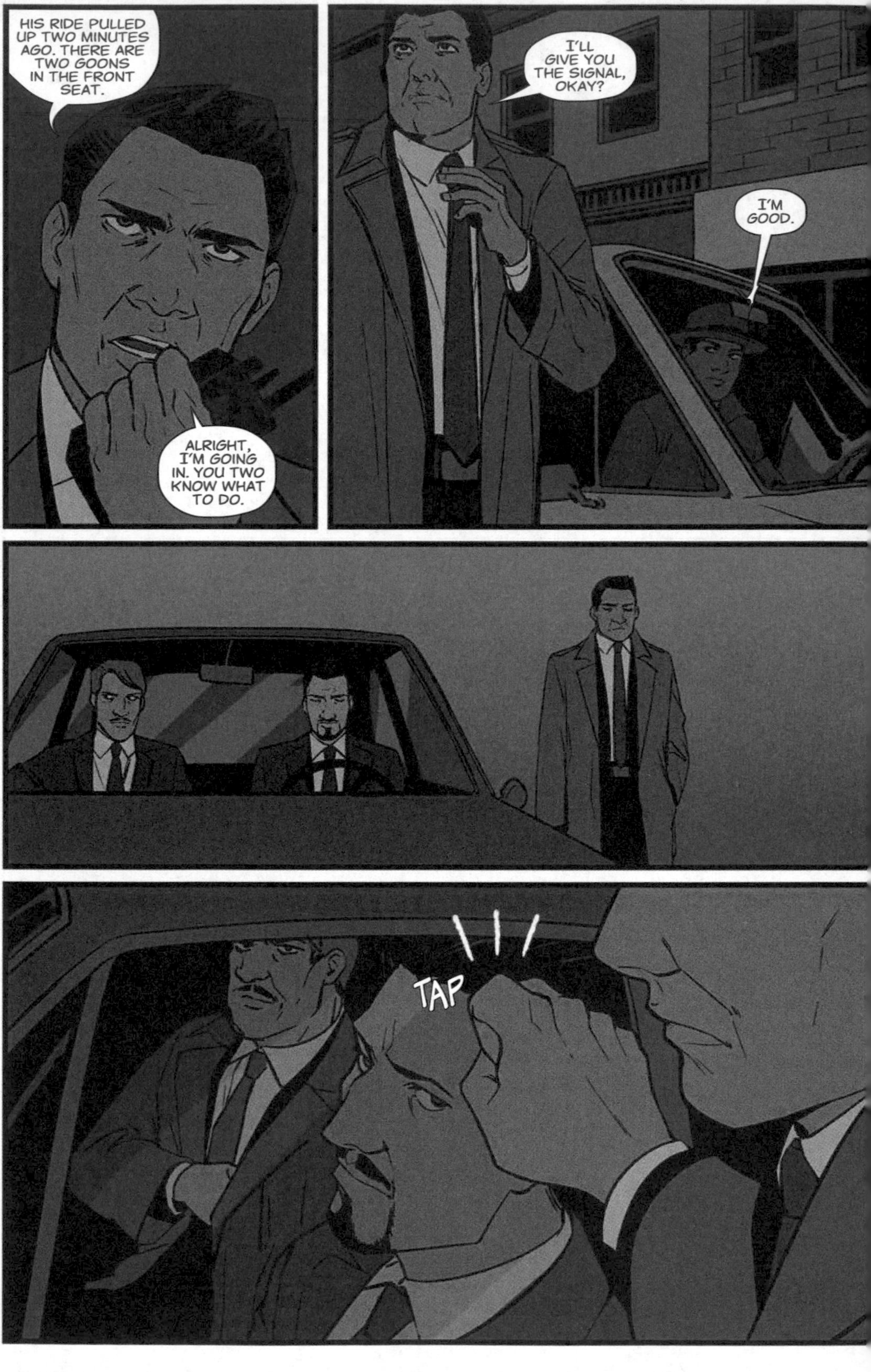
HIS RIDE PULLED UP TWO MINUTES AGO. THERE ARE TWO GOONS IN THE FRONT SEAT.
ALRIGHT, I'M GOING IN. YOU TWO KNOW WHAT TO DO.
I'LL GIVE YOU THE SIGNAL, OKAY?
I'M GOOD.
TAP

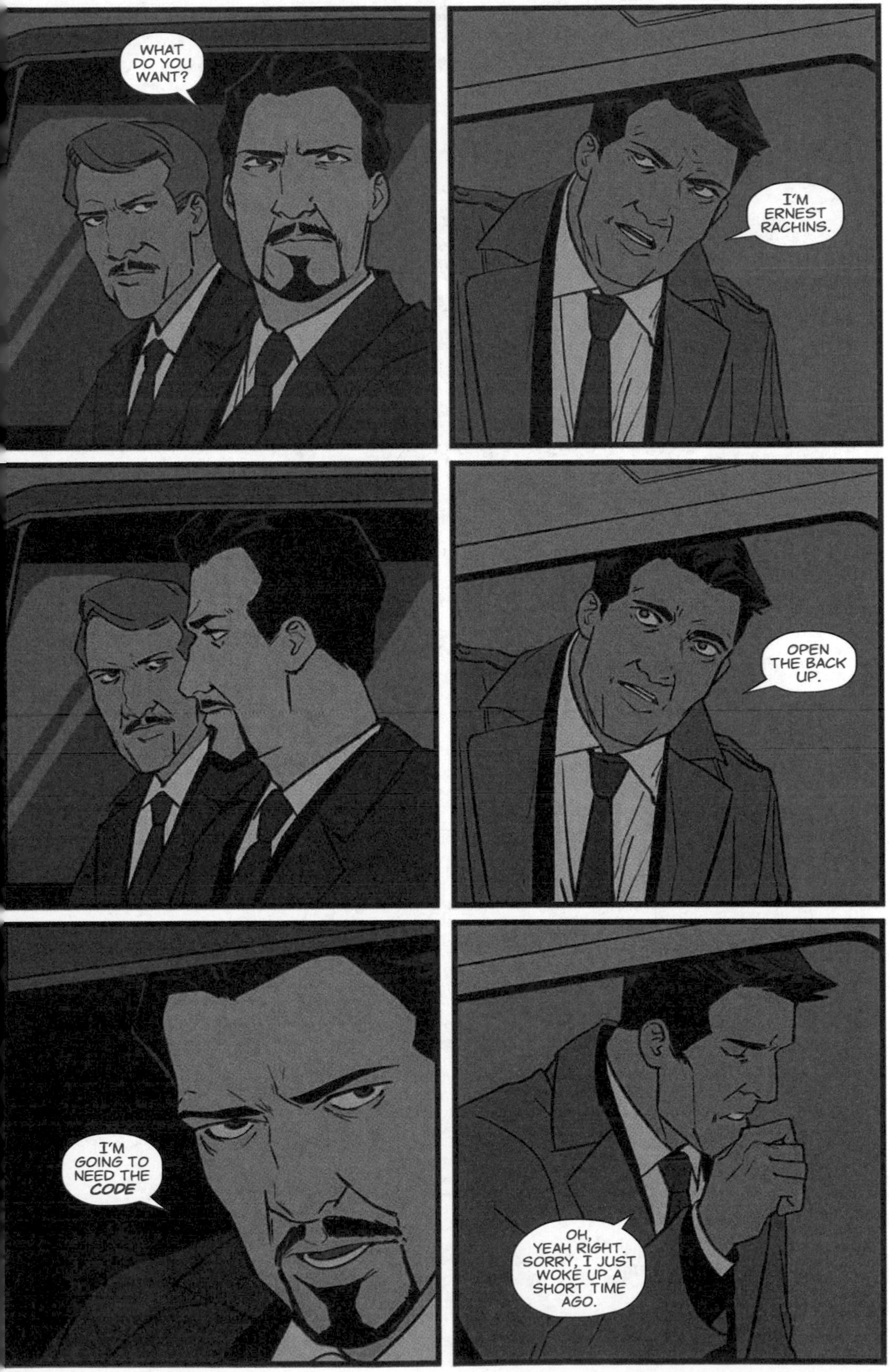
WHAT DO YOU WANT?
I'M ERNEST RACHINS.
OPEN THE BACK UP.
I'M GOING TO NEED THE *CODE*
OH, YEAH RIGHT. SORRY, I JUST WOKE UP A SHORT TIME AGO.

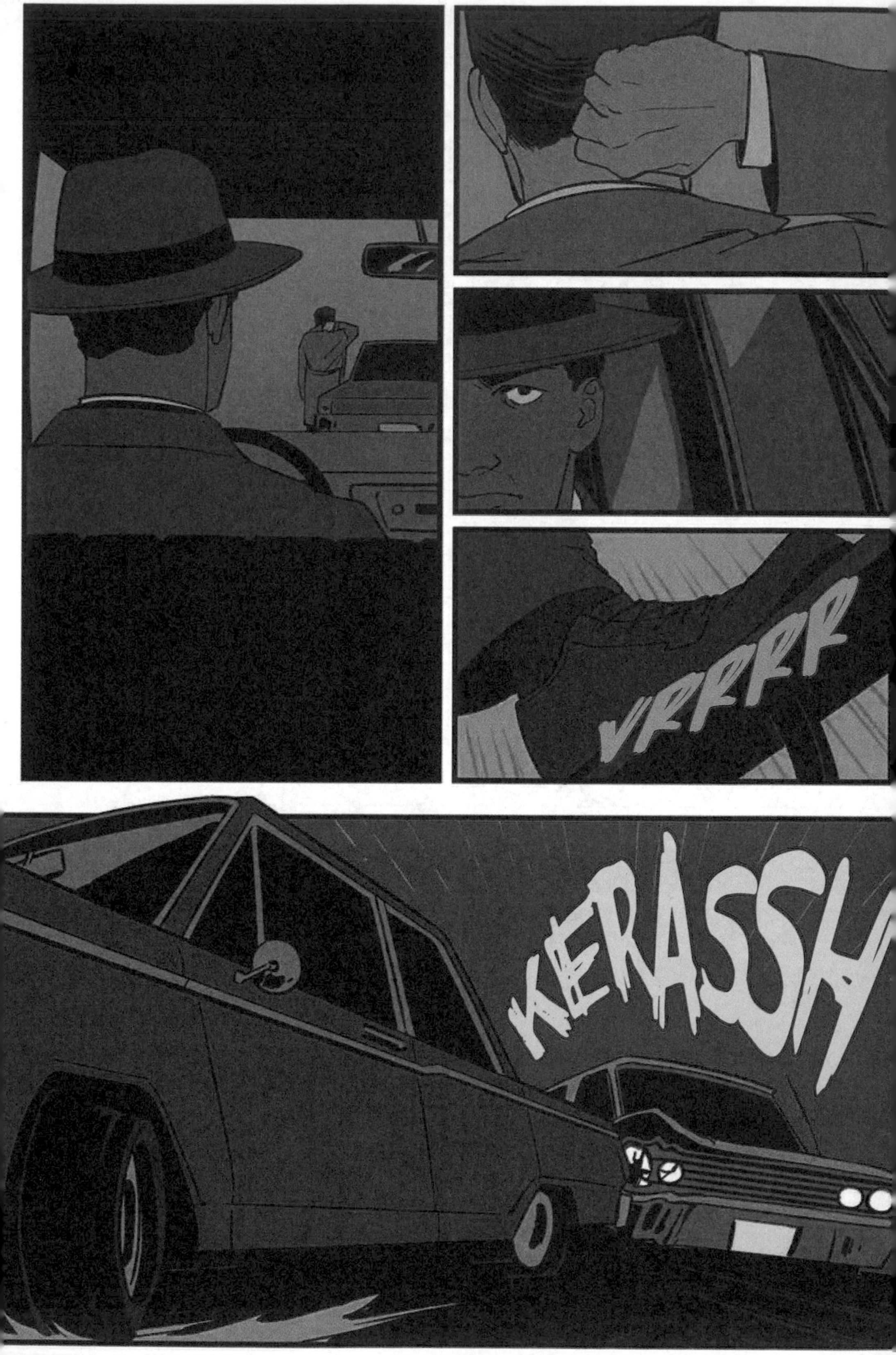
VRRRR
KERASSH

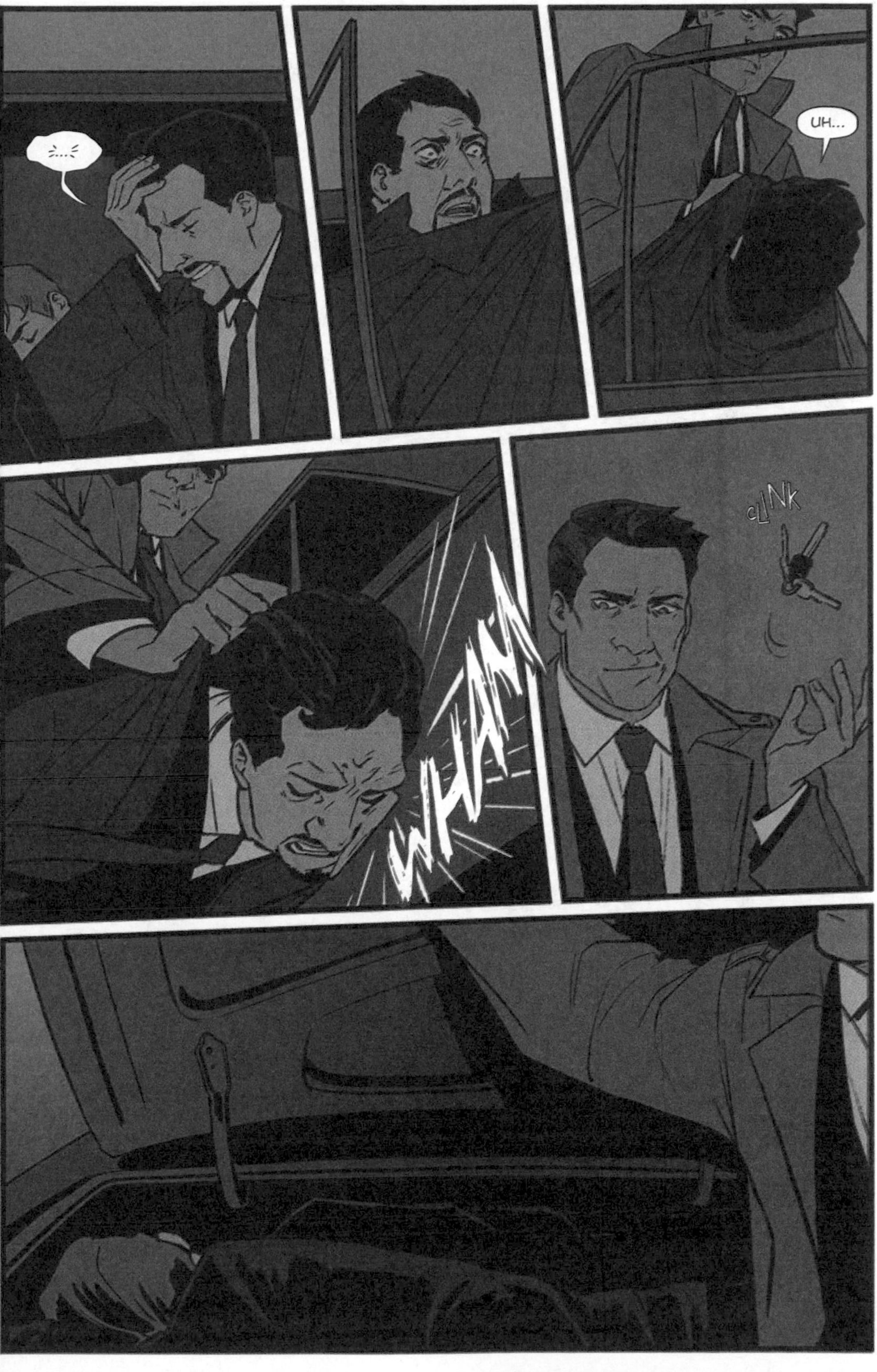
...
UH...
WHAM
CLINK

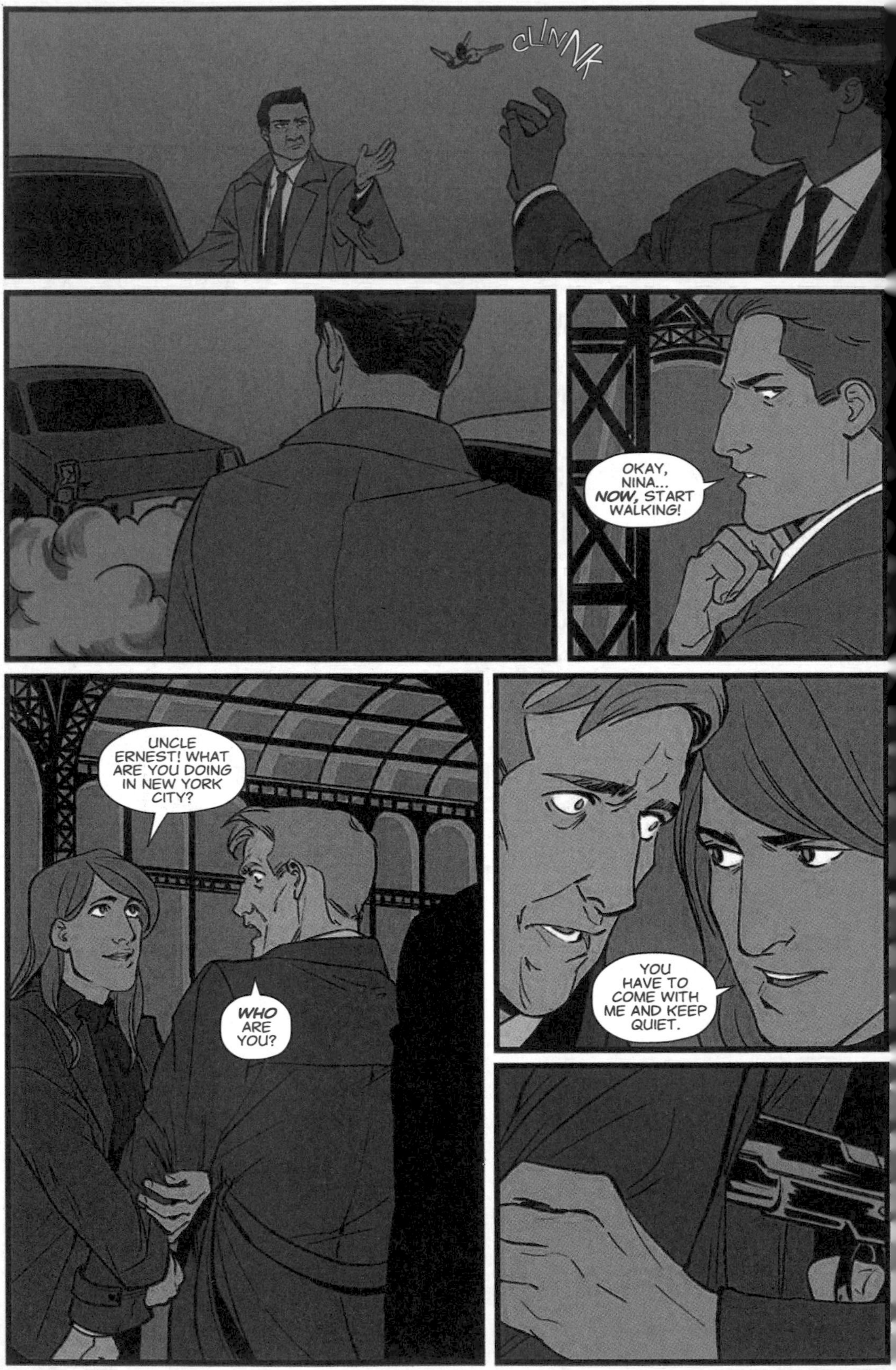
CLINNK
OKAY, NINA... NOW, START WALKING!
UNCLE ERNEST! WHAT ARE YOU DOING IN NEW YORK CITY?
WHO ARE YOU?
YOU HAVE TO COME WITH ME AND KEEP QUIET.

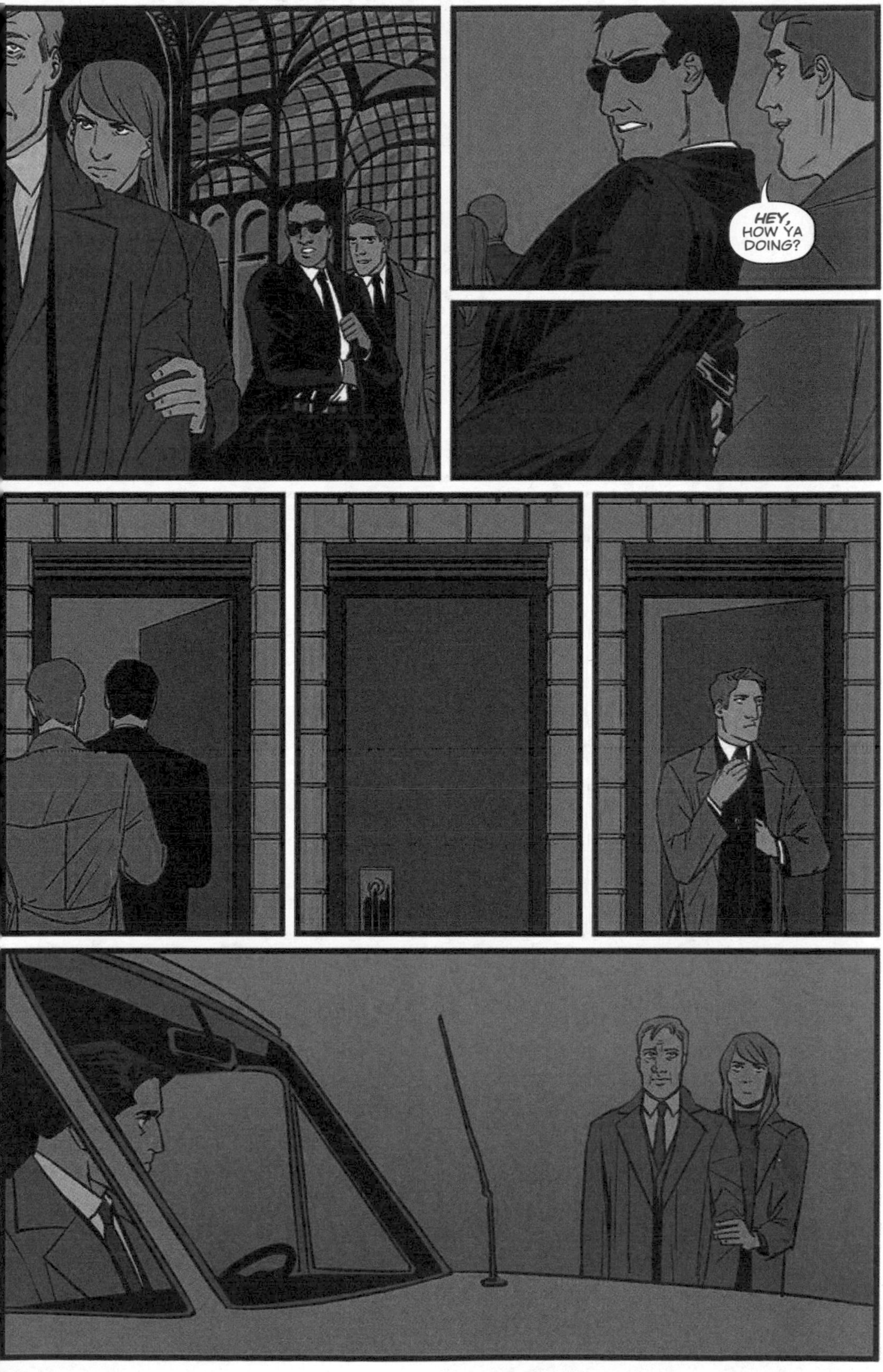
HEY, HOW YA DOING?

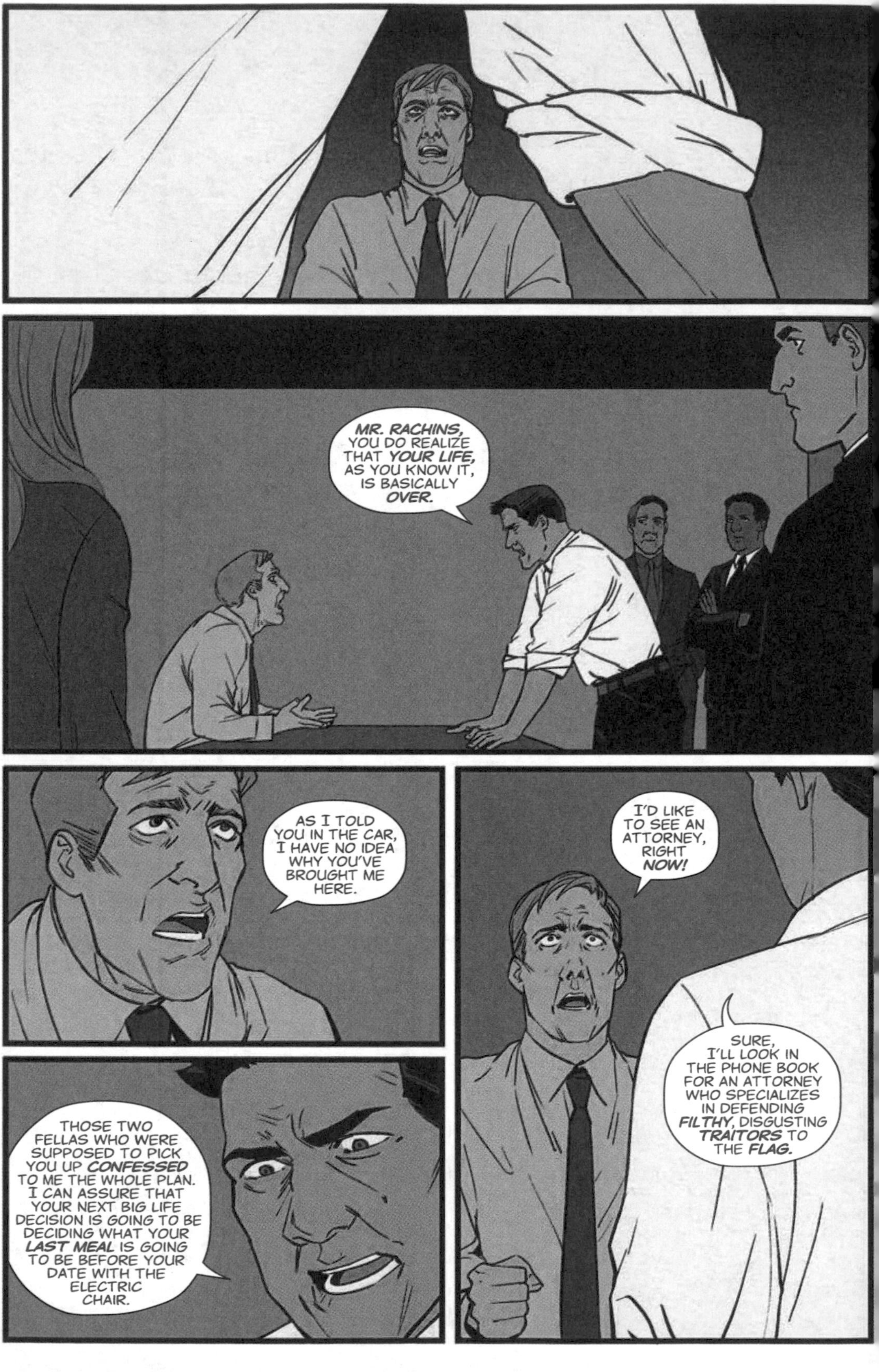
MR. RACHINS, YOU DO REALIZE THAT YOUR LIFE, AS YOU KNOW IT, IS BASICALLY OVER.
AS I TOLD YOU IN THE CAR, I HAVE NO IDEA WHY YOU'VE BROUGHT ME HERE.
THOSE TWO FELLAS WHO WERE SUPPOSED TO PICK YOU UP CONFESSED TO ME THE WHOLE PLAN. I CAN ASSURE THAT YOUR NEXT BIG LIFE DECISION IS GOING TO BE DECIDING WHAT YOUR LAST MEAL IS GOING TO BE BEFORE YOUR DATE WITH THE ELECTRIC CHAIR.
I'D LIKE TO SEE AN ATTORNEY, RIGHT NOW!
SURE, I'LL LOOK IN THE PHONE BOOK FOR AN ATTORNEY WHO SPECIALIZES IN DEFENDING FILTHY, DISGUSTING TRAITORS TO THE FLAG.

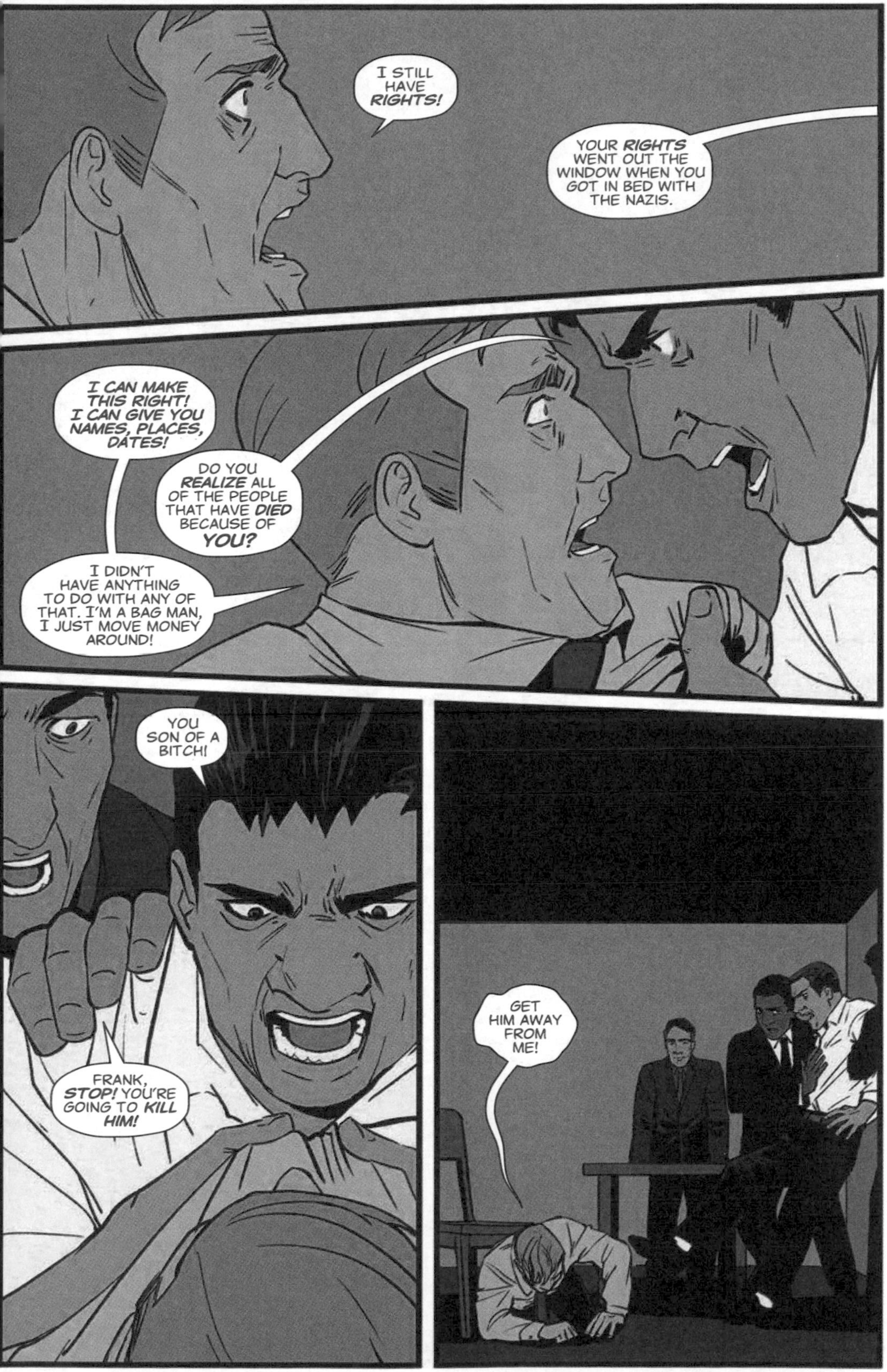
I STILL HAVE RIGHTS!
YOUR RIGHTS WENT OUT THE WINDOW WHEN YOU GOT IN BED WITH THE NAZIS.
I CAN MAKE THIS RIGHT! I CAN GIVE YOU NAMES, PLACES, DATES!
DO YOU REALIZE ALL OF THE PEOPLE THAT HAVE DIED BECAUSE OF YOU?
I DIDN'T HAVE ANYTHING TO DO WITH ANY OF THAT. I'M A BAG MAN, I JUST MOVE MONEY AROUND!
YOU SON OF A BITCH!
FRANK, STOP! YOU'RE GOING TO KILL HIM!
GET HIM AWAY FROM ME!

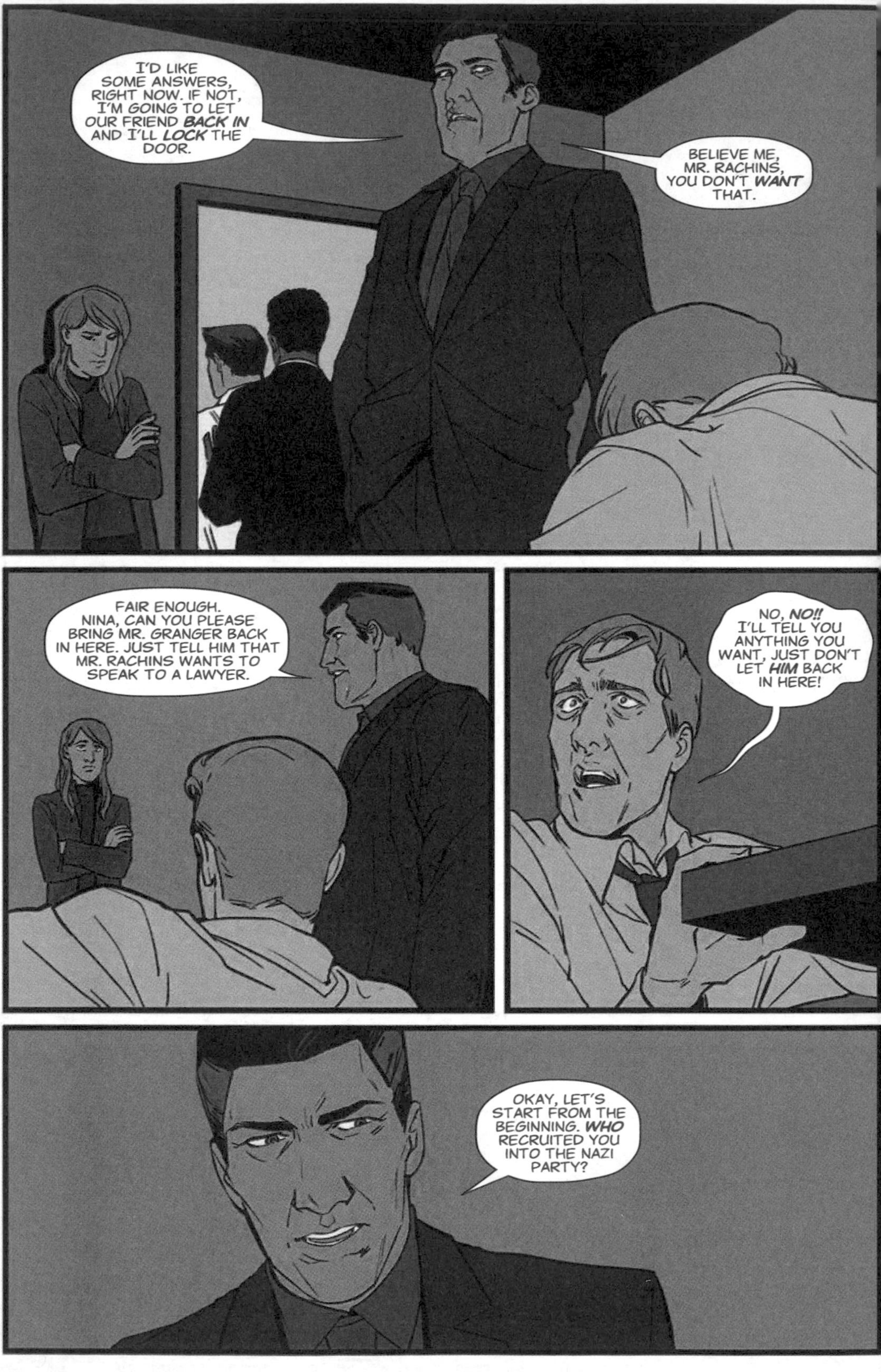
I'D LIKE SOME ANSWERS, RIGHT NOW. IF NOT, I'M GOING TO LET OUR FRIEND BACK IN AND I'LL LOCK THE DOOR.
BELIEVE ME, MR. RACHINS, YOU DON'T WANT THAT.
FAIR ENOUGH. NINA, CAN YOU PLEASE BRING MR. GRANGER BACK IN HERE. JUST TELL HIM THAT MR. RACHINS WANTS TO SPEAK TO A LAWYER.
NO, NO!! I'LL TELL YOU ANYTHING YOU WANT, JUST DON'T LET HIM BACK IN HERE!
OKAY, LET'S START FROM THE BEGINNING. WHO RECRUITED YOU INTO THE NAZI PARTY?

RECOMMENDED LISTENING:

YOU LET ME DOWN
BY BILLIE HOLIDAY

LIVIN' IN THE FUTURE
BY BRUCE SPRINGSTEEN & THE E STREET BAND

SHIP LIBERTY SAILED AWAY
BY NINA OVERSTREET

CHAPTER
EIGHT
Rendition,
Suppression
and
Intentional
Omissions

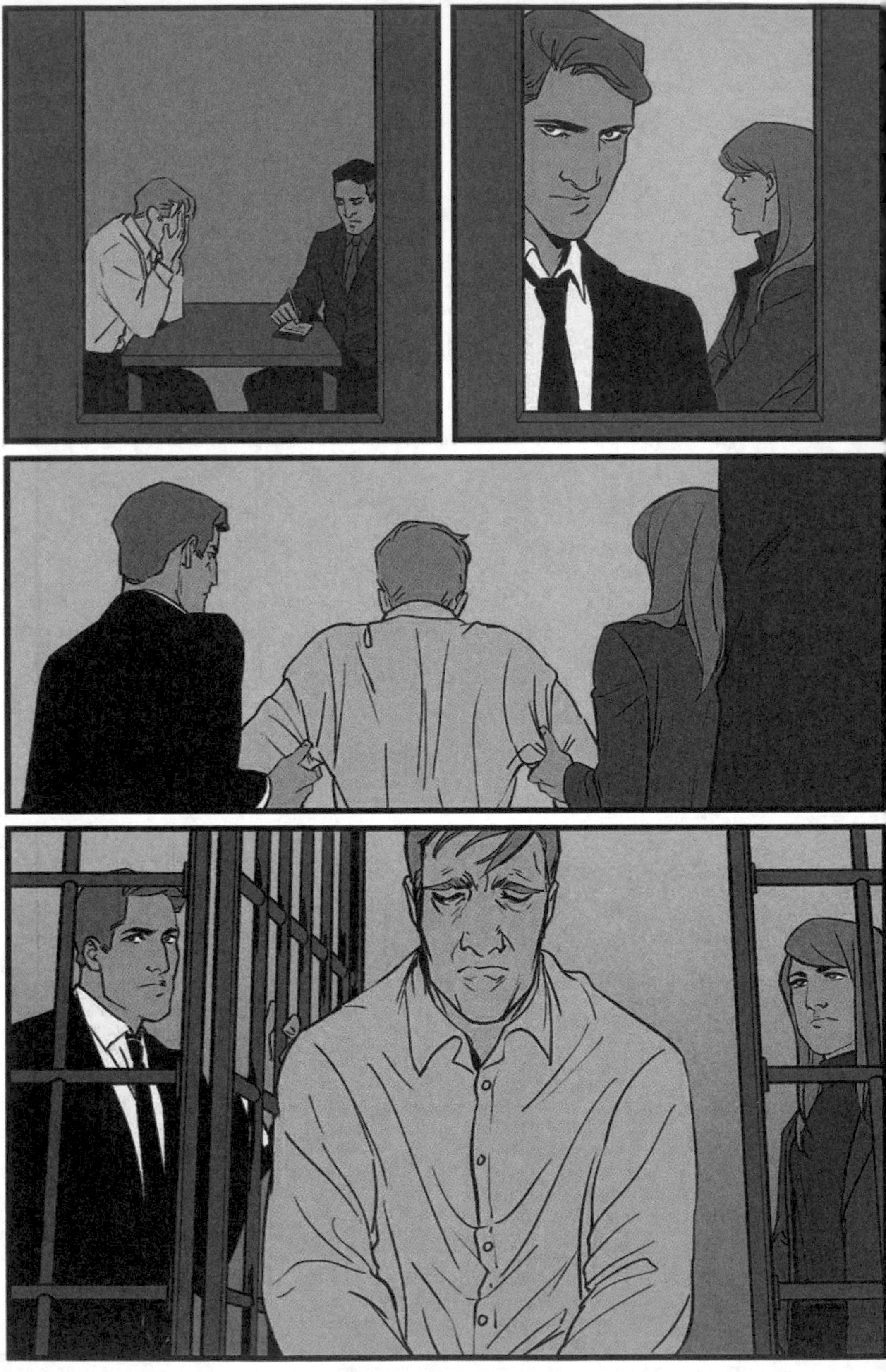

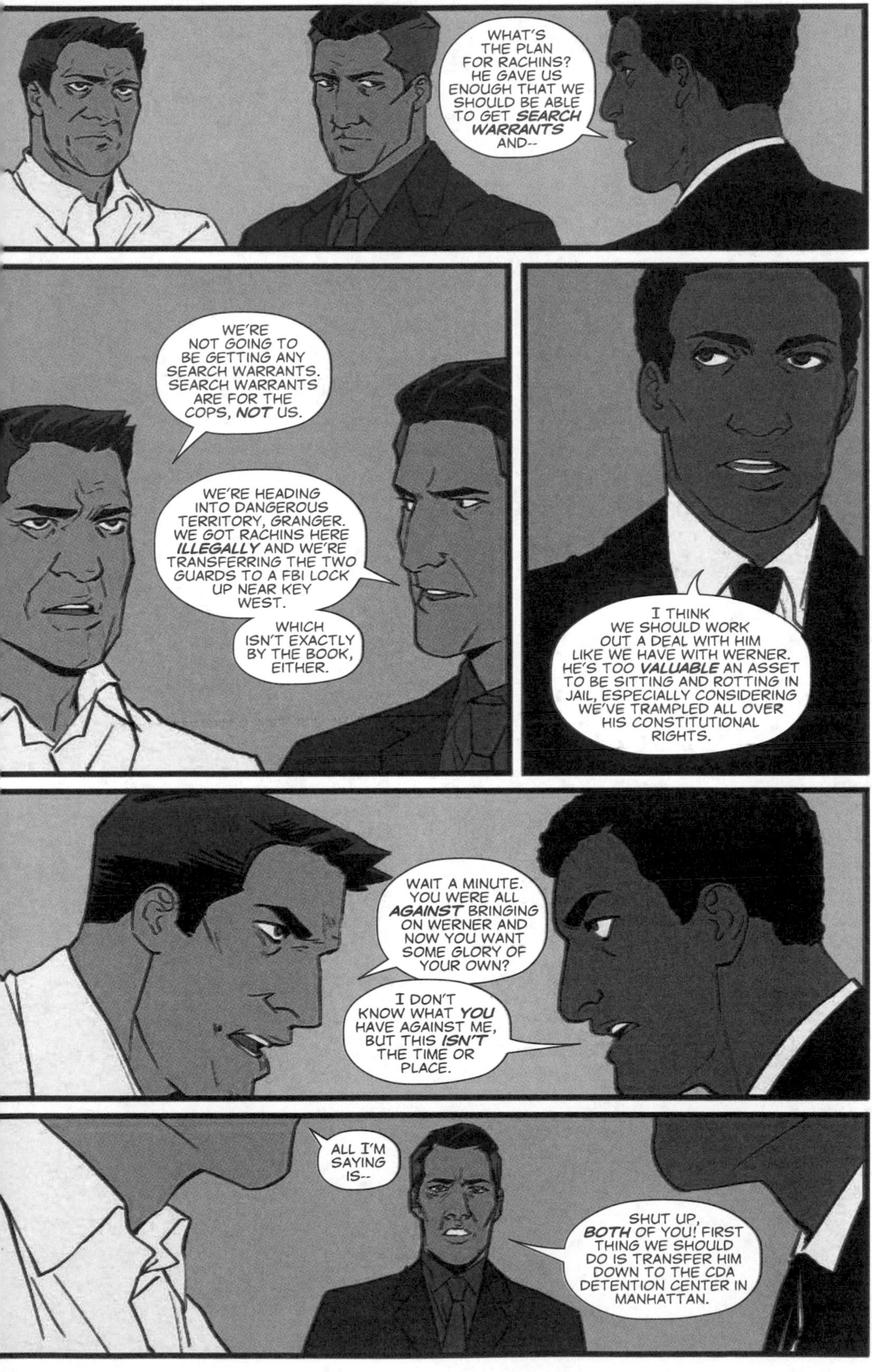
WHAT'S THE PLAN FOR RACHINS? HE GAVE US ENOUGH THAT WE SHOULD BE ABLE TO GET SEARCH WARRANTS AND--
WE'RE NOT GOING TO BE GETTING ANY SEARCH WARRANTS. SEARCH WARRANTS ARE FOR THE COPS, NOT US.
WE'RE HEADING INTO DANGEROUS TERRITORY, GRANGER. WE GOT RACHINS HERE ILLEGALLY AND WE'RE TRANSFERRING THE TWO GUARDS TO A FBI LOCK UP NEAR KEY WEST.
WHICH ISN'T EXACTLY BY THE BOOK, EITHER.
I THINK WE SHOULD WORK OUT A DEAL WITH HIM LIKE WE HAVE WITH WERNER. HE'S TOO VALUABLE AN ASSET TO BE SITTING AND ROTTING IN JAIL, ESPECIALLY CONSIDERING WE'VE TRAMPLED ALL OVER HIS CONSTITUTIONAL RIGHTS.
WAIT A MINUTE. YOU WERE ALL AGAINST BRINGING ON WERNER AND NOW YOU WANT SOME GLORY OF YOUR OWN?
I DON'T KNOW WHAT YOU HAVE AGAINST ME, BUT THIS ISN'T THE TIME OR PLACE.
ALL I'M SAYING IS--
SHUT UP, BOTH OF YOU! FIRST THING WE SHOULD DO IS TRANSFER HIM DOWN TO THE CDA DETENTION CENTER IN MANHATTAN.

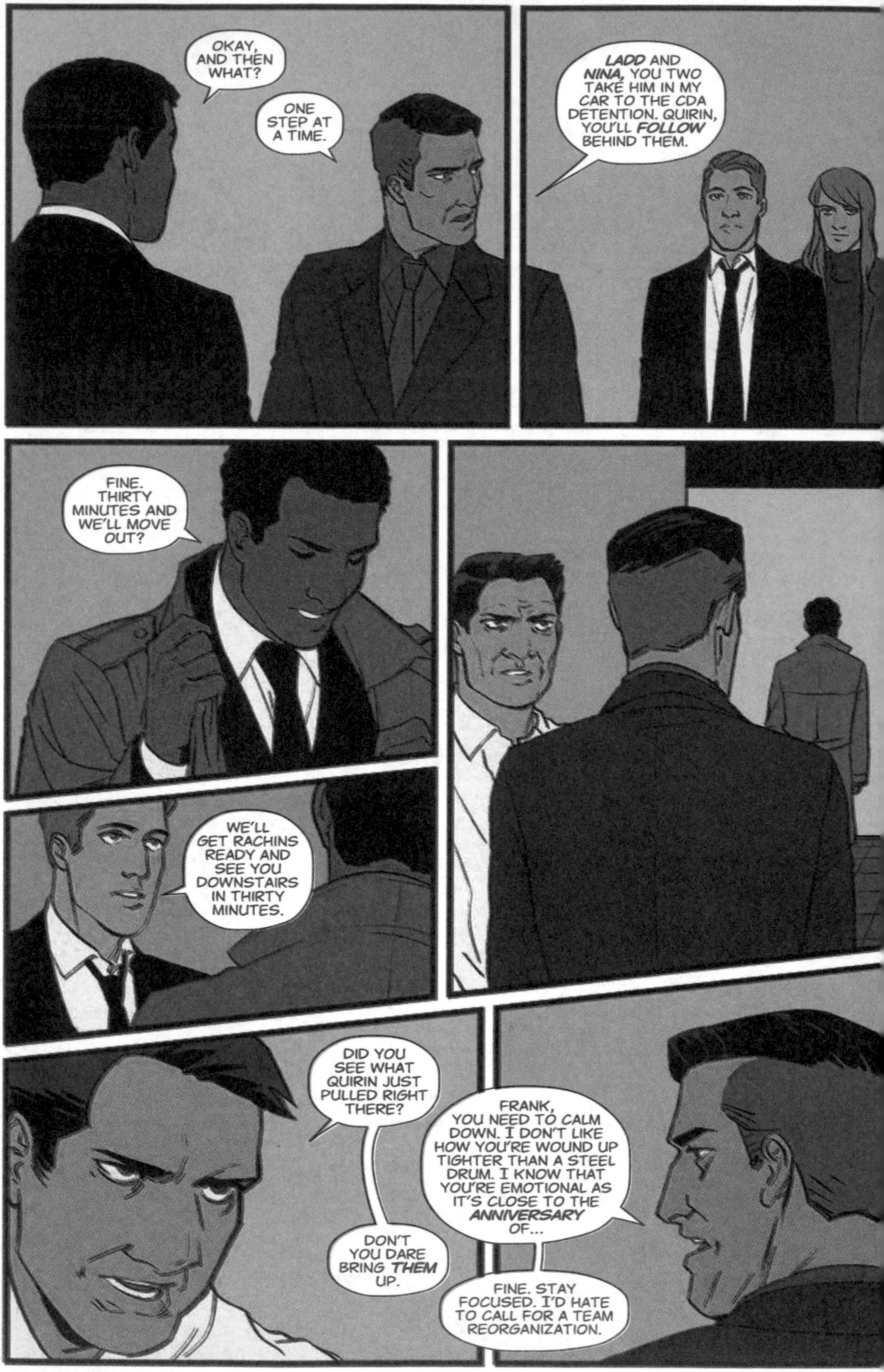

OKAY, AND THEN WHAT?
ONE STEP AT A TIME.
LADD AND NINA, YOU TWO TAKE HIM IN MY CAR TO THE CDA DETENTION. QUIRIN, YOU'LL FOLLOW BEHIND THEM.
FINE. THIRTY MINUTES AND WE'LL MOVE OUT?
WE'LL GET RACHINS READY AND SEE YOU DOWNSTAIRS IN THIRTY MINUTES.
DID YOU SEE WHAT QUIRIN JUST PULLED RIGHT THERE?
FRANK, YOU NEED TO CALM DOWN. I DON'T LIKE HOW YOU'RE WOUND UP TIGHTER THAN A STEEL DRUM. I KNOW THAT YOU'RE EMOTIONAL AS IT'S CLOSE TO THE ANNIVERSARY OF...
DON'T YOU DARE BRING THEM UP.
FINE. STAY FOCUSED. I'D HATE TO CALL FOR A TEAM REORGANIZATION.

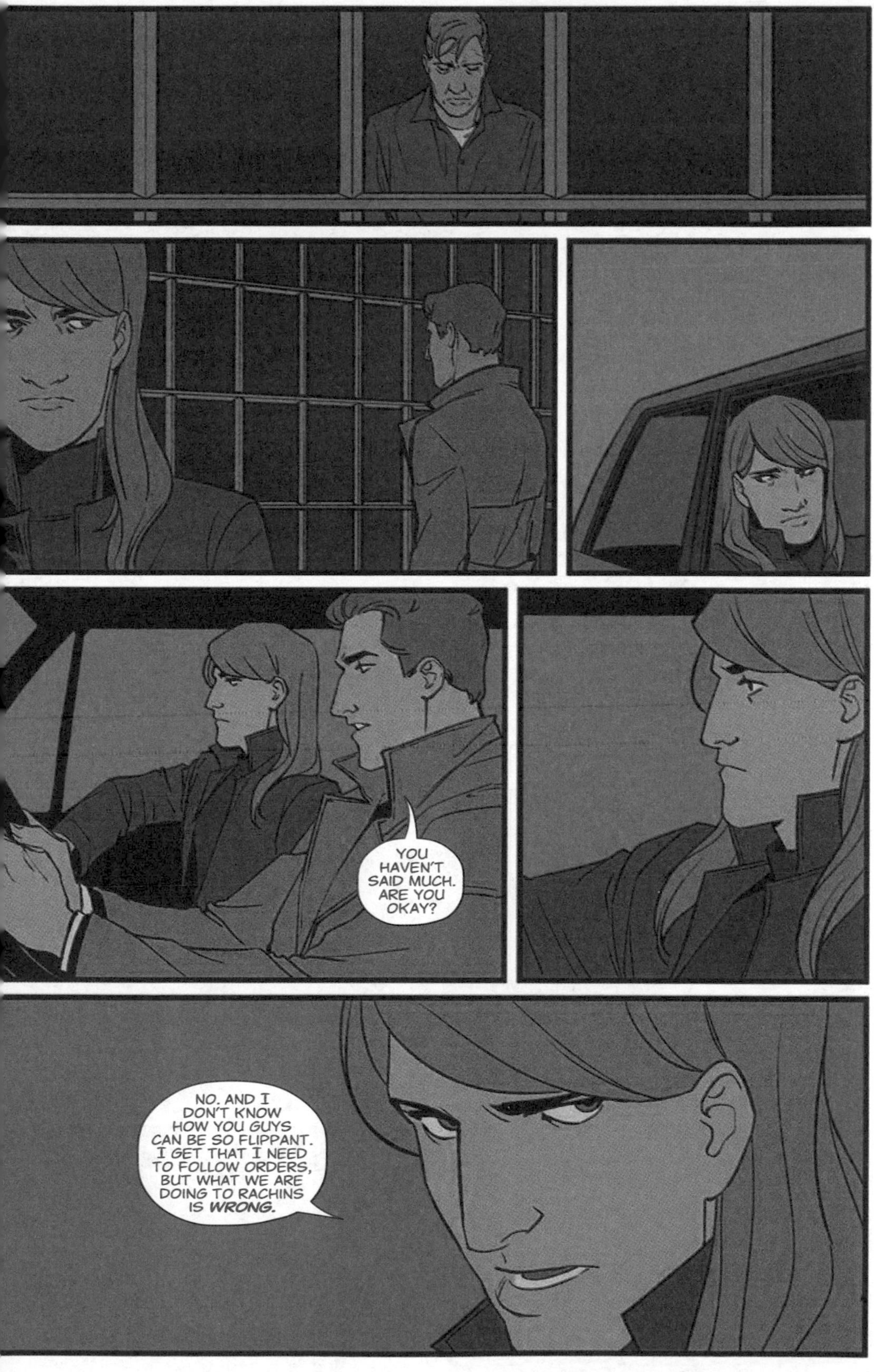
YOU HAVEN'T SAID MUCH. ARE YOU OKAY?
NO. AND I DON'T KNOW HOW YOU GUYS CAN BE SO FLIPPANT. I GET THAT I NEED TO FOLLOW ORDERS, BUT WHAT WE ARE DOING TO RACHINS IS *WRONG.*

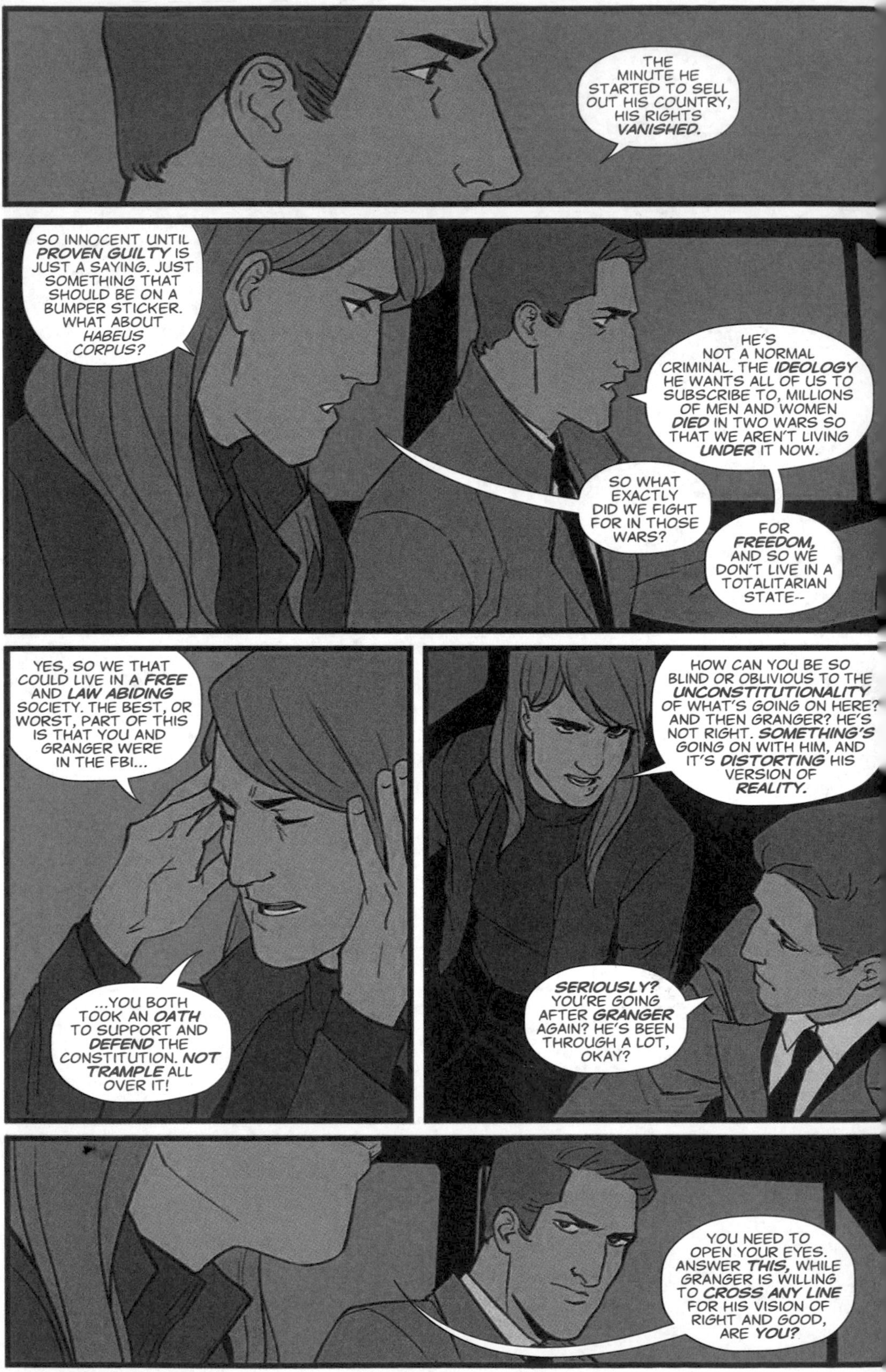
THE MINUTE HE STARTED TO SELL OUT HIS COUNTRY, HIS RIGHTS VANISHED.
SO INNOCENT UNTIL PROVEN GUILTY IS JUST A SAYING. JUST SOMETHING THAT SHOULD BE ON A BUMPER STICKER. WHAT ABOUT HABEUS CORPUS?
HE'S NOT A NORMAL CRIMINAL. THE IDEOLOGY HE WANTS ALL OF US TO SUBSCRIBE TO, MILLIONS OF MEN AND WOMEN DIED IN TWO WARS SO THAT WE AREN'T LIVING UNDER IT NOW.
SO WHAT EXACTLY DID WE FIGHT FOR IN THOSE WARS?
FOR FREEDOM, AND SO WE DON'T LIVE IN A TOTALITARIAN STATE--
YES, SO WE THAT COULD LIVE IN A FREE AND LAW ABIDING SOCIETY. THE BEST, OR WORST, PART OF THIS IS THAT YOU AND GRANGER WERE IN THE FBI...
...YOU BOTH TOOK AN OATH TO SUPPORT AND DEFEND THE CONSTITUTION. NOT TRAMPLE ALL OVER IT!
HOW CAN YOU BE SO BLIND OR OBLIVIOUS TO THE UNCONSTITUTIONALITY OF WHAT'S GOING ON HERE? AND THEN GRANGER? HE'S NOT RIGHT. SOMETHING'S GOING ON WITH HIM, AND IT'S DISTORTING HIS VERSION OF REALITY.
SERIOUSLY? YOU'RE GOING AFTER GRANGER AGAIN? HE'S BEEN THROUGH A LOT, OKAY?
YOU NEED TO OPEN YOUR EYES. ANSWER THIS, WHILE GRANGER IS WILLING TO CROSS ANY LINE FOR HIS VISION OF RIGHT AND GOOD, ARE YOU?

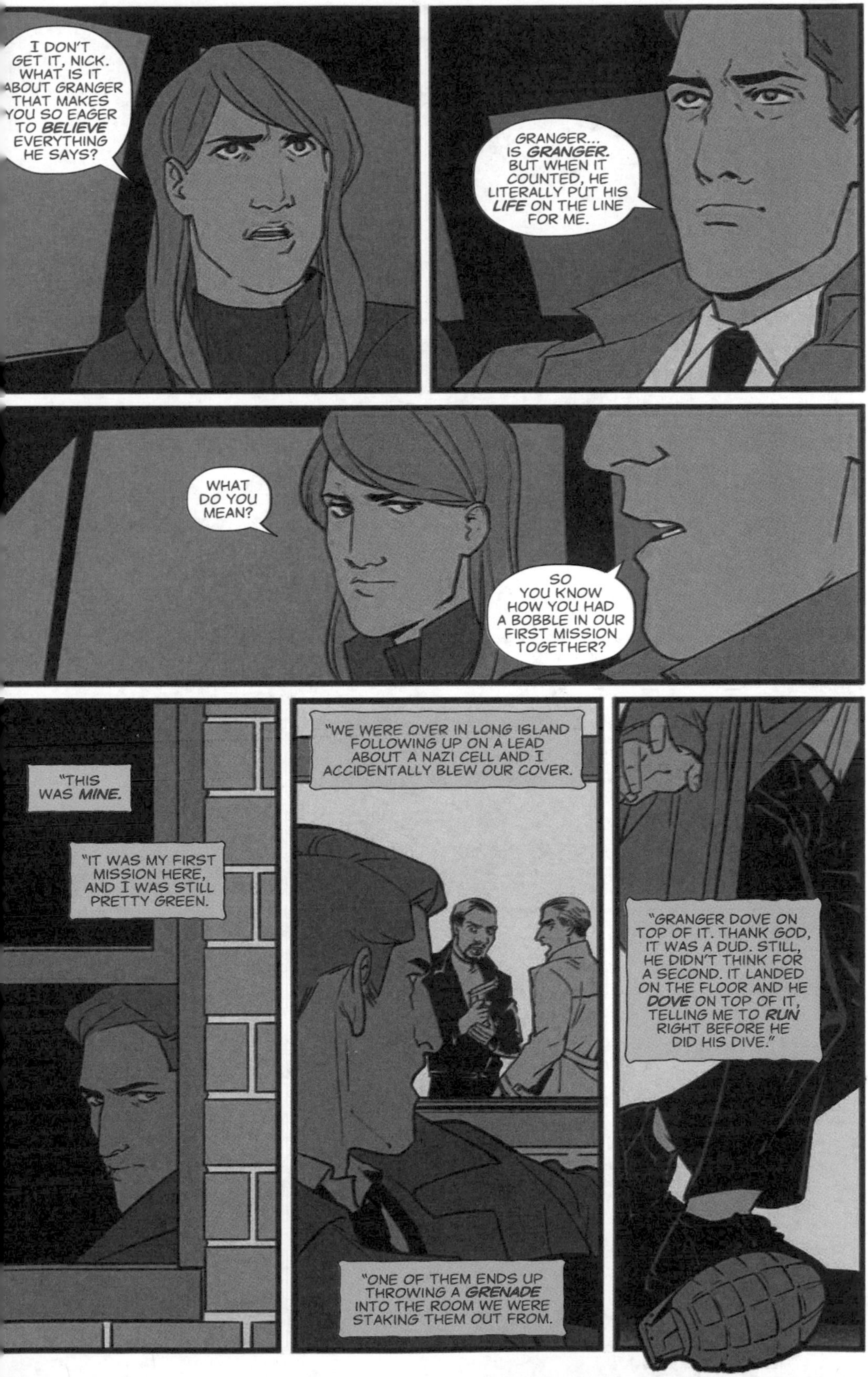
I DON'T GET IT, NICK. WHAT IS IT ABOUT GRANGER THAT MAKES YOU SO EAGER TO BELIEVE EVERYTHING HE SAYS?
GRANGER... IS GRANGER. BUT WHEN IT COUNTED, HE LITERALLY PUT HIS LIFE ON THE LINE FOR ME.
WHAT DO YOU MEAN?
SO YOU KNOW HOW YOU HAD A BOBBLE IN OUR FIRST MISSION TOGETHER?
"THIS WAS MINE.
"IT WAS MY FIRST MISSION HERE, AND I WAS STILL PRETTY GREEN.
"WE WERE OVER IN LONG ISLAND FOLLOWING UP ON A LEAD ABOUT A NAZI CELL AND I ACCIDENTALLY BLEW OUR COVER.
"ONE OF THEM ENDS UP THROWING A GRENADE INTO THE ROOM WE WERE STAKING THEM OUT FROM.
"GRANGER DOVE ON TOP OF IT. THANK GOD, IT WAS A DUD. STILL, HE DIDN'T THINK FOR A SECOND. IT LANDED ON THE FLOOR AND HE DOVE ON TOP OF IT, TELLING ME TO RUN RIGHT BEFORE HE DID HIS DIVE."

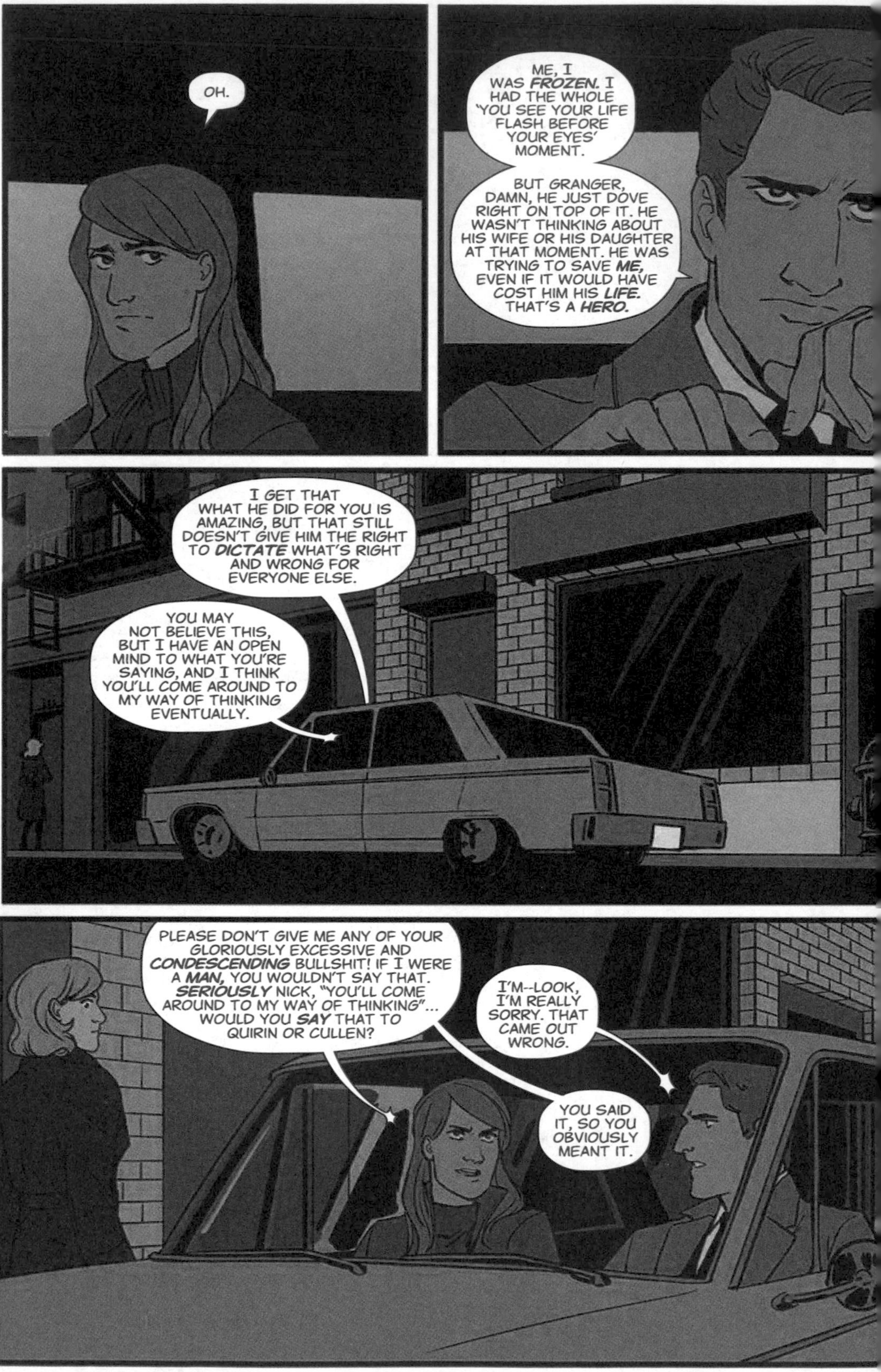
OH.
ME, I WAS FROZEN. I HAD THE WHOLE 'YOU SEE YOUR LIFE FLASH BEFORE YOUR EYES' MOMENT.
BUT GRANGER, DAMN, HE JUST DOVE RIGHT ON TOP OF IT. HE WASN'T THINKING ABOUT HIS WIFE OR HIS DAUGHTER AT THAT MOMENT. HE WAS TRYING TO SAVE ME, EVEN IF IT WOULD HAVE COST HIM HIS LIFE. THAT'S A HERO.
I GET THAT WHAT HE DID FOR YOU IS AMAZING, BUT THAT STILL DOESN'T GIVE HIM THE RIGHT TO DICTATE WHAT'S RIGHT AND WRONG FOR EVERYONE ELSE.
YOU MAY NOT BELIEVE THIS, BUT I HAVE AN OPEN MIND TO WHAT YOU'RE SAYING, AND I THINK YOU'LL COME AROUND TO MY WAY OF THINKING EVENTUALLY.
PLEASE DON'T GIVE ME ANY OF YOUR GLORIOUSLY EXCESSIVE AND CONDESCENDING BULLSHIT! IF I WERE A MAN, YOU WOULDN'T SAY THAT. SERIOUSLY NICK, "YOU'LL COME AROUND TO MY WAY OF THINKING"... WOULD YOU SAY THAT TO QUIRIN OR CULLEN?
I'M--LOOK, I'M REALLY SORRY. THAT CAME OUT WRONG.
YOU SAID IT, SO YOU OBVIOUSLY MEANT IT.

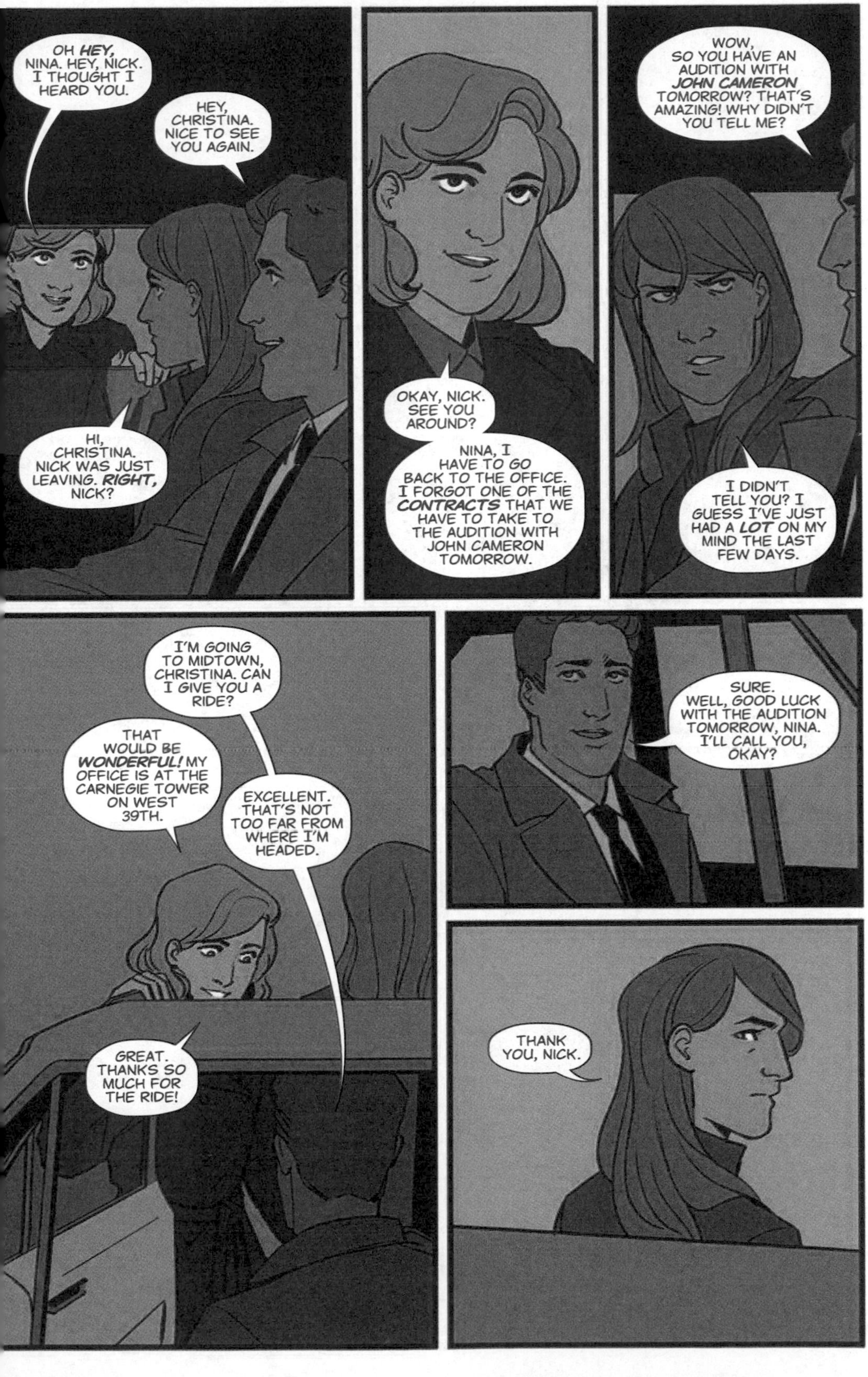
OH HEY, NINA. HEY, NICK. I THOUGHT I HEARD YOU.
HEY, CHRISTINA. NICE TO SEE YOU AGAIN.
HI, CHRISTINA. NICK WAS JUST LEAVING. RIGHT, NICK?
OKAY, NICK. SEE YOU AROUND?
NINA, I HAVE TO GO BACK TO THE OFFICE. I FORGOT ONE OF THE CONTRACTS THAT WE HAVE TO TAKE TO THE AUDITION WITH JOHN CAMERON TOMORROW.
WOW, SO YOU HAVE AN AUDITION WITH JOHN CAMERON TOMORROW? THAT'S AMAZING! WHY DIDN'T YOU TELL ME?
I DIDN'T TELL YOU? I GUESS I'VE JUST HAD A LOT ON MY MIND THE LAST FEW DAYS.
I'M GOING TO MIDTOWN, CHRISTINA. CAN I GIVE YOU A RIDE?
THAT WOULD BE WONDERFUL! MY OFFICE IS AT THE CARNEGIE TOWER ON WEST 39TH.
EXCELLENT. THAT'S NOT TOO FAR FROM WHERE I'M HEADED.
GREAT. THANKS SO MUCH FOR THE RIDE!
SURE. WELL, GOOD LUCK WITH THE AUDITION TOMORROW, NINA. I'LL CALL YOU, OKAY?
THANK YOU, NICK.

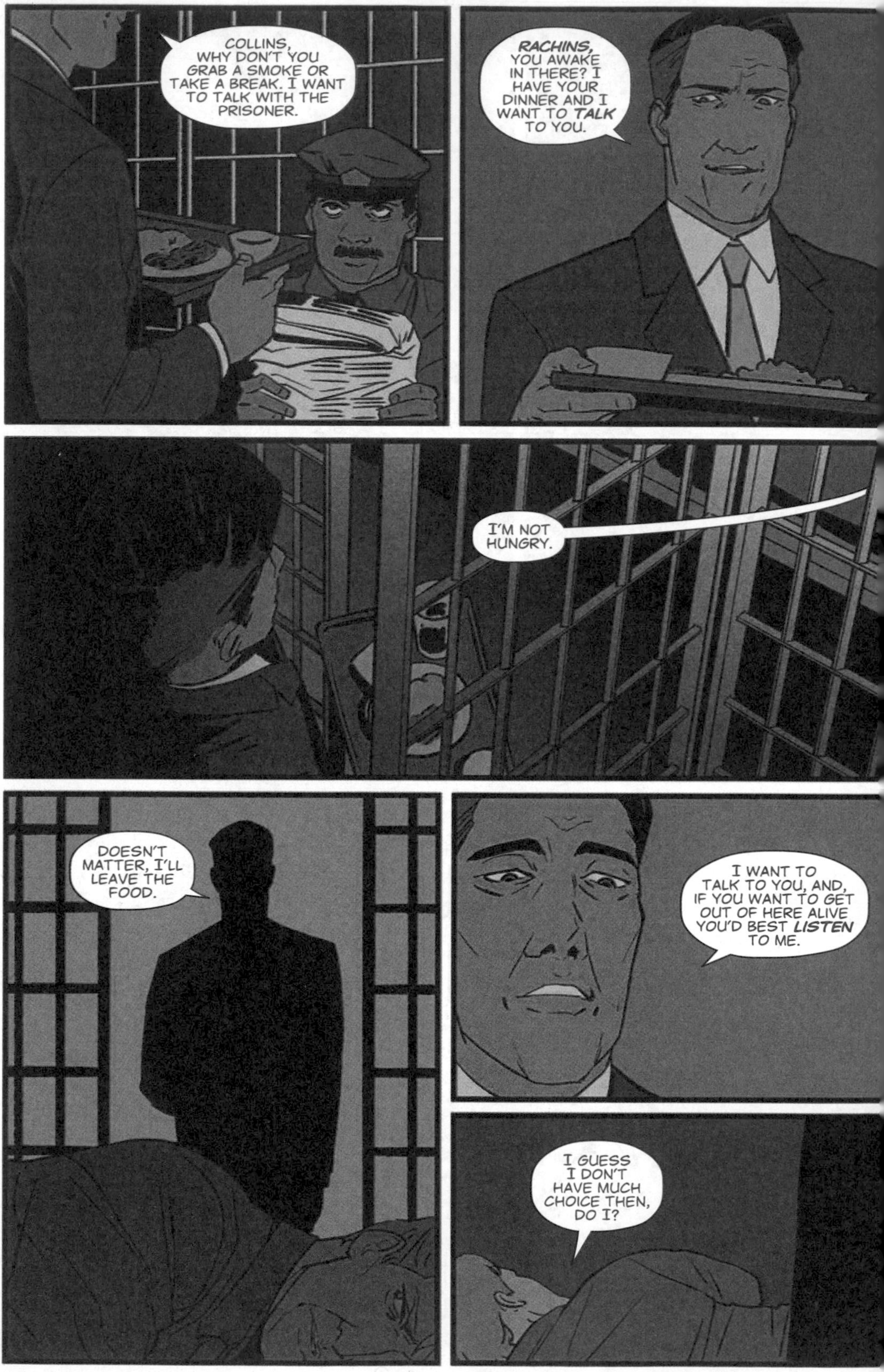
COLLINS, WHY DON'T YOU GRAB A SMOKE OR TAKE A BREAK. I WANT TO TALK WITH THE PRISONER.
RACHINS, YOU AWAKE IN THERE? I HAVE YOUR DINNER AND I WANT TO TALK TO YOU.
I'M NOT HUNGRY.
DOESN'T MATTER, I'LL LEAVE THE FOOD.
I WANT TO TALK TO YOU, AND, IF YOU WANT TO GET OUT OF HERE ALIVE YOU'D BEST LISTEN TO ME.
I GUESS I DON'T HAVE MUCH CHOICE THEN, DO I?

RECOMMENDED LISTENING:

DOO WOP [THAT THING]
BY LAURYN HILL

HAND TO MOUTH
BY THE GEORGIA SATELLITES

BABY, YOU'RE A RICH MAN
BY THE BEATLES

YOU MADE IT THERE SOMEHOW
BY NINA OVERSTREET

CHAPTER NINE

No Overnight Sensation

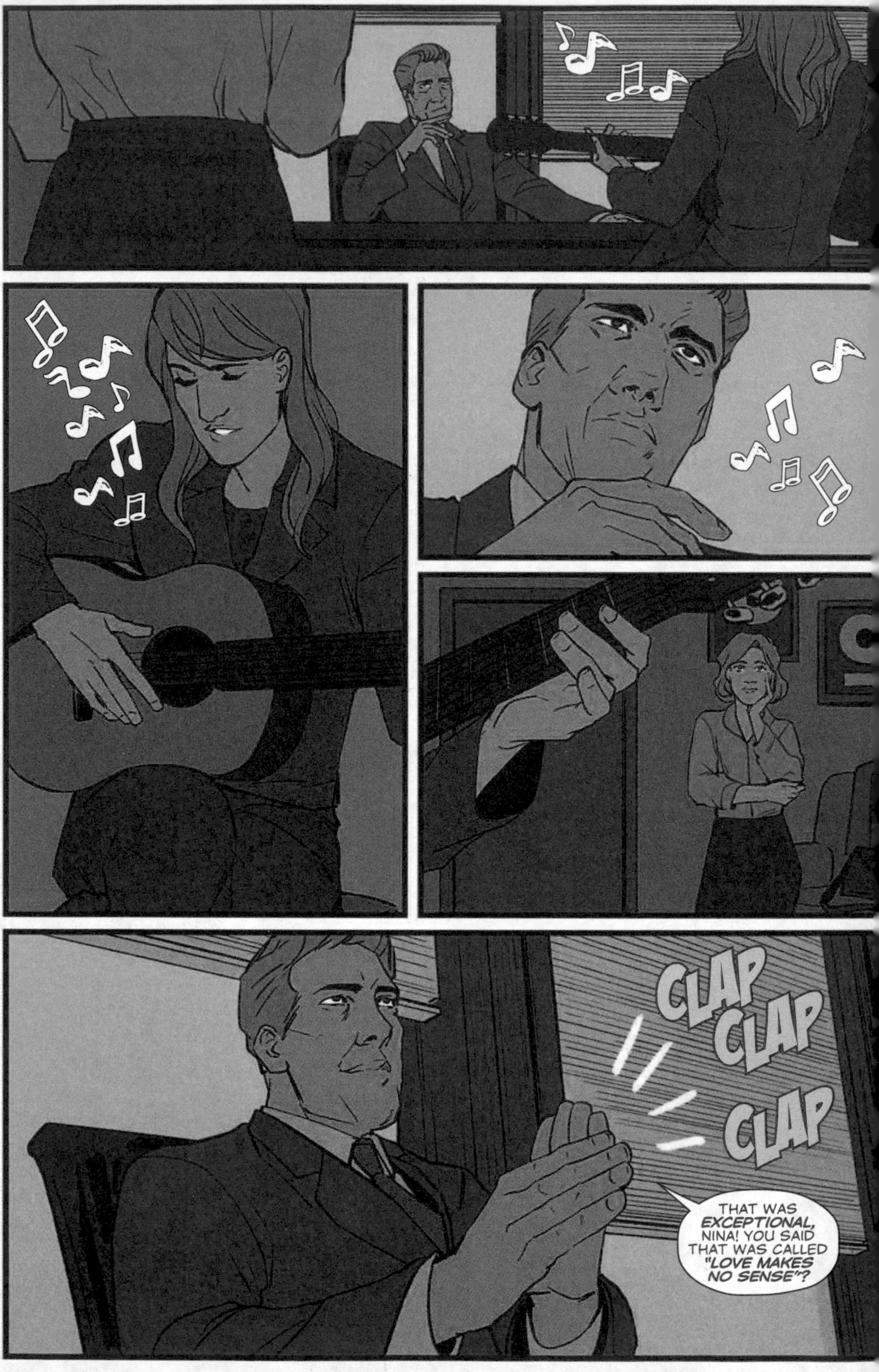
CLAP
CLAP
CLAP
THAT WAS EXCEPTIONAL, NINA! YOU SAID THAT WAS CALLED "LOVE MAKES NO SENSE"?

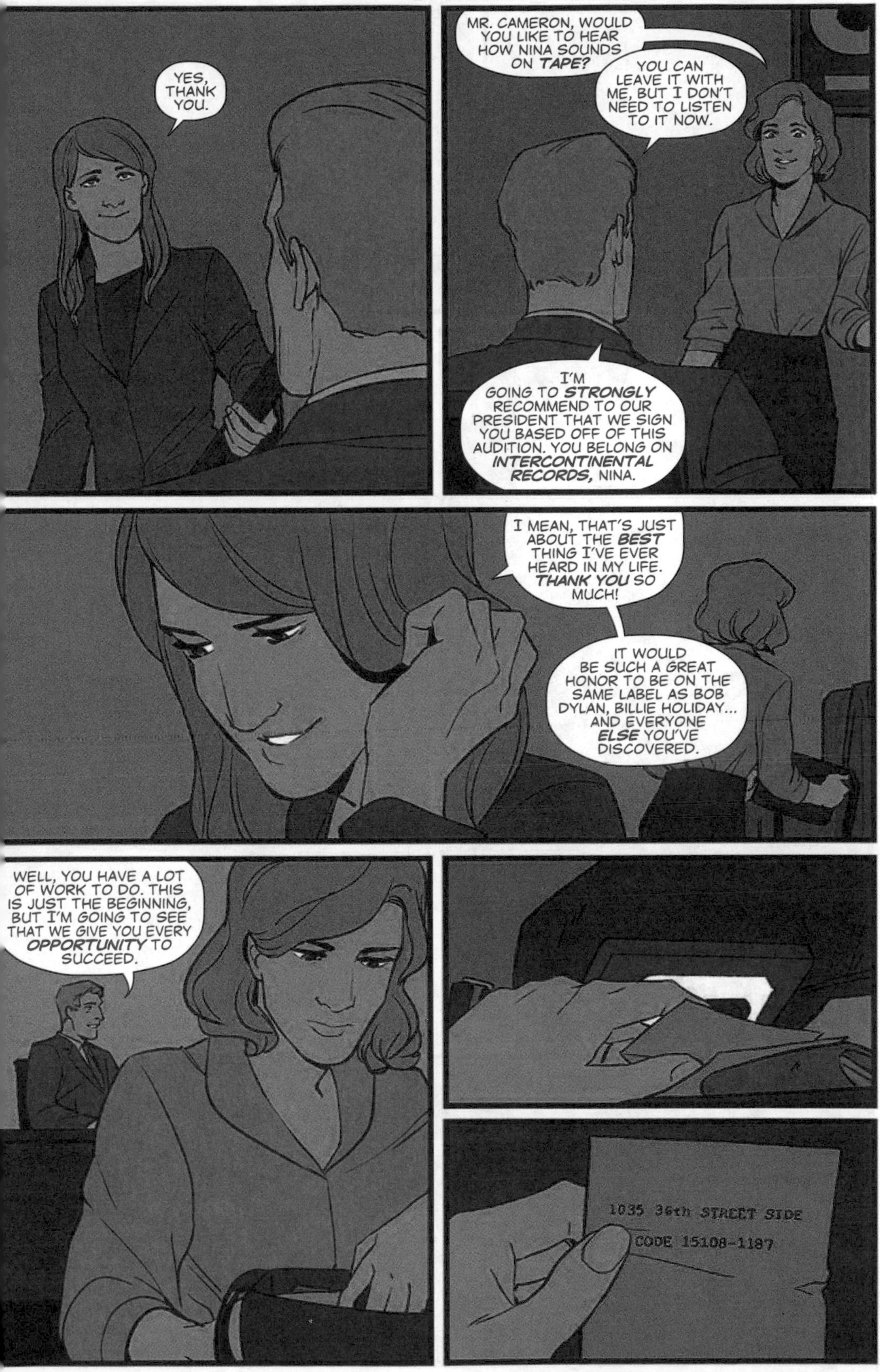
YES, THANK YOU.
MR. CAMERON, WOULD YOU LIKE TO HEAR HOW NINA SOUNDS ON TAPE?
YOU CAN LEAVE IT WITH ME, BUT I DON'T NEED TO LISTEN TO IT NOW.
I'M GOING TO STRONGLY RECOMMEND TO OUR PRESIDENT THAT WE SIGN YOU BASED OFF OF THIS AUDITION. YOU BELONG ON INTERCONTINENTAL RECORDS, NINA.
I MEAN, THAT'S JUST ABOUT THE BEST THING I'VE EVER HEARD IN MY LIFE. THANK YOU SO MUCH!
IT WOULD BE SUCH A GREAT HONOR TO BE ON THE SAME LABEL AS BOB DYLAN, BILLIE HOLIDAY... AND EVERYONE ELSE YOU'VE DISCOVERED.
WELL, YOU HAVE A LOT OF WORK TO DO. THIS IS JUST THE BEGINNING, BUT I'M GOING TO SEE THAT WE GIVE YOU EVERY OPPORTUNITY TO SUCCEED.
1035 36th STREET SIDE
CODE 15108-1187

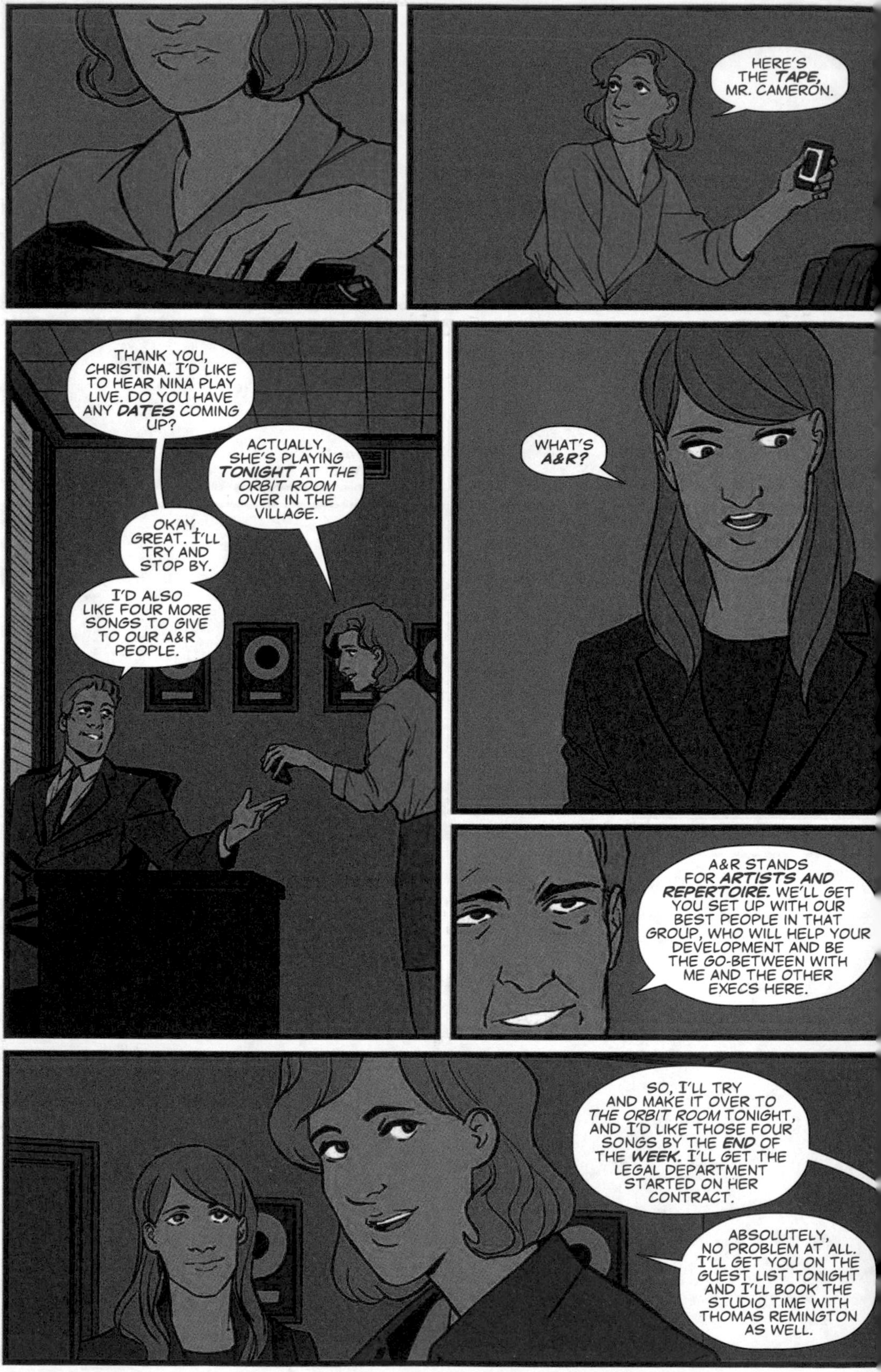
HERE'S THE TAPE, MR. CAMERON.
THANK YOU, CHRISTINA. I'D LIKE TO HEAR NINA PLAY LIVE. DO YOU HAVE ANY DATES COMING UP?
ACTUALLY, SHE'S PLAYING TONIGHT AT THE ORBIT ROOM OVER IN THE VILLAGE.
OKAY, GREAT. I'LL TRY AND STOP BY.
I'D ALSO LIKE FOUR MORE SONGS TO GIVE TO OUR A&R PEOPLE.
WHAT'S A&R?
A&R STANDS FOR ARTISTS AND REPERTOIRE. WE'LL GET YOU SET UP WITH OUR BEST PEOPLE IN THAT GROUP, WHO WILL HELP YOUR DEVELOPMENT AND BE THE GO-BETWEEN WITH ME AND THE OTHER EXECS HERE.
SO, I'LL TRY AND MAKE IT OVER TO THE ORBIT ROOM TONIGHT, AND I'D LIKE THOSE FOUR SONGS BY THE END OF THE WEEK. I'LL GET THE LEGAL DEPARTMENT STARTED ON HER CONTRACT.
ABSOLUTELY, NO PROBLEM AT ALL. I'LL GET YOU ON THE GUEST LIST TONIGHT AND I'LL BOOK THE STUDIO TIME WITH THOMAS REMINGTON AS WELL.

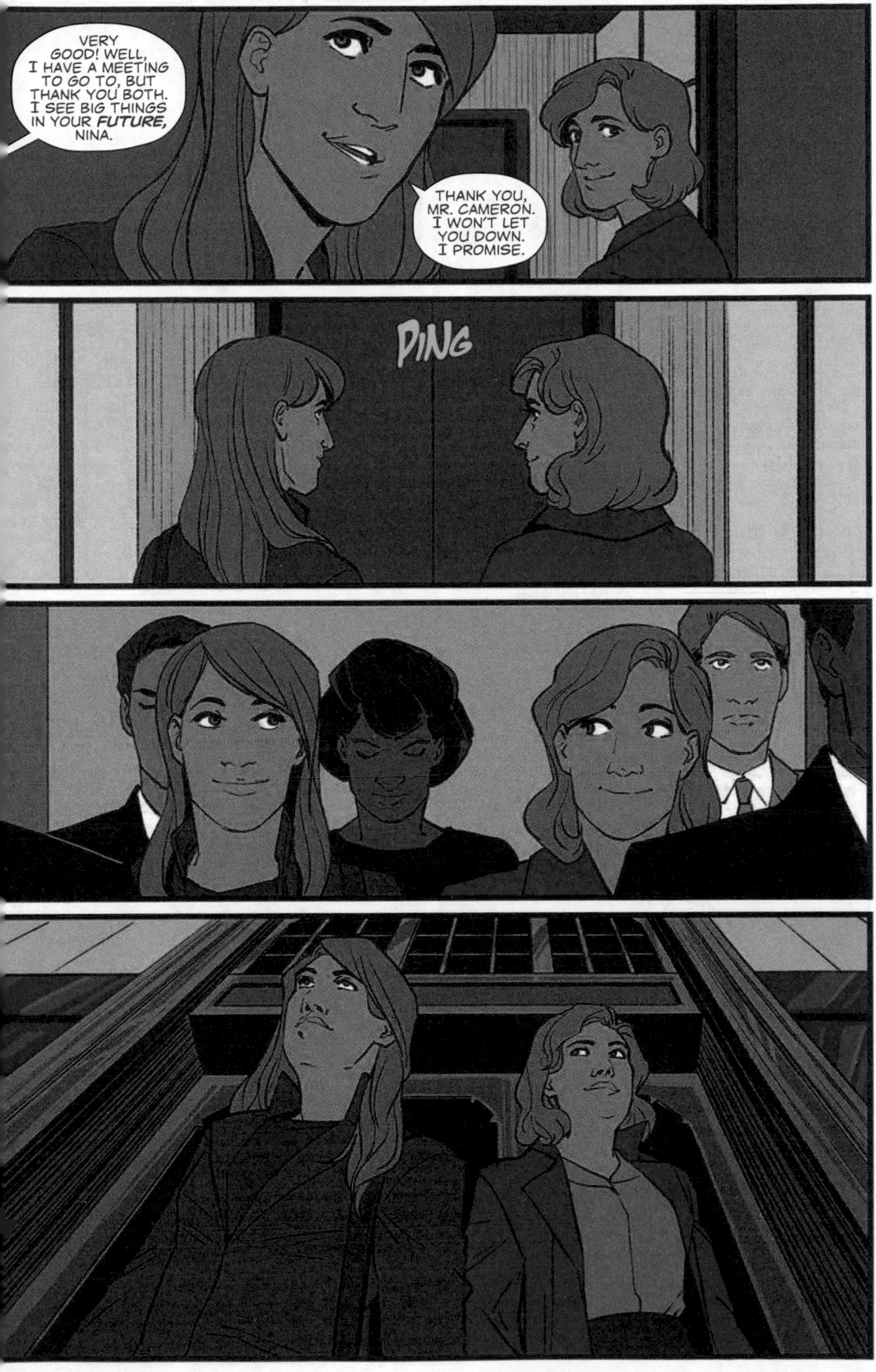
VERY GOOD! WELL, I HAVE A MEETING TO GO TO, BUT THANK YOU BOTH. I SEE BIG THINGS IN YOUR *FUTURE,* NINA.
THANK YOU, MR. CAMERON. I WON'T LET YOU DOWN. I PROMISE.
DING

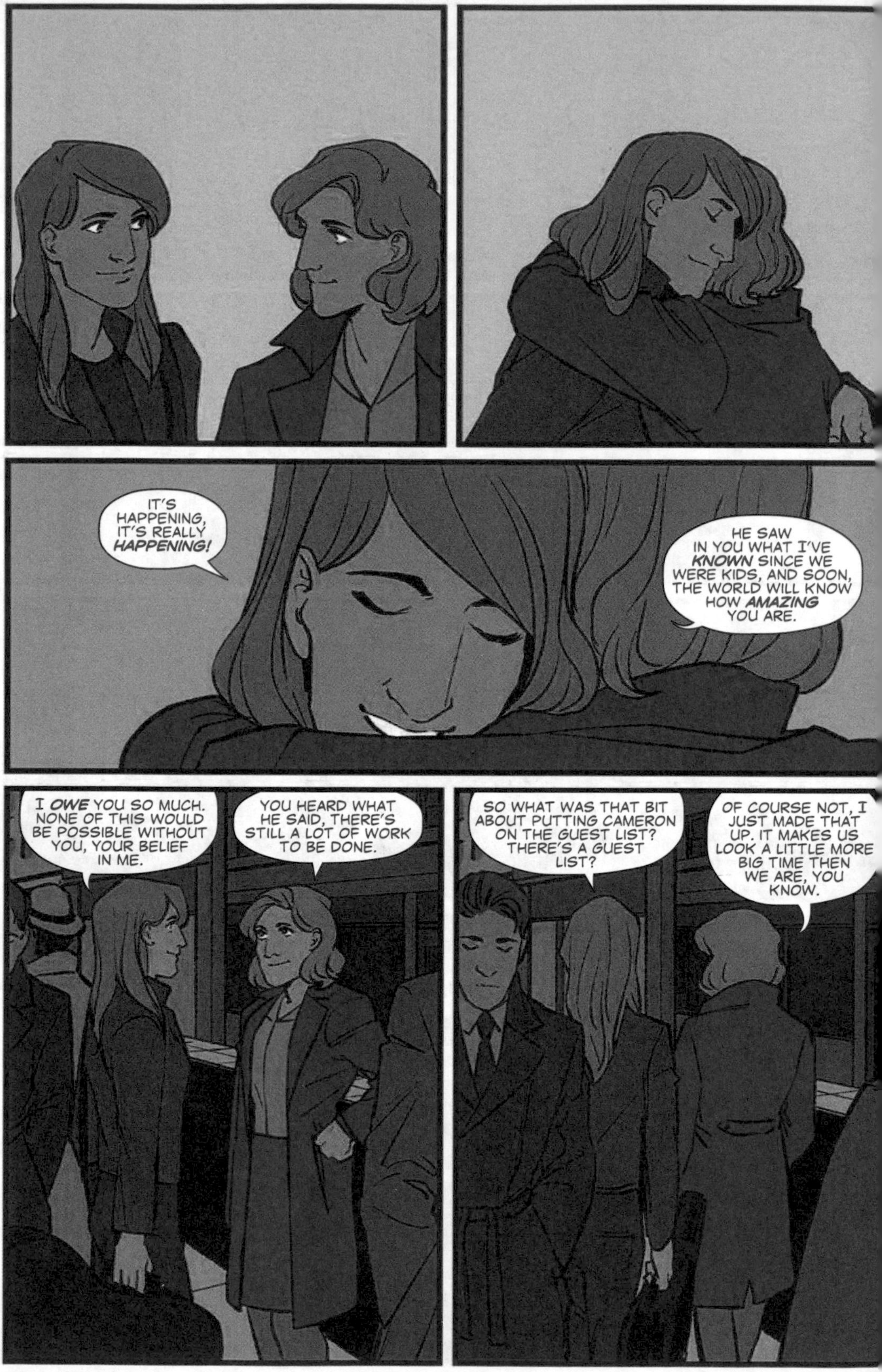
IT'S HAPPENING, IT'S REALLY HAPPENING!
HE SAW IN YOU WHAT I'VE KNOWN SINCE WE WERE KIDS, AND SOON, THE WORLD WILL KNOW HOW AMAZING YOU ARE.
I OWE YOU SO MUCH. NONE OF THIS WOULD BE POSSIBLE WITHOUT YOU, YOUR BELIEF IN ME.
YOU HEARD WHAT HE SAID, THERE'S STILL A LOT OF WORK TO BE DONE.
SO WHAT WAS THAT BIT ABOUT PUTTING CAMERON ON THE GUEST LIST? THERE'S A GUEST LIST?
OF COURSE NOT, I JUST MADE THAT UP. IT MAKES US LOOK A LITTLE MORE BIG TIME THEN WE ARE, YOU KNOW.

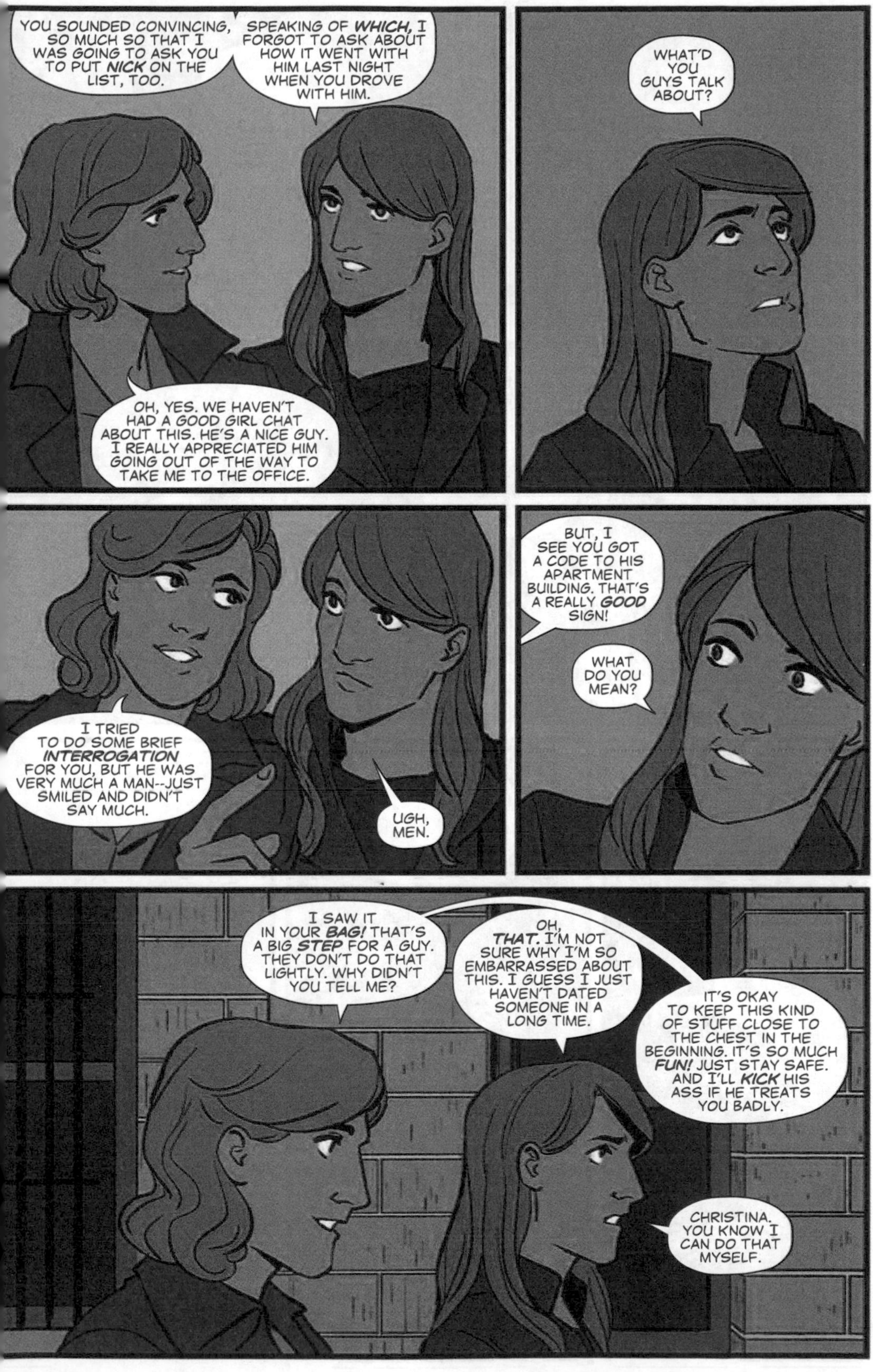
YOU SOUNDED CONVINCING, SO MUCH SO THAT I WAS GOING TO ASK YOU TO PUT NICK ON THE LIST, TOO.
SPEAKING OF WHICH, I FORGOT TO ASK ABOUT HOW IT WENT WITH HIM LAST NIGHT WHEN YOU DROVE WITH HIM.
OH, YES. WE HAVEN'T HAD A GOOD GIRL CHAT ABOUT THIS. HE'S A NICE GUY. I REALLY APPRECIATED HIM GOING OUT OF THE WAY TO TAKE ME TO THE OFFICE.
WHAT'D YOU GUYS TALK ABOUT?
I TRIED TO DO SOME BRIEF INTERROGATION FOR YOU, BUT HE WAS VERY MUCH A MAN--JUST SMILED AND DIDN'T SAY MUCH.
UGH, MEN.
BUT, I SEE YOU GOT A CODE TO HIS APARTMENT BUILDING. THAT'S A REALLY GOOD SIGN!
WHAT DO YOU MEAN?
I SAW IT IN YOUR BAG! THAT'S A BIG STEP FOR A GUY. THEY DON'T DO THAT LIGHTLY. WHY DIDN'T YOU TELL ME?
OH, THAT. I'M NOT SURE WHY I'M SO EMBARRASSED ABOUT THIS. I GUESS I JUST HAVEN'T DATED SOMEONE IN A LONG TIME.
IT'S OKAY TO KEEP THIS KIND OF STUFF CLOSE TO THE CHEST IN THE BEGINNING. IT'S SO MUCH FUN! JUST STAY SAFE. AND I'LL KICK HIS ASS IF HE TREATS YOU BADLY.
CHRISTINA. YOU KNOW I CAN DO THAT MYSELF.

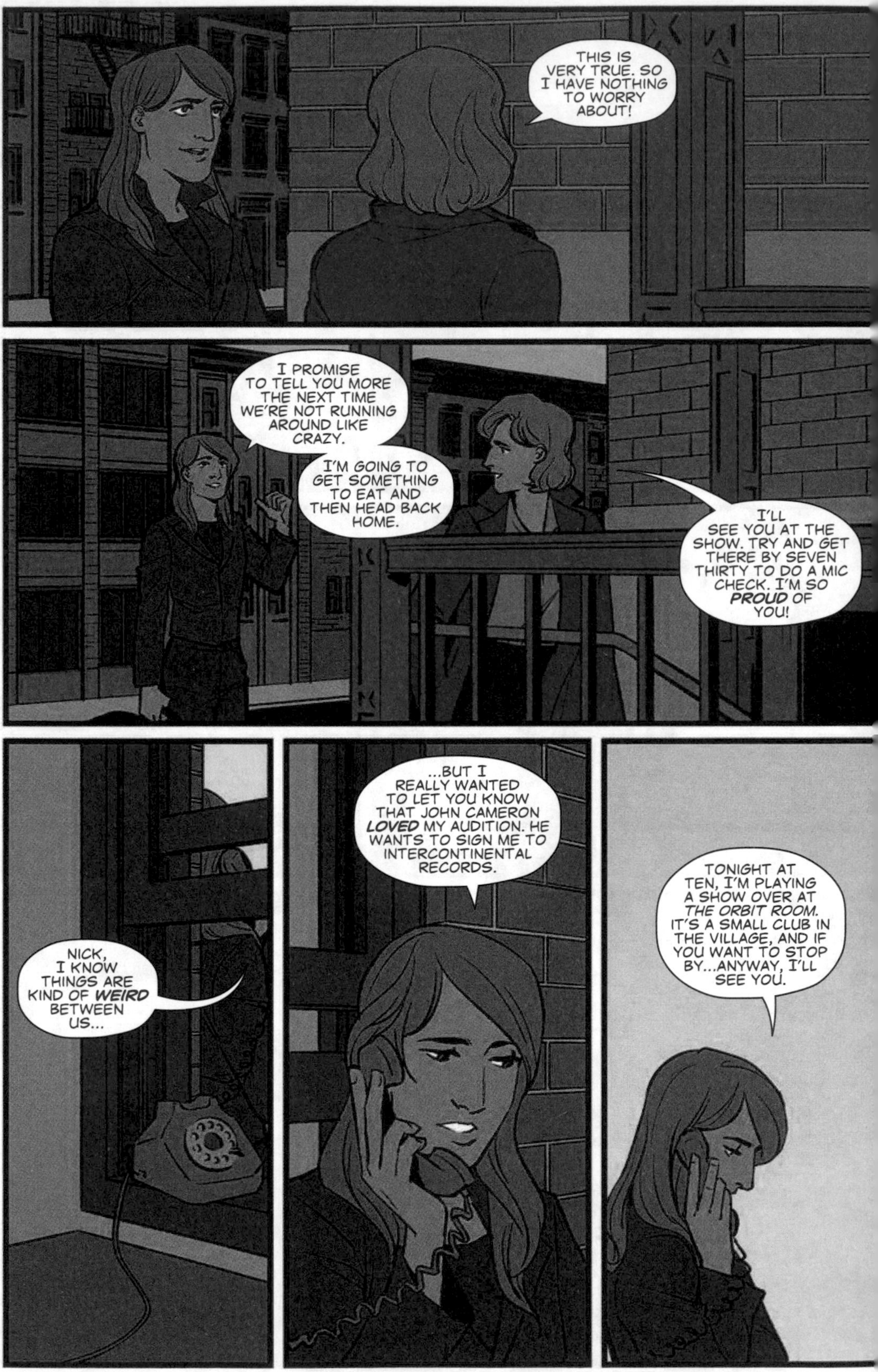
THIS IS VERY TRUE. SO I HAVE NOTHING TO WORRY ABOUT!
I PROMISE TO TELL YOU MORE THE NEXT TIME WE'RE NOT RUNNING AROUND LIKE CRAZY.
I'M GOING TO GET SOMETHING TO EAT AND THEN HEAD BACK HOME.
I'LL SEE YOU AT THE SHOW. TRY AND GET THERE BY SEVEN THIRTY TO DO A MIC CHECK. I'M SO *PROUD* OF YOU!
NICK, I KNOW THINGS ARE KIND OF *WEIRD* BETWEEN US...
...BUT I REALLY WANTED TO LET YOU KNOW THAT JOHN CAMERON *LOVED* MY AUDITION. HE WANTS TO SIGN ME TO INTERCONTINENTAL RECORDS.
TONIGHT AT TEN, I'M PLAYING A SHOW OVER AT *THE ORBIT ROOM.* IT'S A SMALL CLUB IN THE VILLAGE, AND IF YOU WANT TO STOP BY...ANYWAY, I'LL SEE YOU.

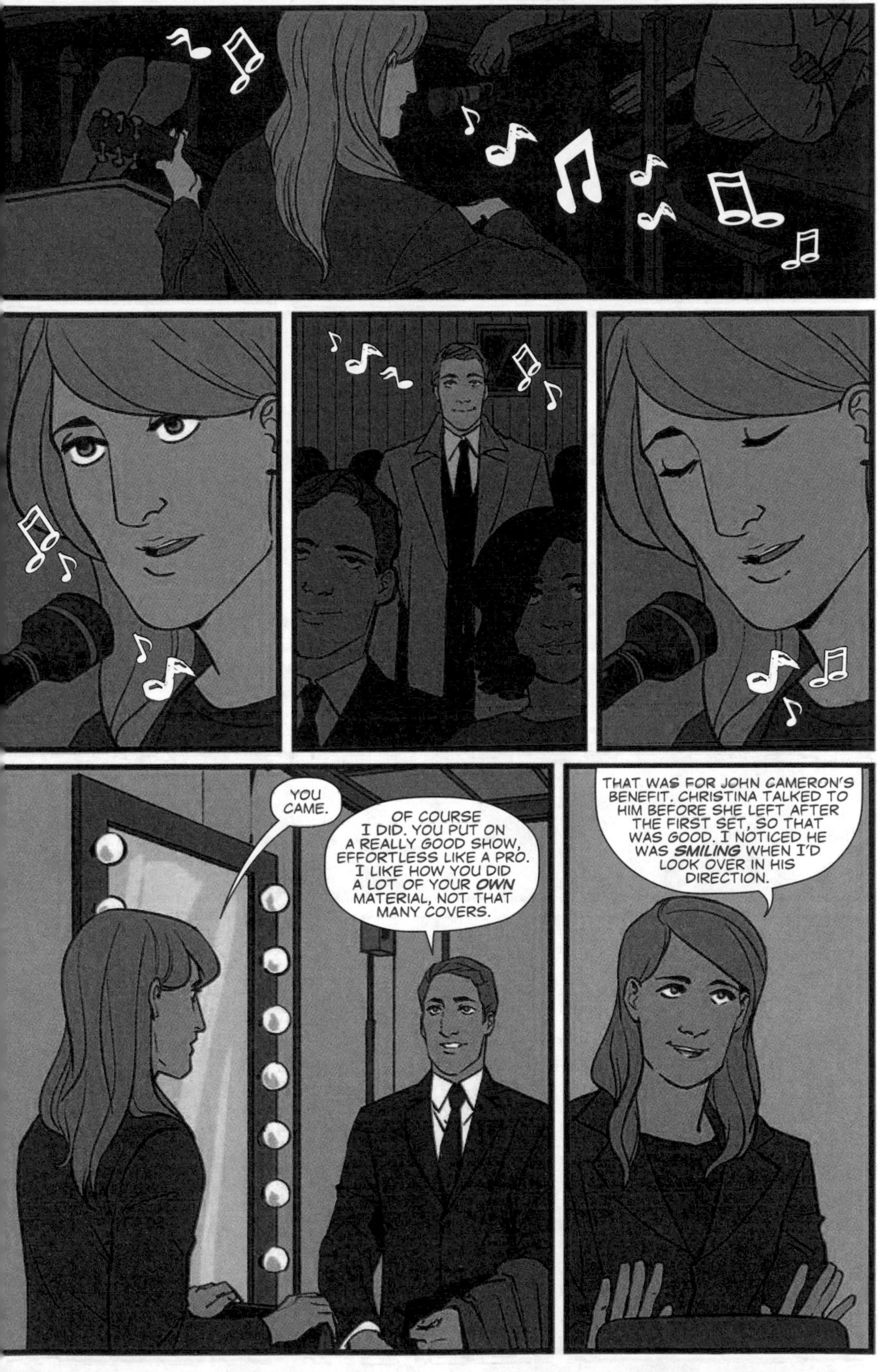
YOU CAME.
OF COURSE I DID. YOU PUT ON A REALLY GOOD SHOW, EFFORTLESS LIKE A PRO. I LIKE HOW YOU DID A LOT OF YOUR *OWN* MATERIAL, NOT THAT MANY COVERS.
THAT WAS FOR JOHN CAMERON'S BENEFIT. CHRISTINA TALKED TO HIM BEFORE SHE LEFT AFTER THE FIRST SET, SO THAT WAS GOOD. I NOTICED HE WAS *SMILING* WHEN I'D LOOK OVER IN HIS DIRECTION.

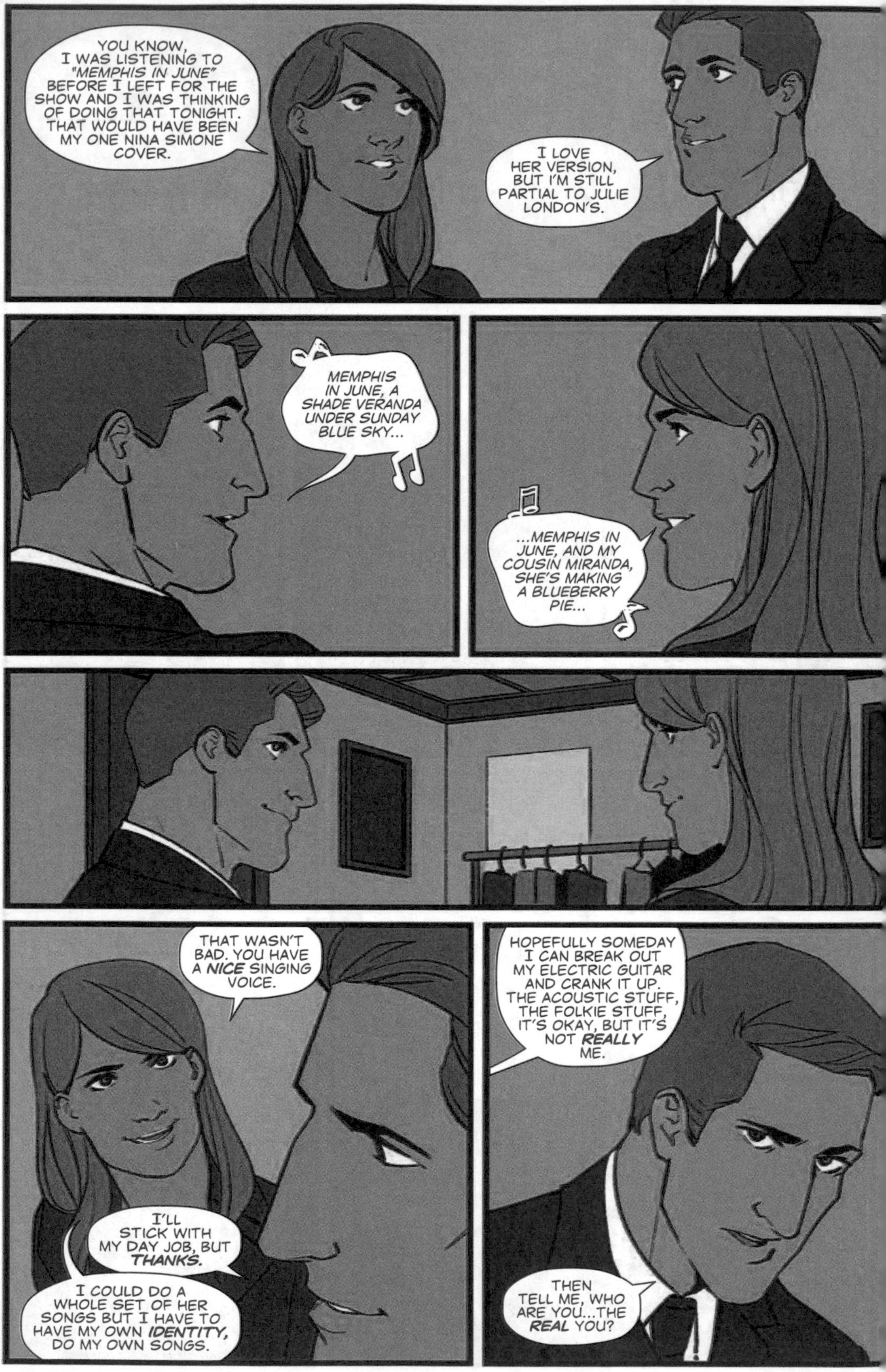
YOU KNOW, I WAS LISTENING TO "MEMPHIS IN JUNE" BEFORE I LEFT FOR THE SHOW AND I WAS THINKING OF DOING THAT TONIGHT. THAT WOULD HAVE BEEN MY ONE NINA SIMONE COVER.
I LOVE HER VERSION, BUT I'M STILL PARTIAL TO JULIE LONDON'S.
MEMPHIS IN JUNE, A SHADE VERANDA UNDER SUNDAY BLUE SKY...
...MEMPHIS IN JUNE, AND MY COUSIN MIRANDA, SHE'S MAKING A BLUEBERRY PIE...
THAT WASN'T BAD. YOU HAVE A NICE SINGING VOICE.
I'LL STICK WITH MY DAY JOB, BUT THANKS.
I COULD DO A WHOLE SET OF HER SONGS BUT I HAVE TO HAVE MY OWN IDENTITY, DO MY OWN SONGS.
HOPEFULLY SOMEDAY I CAN BREAK OUT MY ELECTRIC GUITAR AND CRANK IT UP. THE ACOUSTIC STUFF, THE FOLKIE STUFF, IT'S OKAY, BUT IT'S NOT REALLY ME.
THEN TELL ME, WHO ARE YOU...THE REAL YOU?

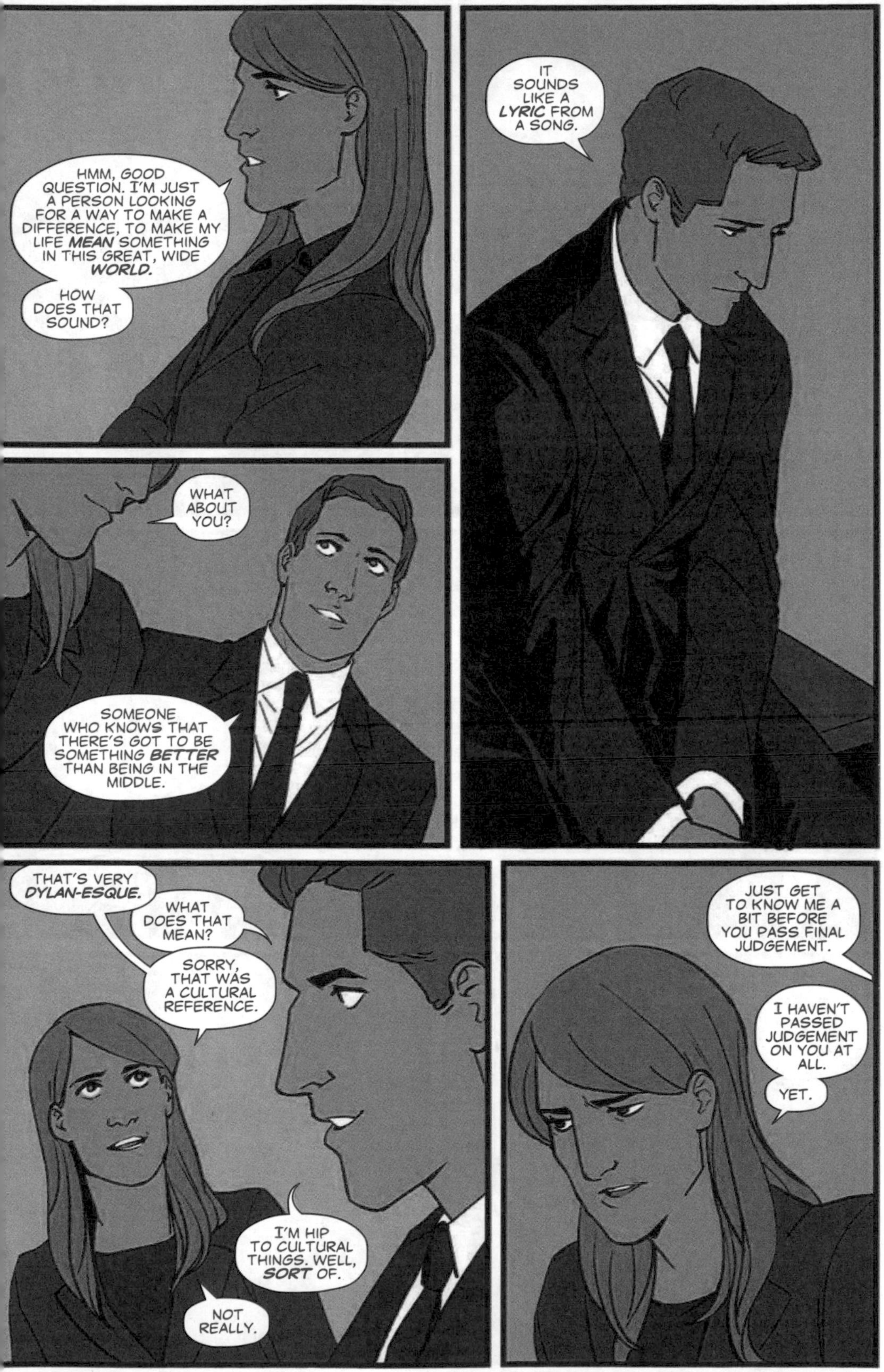
HMM, GOOD QUESTION. I'M JUST A PERSON LOOKING FOR A WAY TO MAKE A DIFFERENCE, TO MAKE MY LIFE MEAN SOMETHING IN THIS GREAT, WIDE WORLD.
HOW DOES THAT SOUND?
IT SOUNDS LIKE A LYRIC FROM A SONG.
WHAT ABOUT YOU?
SOMEONE WHO KNOWS THAT THERE'S GOT TO BE SOMETHING BETTER THAN BEING IN THE MIDDLE.
THAT'S VERY DYLAN-ESQUE.
WHAT DOES THAT MEAN?
SORRY, THAT WAS A CULTURAL REFERENCE.
I'M HIP TO CULTURAL THINGS. WELL, SORT OF.
NOT REALLY.
JUST GET TO KNOW ME A BIT BEFORE YOU PASS FINAL JUDGEMENT.
I HAVEN'T PASSED JUDGEMENT ON YOU AT ALL.
YET.

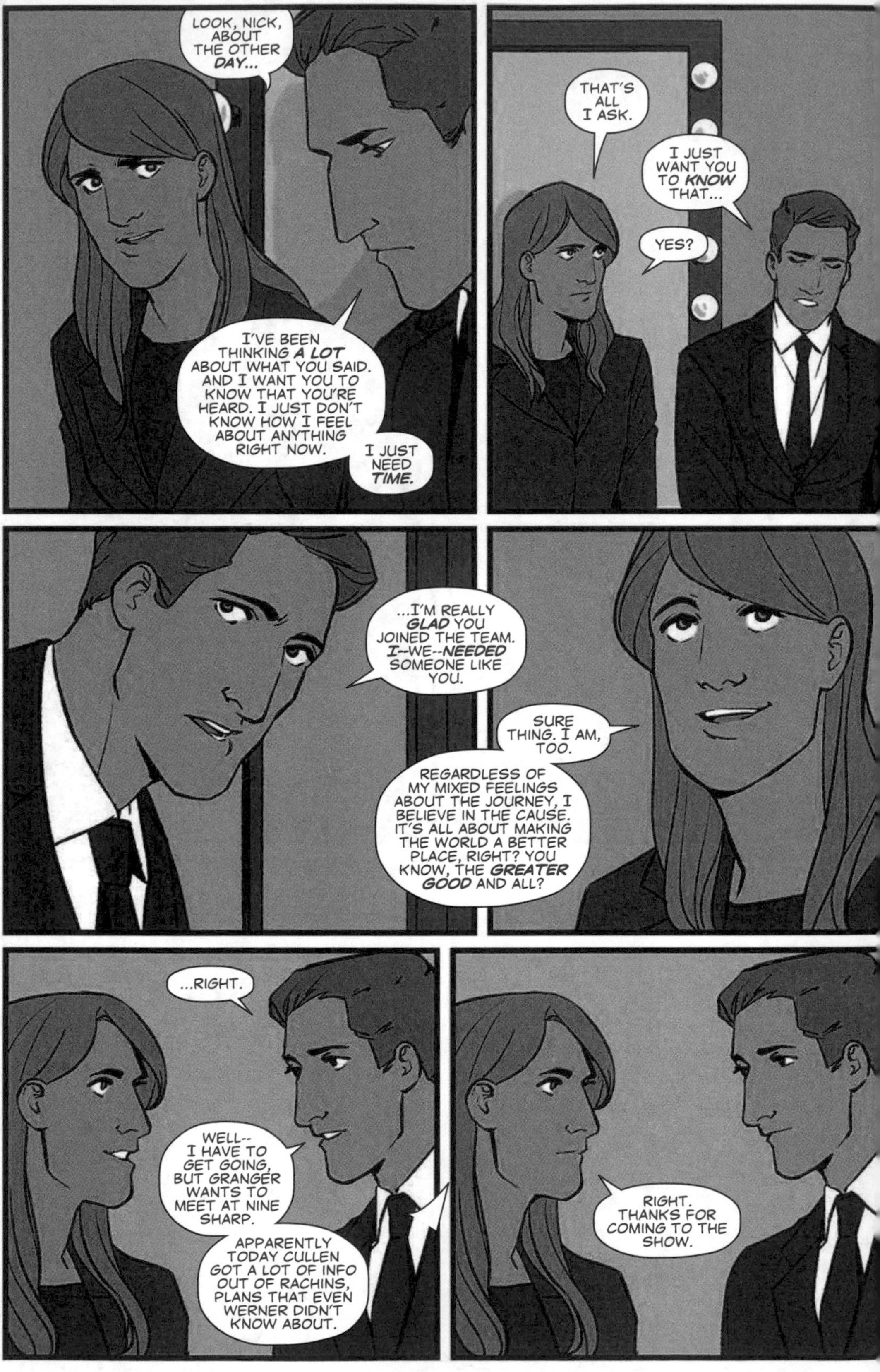
LOOK, NICK, ABOUT THE OTHER DAY...
I'VE BEEN THINKING A LOT ABOUT WHAT YOU SAID. AND I WANT YOU TO KNOW THAT YOU'RE HEARD. I JUST DON'T KNOW HOW I FEEL ABOUT ANYTHING RIGHT NOW.
I JUST NEED TIME.
THAT'S ALL I ASK.
I JUST WANT YOU TO KNOW THAT...
YES?
...I'M REALLY GLAD YOU JOINED THE TEAM. I--WE--NEEDED SOMEONE LIKE YOU.
SURE THING. I AM, TOO.
REGARDLESS OF MY MIXED FEELINGS ABOUT THE JOURNEY, I BELIEVE IN THE CAUSE. IT'S ALL ABOUT MAKING THE WORLD A BETTER PLACE, RIGHT? YOU KNOW, THE GREATER GOOD AND ALL?
...RIGHT.
WELL-- I HAVE TO GET GOING, BUT GRANGER WANTS TO MEET AT NINE SHARP.
APPARENTLY TODAY CULLEN GOT A LOT OF INFO OUT OF RACHINS, PLANS THAT EVEN WERNER DIDN'T KNOW ABOUT.
RIGHT. THANKS FOR COMING TO THE SHOW.

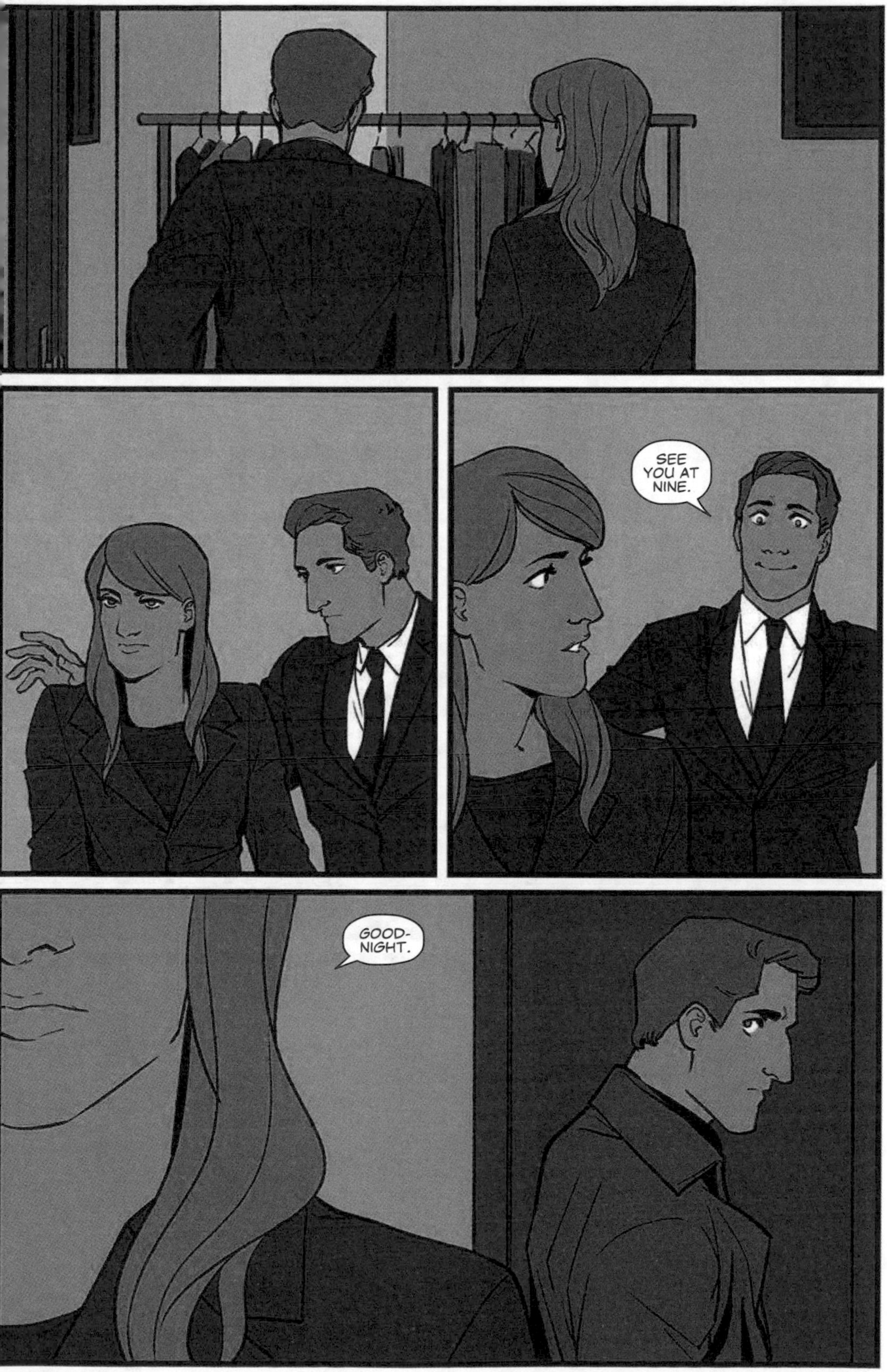
SEE YOU AT NINE.
GOOD-NIGHT.

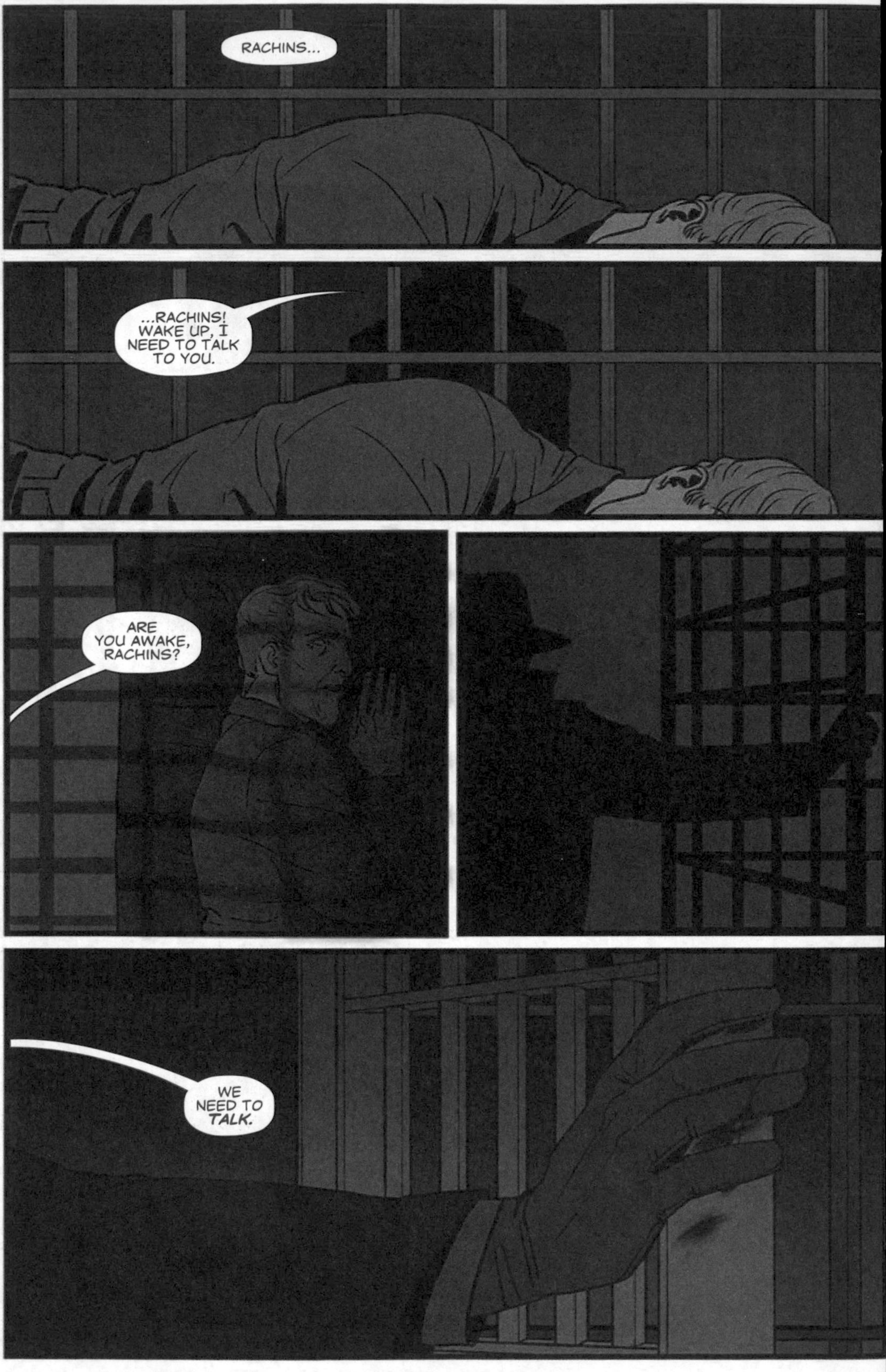
RACHINS...
...RACHINS! WAKE UP, I NEED TO TALK TO YOU.
ARE YOU AWAKE, RACHINS?
WE NEED TO *TALK.*

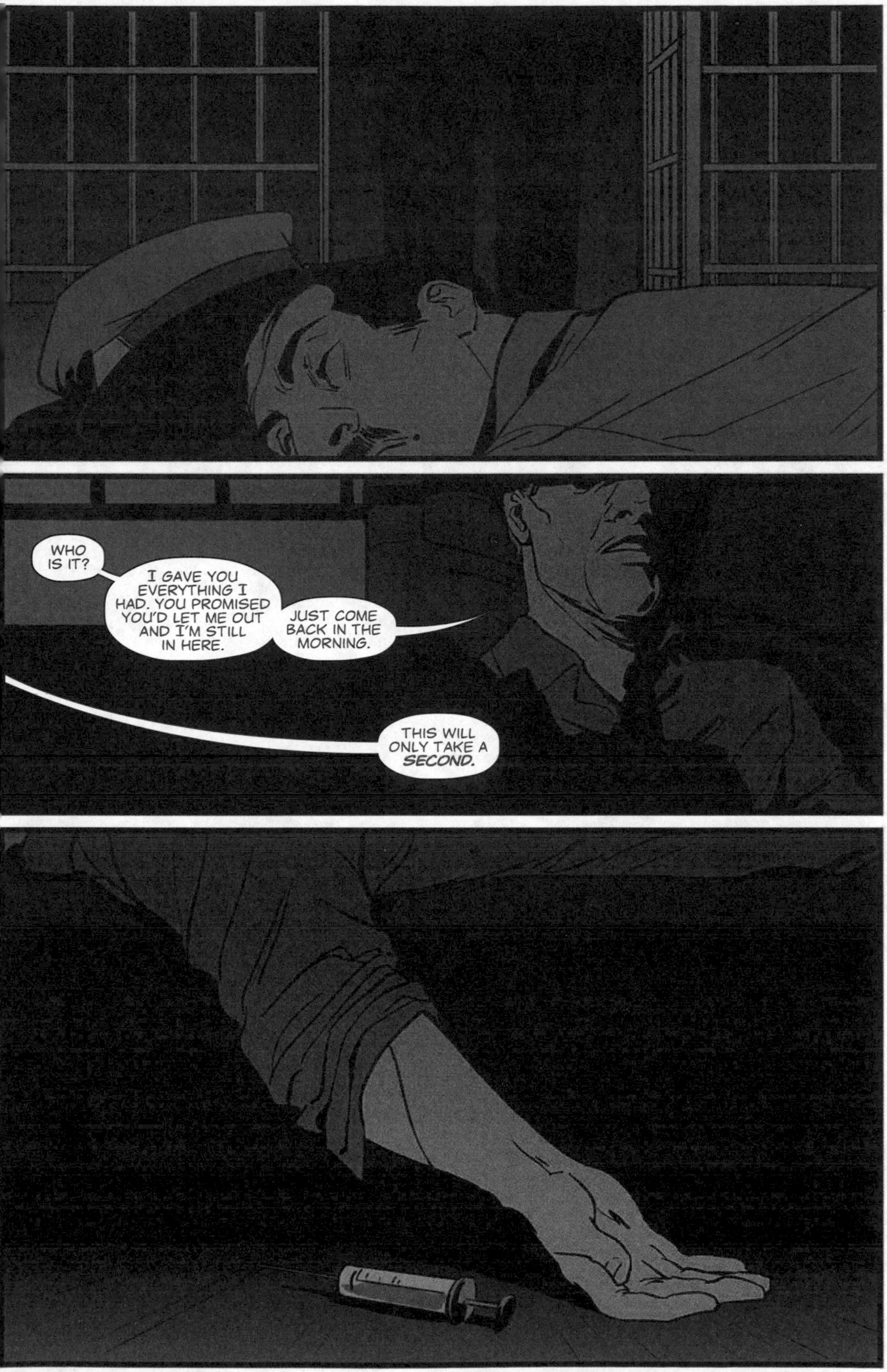
WHO IS IT?
I GAVE YOU EVERYTHING I HAD. YOU PROMISED YOU'D LET ME OUT AND I'M STILL IN HERE.
JUST COME BACK IN THE MORNING.
THIS WILL ONLY TAKE A ***SECOND.***

RECOMMENDED LISTENING:

HIDE AWAY
BY DAVA

BIRD ON A WIRE
BY LEONARD COHEN

QUIET NO MORE
BY NINA OVERSTREET

CHAPTER TEN

The Deepest of Cover (Nina Sheds Her Skin)

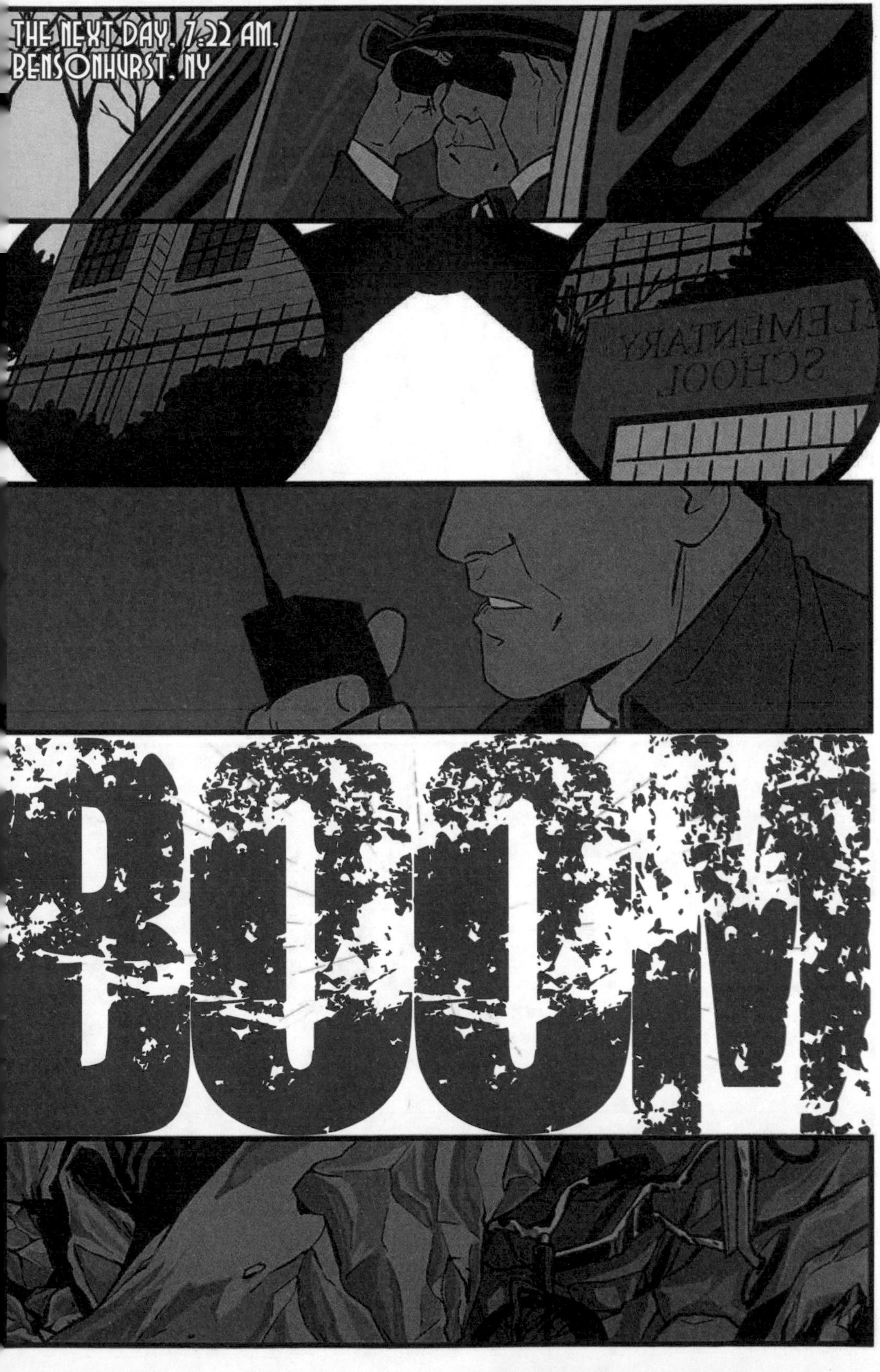
THE NEXT DAY, 7:22 AM,
BENSONHURST, NY
ELEMENTARY
SCHOOL
BOOM

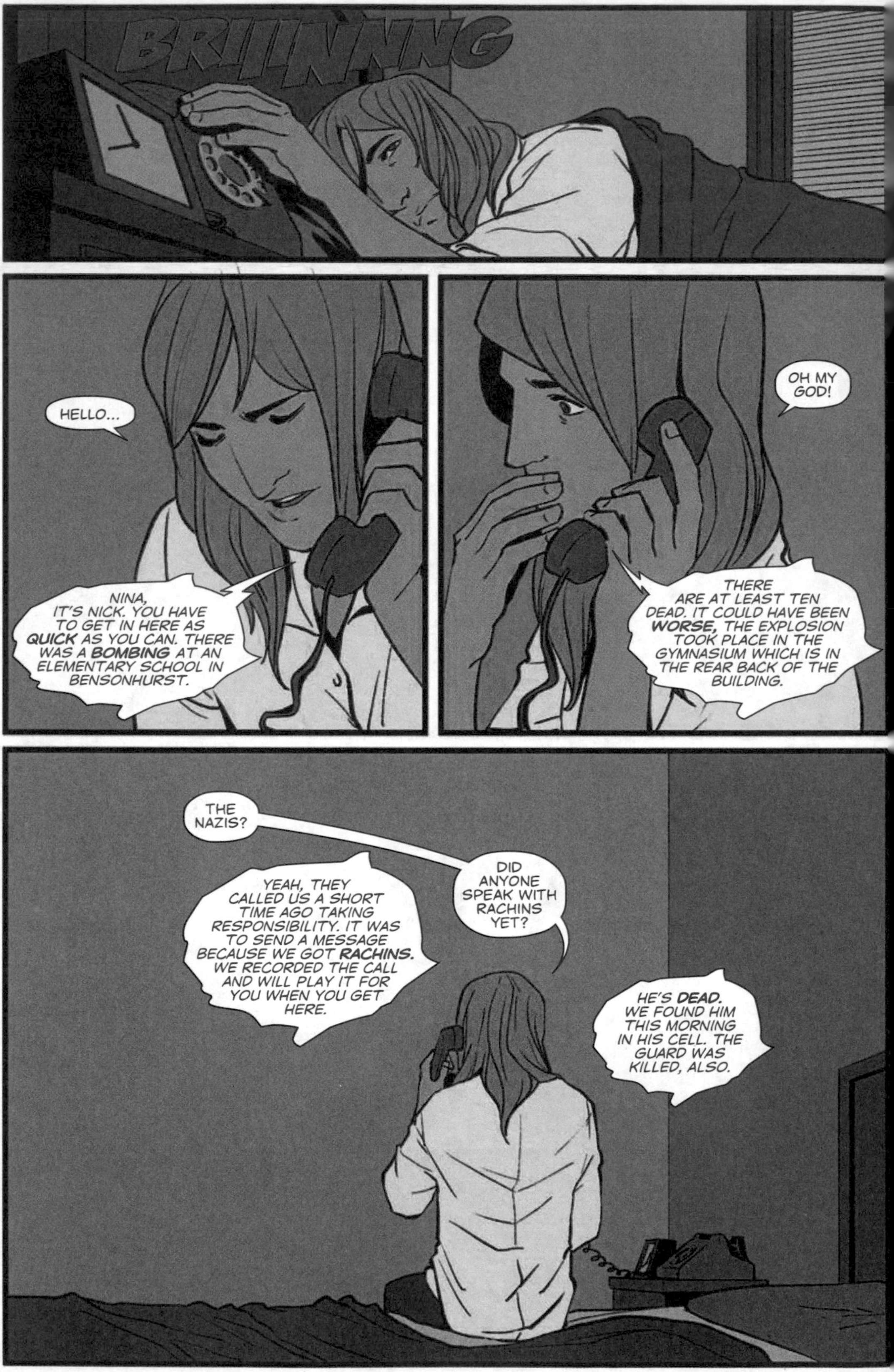
BRIIINNNG
HELLO...
NINA, IT'S NICK. YOU HAVE TO GET IN HERE AS QUICK AS YOU CAN. THERE WAS A BOMBING AT AN ELEMENTARY SCHOOL IN BENSONHURST.
OH MY GOD!
THERE ARE AT LEAST TEN DEAD. IT COULD HAVE BEEN WORSE, THE EXPLOSION TOOK PLACE IN THE GYMNASIUM WHICH IS IN THE REAR BACK OF THE BUILDING.
THE NAZIS?
YEAH, THEY CALLED US A SHORT TIME AGO TAKING RESPONSIBILITY. IT WAS TO SEND A MESSAGE BECAUSE WE GOT RACHINS. WE RECORDED THE CALL AND WILL PLAY IT FOR YOU WHEN YOU GET HERE.
DID ANYONE SPEAK WITH RACHINS YET?
HE'S DEAD. WE FOUND HIM THIS MORNING IN HIS CELL. THE GUARD WAS KILLED, ALSO.

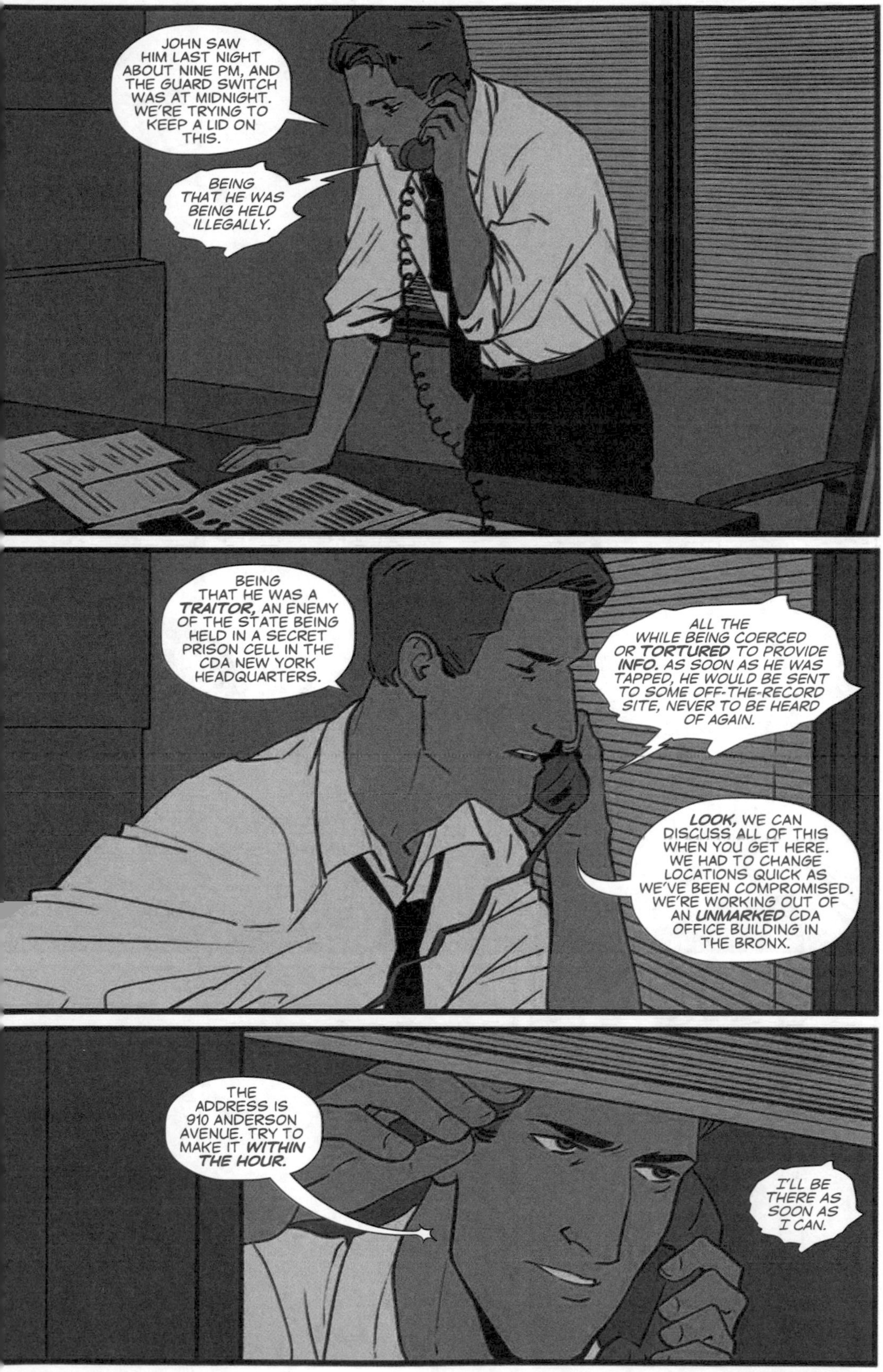
JOHN SAW HIM LAST NIGHT ABOUT NINE PM, AND THE GUARD SWITCH WAS AT MIDNIGHT. WE'RE TRYING TO KEEP A LID ON THIS.
BEING THAT HE WAS BEING HELD ILLEGALLY.
BEING THAT HE WAS A TRAITOR, AN ENEMY OF THE STATE BEING HELD IN A SECRET PRISON CELL IN THE CDA NEW YORK HEADQUARTERS.
ALL THE WHILE BEING COERCED OR TORTURED TO PROVIDE INFO. AS SOON AS HE WAS TAPPED, HE WOULD BE SENT TO SOME OFF-THE-RECORD SITE, NEVER TO BE HEARD OF AGAIN.
LOOK, WE CAN DISCUSS ALL OF THIS WHEN YOU GET HERE. WE HAD TO CHANGE LOCATIONS QUICK AS WE'VE BEEN COMPROMISED. WE'RE WORKING OUT OF AN UNMARKED CDA OFFICE BUILDING IN THE BRONX.
THE ADDRESS IS 910 ANDERSON AVENUE. TRY TO MAKE IT WITHIN THE HOUR.
I'LL BE THERE AS SOON AS I CAN.

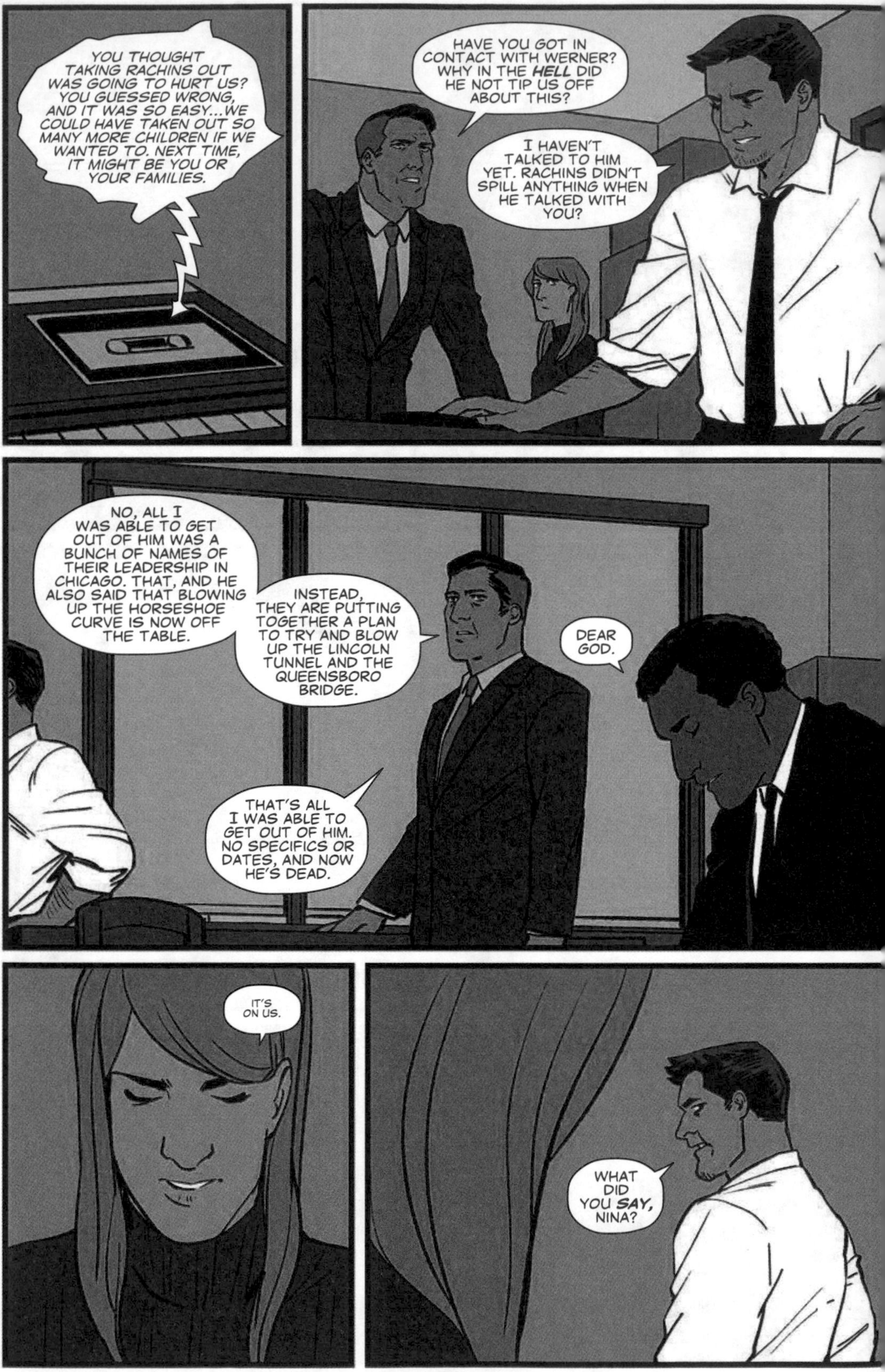
YOU THOUGHT TAKING RACHINS OUT WAS GOING TO HURT US? YOU GUESSED WRONG, AND IT WAS SO EASY...WE COULD HAVE TAKEN OUT SO MANY MORE CHILDREN IF WE WANTED TO. NEXT TIME, IT MIGHT BE YOU OR YOUR FAMILIES.
HAVE YOU GOT IN CONTACT WITH WERNER? WHY IN THE **HELL** DID HE NOT TIP US OFF ABOUT THIS?
I HAVEN'T TALKED TO HIM YET. RACHINS DIDN'T SPILL ANYTHING WHEN HE TALKED WITH YOU?
NO, ALL I WAS ABLE TO GET OUT OF HIM WAS A BUNCH OF NAMES OF THEIR LEADERSHIP IN CHICAGO. THAT, AND HE ALSO SAID THAT BLOWING UP THE HORSESHOE CURVE IS NOW OFF THE TABLE.
INSTEAD, THEY ARE PUTTING TOGETHER A PLAN TO TRY AND BLOW UP THE LINCOLN TUNNEL AND THE QUEENSBORO BRIDGE.
DEAR GOD.
THAT'S ALL I WAS ABLE TO GET OUT OF HIM. NO SPECIFICS OR DATES, AND NOW HE'S DEAD.
IT'S ON US.
WHAT DID YOU **SAY,** NINA?

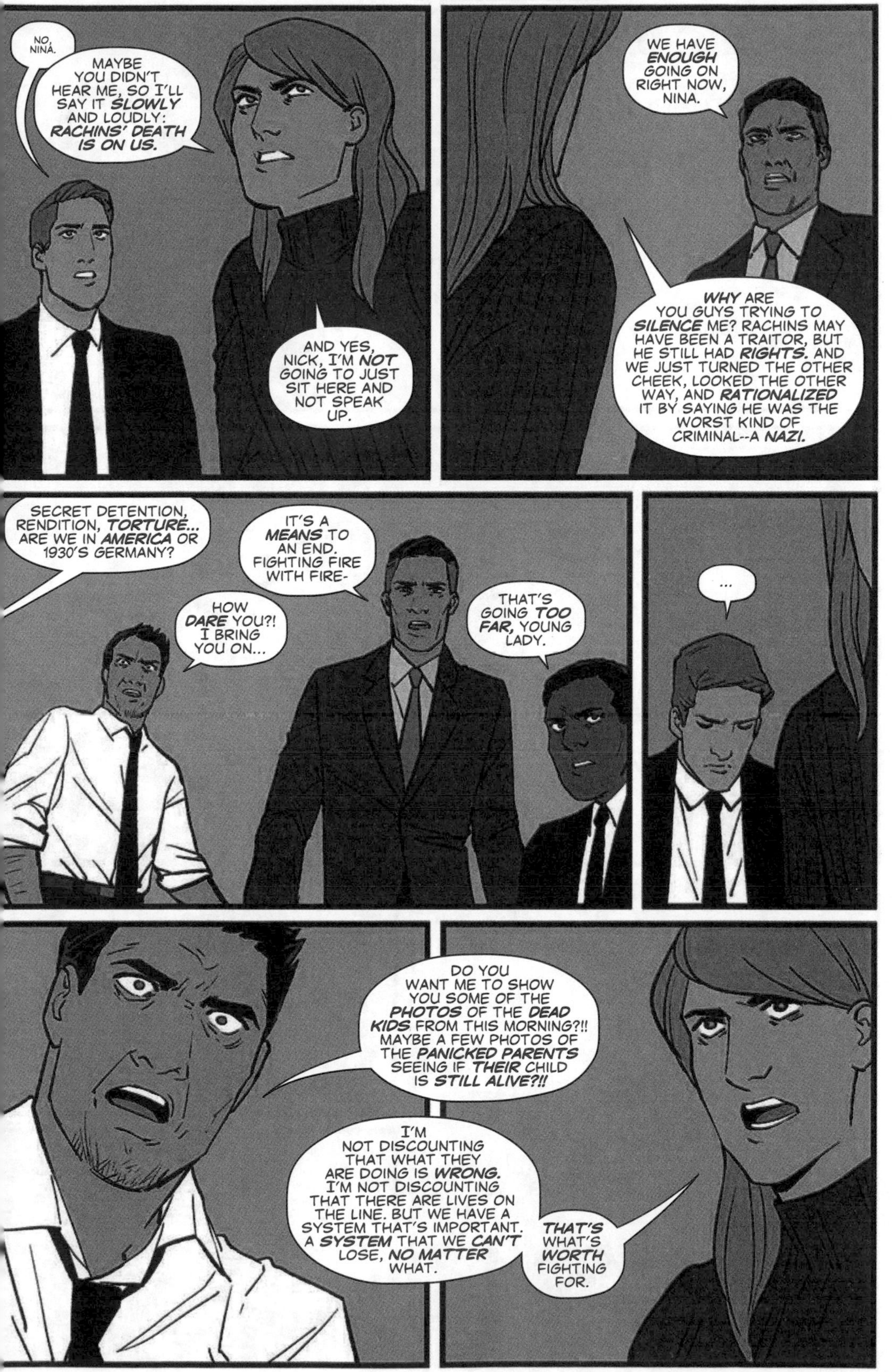
NO, NINA.
MAYBE YOU DIDN'T HEAR ME, SO I'LL SAY IT SLOWLY AND LOUDLY: RACHINS' DEATH IS ON US.
AND YES, NICK, I'M NOT GOING TO JUST SIT HERE AND NOT SPEAK UP.
WE HAVE ENOUGH GOING ON RIGHT NOW, NINA.
WHY ARE YOU GUYS TRYING TO SILENCE ME? RACHINS MAY HAVE BEEN A TRAITOR, BUT HE STILL HAD RIGHTS. AND WE JUST TURNED THE OTHER CHEEK, LOOKED THE OTHER WAY, AND RATIONALIZED IT BY SAYING HE WAS THE WORST KIND OF CRIMINAL--A NAZI.
SECRET DETENTION, RENDITION, TORTURE... ARE WE IN AMERICA OR 1930'S GERMANY?
IT'S A MEANS TO AN END. FIGHTING FIRE WITH FIRE-
HOW DARE YOU?! I BRING YOU ON...
THAT'S GOING TOO FAR, YOUNG LADY.
...
DO YOU WANT ME TO SHOW YOU SOME OF THE PHOTOS OF THE DEAD KIDS FROM THIS MORNING?!! MAYBE A FEW PHOTOS OF THE PANICKED PARENTS SEEING IF THEIR CHILD IS STILL ALIVE?!!
I'M NOT DISCOUNTING THAT WHAT THEY ARE DOING IS WRONG. I'M NOT DISCOUNTING THAT THERE ARE LIVES ON THE LINE. BUT WE HAVE A SYSTEM THAT'S IMPORTANT. A SYSTEM THAT WE CAN'T LOSE, NO MATTER WHAT.
THAT'S WHAT'S WORTH FIGHTING FOR.

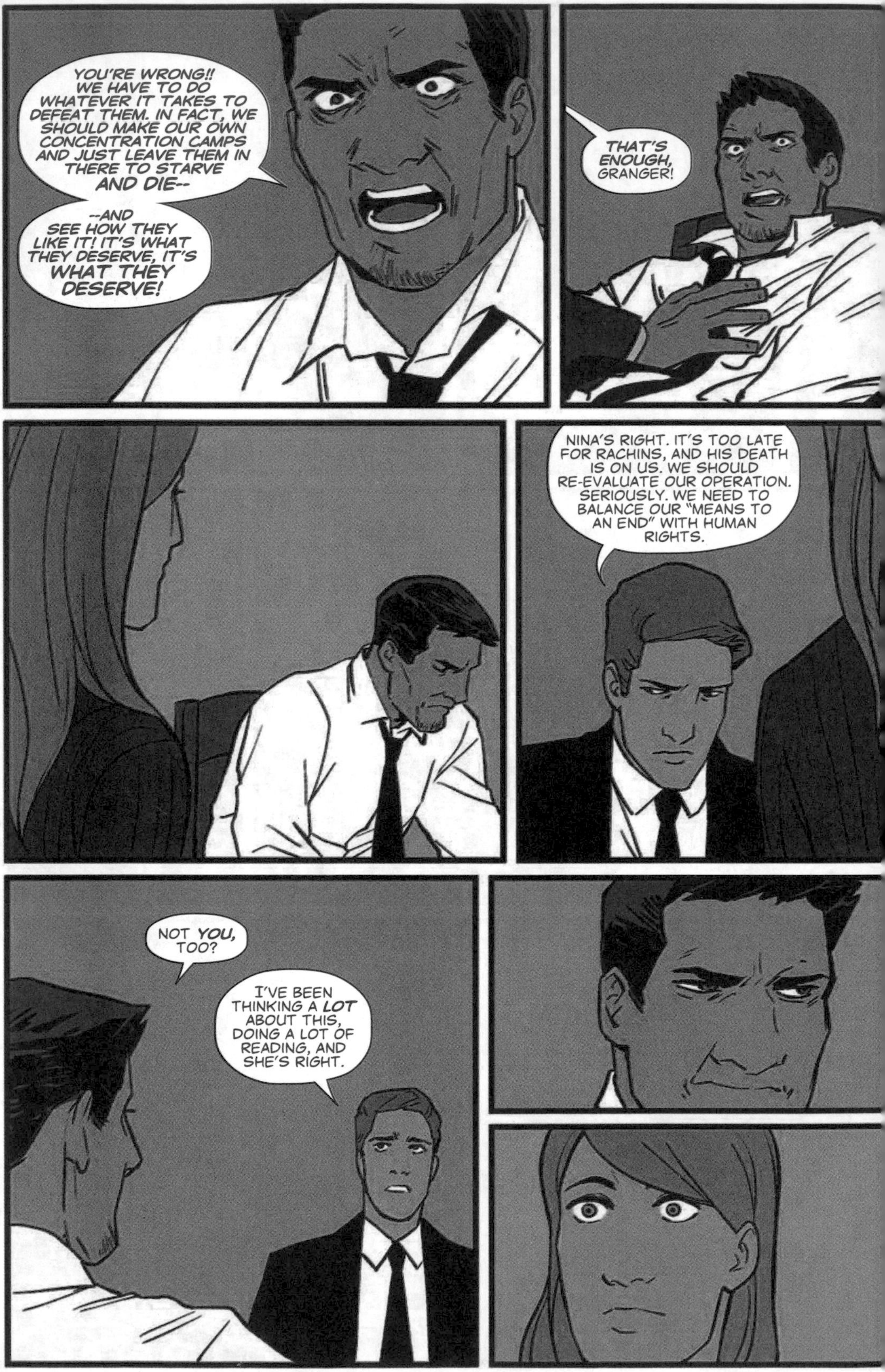
YOU'RE WRONG!! WE HAVE TO DO WHATEVER IT TAKES TO DEFEAT THEM. IN FACT, WE SHOULD MAKE OUR OWN CONCENTRATION CAMPS AND JUST LEAVE THEM IN THERE TO STARVE AND DIE--
--AND SEE HOW THEY LIKE IT! IT'S WHAT THEY DESERVE, IT'S WHAT THEY DESERVE!
THAT'S ENOUGH, GRANGER!
NINA'S RIGHT. IT'S TOO LATE FOR RACHINS, AND HIS DEATH IS ON US. WE SHOULD RE-EVALUATE OUR OPERATION. SERIOUSLY. WE NEED TO BALANCE OUR "MEANS TO AN END" WITH HUMAN RIGHTS.
NOT YOU, TOO?
I'VE BEEN THINKING A LOT ABOUT THIS, DOING A LOT OF READING, AND SHE'S RIGHT.

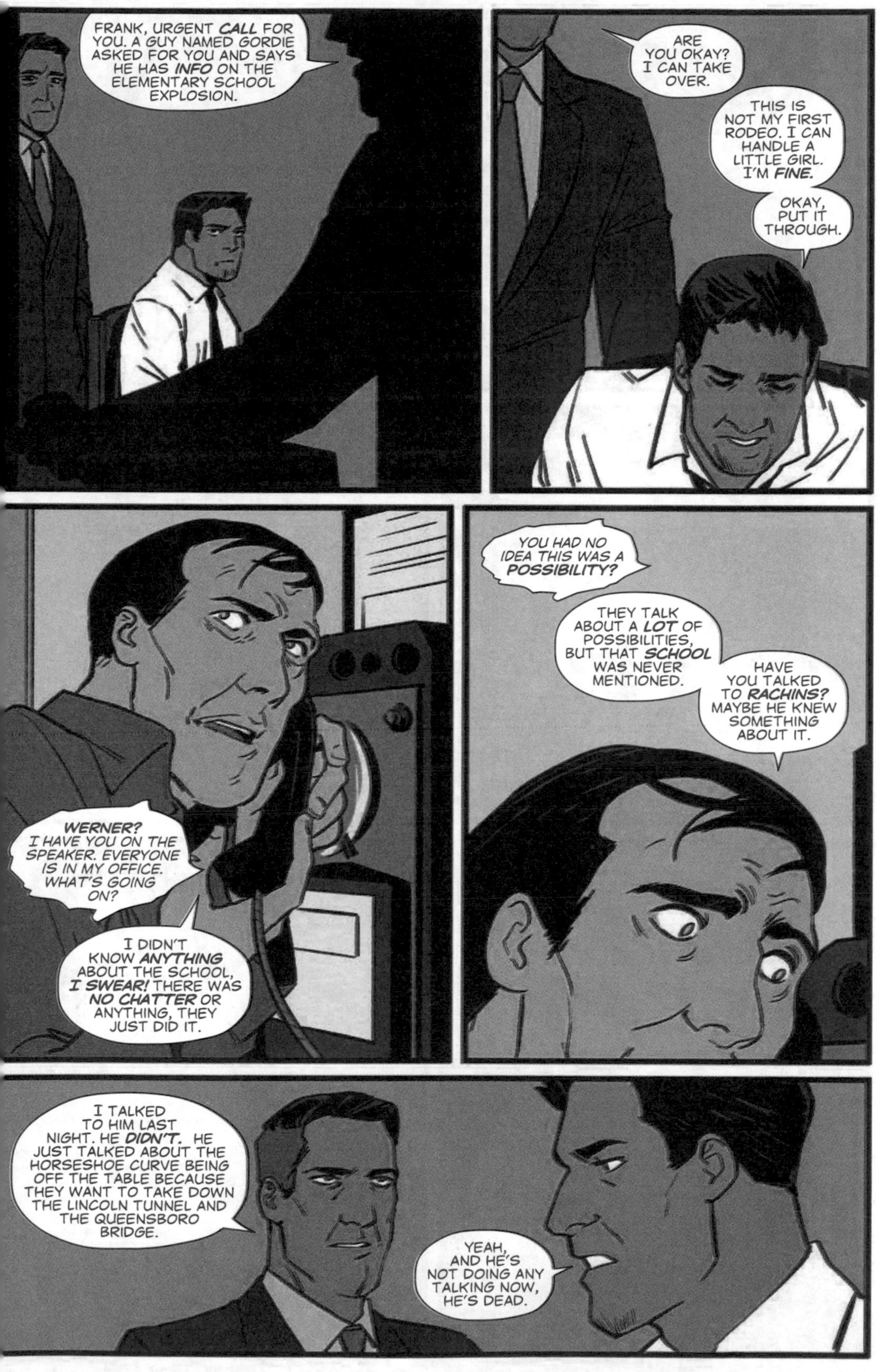
FRANK, URGENT CALL FOR YOU. A GUY NAMED GORDIE ASKED FOR YOU AND SAYS HE HAS INFO ON THE ELEMENTARY SCHOOL EXPLOSION.
ARE YOU OKAY? I CAN TAKE OVER.
THIS IS NOT MY FIRST RODEO. I CAN HANDLE A LITTLE GIRL. I'M FINE.
OKAY, PUT IT THROUGH.
WERNER? I HAVE YOU ON THE SPEAKER. EVERYONE IS IN MY OFFICE. WHAT'S GOING ON?
I DIDN'T KNOW ANYTHING ABOUT THE SCHOOL, I SWEAR! THERE WAS NO CHATTER OR ANYTHING, THEY JUST DID IT.
YOU HAD NO IDEA THIS WAS A POSSIBILITY?
THEY TALK ABOUT A LOT OF POSSIBILITIES, BUT THAT SCHOOL WAS NEVER MENTIONED.
HAVE YOU TALKED TO RACHINS? MAYBE HE KNEW SOMETHING ABOUT IT.
I TALKED TO HIM LAST NIGHT. HE DIDN'T. HE JUST TALKED ABOUT THE HORSESHOE CURVE BEING OFF THE TABLE BECAUSE THEY WANT TO TAKE DOWN THE LINCOLN TUNNEL AND THE QUEENSBORO BRIDGE.
YEAH, AND HE'S NOT DOING ANY TALKING NOW, HE'S DEAD.

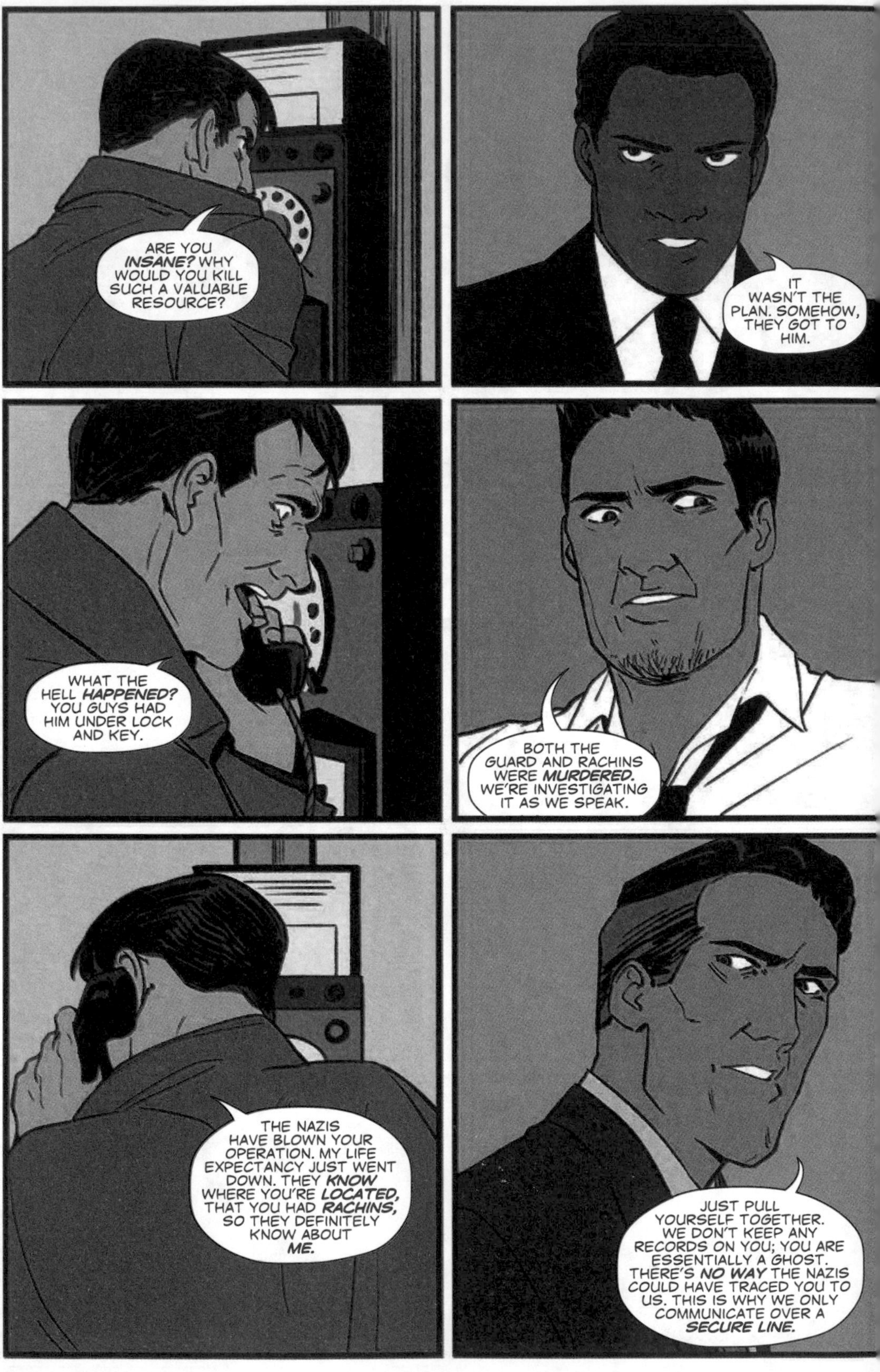
ARE YOU ***INSANE?*** WHY WOULD YOU KILL SUCH A VALUABLE RESOURCE?
IT WASN'T THE PLAN. SOMEHOW, THEY GOT TO HIM.
WHAT THE HELL ***HAPPENED?*** YOU GUYS HAD HIM UNDER LOCK AND KEY.
BOTH THE GUARD AND RACHINS WERE ***MURDERED.*** WE'RE INVESTIGATING IT AS WE SPEAK.
THE NAZIS HAVE BLOWN YOUR OPERATION. MY LIFE EXPECTANCY JUST WENT DOWN. THEY ***KNOW*** WHERE YOU'RE ***LOCATED,*** THAT YOU HAD ***RACHINS,*** SO THEY DEFINITELY KNOW ABOUT ***ME.***
JUST PULL YOURSELF TOGETHER. WE DON'T KEEP ANY RECORDS ON YOU; YOU ARE ESSENTIALLY A GHOST. THERE'S ***NO WAY*** THE NAZIS COULD HAVE TRACED YOU TO US. THIS IS WHY WE ONLY COMMUNICATE OVER A ***SECURE LINE.***

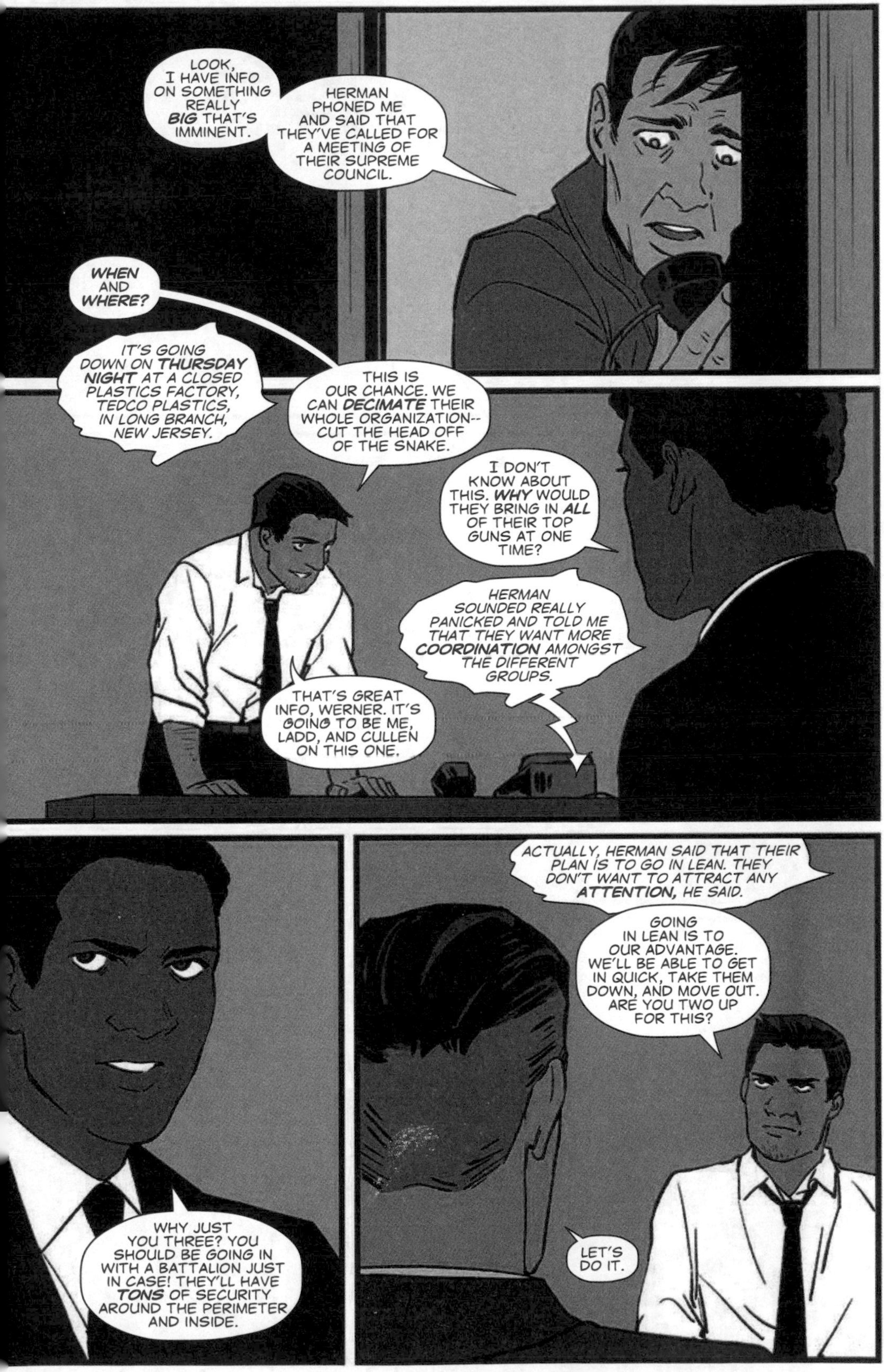
LOOK, I HAVE INFO ON SOMETHING REALLY BIG THAT'S IMMINENT.
HERMAN PHONED ME AND SAID THAT THEY'VE CALLED FOR A MEETING OF THEIR SUPREME COUNCIL.
WHEN AND WHERE?
IT'S GOING DOWN ON THURSDAY NIGHT AT A CLOSED PLASTICS FACTORY, TEDCO PLASTICS, IN LONG BRANCH, NEW JERSEY.
THIS IS OUR CHANCE. WE CAN DECIMATE THEIR WHOLE ORGANIZATION-- CUT THE HEAD OFF OF THE SNAKE.
I DON'T KNOW ABOUT THIS. WHY WOULD THEY BRING IN ALL OF THEIR TOP GUNS AT ONE TIME?
HERMAN SOUNDED REALLY PANICKED AND TOLD ME THAT THEY WANT MORE COORDINATION AMONGST THE DIFFERENT GROUPS.
THAT'S GREAT INFO, WERNER. IT'S GOING TO BE ME, LADD, AND CULLEN ON THIS ONE.
WHY JUST YOU THREE? YOU SHOULD BE GOING IN WITH A BATTALION JUST IN CASE! THEY'LL HAVE TONS OF SECURITY AROUND THE PERIMETER AND INSIDE.
ACTUALLY, HERMAN SAID THAT THEIR PLAN IS TO GO IN LEAN. THEY DON'T WANT TO ATTRACT ANY ATTENTION, HE SAID.
GOING IN LEAN IS TO OUR ADVANTAGE. WE'LL BE ABLE TO GET IN QUICK, TAKE THEM DOWN, AND MOVE OUT. ARE YOU TWO UP FOR THIS?
LET'S DO IT.

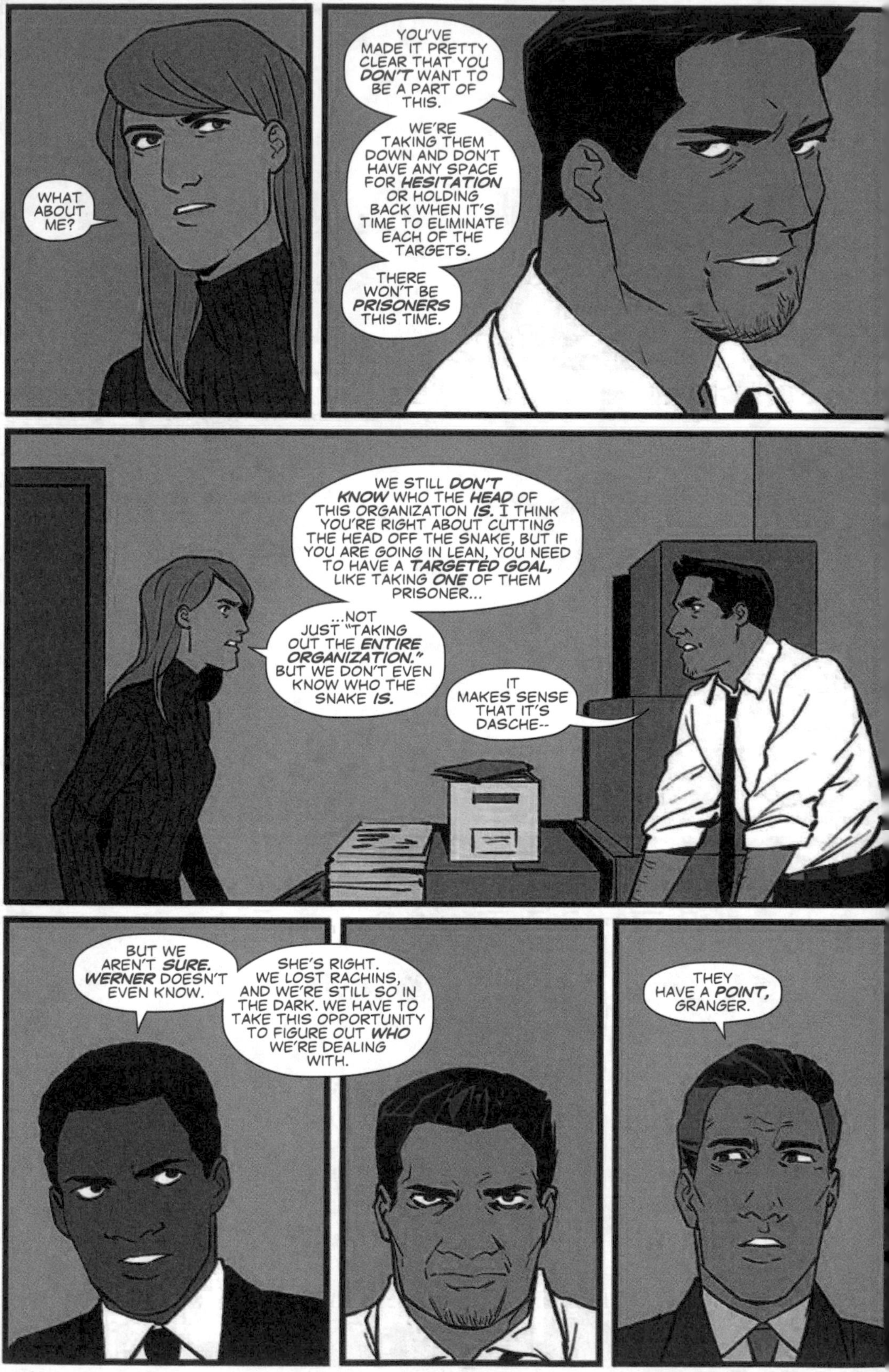
WHAT ABOUT ME?
YOU'VE MADE IT PRETTY CLEAR THAT YOU DON'T WANT TO BE A PART OF THIS.
WE'RE TAKING THEM DOWN AND DON'T HAVE ANY SPACE FOR HESITATION OR HOLDING BACK WHEN IT'S TIME TO ELIMINATE EACH OF THE TARGETS.
THERE WON'T BE PRISONERS THIS TIME.
WE STILL DON'T KNOW WHO THE HEAD OF THIS ORGANIZATION IS. I THINK YOU'RE RIGHT ABOUT CUTTING THE HEAD OFF THE SNAKE, BUT IF YOU ARE GOING IN LEAN, YOU NEED TO HAVE A TARGETED GOAL, LIKE TAKING ONE OF THEM PRISONER...
...NOT JUST "TAKING OUT THE ENTIRE ORGANIZATION." BUT WE DON'T EVEN KNOW WHO THE SNAKE IS.
IT MAKES SENSE THAT IT'S DASCHE--
BUT WE AREN'T SURE. WERNER DOESN'T EVEN KNOW.
SHE'S RIGHT. WE LOST RACHINS, AND WE'RE STILL SO IN THE DARK. WE HAVE TO TAKE THIS OPPORTUNITY TO FIGURE OUT WHO WE'RE DEALING WITH.
THEY HAVE A POINT, GRANGER.

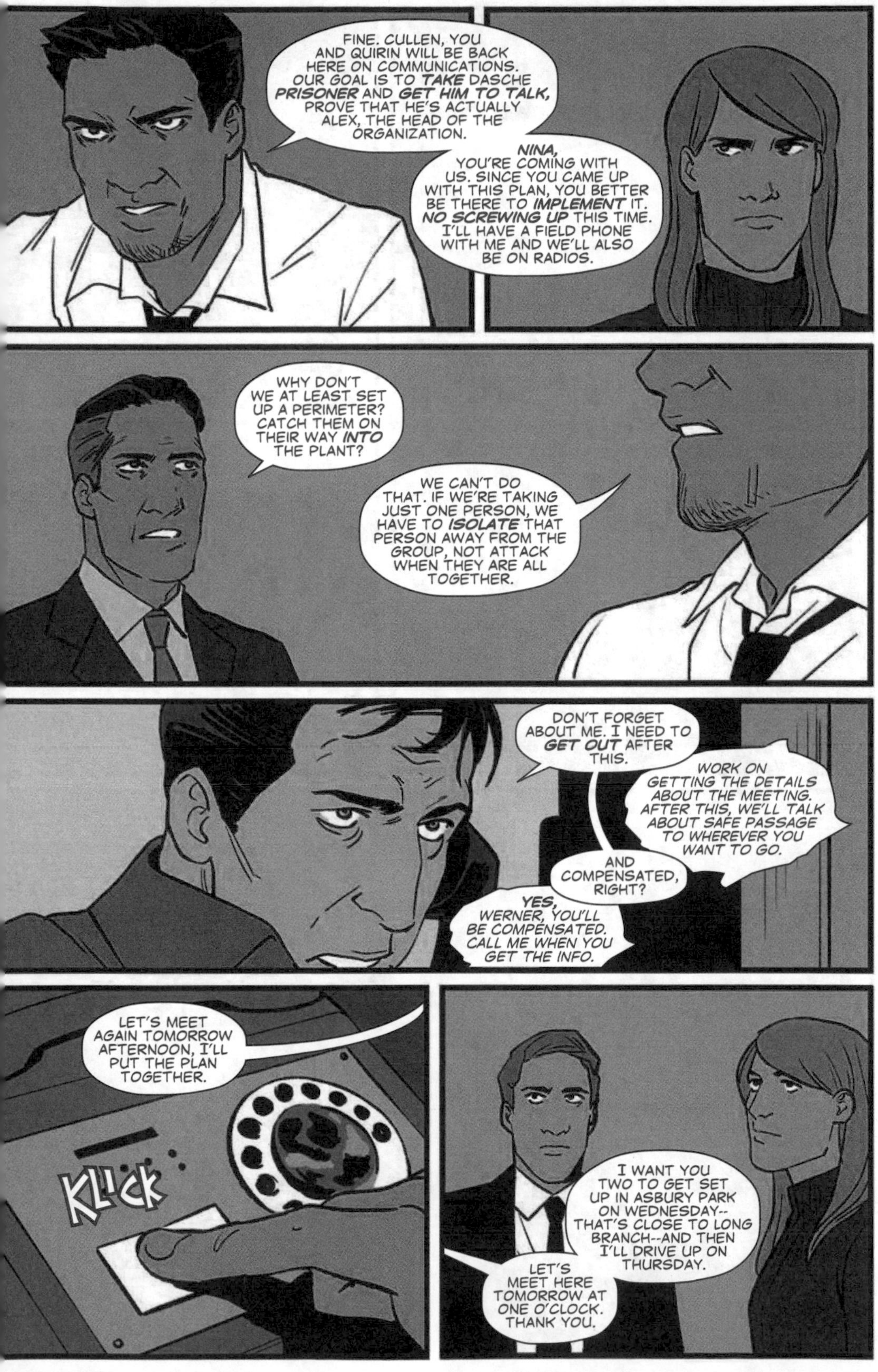
FINE. CULLEN, YOU AND QUIRIN WILL BE BACK HERE ON COMMUNICATIONS. OUR GOAL IS TO TAKE DASCHE PRISONER AND GET HIM TO TALK, PROVE THAT HE'S ACTUALLY ALEX, THE HEAD OF THE ORGANIZATION.
NINA, YOU'RE COMING WITH US. SINCE YOU CAME UP WITH THIS PLAN, YOU BETTER BE THERE TO IMPLEMENT IT. NO SCREWING UP THIS TIME. I'LL HAVE A FIELD PHONE WITH ME AND WE'LL ALSO BE ON RADIOS.
WHY DON'T WE AT LEAST SET UP A PERIMETER? CATCH THEM ON THEIR WAY INTO THE PLANT?
WE CAN'T DO THAT. IF WE'RE TAKING JUST ONE PERSON, WE HAVE TO ISOLATE THAT PERSON AWAY FROM THE GROUP, NOT ATTACK WHEN THEY ARE ALL TOGETHER.
DON'T FORGET ABOUT ME. I NEED TO GET OUT AFTER THIS.
WORK ON GETTING THE DETAILS ABOUT THE MEETING. AFTER THIS, WE'LL TALK ABOUT SAFE PASSAGE TO WHEREVER YOU WANT TO GO.
AND COMPENSATED, RIGHT?
YES, WERNER, YOU'LL BE COMPENSATED. CALL ME WHEN YOU GET THE INFO.
LET'S MEET AGAIN TOMORROW AFTERNOON, I'LL PUT THE PLAN TOGETHER.
KLICK
I WANT YOU TWO TO GET SET UP IN ASBURY PARK ON WEDNESDAY-- THAT'S CLOSE TO LONG BRANCH--AND THEN I'LL DRIVE UP ON THURSDAY.
LET'S MEET HERE TOMORROW AT ONE O'CLOCK. THANK YOU.

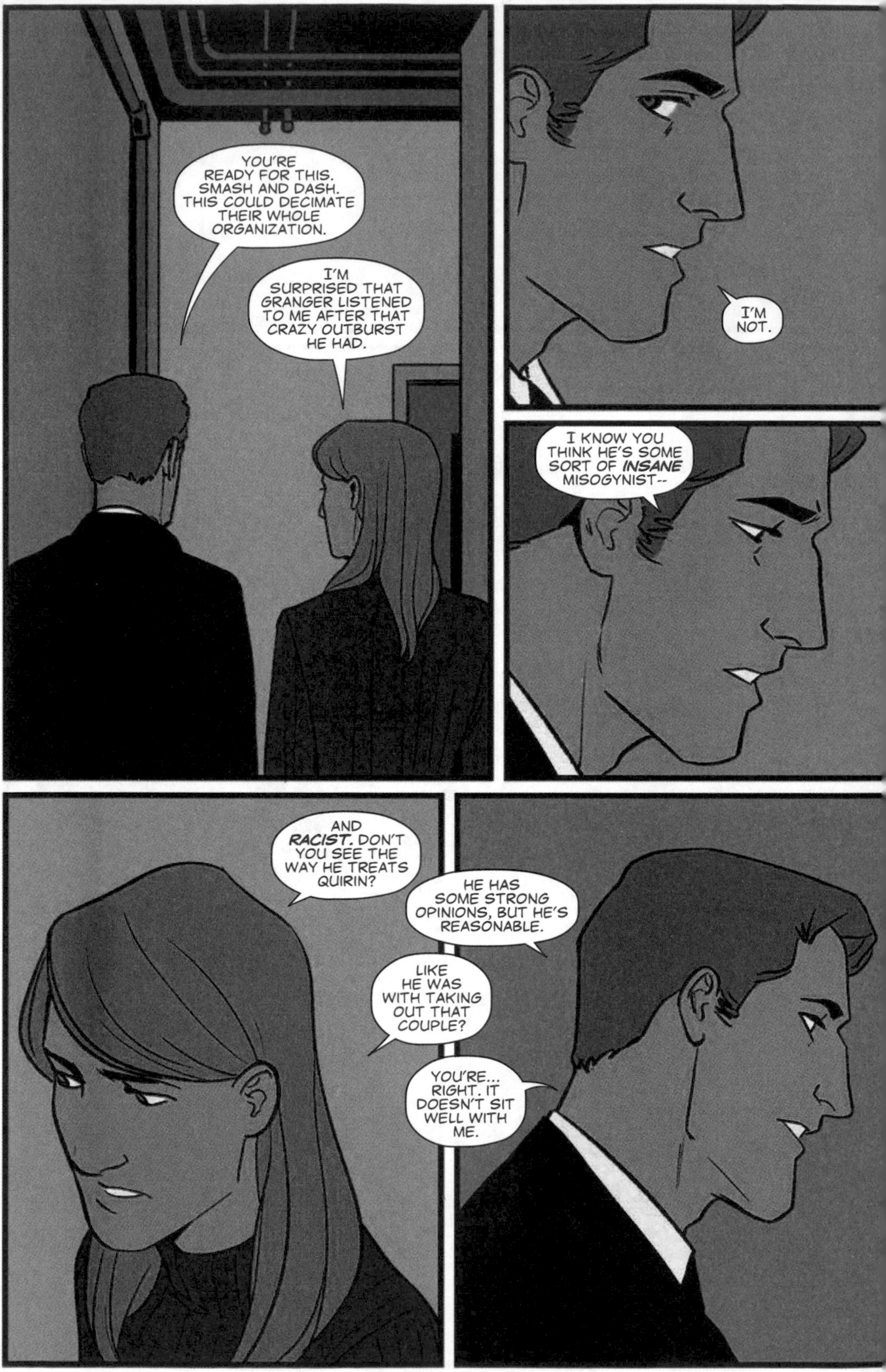
YOU'RE READY FOR THIS. SMASH AND DASH. THIS COULD DECIMATE THEIR WHOLE ORGANIZATION.
I'M SURPRISED THAT GRANGER LISTENED TO ME AFTER THAT CRAZY OUTBURST HE HAD.
I'M NOT.
I KNOW YOU THINK HE'S SOME SORT OF *INSANE* MISOGYNIST--
AND *RACIST.* DON'T YOU SEE THE WAY HE TREATS QUIRIN?
HE HAS SOME STRONG OPINIONS, BUT HE'S REASONABLE.
LIKE HE WAS WITH TAKING OUT THAT COUPLE?
YOU'RE... RIGHT. IT DOESN'T SIT WELL WITH ME.

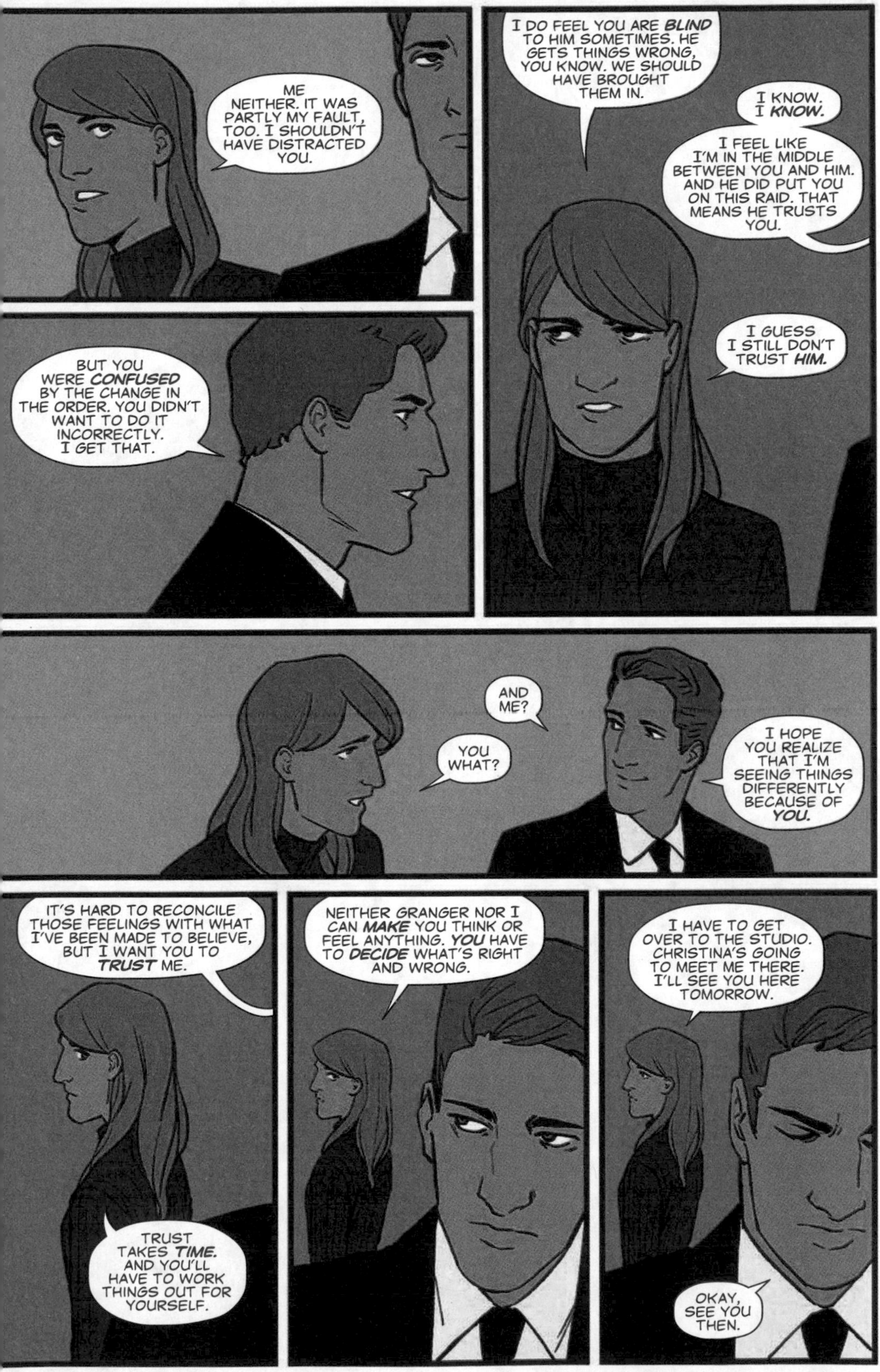
ME NEITHER. IT WAS PARTLY MY FAULT, TOO. I SHOULDN'T HAVE DISTRACTED YOU.
BUT YOU WERE CONFUSED BY THE CHANGE IN THE ORDER. YOU DIDN'T WANT TO DO IT INCORRECTLY. I GET THAT.
I DO FEEL YOU ARE BLIND TO HIM SOMETIMES. HE GETS THINGS WRONG, YOU KNOW. WE SHOULD HAVE BROUGHT THEM IN.
I KNOW. I KNOW.
I FEEL LIKE I'M IN THE MIDDLE BETWEEN YOU AND HIM. AND HE DID PUT YOU ON THIS RAID. THAT MEANS HE TRUSTS YOU.
I GUESS I STILL DON'T TRUST HIM.
AND ME?
YOU WHAT?
I HOPE YOU REALIZE THAT I'M SEEING THINGS DIFFERENTLY BECAUSE OF YOU.
IT'S HARD TO RECONCILE THOSE FEELINGS WITH WHAT I'VE BEEN MADE TO BELIEVE, BUT I WANT YOU TO TRUST ME.
TRUST TAKES TIME. AND YOU'LL HAVE TO WORK THINGS OUT FOR YOURSELF.
NEITHER GRANGER NOR I CAN MAKE YOU THINK OR FEEL ANYTHING. YOU HAVE TO DECIDE WHAT'S RIGHT AND WRONG.
I HAVE TO GET OVER TO THE STUDIO. CHRISTINA'S GOING TO MEET ME THERE. I'LL SEE YOU HERE TOMORROW.
OKAY, SEE YOU THEN.

RECOMMENDED LISTENING:

RIGHT IN TIME
BY LUCINDA WILLIAMS

MAY THIS BE LOVE [WATERFALL]
BY JIMI HENDRIX

ROMEO AND JULIET
BY DIRE STRAITS

NOTHING CAN HARM ME
BY BY NINA OVERSTREET

CHAPTER
ELEVEN

May
This Be
Love?

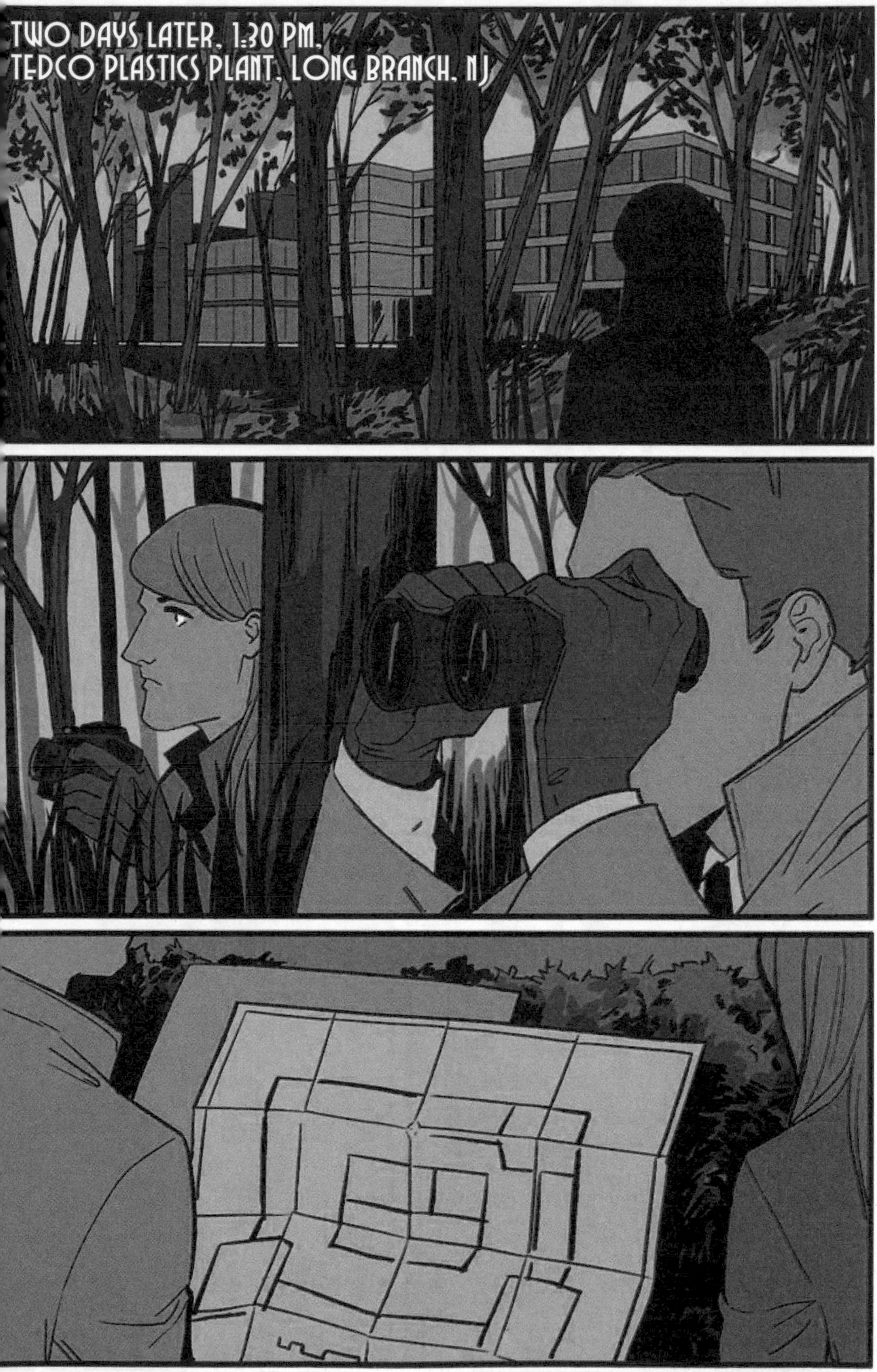
TWO DAYS LATER, 1:30 PM.
TEDCO PLASTICS PLANT, LONG BRANCH, NJ

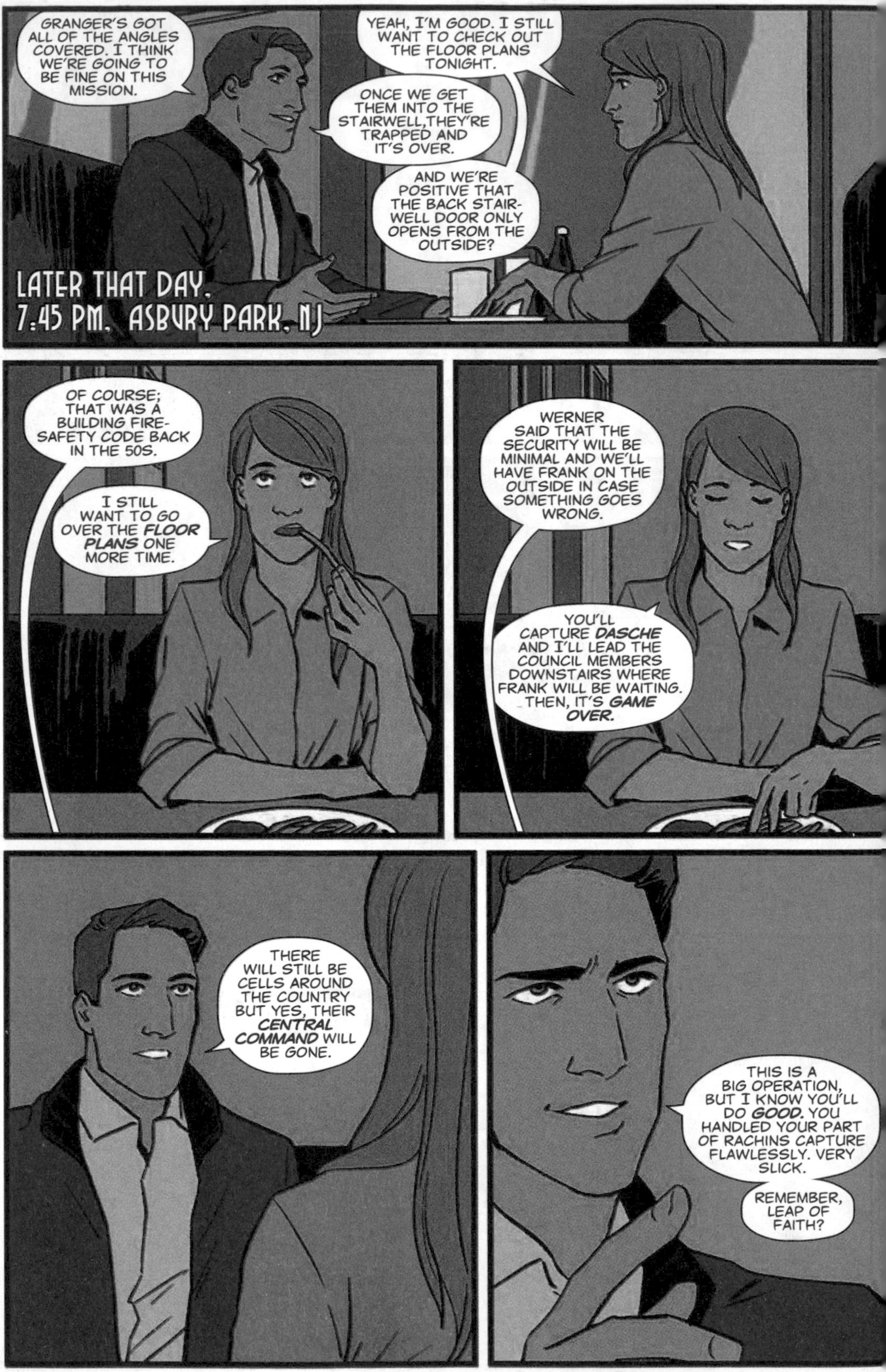
LATER THAT DAY.
7:45 PM. ASBURY PARK, NJ
GRANGER'S GOT ALL OF THE ANGLES COVERED. I THINK WE'RE GOING TO BE FINE ON THIS MISSION.
YEAH, I'M GOOD. I STILL WANT TO CHECK OUT THE FLOOR PLANS TONIGHT.
ONCE WE GET THEM INTO THE STAIRWELL,THEY'RE TRAPPED AND IT'S OVER.
AND WE'RE POSITIVE THAT THE BACK STAIR-WELL DOOR ONLY OPENS FROM THE OUTSIDE?
OF COURSE; THAT WAS A BUILDING FIRE-SAFETY CODE BACK IN THE 50S.
I STILL WANT TO GO OVER THE FLOOR PLANS ONE MORE TIME.
WERNER SAID THAT THE SECURITY WILL BE MINIMAL AND WE'LL HAVE FRANK ON THE OUTSIDE IN CASE SOMETHING GOES WRONG.
YOU'LL CAPTURE DASCHE AND I'LL LEAD THE COUNCIL MEMBERS DOWNSTAIRS WHERE FRANK WILL BE WAITING. THEN, IT'S GAME OVER.
THERE WILL STILL BE CELLS AROUND THE COUNTRY BUT YES, THEIR CENTRAL COMMAND WILL BE GONE.
THIS IS A BIG OPERATION, BUT I KNOW YOU'LL DO GOOD. YOU HANDLED YOUR PART OF RACHINS CAPTURE FLAWLESSLY. VERY SLICK.
REMEMBER, LEAP OF FAITH?

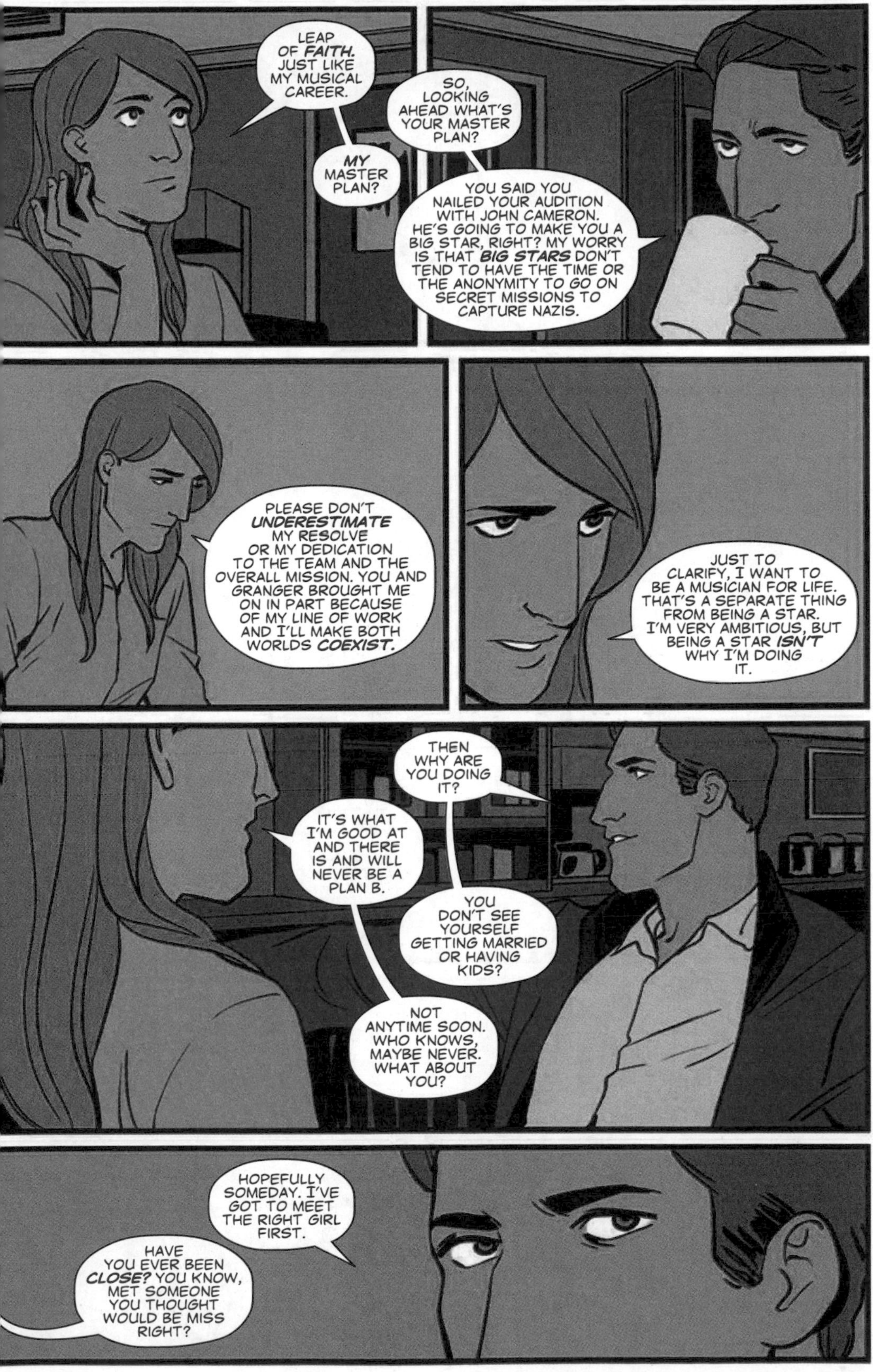
LEAP OF *FAITH.* JUST LIKE MY MUSICAL CAREER.
SO, LOOKING AHEAD WHAT'S YOUR MASTER PLAN?
MY MASTER PLAN?
YOU SAID YOU NAILED YOUR AUDITION WITH JOHN CAMERON. HE'S GOING TO MAKE YOU A BIG STAR, RIGHT? MY WORRY IS THAT ***BIG STARS*** DON'T TEND TO HAVE THE TIME OR THE ANONYMITY TO *GO ON* SECRET MISSIONS TO CAPTURE NAZIS.
PLEASE DON'T ***UNDERESTIMATE*** MY RESOLVE OR MY DEDICATION TO THE TEAM AND THE OVERALL MISSION. YOU AND GRANGER BROUGHT ME ON IN PART BECAUSE OF MY LINE OF WORK AND I'LL MAKE BOTH WORLDS ***COEXIST.***
JUST TO CLARIFY, I WANT TO BE A MUSICIAN FOR LIFE. THAT'S A SEPARATE THING FROM BEING A STAR. I'M VERY AMBITIOUS, BUT BEING A STAR ***ISN'T*** WHY I'M DOING IT.
THEN WHY ARE YOU DOING IT?
IT'S WHAT I'M GOOD AT AND THERE IS AND WILL NEVER BE A PLAN B.
YOU DON'T SEE YOURSELF GETTING MARRIED OR HAVING KIDS?
NOT ANYTIME SOON. WHO KNOWS, MAYBE NEVER. WHAT ABOUT YOU?
HOPEFULLY SOMEDAY. I'VE GOT TO MEET THE RIGHT GIRL FIRST.
HAVE YOU EVER BEEN ***CLOSE?*** YOU KNOW, MET SOMEONE YOU THOUGHT WOULD BE MISS RIGHT?

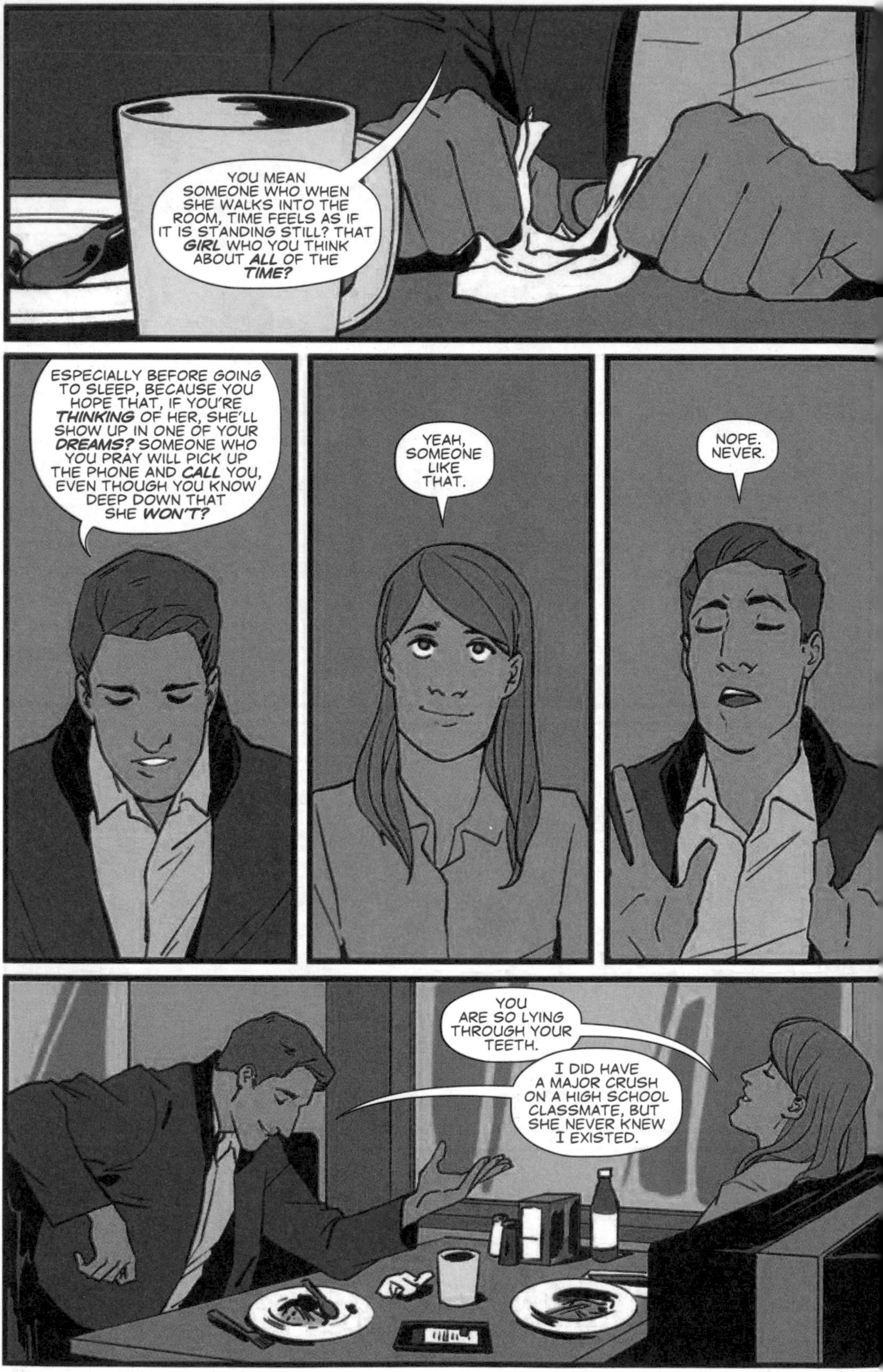
YOU MEAN SOMEONE WHO WHEN SHE WALKS INTO THE ROOM, TIME FEELS AS IF IT IS STANDING STILL? THAT GIRL WHO YOU THINK ABOUT ALL OF THE TIME?
ESPECIALLY BEFORE GOING TO SLEEP, BECAUSE YOU HOPE THAT, IF YOU'RE THINKING OF HER, SHE'LL SHOW UP IN ONE OF YOUR DREAMS? SOMEONE WHO YOU PRAY WILL PICK UP THE PHONE AND CALL YOU, EVEN THOUGH YOU KNOW DEEP DOWN THAT SHE WON'T?
YEAH, SOMEONE LIKE THAT.
NOPE. NEVER.
YOU ARE SO LYING THROUGH YOUR TEETH.
I DID HAVE A MAJOR CRUSH ON A HIGH SCHOOL CLASSMATE, BUT SHE NEVER KNEW I EXISTED.

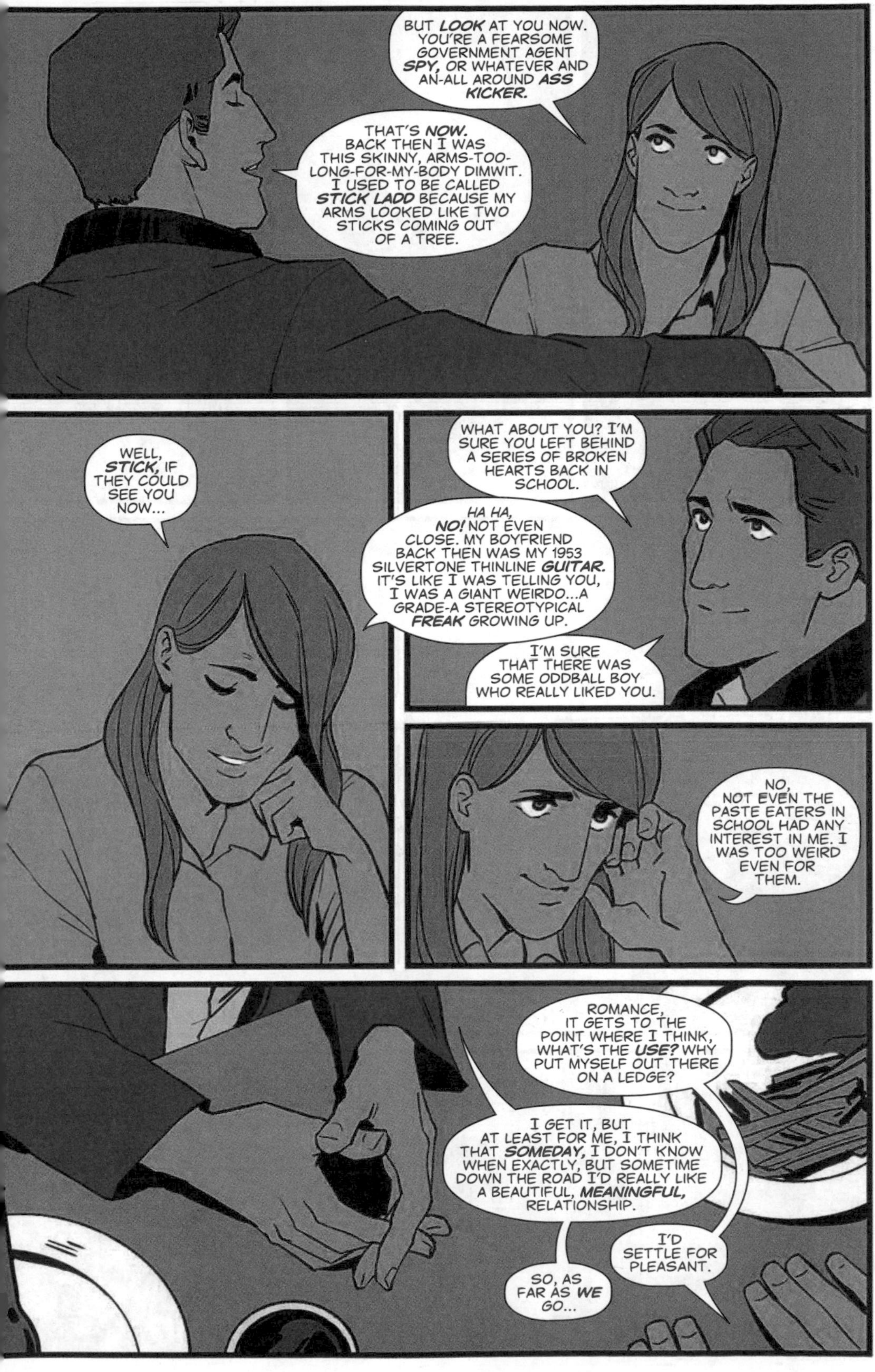
BUT LOOK AT YOU NOW. YOU'RE A FEARSOME GOVERNMENT AGENT SPY, OR WHATEVER AND AN-ALL AROUND ASS KICKER.
THAT'S NOW. BACK THEN I WAS THIS SKINNY, ARMS-TOO-LONG-FOR-MY-BODY DIMWIT. I USED TO BE CALLED STICK LADD BECAUSE MY ARMS LOOKED LIKE TWO STICKS COMING OUT OF A TREE.
WELL, STICK, IF THEY COULD SEE YOU NOW...
WHAT ABOUT YOU? I'M SURE YOU LEFT BEHIND A SERIES OF BROKEN HEARTS BACK IN SCHOOL.
HA HA, NO! NOT EVEN CLOSE. MY BOYFRIEND BACK THEN WAS MY 1953 SILVERTONE THINLINE GUITAR. IT'S LIKE I WAS TELLING YOU, I WAS A GIANT WEIRDO...A GRADE-A STEREOTYPICAL FREAK GROWING UP.
I'M SURE THAT THERE WAS SOME ODDBALL BOY WHO REALLY LIKED YOU.
NO, NOT EVEN THE PASTE EATERS IN SCHOOL HAD ANY INTEREST IN ME. I WAS TOO WEIRD EVEN FOR THEM.
ROMANCE, IT GETS TO THE POINT WHERE I THINK, WHAT'S THE USE? WHY PUT MYSELF OUT THERE ON A LEDGE?
I GET IT, BUT AT LEAST FOR ME, I THINK THAT SOMEDAY, I DON'T KNOW WHEN EXACTLY, BUT SOMETIME DOWN THE ROAD I'D REALLY LIKE A BEAUTIFUL, MEANINGFUL, RELATIONSHIP.
I'D SETTLE FOR PLEASANT.
SO, AS FAR AS WE GO...

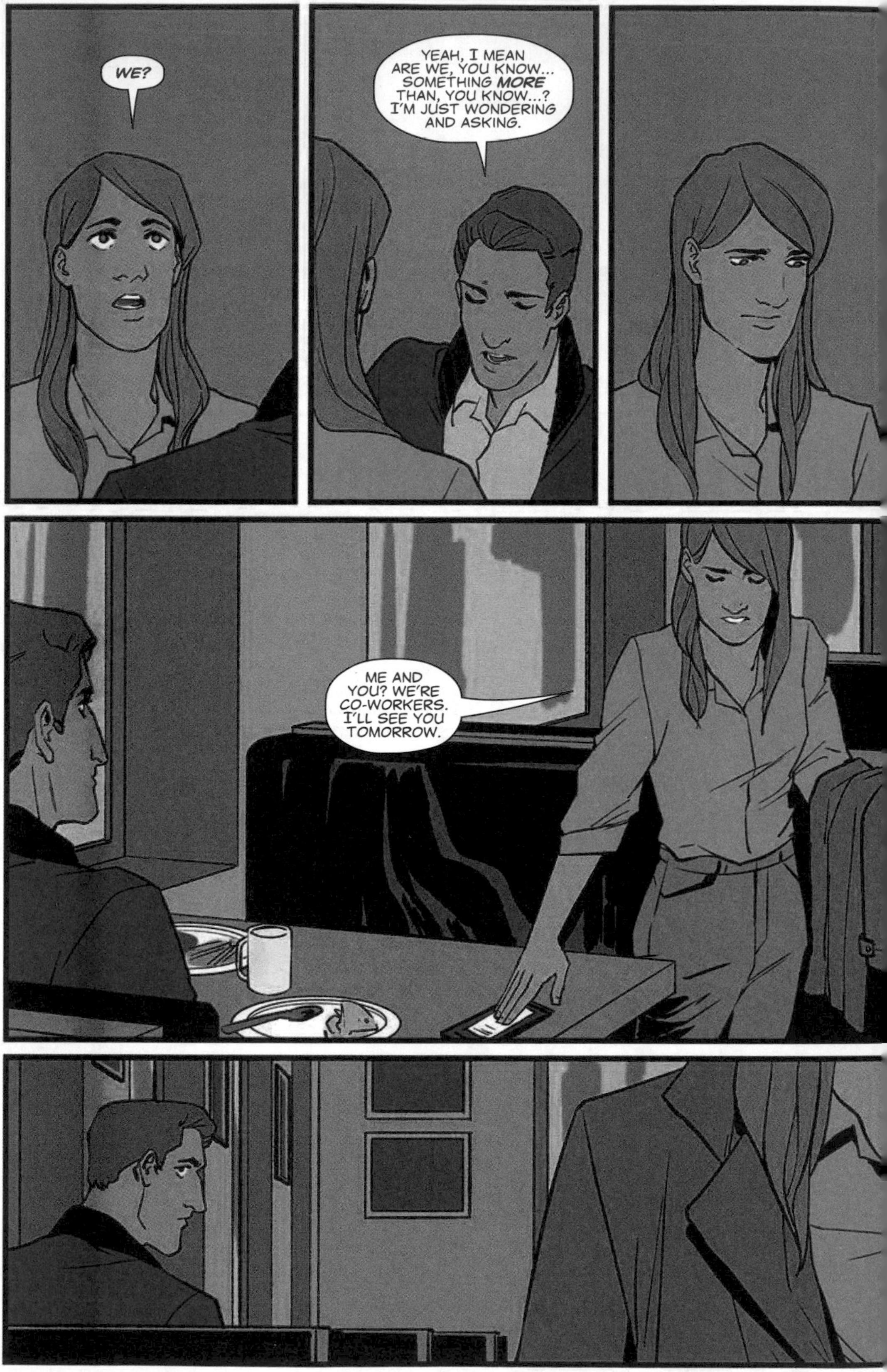
WE?
YEAH, I MEAN ARE WE, YOU KNOW... SOMETHING MORE THAN, YOU KNOW...? I'M JUST WONDERING AND ASKING.
ME AND YOU? WE'RE CO-WORKERS. I'LL SEE YOU TOMORROW.

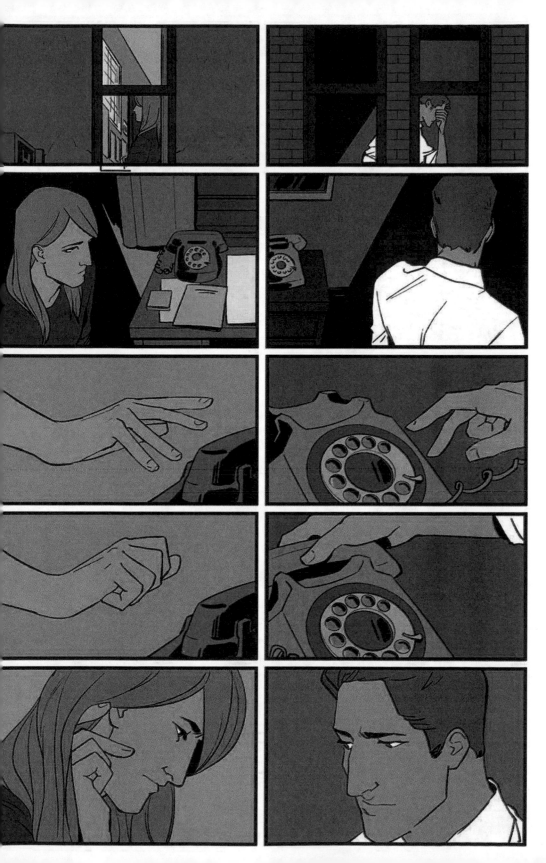

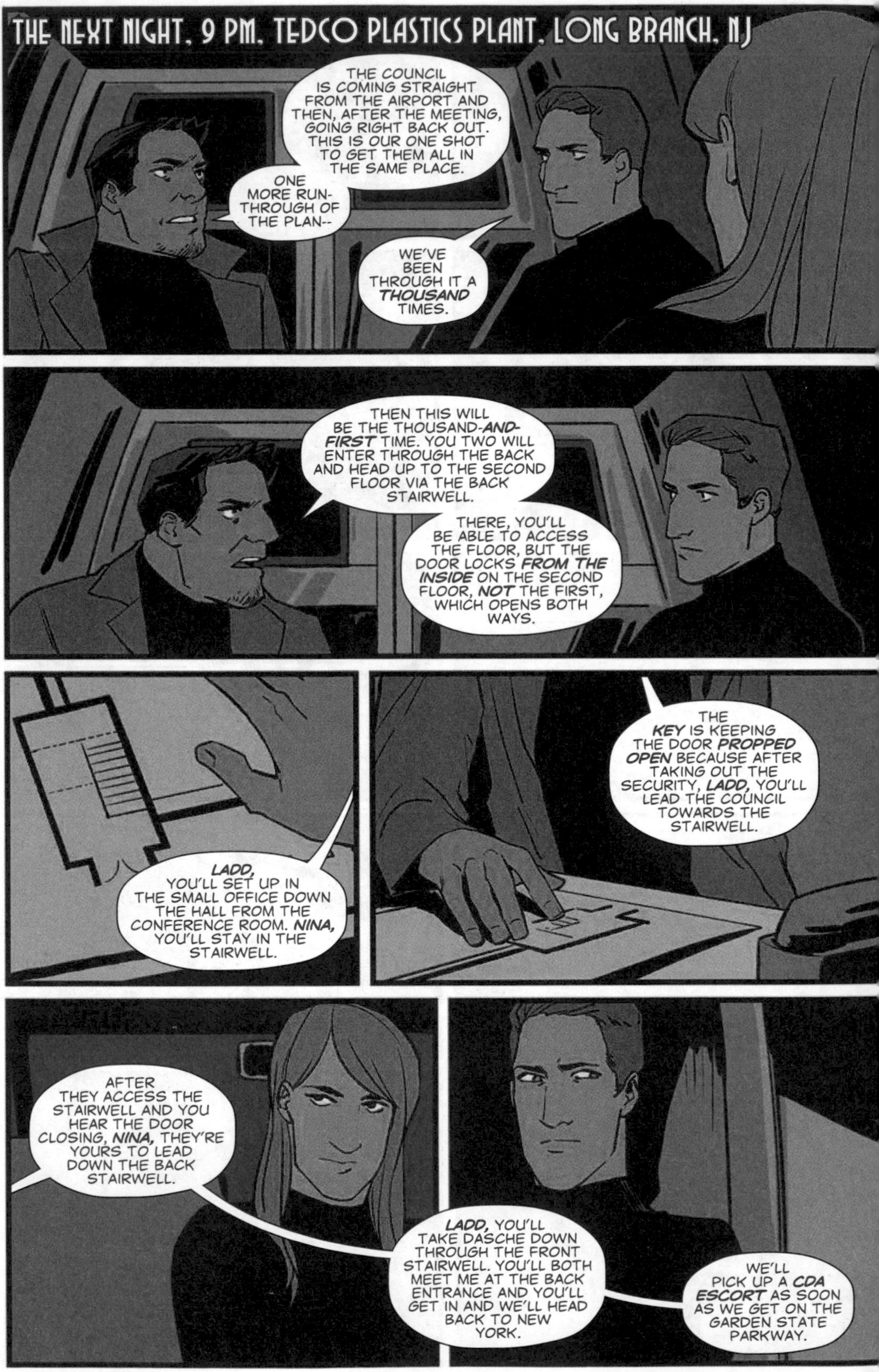
THE NEXT NIGHT, 9 PM, TEDCO PLASTICS PLANT, LONG BRANCH, NJ
THE COUNCIL IS COMING STRAIGHT FROM THE AIRPORT AND THEN, AFTER THE MEETING, GOING RIGHT BACK OUT. THIS IS OUR ONE SHOT TO GET THEM ALL IN THE SAME PLACE.
ONE MORE RUN-THROUGH OF THE PLAN--
WE'VE BEEN THROUGH IT A THOUSAND TIMES.
THEN THIS WILL BE THE THOUSAND-AND-FIRST TIME. YOU TWO WILL ENTER THROUGH THE BACK AND HEAD UP TO THE SECOND FLOOR VIA THE BACK STAIRWELL.
THERE, YOU'LL BE ABLE TO ACCESS THE FLOOR, BUT THE DOOR LOCKS FROM THE INSIDE ON THE SECOND FLOOR, NOT THE FIRST, WHICH OPENS BOTH WAYS.
LADD, YOU'LL SET UP IN THE SMALL OFFICE DOWN THE HALL FROM THE CONFERENCE ROOM. NINA, YOU'LL STAY IN THE STAIRWELL.
THE KEY IS KEEPING THE DOOR PROPPED OPEN BECAUSE AFTER TAKING OUT THE SECURITY, LADD, YOU'LL LEAD THE COUNCIL TOWARDS THE STAIRWELL.
AFTER THEY ACCESS THE STAIRWELL AND YOU HEAR THE DOOR CLOSING, NINA, THEY'RE YOURS TO LEAD DOWN THE BACK STAIRWELL.
LADD, YOU'LL TAKE DASCHE DOWN THROUGH THE FRONT STAIRWELL. YOU'LL BOTH MEET ME AT THE BACK ENTRANCE AND YOU'LL GET IN AND WE'LL HEAD BACK TO NEW YORK.
WE'LL PICK UP A CDA ESCORT AS SOON AS WE GET ON THE GARDEN STATE PARKWAY.

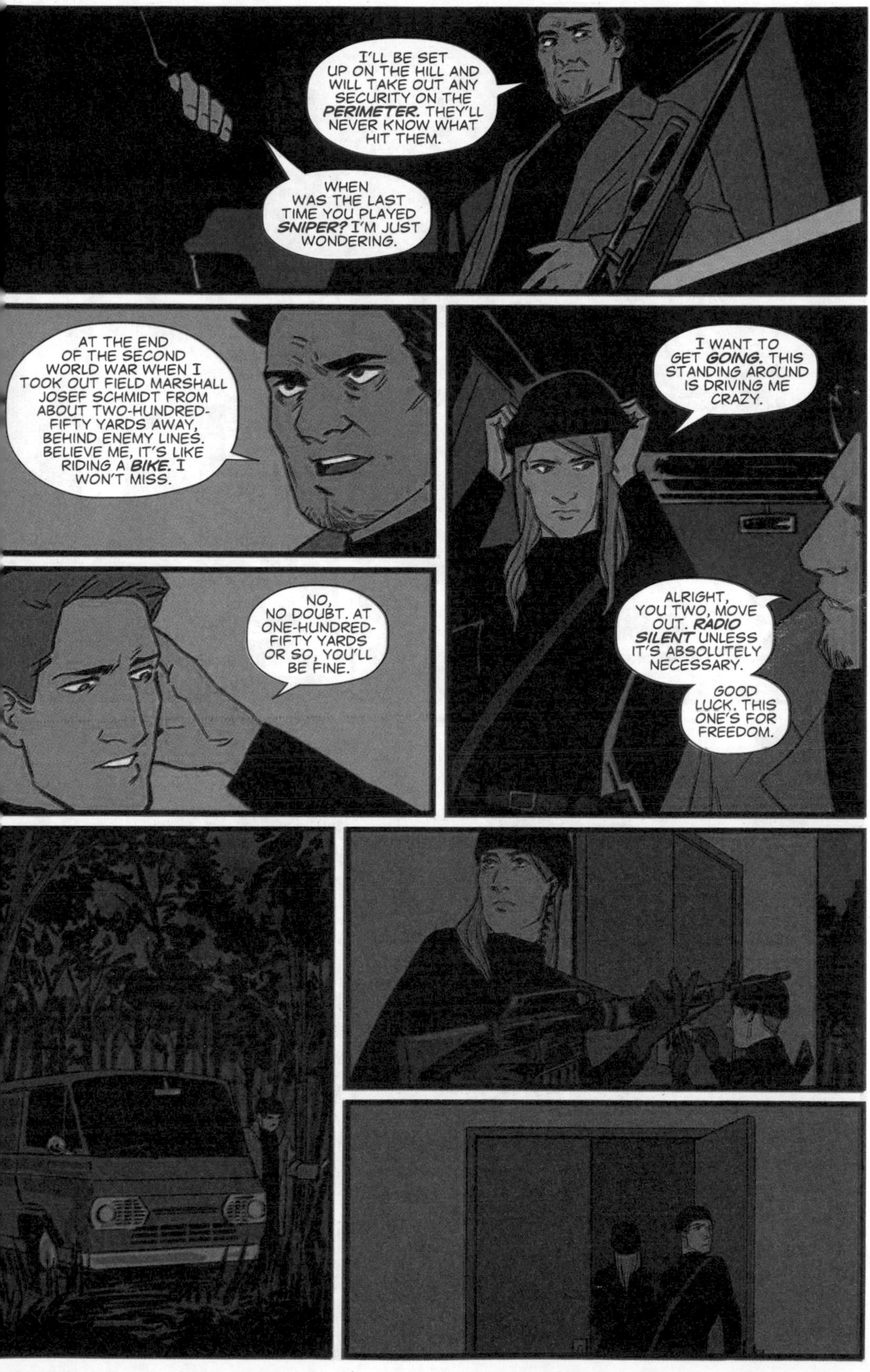
I'LL BE SET UP ON THE HILL AND WILL TAKE OUT ANY SECURITY ON THE PERIMETER. THEY'LL NEVER KNOW WHAT HIT THEM.
WHEN WAS THE LAST TIME YOU PLAYED SNIPER? I'M JUST WONDERING.
AT THE END OF THE SECOND WORLD WAR WHEN I TOOK OUT FIELD MARSHALL JOSEF SCHMIDT FROM ABOUT TWO-HUNDRED-FIFTY YARDS AWAY, BEHIND ENEMY LINES. BELIEVE ME, IT'S LIKE RIDING A BIKE. I WON'T MISS.
NO, NO DOUBT. AT ONE-HUNDRED-FIFTY YARDS OR SO, YOU'LL BE FINE.
I WANT TO GET GOING. THIS STANDING AROUND IS DRIVING ME CRAZY.
ALRIGHT, YOU TWO, MOVE OUT. RADIO SILENT UNLESS IT'S ABSOLUTELY NECESSARY.
GOOD LUCK. THIS ONE'S FOR FREEDOM.

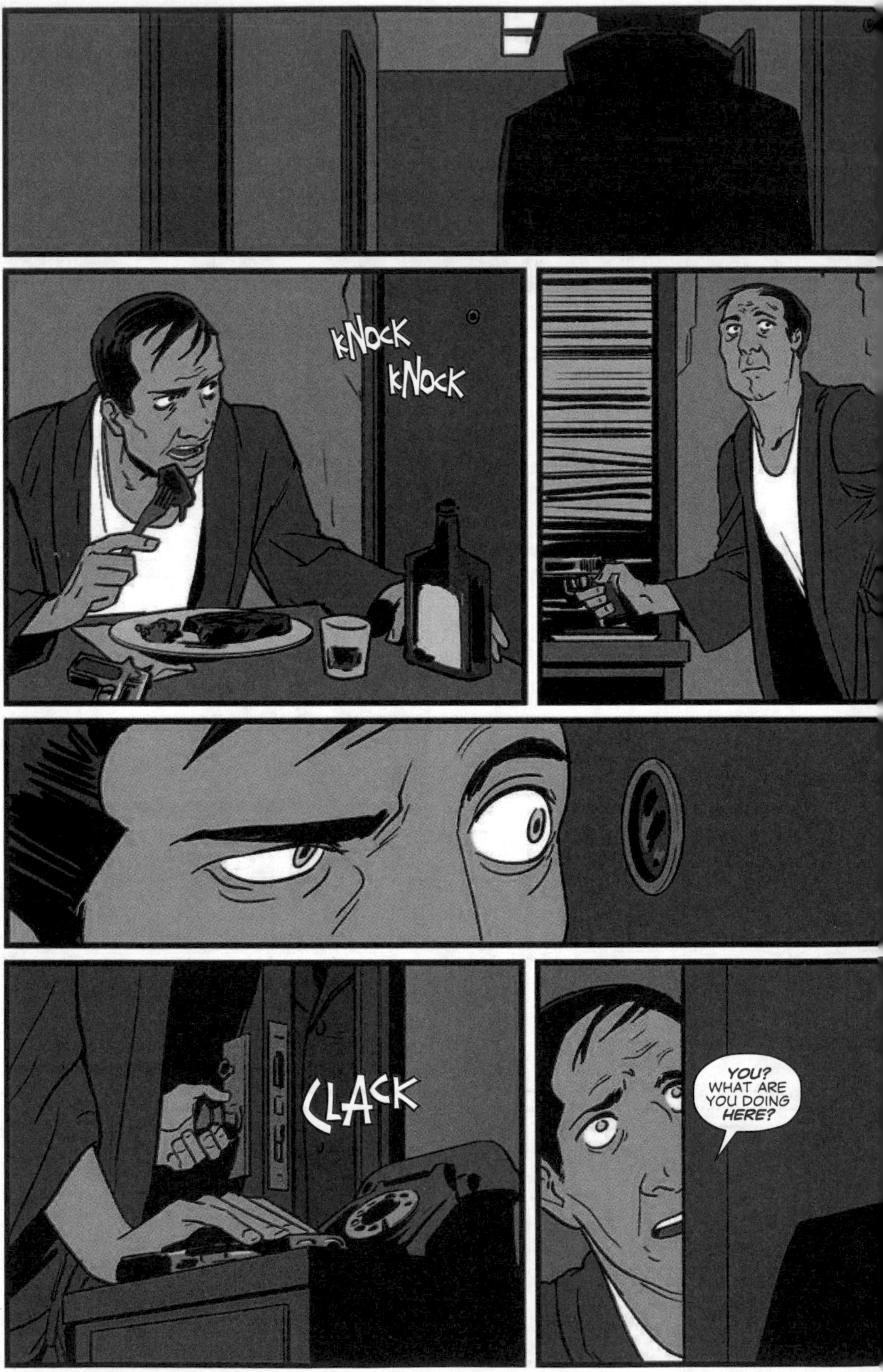
KNOCK
KNOCK
CLACK
YOU? WHAT ARE YOU DOING HERE?

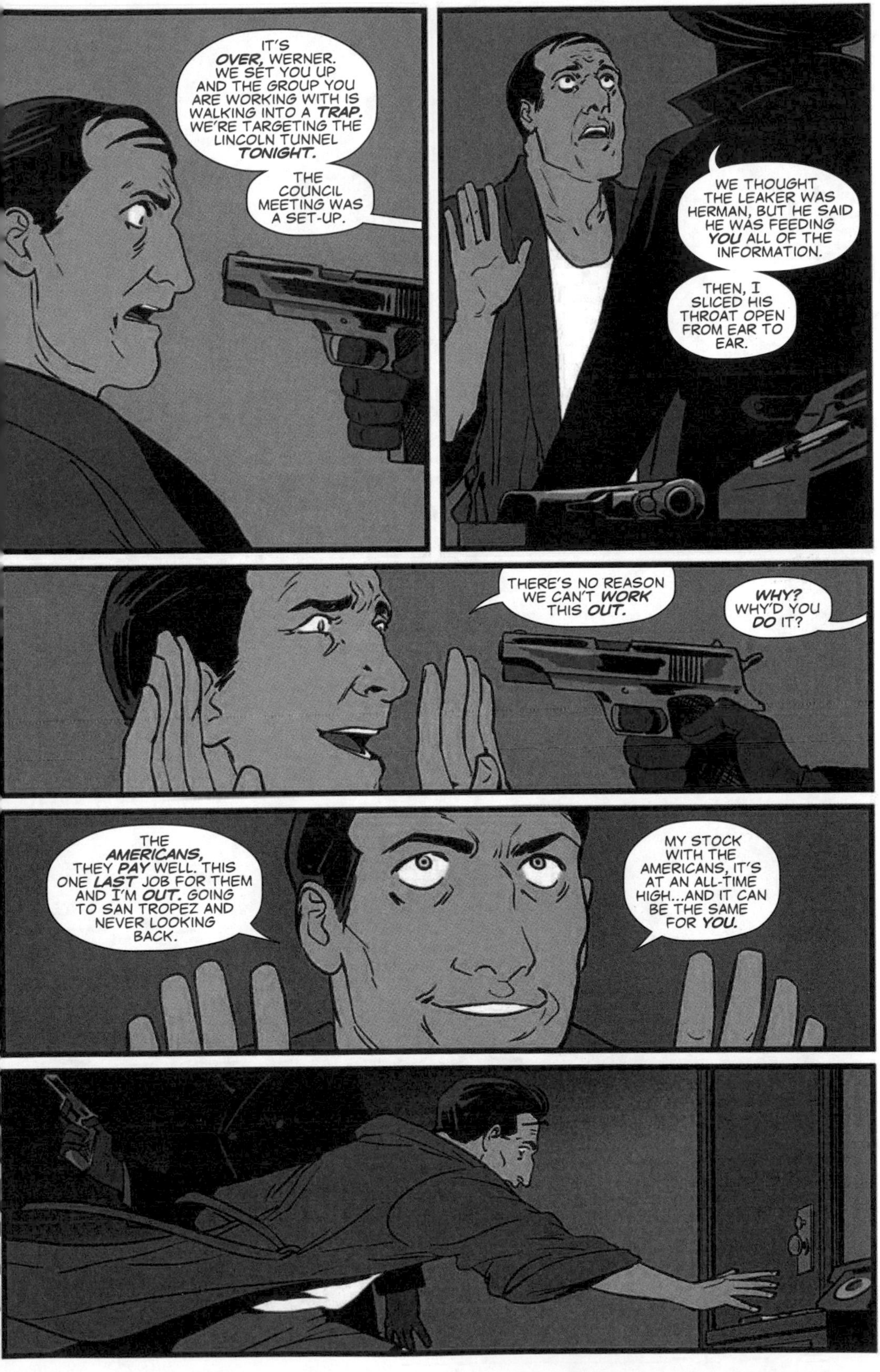
IT'S OVER, WERNER. WE SET YOU UP AND THE GROUP YOU ARE WORKING WITH IS WALKING INTO A TRAP. WE'RE TARGETING THE LINCOLN TUNNEL TONIGHT.
THE COUNCIL MEETING WAS A SET-UP.
WE THOUGHT THE LEAKER WAS HERMAN, BUT HE SAID HE WAS FEEDING YOU ALL OF THE INFORMATION.
THEN, I SLICED HIS THROAT OPEN FROM EAR TO EAR.
WHY? WHY'D YOU DO IT?
THERE'S NO REASON WE CAN'T WORK THIS OUT.
THE AMERICANS, THEY PAY WELL. THIS ONE LAST JOB FOR THEM AND I'M OUT. GOING TO SAN TROPEZ AND NEVER LOOKING BACK.
MY STOCK WITH THE AMERICANS, IT'S AT AN ALL-TIME HIGH...AND IT CAN BE THE SAME FOR YOU.

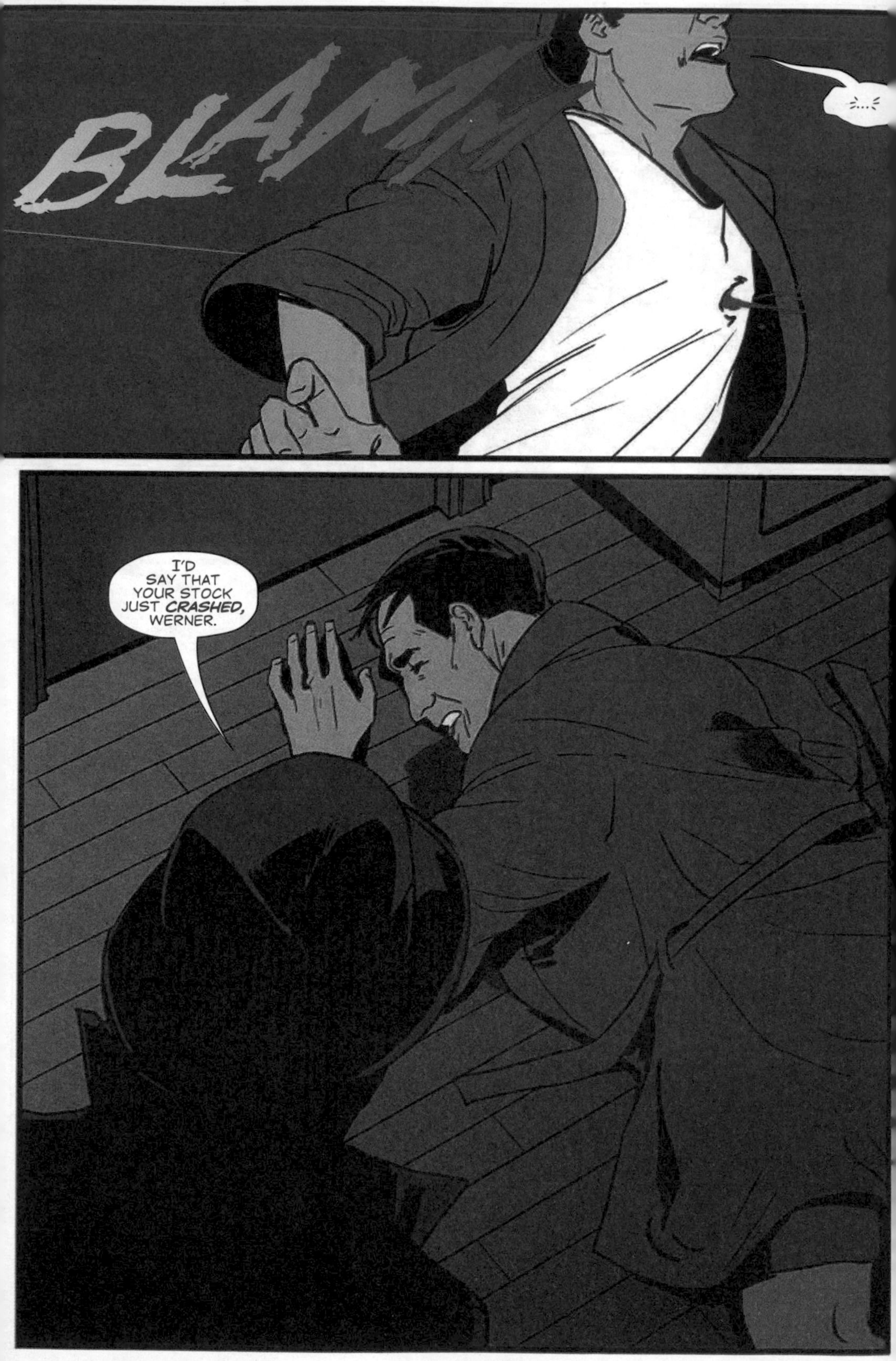
BLAM
...
I'D SAY THAT YOUR STOCK JUST ***CRASHED,*** WERNER.

RECOMMENDED LISTENING:

I FEEL IT ALL
BY FEIST

THE BORDER
BY JÓHANN JÓHANNSSON

THE PRICE WAS LOADED
FROM THE START
BY NINA OVERSTREET

CHAPTER TWELVE

Not In Vain

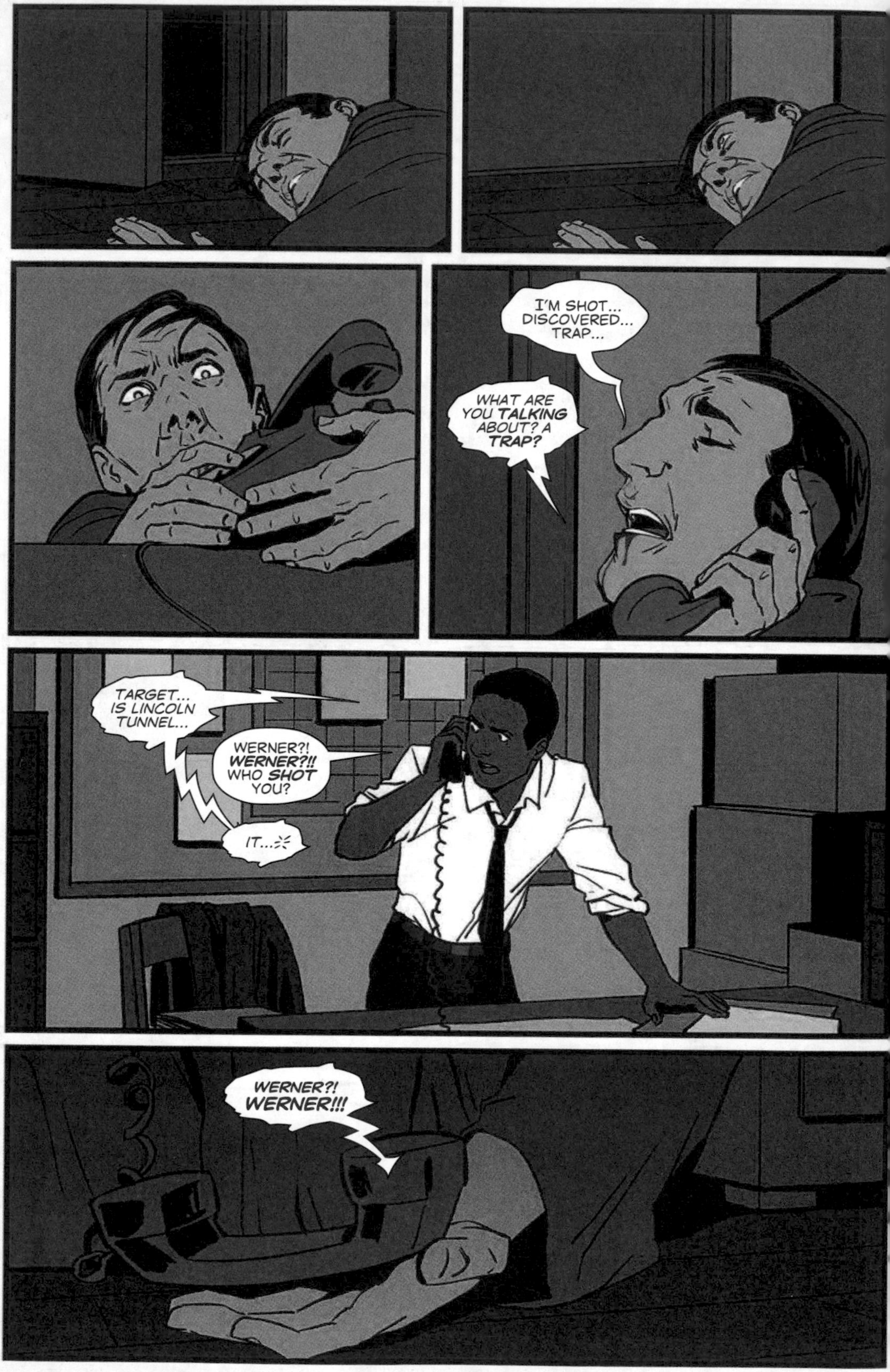
I'M SHOT... DISCOVERED... TRAP...
WHAT ARE YOU TALKING ABOUT? A TRAP?
TARGET... IS LINCOLN TUNNEL...
WERNER?! WERNER?!! WHO SHOT YOU?
IT...
WERNER?! WERNER!!!

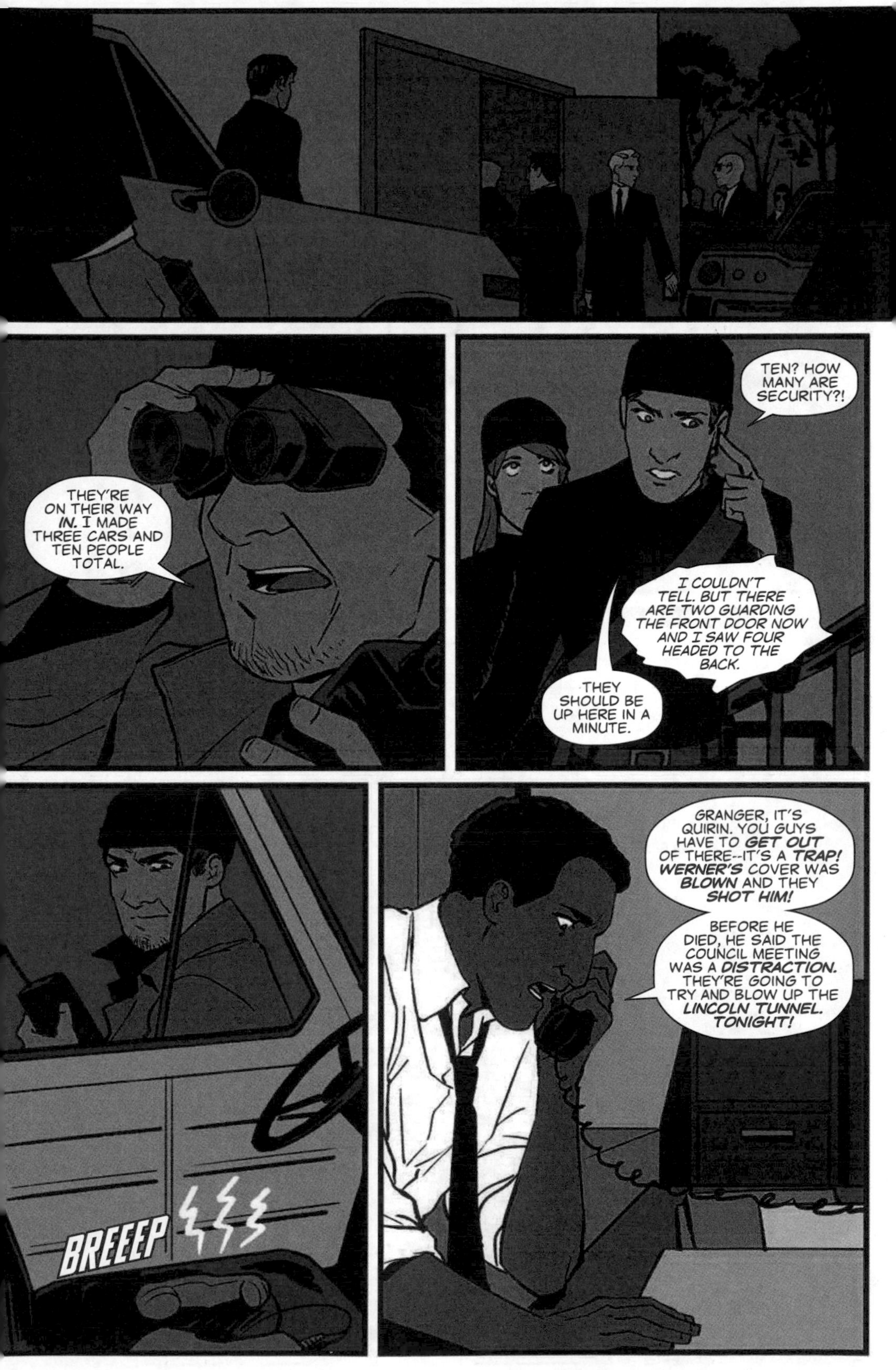
THEY'RE ON THEIR WAY *IN.* I MADE THREE CARS AND TEN PEOPLE TOTAL.
TEN? HOW MANY ARE SECURITY?!
I COULDN'T TELL. BUT THERE ARE TWO GUARDING THE FRONT DOOR NOW AND I SAW FOUR HEADED TO THE BACK.
THEY SHOULD BE UP HERE IN A MINUTE.
BREEEP
GRANGER, IT'S QUIRIN. YOU GUYS HAVE TO ***GET OUT*** OF THERE--IT'S A ***TRAP! WERNER'S*** COVER WAS ***BLOWN*** AND THEY ***SHOT HIM!***
BEFORE HE DIED, HE SAID THE COUNCIL MEETING WAS A ***DISTRACTION.*** THEY'RE GOING TO TRY AND BLOW UP THE ***LINCOLN TUNNEL. TONIGHT!***

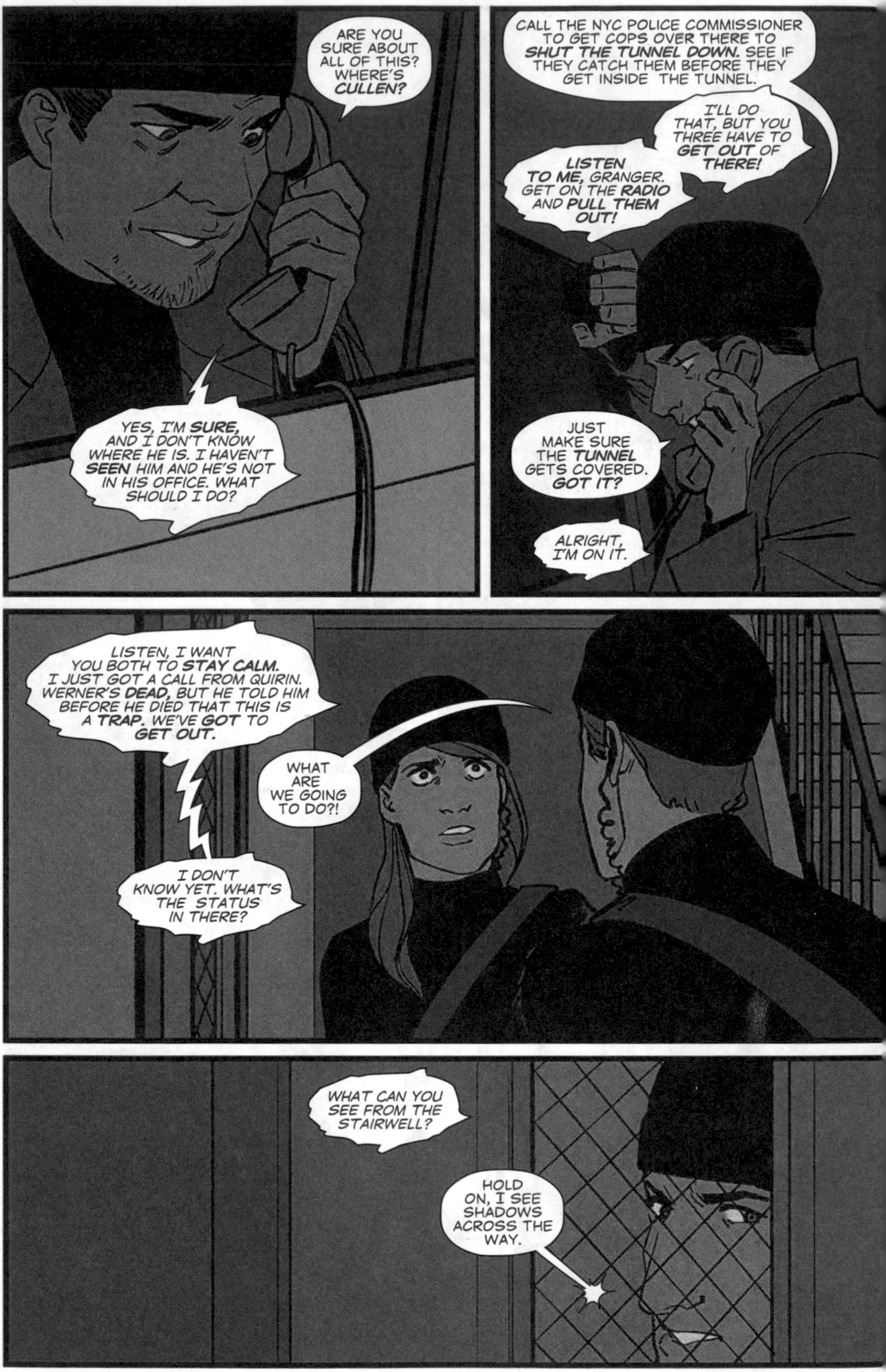
ARE YOU SURE ABOUT ALL OF THIS? WHERE'S CULLEN?
YES, I'M SURE, AND I DON'T KNOW WHERE HE IS. I HAVEN'T SEEN HIM AND HE'S NOT IN HIS OFFICE. WHAT SHOULD I DO?
CALL THE NYC POLICE COMMISSIONER TO GET COPS OVER THERE TO SHUT THE TUNNEL DOWN. SEE IF THEY CATCH THEM BEFORE THEY GET INSIDE THE TUNNEL.
I'LL DO THAT, BUT YOU THREE HAVE TO GET OUT OF THERE!
LISTEN TO ME, GRANGER. GET ON THE RADIO AND PULL THEM OUT!
JUST MAKE SURE THE TUNNEL GETS COVERED. GOT IT?
ALRIGHT, I'M ON IT.
LISTEN, I WANT YOU BOTH TO STAY CALM. I JUST GOT A CALL FROM QUIRIN. WERNER'S DEAD, BUT HE TOLD HIM BEFORE HE DIED THAT THIS IS A TRAP. WE'VE GOT TO GET OUT.
WHAT ARE WE GOING TO DO?!
I DON'T KNOW YET. WHAT'S THE STATUS IN THERE?
WHAT CAN YOU SEE FROM THE STAIRWELL?
HOLD ON, I SEE SHADOWS ACROSS THE WAY.

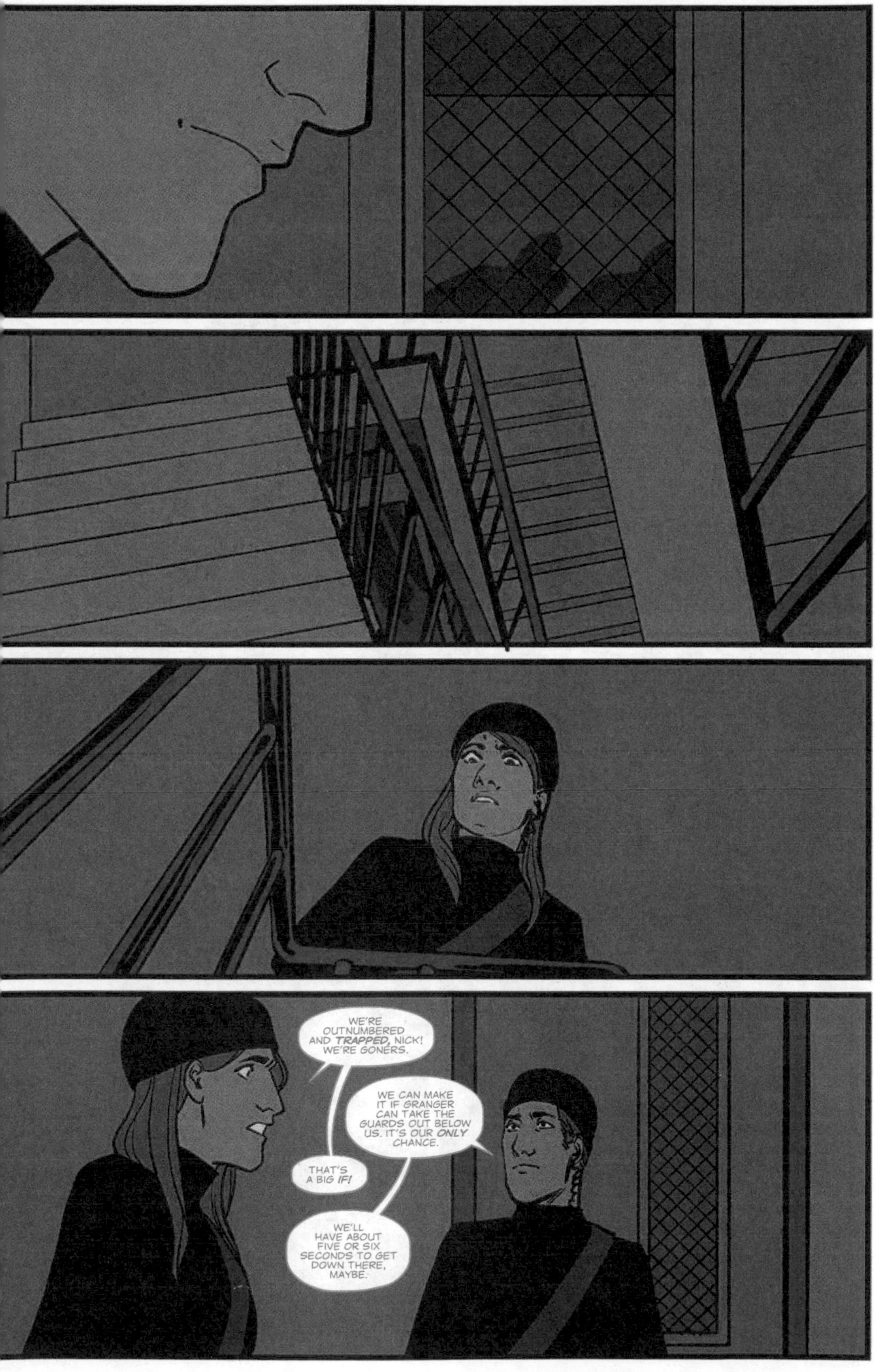
WE'RE OUTNUMBERED AND TRAPPED, NICK! WE'RE GONERS.
WE CAN MAKE IT IF GRANGER CAN TAKE THE GUARDS OUT BELOW US. IT'S OUR ONLY CHANCE.
THAT'S A BIG IF!
WE'LL HAVE ABOUT FIVE OR SIX SECONDS TO GET DOWN THERE, MAYBE.

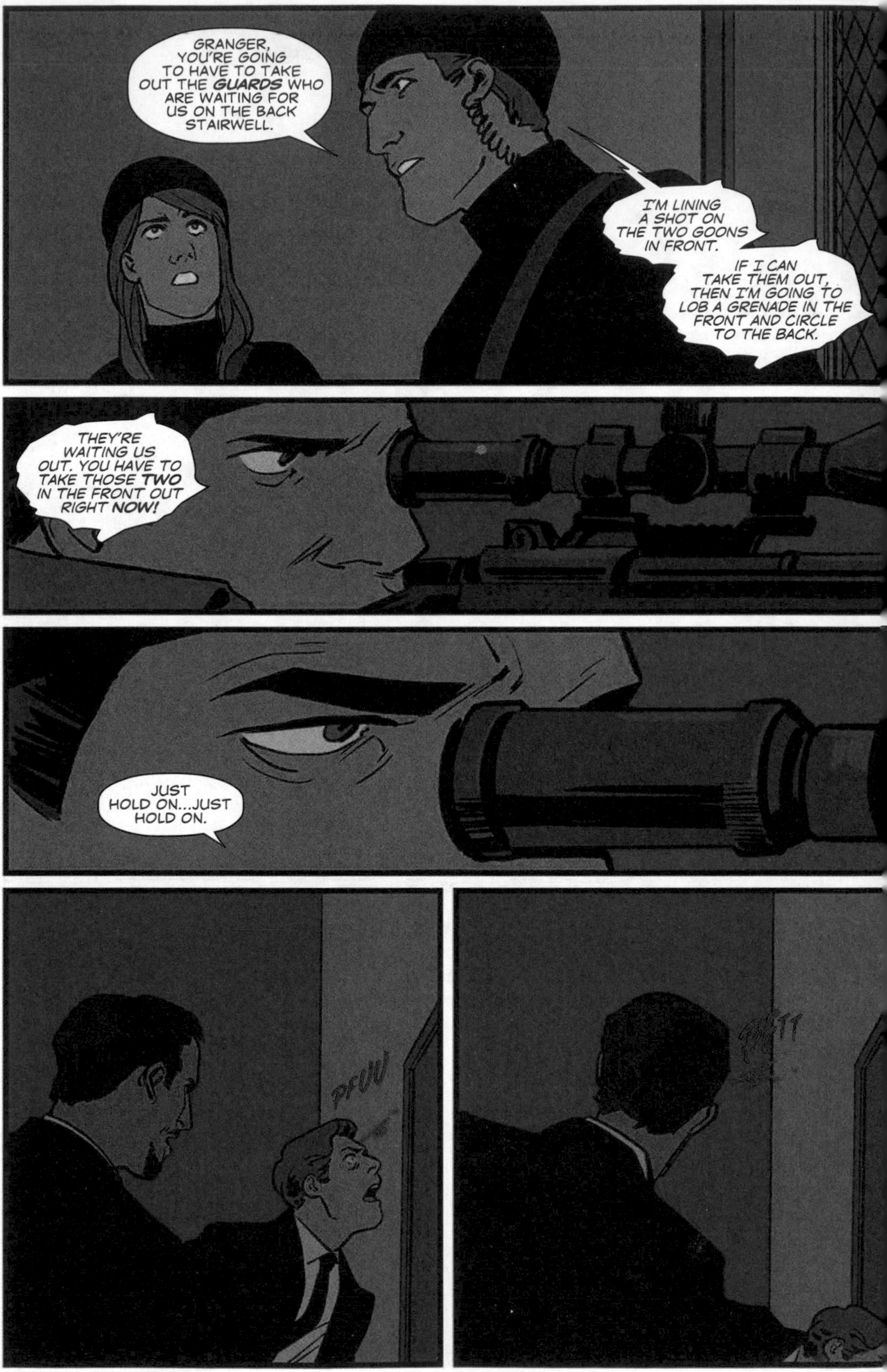

GRANGER, YOU'RE GOING TO HAVE TO TAKE OUT THE ***GUARDS*** WHO ARE WAITING FOR US ON THE BACK STAIRWELL.
I'M LINING A SHOT ON THE TWO GOONS IN FRONT.
IF I CAN TAKE THEM OUT, THEN I'M GOING TO LOB A GRENADE IN THE FRONT AND CIRCLE TO THE BACK.
*THEY'RE WAITING US OUT. YOU HAVE TO TAKE THOSE **TWO** IN THE FRONT OUT RIGHT **NOW!***
JUST HOLD ON...JUST HOLD ON.
PFUU

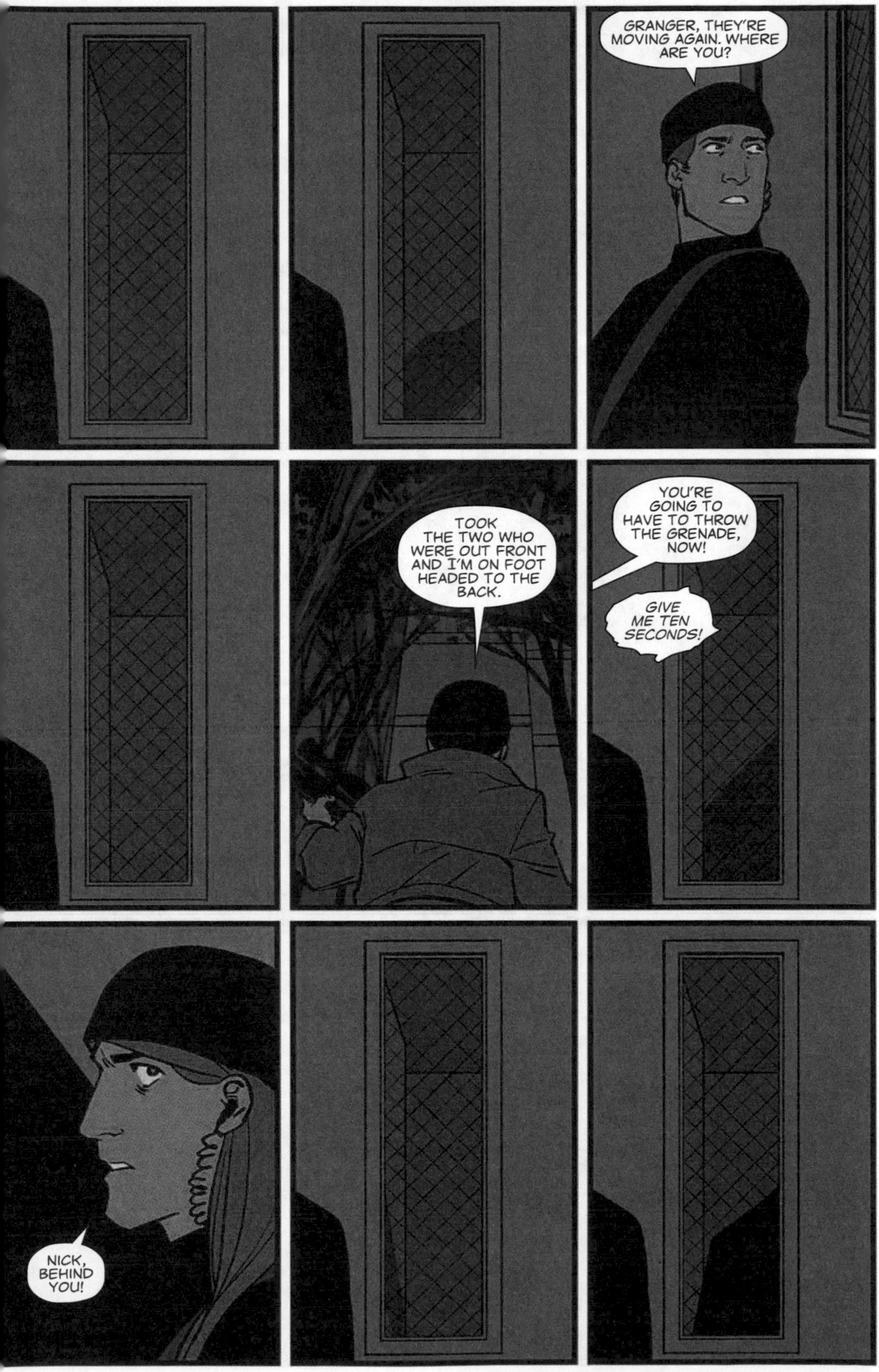
GRANGER, THEY'RE MOVING AGAIN. WHERE ARE YOU?
TOOK THE TWO WHO WERE OUT FRONT AND I'M ON FOOT HEADED TO THE BACK.
YOU'RE GOING TO HAVE TO THROW THE GRENADE, NOW!
GIVE ME TEN SECONDS!
NICK, BEHIND YOU!

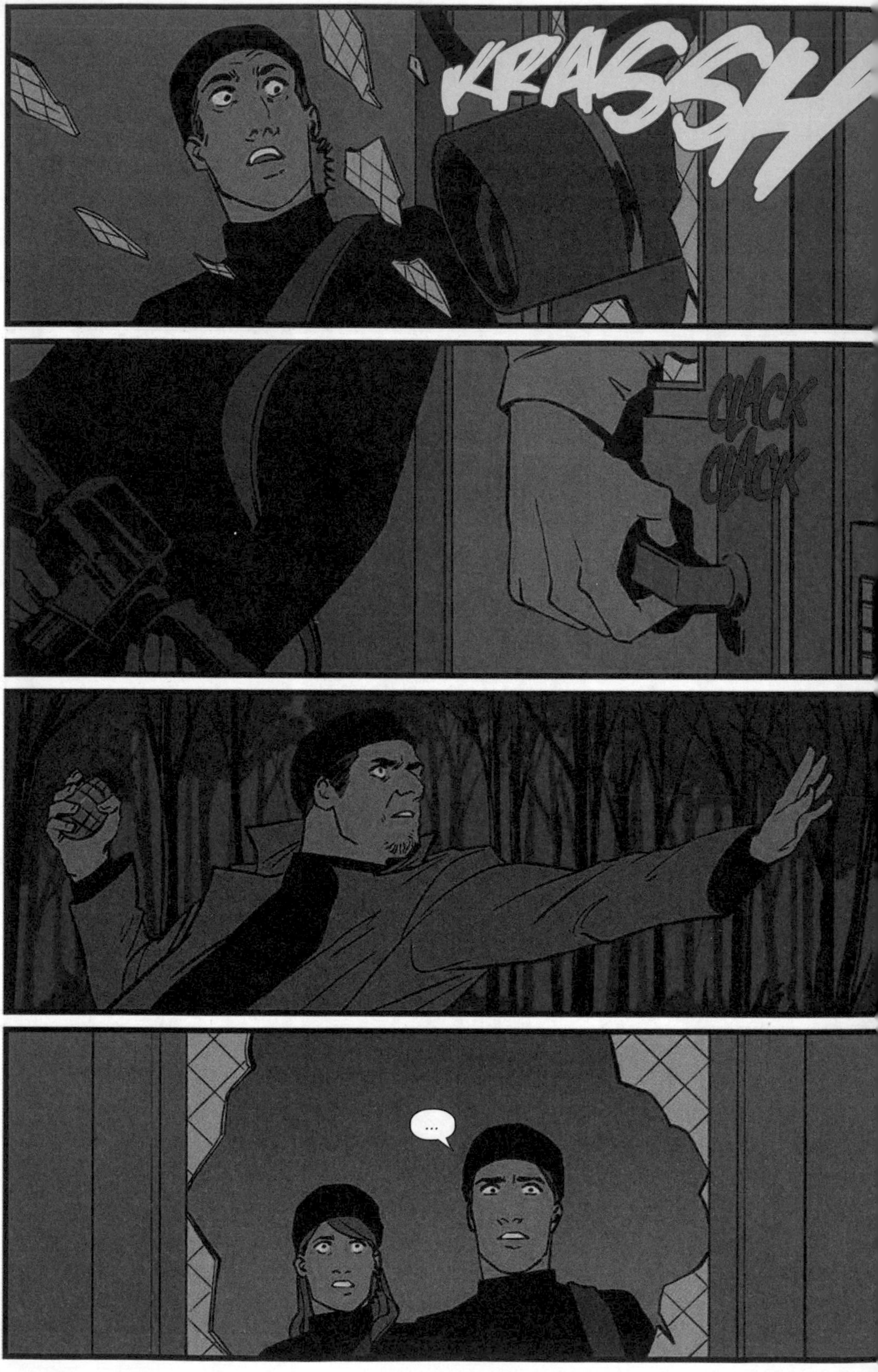
KRASSH
CLACK
CLACK
...

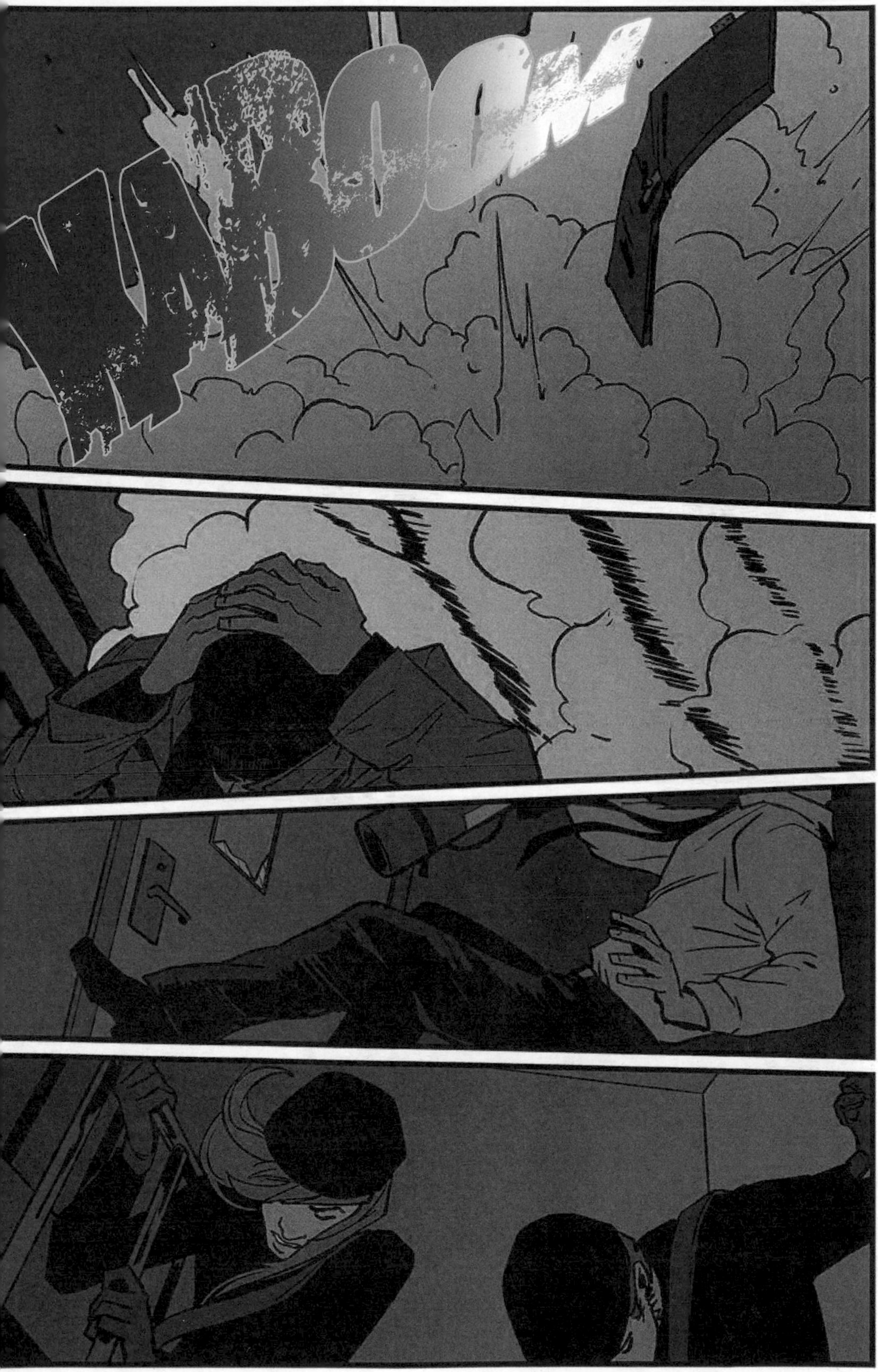
KABOOM

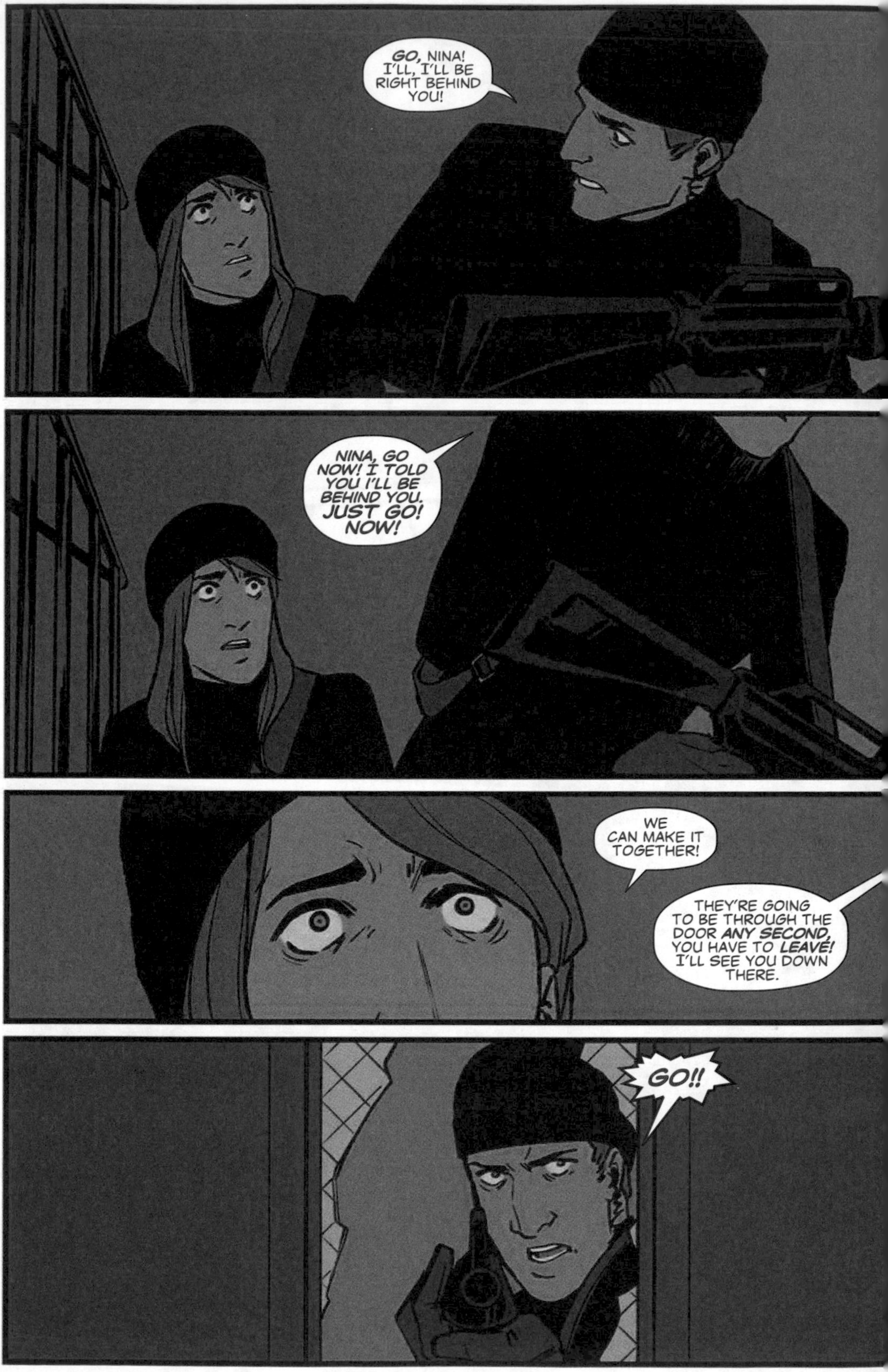
GO, NINA! I'LL, I'LL BE RIGHT BEHIND YOU!
NINA, GO NOW! I TOLD YOU I'LL BE BEHIND YOU. JUST GO! NOW!
WE CAN MAKE IT TOGETHER!
THEY'RE GOING TO BE THROUGH THE DOOR ANY SECOND, YOU HAVE TO LEAVE! I'LL SEE YOU DOWN THERE.
GO!!

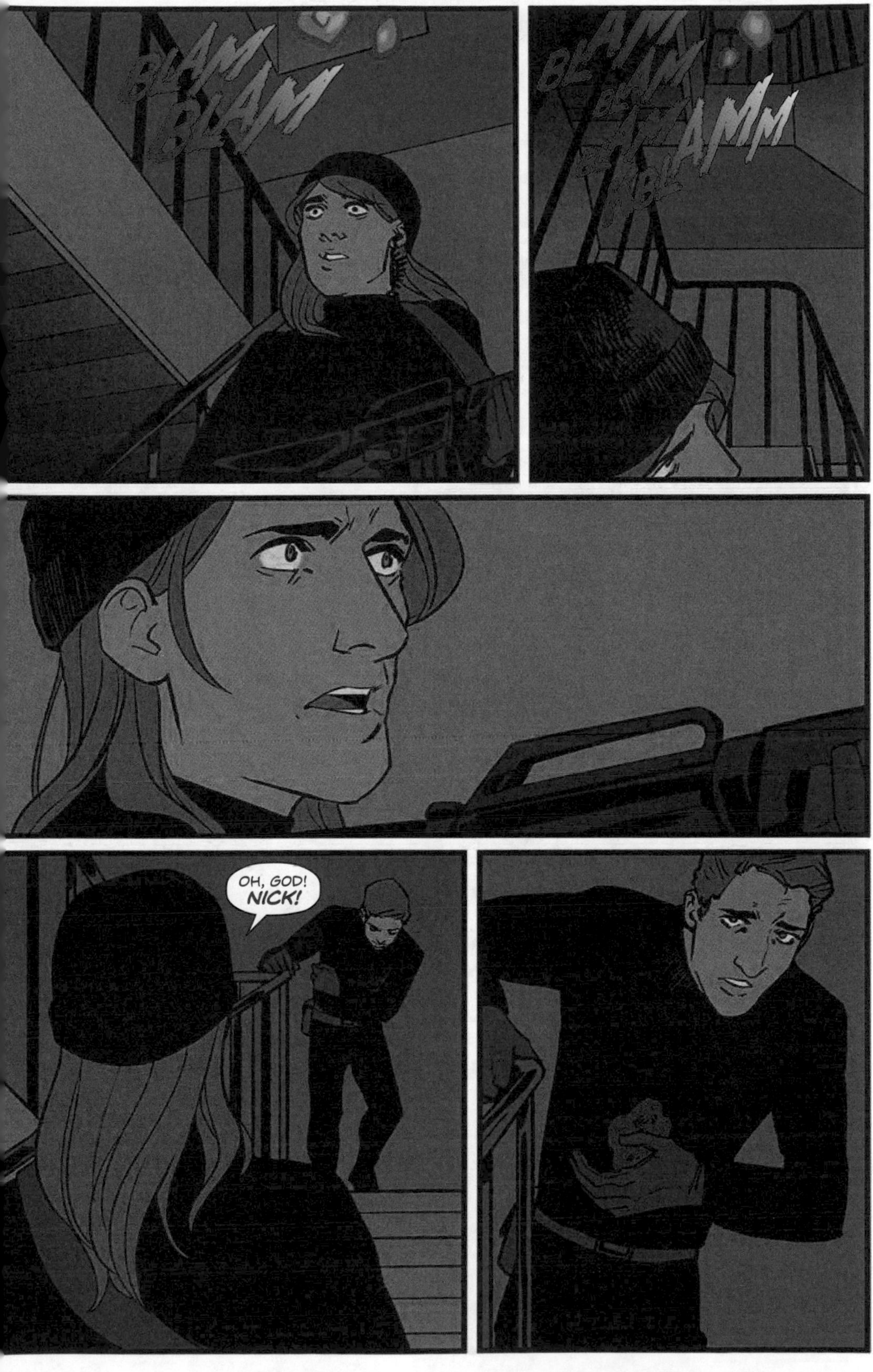
BLAM BLAM
BLAM BLAM BLAM BLAM KBLAMM
OH, GOD! NICK!

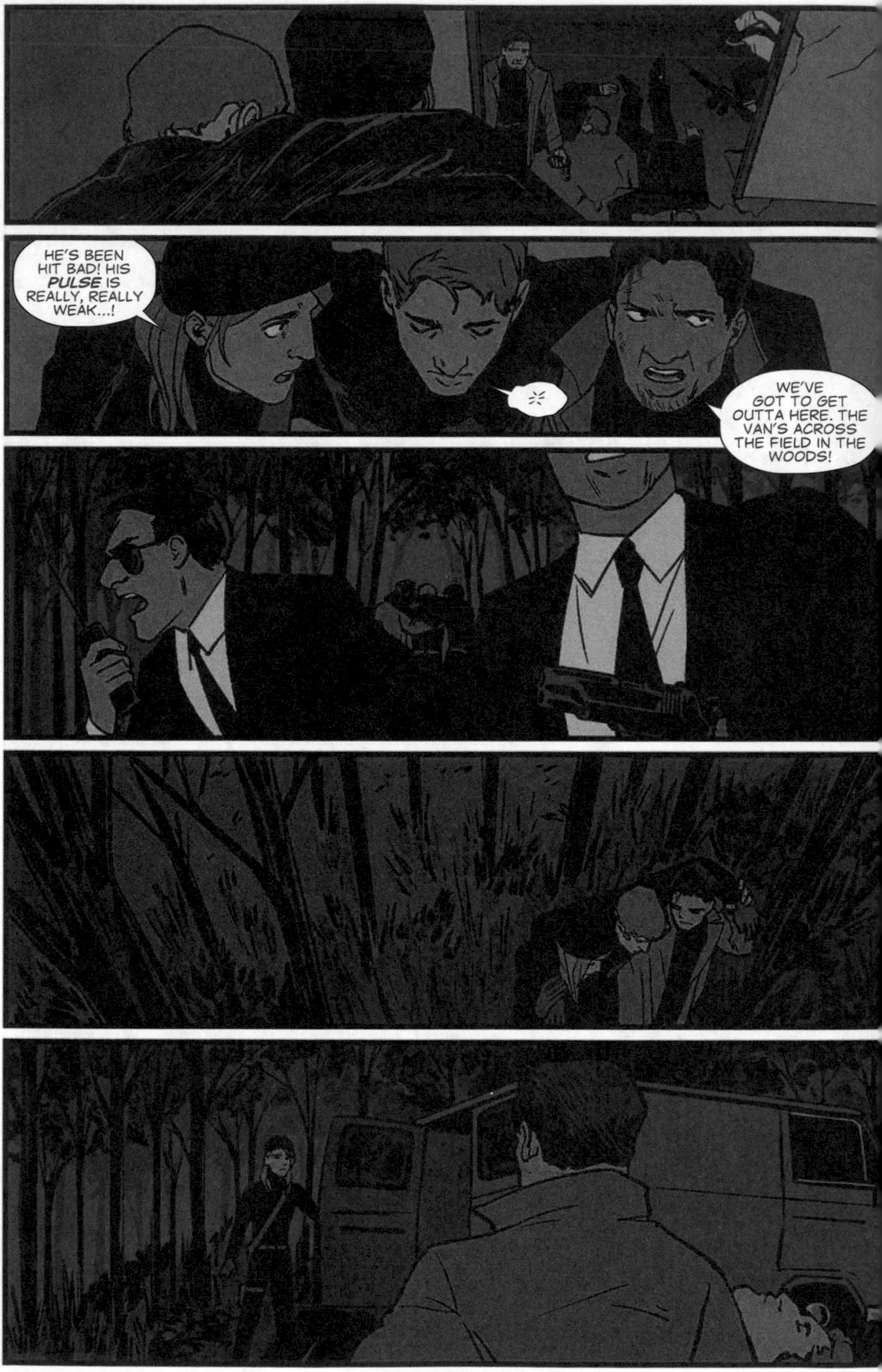

HE'S BEEN HIT BAD! HIS *PULSE* IS REALLY, REALLY WEAK...!
WE'VE GOT TO GET OUTTA HERE. THE VAN'S ACROSS THE FIELD IN THE WOODS!

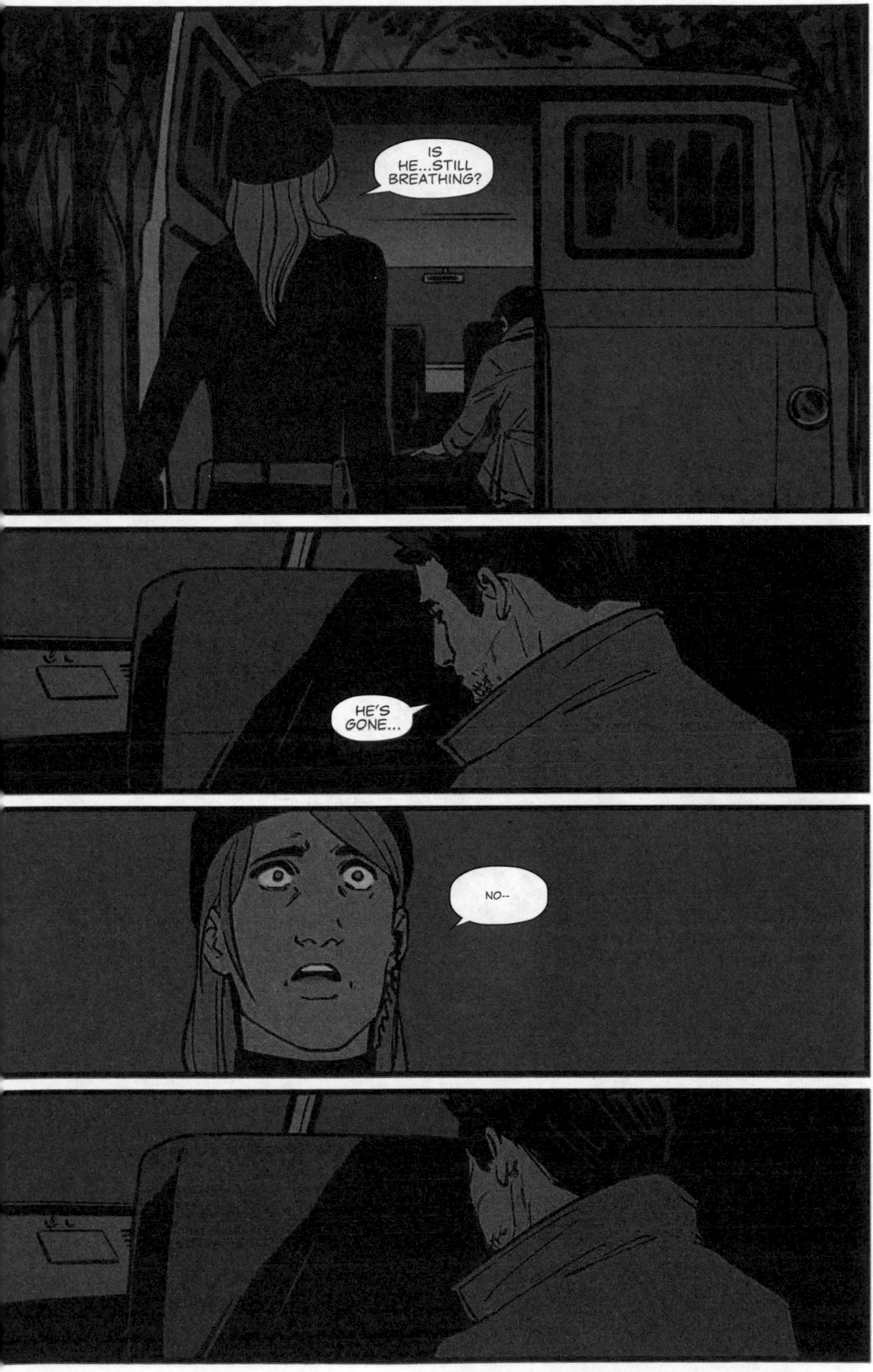
IS HE...STILL BREATHING?
HE'S GONE...
NO--

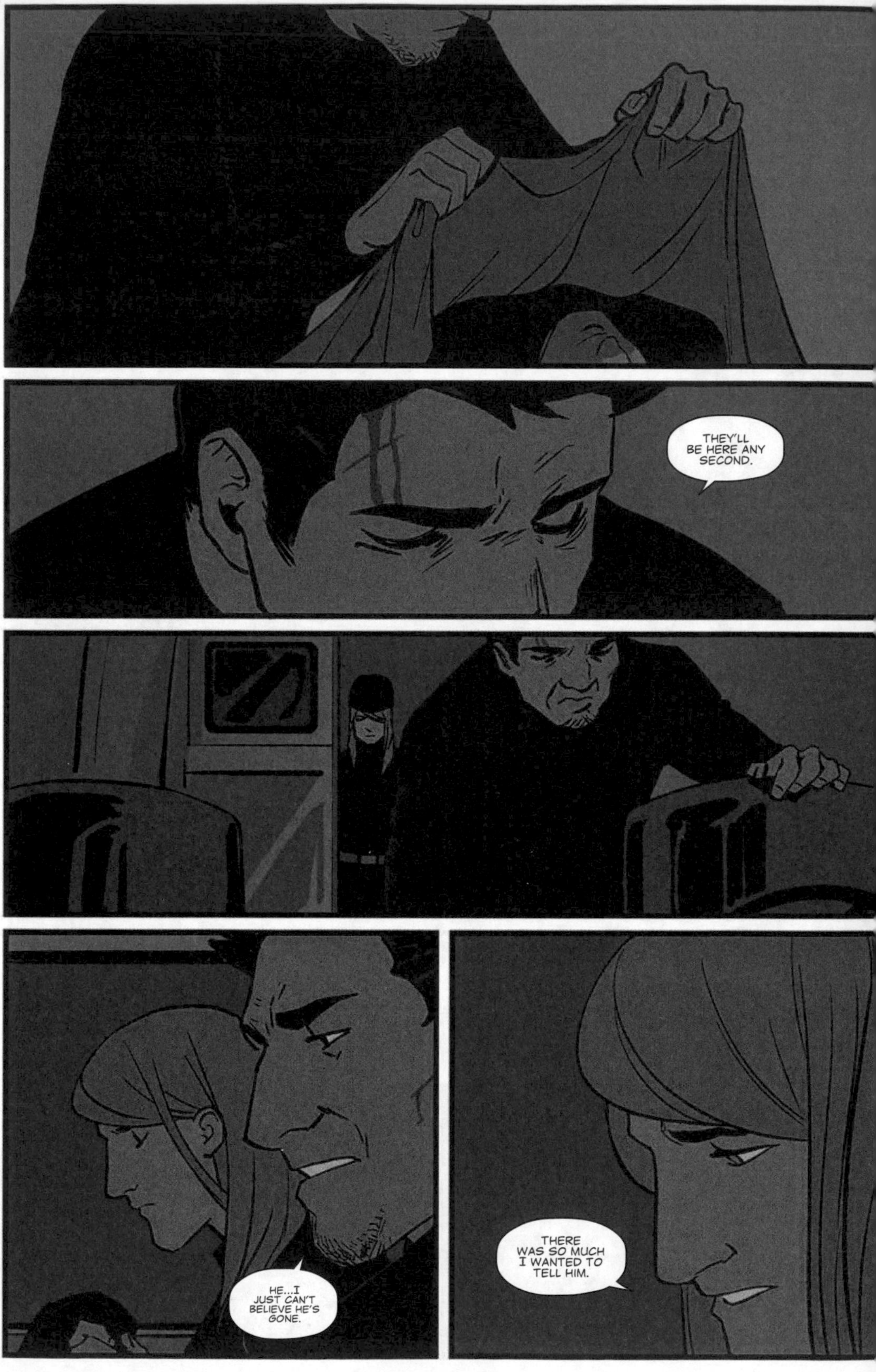
THEY'LL BE HERE ANY SECOND.
HE...I JUST CAN'T BELIEVE HE'S GONE.
THERE WAS SO MUCH I WANTED TO TELL HIM.

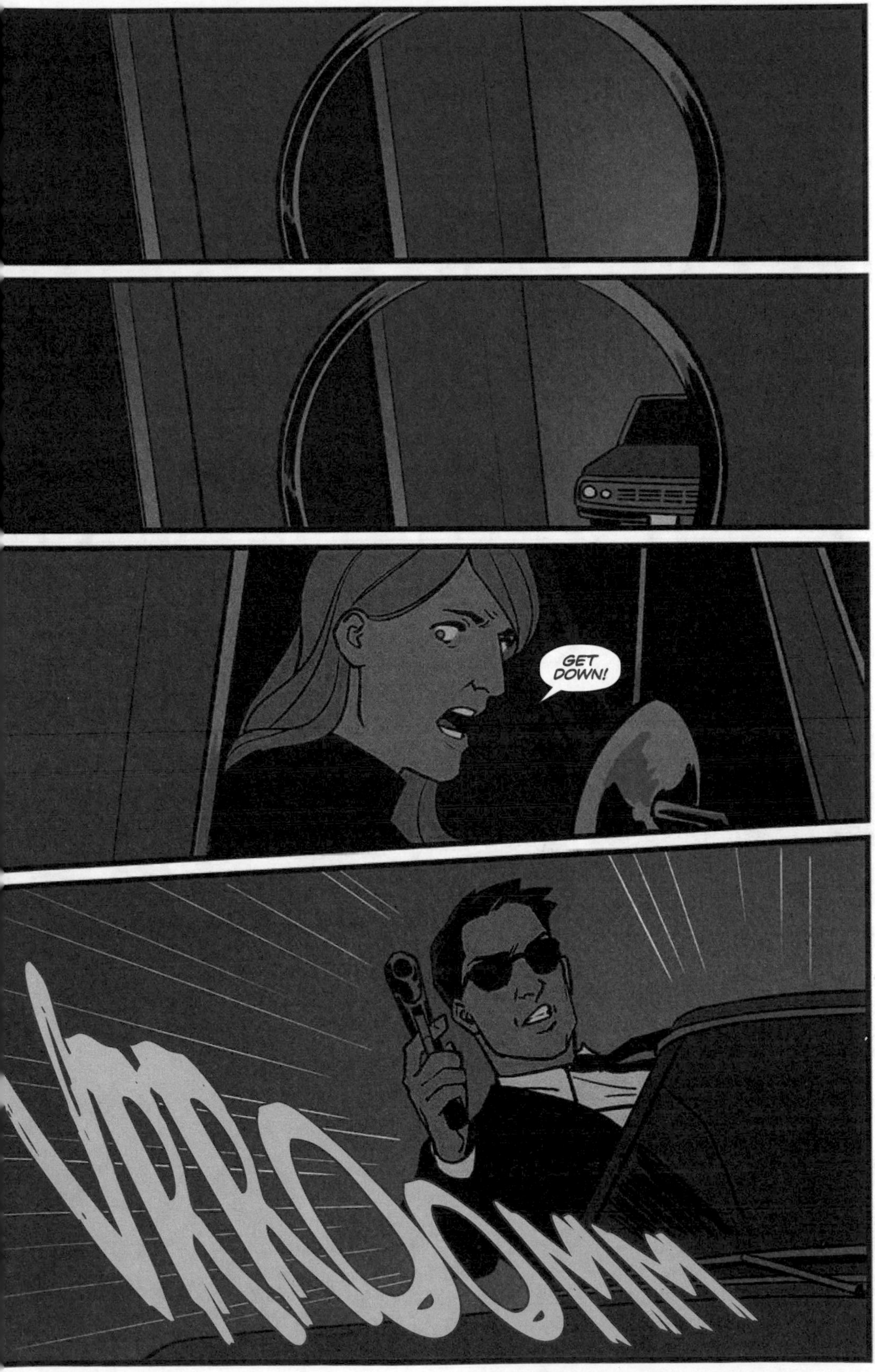
GET DOWN!
VRROOMM

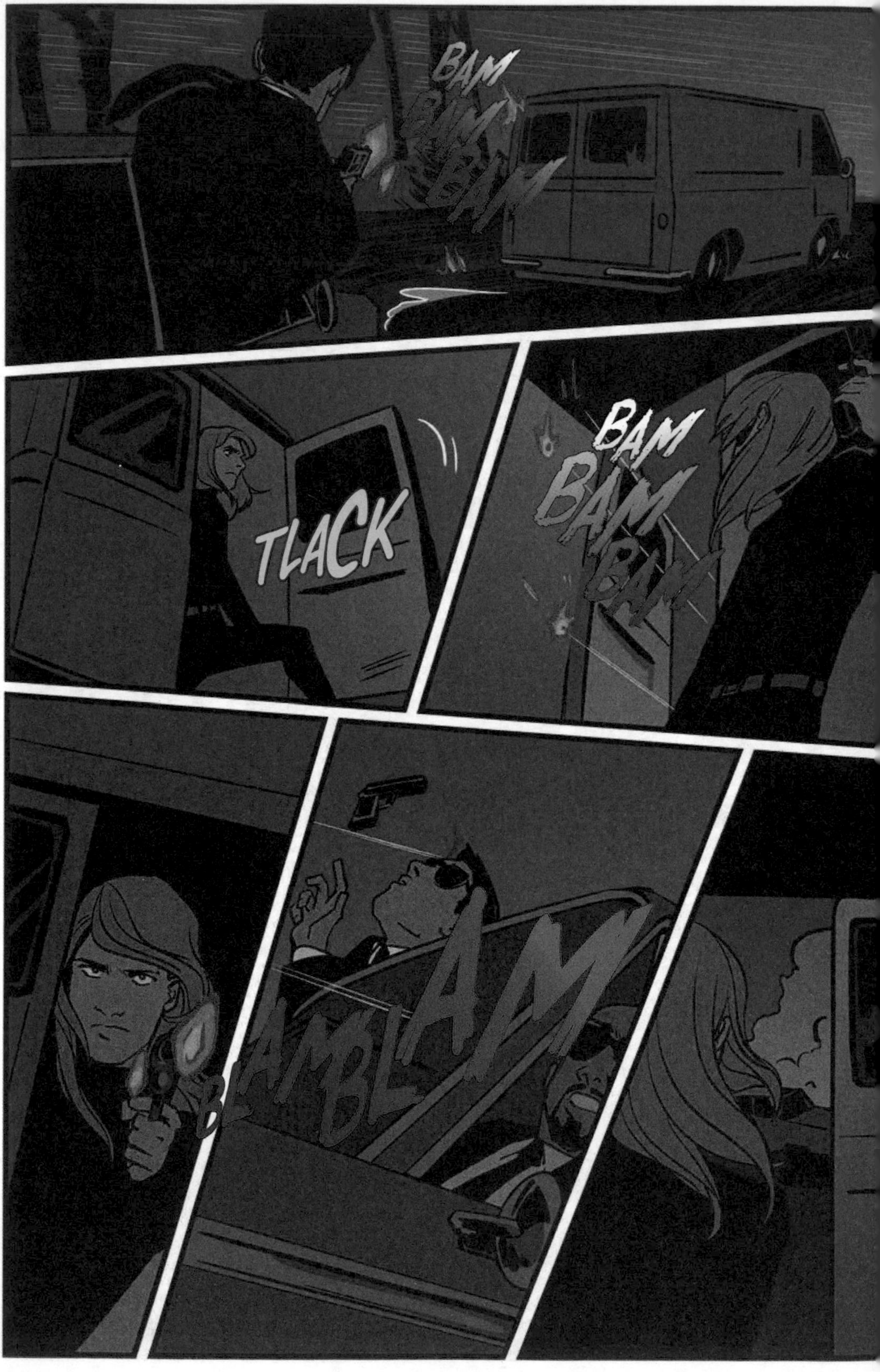
BAM BAM BAM
TLACK
BAM BAM BAM
BLAMBLAM

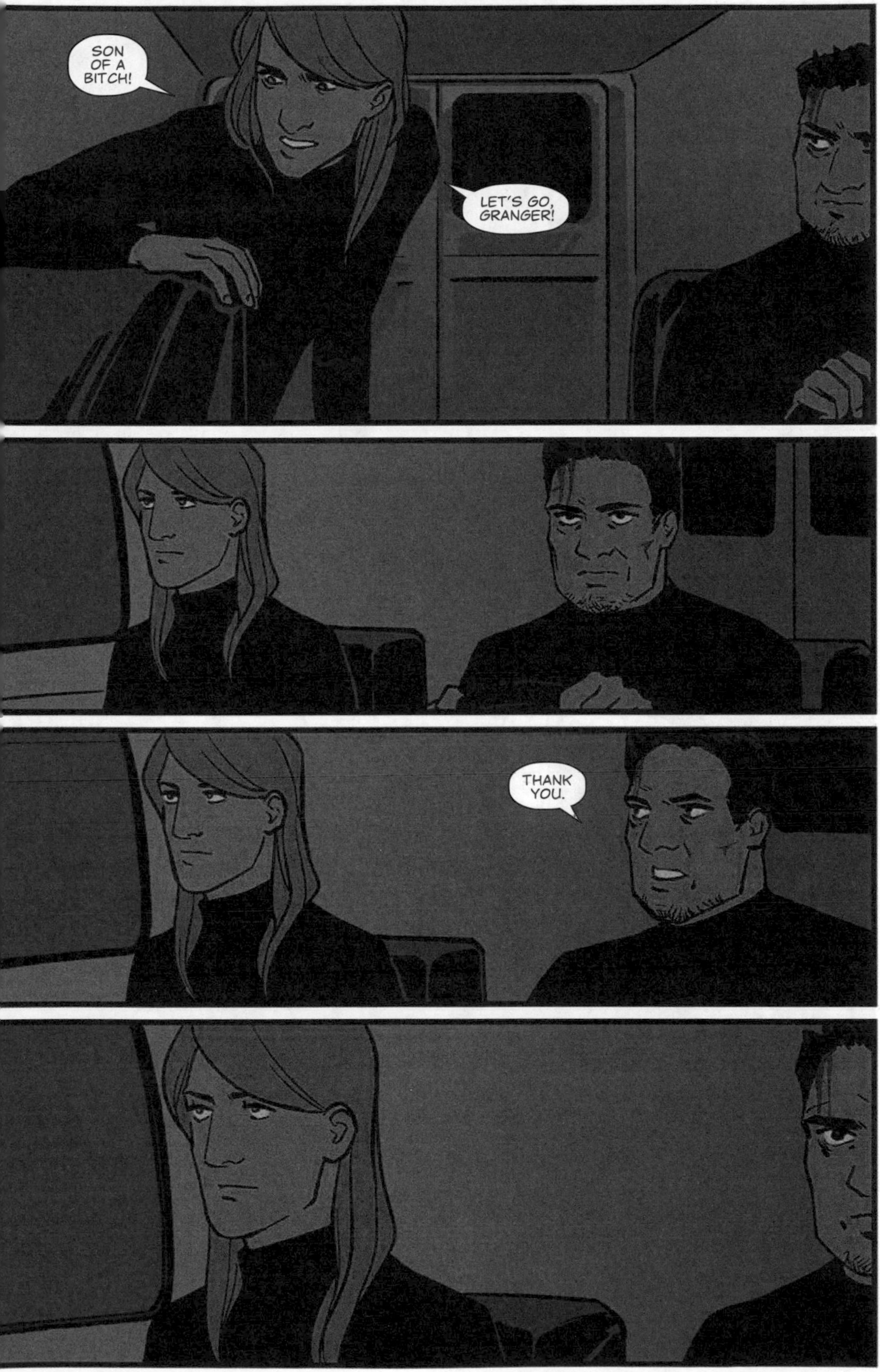
SON OF A BITCH!
LET'S GO, GRANGER!
THANK YOU.

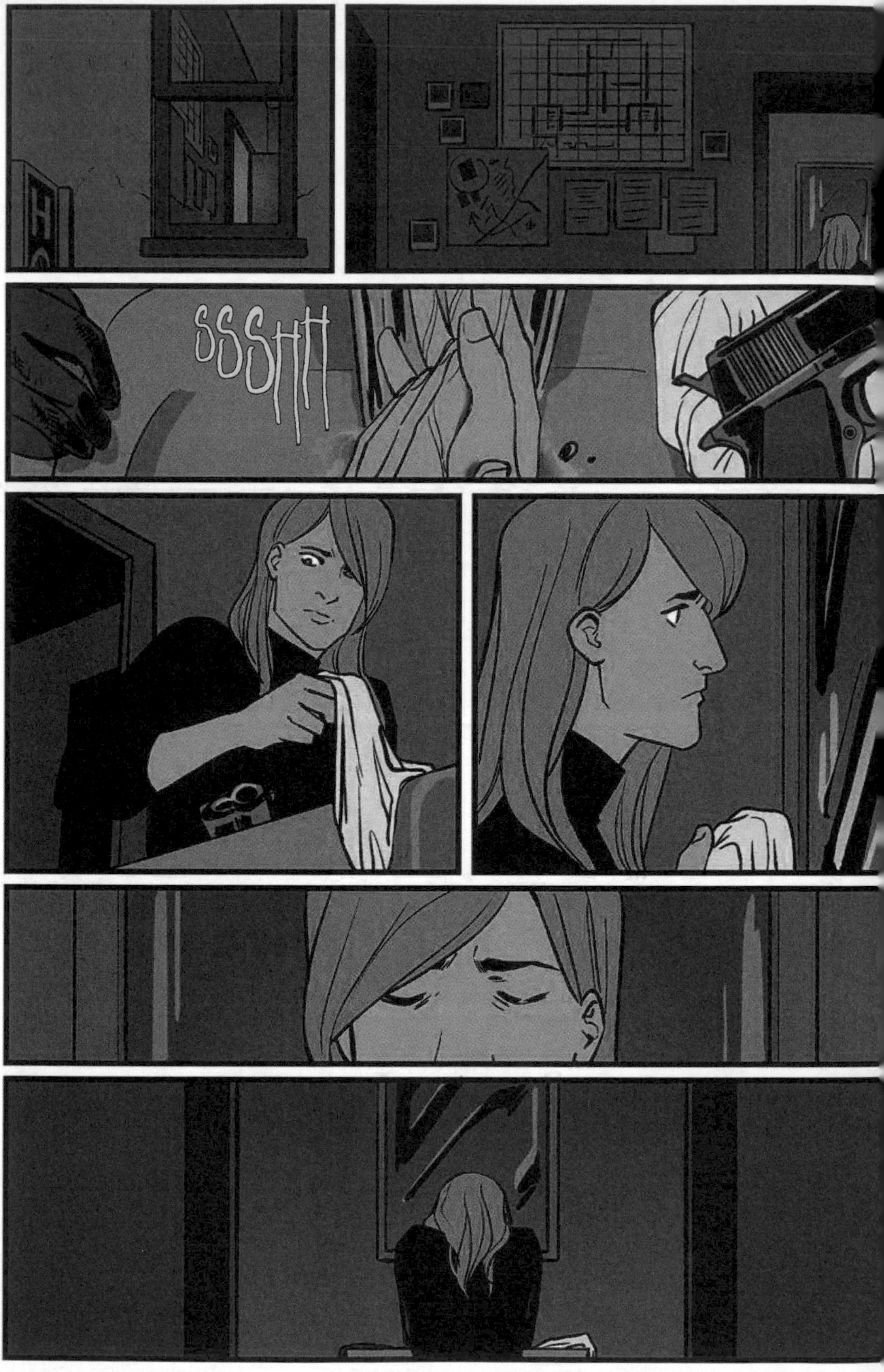
SSSHH

RECOMMENDED LISTENING:

DON'T WORRY 'BOUT ME
BY SARAH VAUGHAN

LITTLE WING
BY JIMI HENDRIX (AS COVERED BY DEREK AND THE DOMINOES)

ONE HEADLIGHT
BY THE WALLFLOWERS

HE'S WALKING THROUGH THE CLOUDS
BY NINA OVERSTREET

CHAPTER THIRTEEN

Drive It Home (Pretty Little Liar)

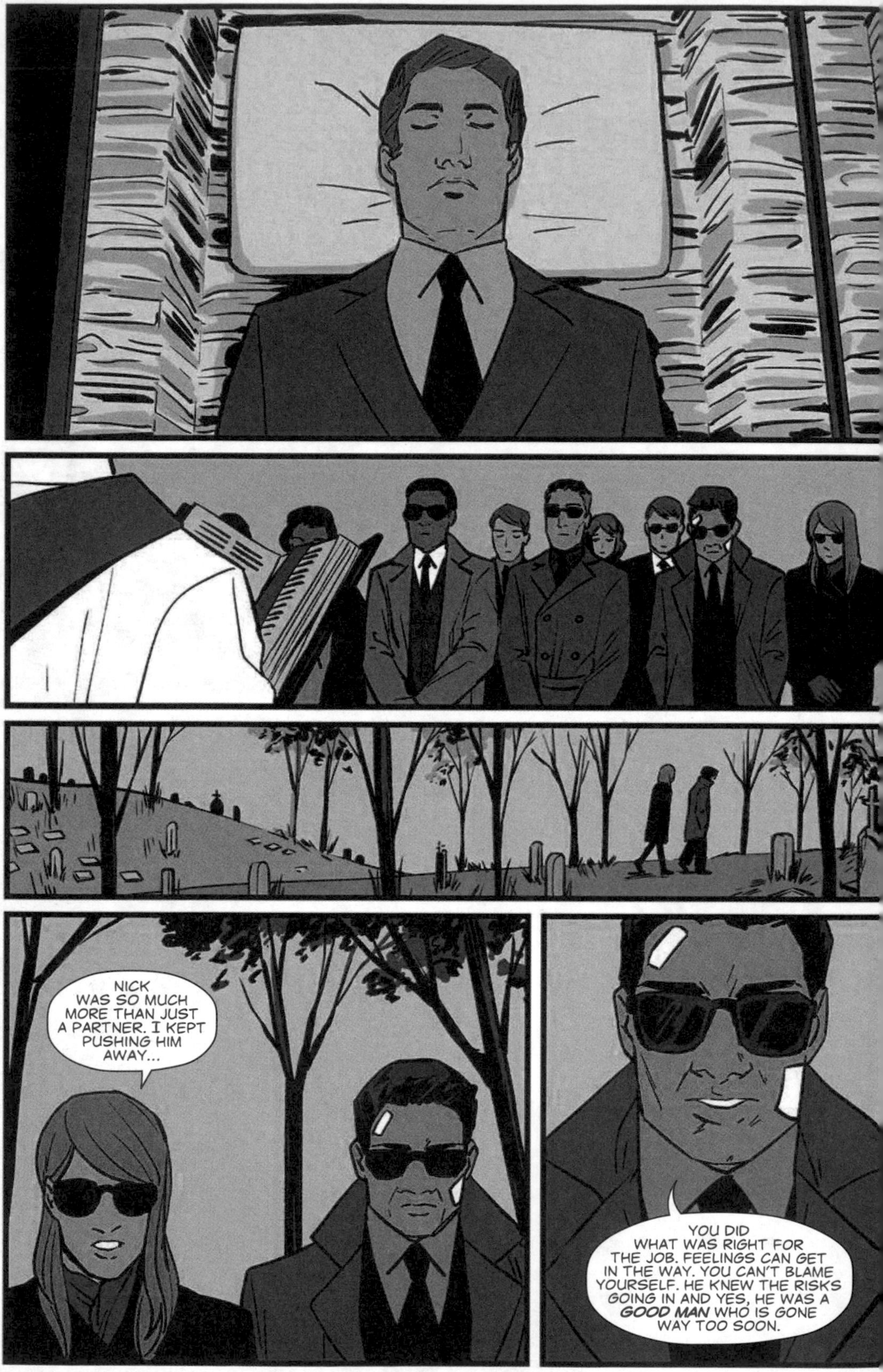
NICK WAS SO MUCH MORE THAN JUST A PARTNER. I KEPT PUSHING HIM AWAY...
YOU DID WHAT WAS RIGHT FOR THE JOB. FEELINGS CAN GET IN THE WAY. YOU CAN'T BLAME YOURSELF. HE KNEW THE RISKS GOING IN AND YES, HE WAS A GOOD MAN WHO IS GONE WAY TOO SOON.

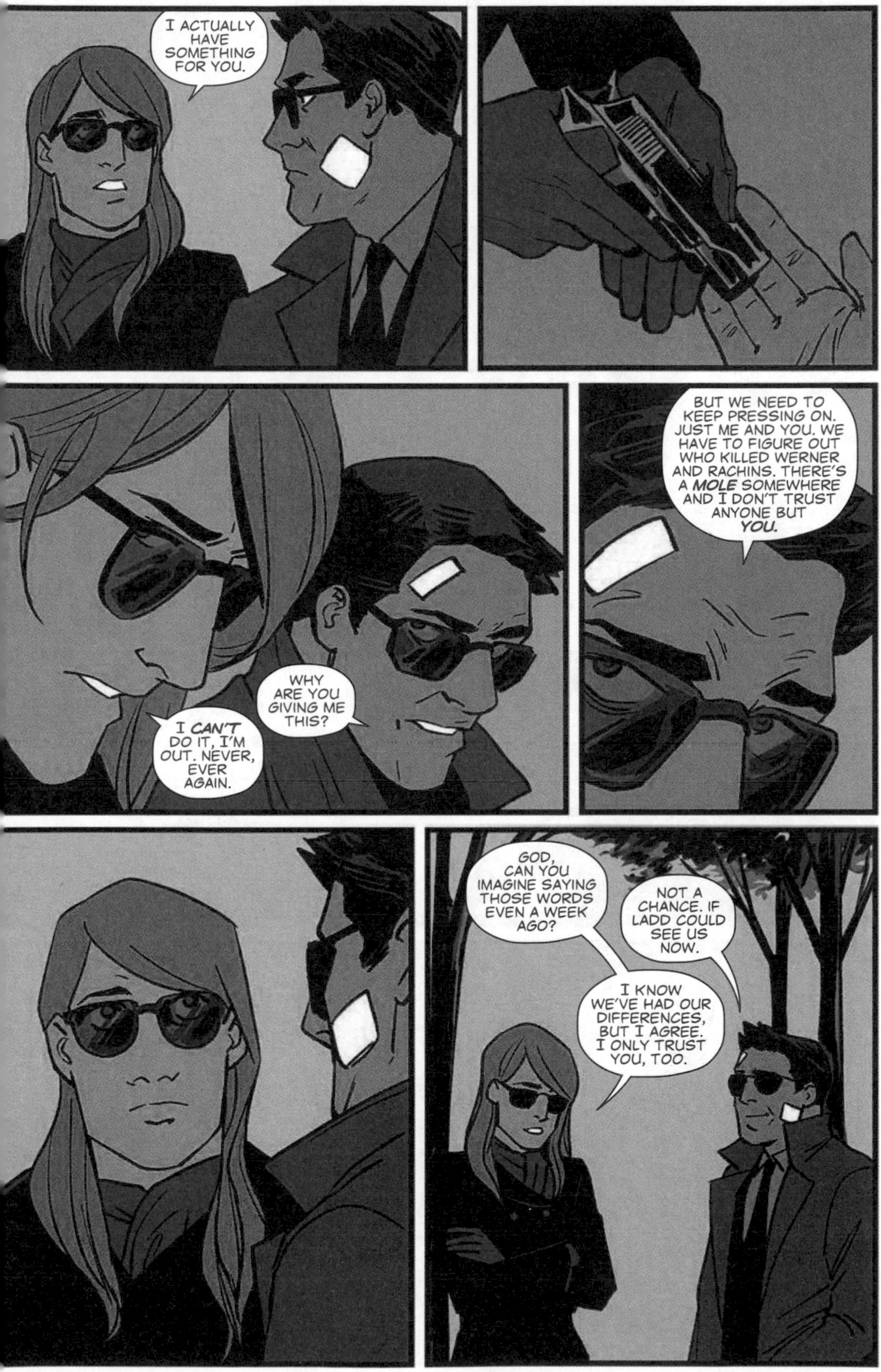
I ACTUALLY HAVE SOMETHING FOR YOU.
WHY ARE YOU GIVING ME THIS?
I *CAN'T* DO IT, I'M OUT. NEVER, EVER AGAIN.
BUT WE NEED TO KEEP PRESSING ON. JUST ME AND YOU. WE HAVE TO FIGURE OUT WHO KILLED WERNER AND RACHINS. THERE'S A *MOLE* SOMEWHERE AND I DON'T TRUST ANYONE BUT *YOU.*
GOD, CAN YOU IMAGINE SAYING THOSE WORDS EVEN A WEEK AGO?
NOT A CHANCE. IF LADD COULD SEE US NOW.
I KNOW WE'VE HAD OUR DIFFERENCES, BUT I AGREE. I ONLY TRUST YOU, TOO.

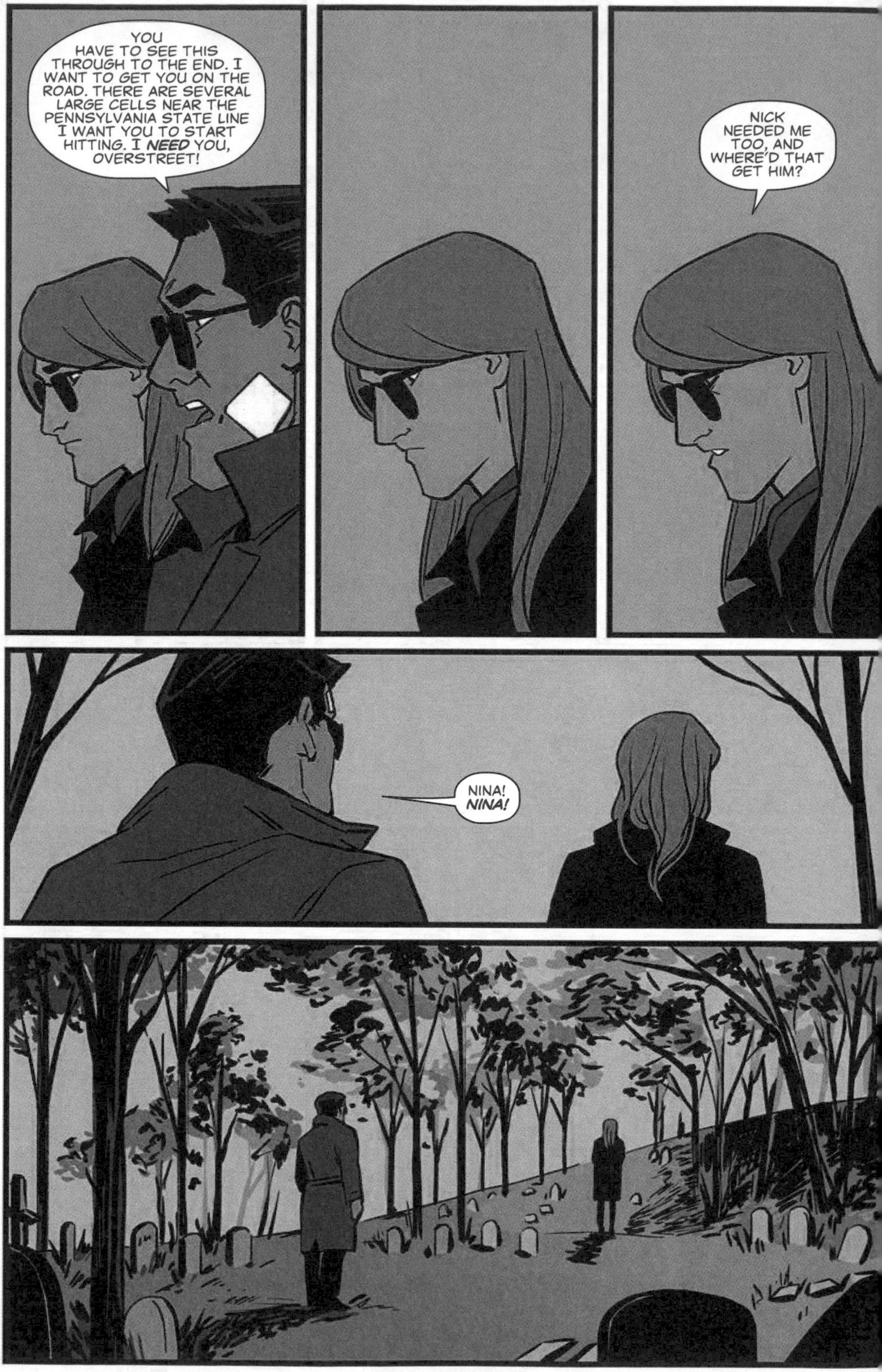
YOU HAVE TO SEE THIS THROUGH TO THE END. I WANT TO GET YOU ON THE ROAD. THERE ARE SEVERAL LARGE CELLS NEAR THE PENNSYLVANIA STATE LINE I WANT YOU TO START HITTING. I *NEED* YOU, OVERSTREET!
NICK NEEDED ME TOO, AND WHERE'D THAT GET HIM?
NINA! *NINA!*

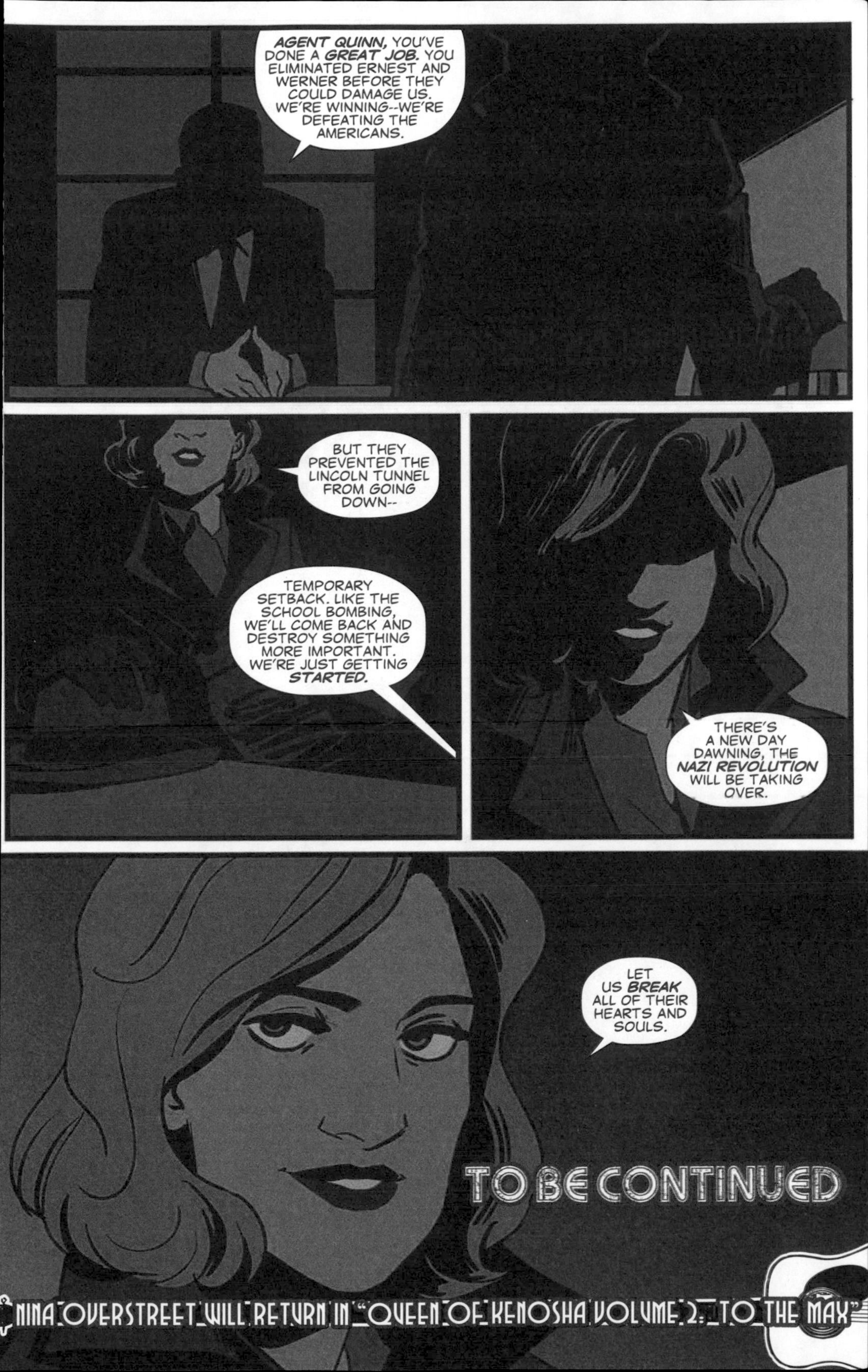
AGENT QUINN, YOU'VE DONE A GREAT JOB. YOU ELIMINATED ERNEST AND WERNER BEFORE THEY COULD DAMAGE US. WE'RE WINNING--WE'RE DEFEATING THE AMERICANS.
BUT THEY PREVENTED THE LINCOLN TUNNEL FROM GOING DOWN--
TEMPORARY SETBACK. LIKE THE SCHOOL BOMBING, WE'LL COME BACK AND DESTROY SOMETHING MORE IMPORTANT. WE'RE JUST GETTING STARTED.
THERE'S A NEW DAY DAWNING, THE NAZI REVOLUTION WILL BE TAKING OVER.
LET US BREAK ALL OF THEIR HEARTS AND SOULS.
TO BE CONTINUED
NINA OVERSTREET WILL RETURN IN "QUEEN OF KENOSHA VOLUME 2: TO THE MAX"

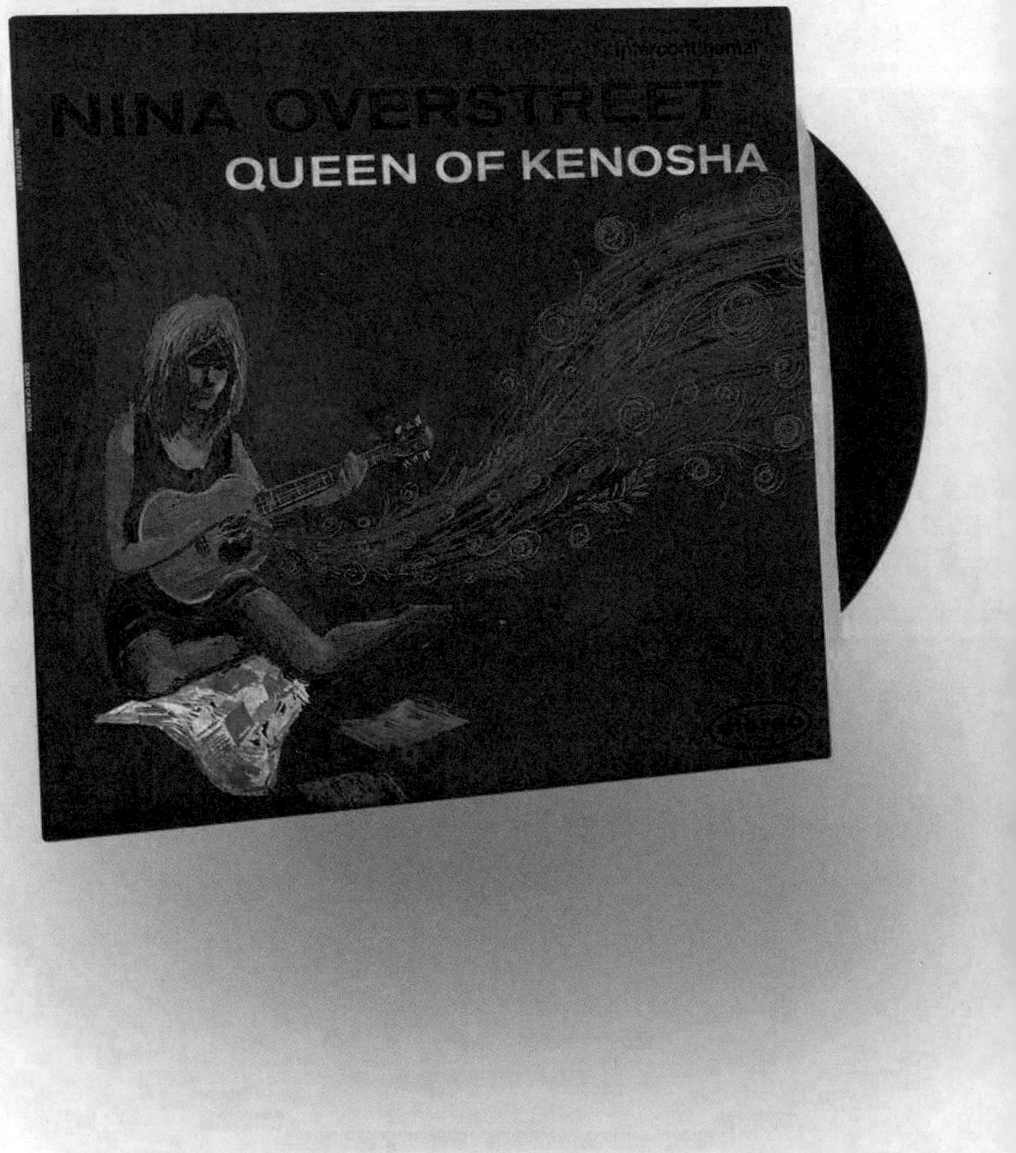
NINA OVERSTREET
QUEEN OF KENOSHA

Love Makes No Sense

You came into the room
Just a few words you had to say
How should I presume
What might have happened if you decided to stay

I don't understand why you can't see
That I'm trying to be who you want me to be
Why do you keep straddling the fence
Is it because you know that love makes no sense

Good person I try to be
Show you how much I care
Questions I ask you are answer free
While I ask the lord to answer my prayer
Please bring him into my life
Instead of this pain cutting like a knife

I don't understand why you can't see
That I'm trying to be who you want me to be
Why do you keep straddling the fence
Is it because you know that love makes no sense

Find myself in New York City
At the bus station there was no welcoming committee
Following a dream
But the hometown boys won't let me join the team
No money to pay for my two leases
Like Patsy sang "I Fall To Pieces"

I'm too far gone and there's no going back
I'm trying to avoid this new kind of heart attack
I think about you and me and what could be
Is it too late for a restart?
A part of you will be in my heart
Even if we are forever apart

Help Me From Myself

Help from myself
As I see my future before my eyes
Make the decision that will haunt me
No choice, no choice at all
Still, let me out alive

As I listen for to the voice inside my head
Saying nothing at all
I lay here and wonder
Does it all end like this?
Promises are made, blood for blood
Why me and why now?
For a moment just tell me you'll end it all
No! Please don't pull the trigger
As the barrel sits next to my temple
I'll handle this one by myself

Oh yeah, oh yeah by myself
Something to live for
Not someone, but I can do this
Not going fall into the trap
And pray to the lord above
To save me, save me from myself

Myself, myself
To whom I may harm
Please forgive me and
Help me from myself
Help me from myself
Help me from myself

(I'm The) Queen of Kenosha

Just like the politician attending the opening of an envelope
I'm all about the attention
And just like addict wanting more dope
I'm all about the hit with no apprehension
I'm foolish and young
From an area that's far flung
That which can never be hurled
I'm going to conquer the world

Stardom, I'm the Queen of Kenosha
So far from home
I'm going to hit you like a supernova
All alone on the street I roam

I'll go where the chosen one goes
And drift around the west side of New York City
A thousand young poets and their beautiful prose
Maybe just one of them will think I'm pretty
But I'm not looking for love
Or somebody to shove
I will not be denied
I want my fame to be worldwide

Stardom, I'm the Queen of Kenosha
Looking for a big time deal
Gonna go straight to number one in Nova Scotia
Look at me now, I've got nothing to conceal

I'm never going back
Never gonna play Franks Diner wearing a backwards Snap On hat
The leader of the pack
The biggest, baddest black cat
Now I'm a tiny fish in the big blue sea
You think futility is my destiny
A thousand locks with no key
You'll see that the power rests with me

Stardom, I'm the Queen of Kenosha
So far from home
I'm going to hit you like a supernova
All alone on the street I roam

A Hostage of the Soul

You and me, we see things differently
My advantage, your roadblock
I say that the circle is unbroken
You hear my words as unspoken

[Chorus:]
A hostage of the soul
Live a day in my shoes you said
See the invisible forces who are in control

Free or freedom
The choice is determined
I think I know you pretty well
You say I haven't scratched the surface
We can play pretend
And act like it doesn't matter
That I want to give you my heart
Because you say we're worlds apart

[Chorus:]
A hostage of the soul
Live a day in my shoes you said
See the invisible forces who are in control

Across the great divide
I can't give you up
I hope you can hear
Hear me say that I can't change the system
But with you, I want to form the resistance

[Chorus:]
A hostage of the soul
Live a day in my shoes you said
See the invisible forces who are in control

Have I Run Too Far To Get Home?

Standing in the shadows
My rapid heartbeat finally slows

Into the fire again
Same old story as before
My mistakes are always on view
But try and see that my aim is true

You pull away and away from me
While all I asked was for some honesty

Into the fire again
Same old story as before
My mistakes are always on view
But try and see that my aim is true

Into the fire again
Same old story as before
My mistakes are always on view
But try and see that my aim is true

[x2:]
Have I run, run too far to get home?
What did I do that was so wrong?
When did it go so far away?

Are you now and forever gone?
You've left me here all alone

This Time Will Pass

You think that it's justified
When nothing is ever wrong, then what is ever right?
Substituting your love for pride
Your black hat turns to white

Let it all slide
Is that what you get to decide?
What a gorgeous song to sing
It must be good to be king

You see things your own way
And look at me crooked
Tell me to stand up straight
That you'll determine my fate
My opinions mean nothing

You say pull yourself together
It's a momentary lapse of reason
As this time will pass

Later is never better
I want it all right now
Because this time will pass

I find you so mesmerizing
Something about you that speaks to me
So much I want to experience
To listen to your voice, to see what you see

I feel like such a fool
To overthink things like I do
I make myself miserable
My love for you is considerable
But you keep pushing me away
Bye, bye baby

You say pull yourself together
It's a momentary lapse of reason
As this time will pass

My love, see what's in front of you
It's a momentary lapse of reason
As this time will pass

I questioned myself, should I take the leap
The climb's not bad 'till you discover how steep

Everytime I'm around you I feel so weak
Ask you questions, but your answers are so oblique

You say pull yourself together
It's a momentary lapse of reason
As this time will pass

Later is never better
I want it all right now
Because this time will pass

And if you go your own way
And if you never look back
And if your better situation wanes
As the winds whip through the great plains

You got caught in a moment
This time must pass

Circle of Deception

Man on the tower
Screaming at the top of his lungs
About fighting the power
And raising all of our guns
"We're all on the firing line
And the killing floor"
The crowd below laughs saying he's asinine
The cop looking up says he's done for

It's the circle of deception
He defies our perception
Maybe we're the crazy ones
We should watch who we shun

The lunatic fringe
And the insane underbelly
Saying things that make you cringe
Like they want the return of Machiavelli
Still, their rights are guaranteed
It's something we can never forget
Their intentions, we cannot misread
Far too many died for us to not pay back that debt

It's the circle of deception
He defies our perception
Maybe we're the crazy ones
We should watch who we shun

Ship Liberty Sailed Away

Lonesome cowboy at sunset
A star spangled true warrior
Collecting a big red white and blue debt
Doesn't realize we are all foreigners

Ship liberty sailed away
Everything built up gets knocked down
Ship liberty sailed away
The good guys have all left town

Losing my faith rapidly
When did upholding the greater good
Turn the strong towards apathy
There goes the entire neighborhood
If that's the case, it's game over
The country is in the midst of a unfriendly takeover
The gatekeeper opened the gates
And let the wild horses run free

(X2)
Ship liberty sailed away
Everything built up gets knocked down
Ship liberty sailed away
The good guys have all left town

I Made it There Somehow

I left it there for you to see, but I don't know if you heard
You are the key to my existence, no pressure or anything
I'll give you my everything, if you'll give me half a chance
Oh those words you said, it's a bit too unreal
Working at it my whole life, none of that matters now
Line them up and I'll slay them all, one by one watch them fall
I made it there somehow

You and I, there seems to be something deep down
I look for the signs, you do too
We spread it here and we spread it there
Hard to get past you being cherry red and I'm true blue

Can't drop my resistance
My stone cold façade
Please understand why I keep my distance
So many close to me have been taken away by God

You wanna be more then friends, that's the signal you send
As we go in for the kill, that's when I get my fill
I made it there somehow

I recognize the symptoms, but I don't know about the cure
Your feelings are so useless, your persistence just keeps time
You think the walls will crumble, the doors will be less secure
I hate the game, I feel like I'm committing a crime

All that heaven will allow
I made it there somehow

Quiet No More

You treat me like a parent to a child
"Keep your thoughts and feelings reconciled"
It's not going to work like that

Like the king on the chessboard
Like the white knight brandishing his silver sword
I had held you in such high esteem
So why change horses in midstream?
I just can't let it go by
Living a giant lie
I won't back down from this war
I'll be quiet no more

Like the bullet loaded into the chamber
The cannonball in the cannon
There will be no fragrant beads of amber
But I will give you my red bandana
As I explode in fists of rage
I swear by this song
The animal is out of the cage
No apologies for I have done nothing wrong

A man behind bars
He said to me "Please come to my rescue."
Tears in my eyes I said "I'm sorry for failing you."
But no more
I won't back down from this war
I'll be quiet no more

Nothing Can Harm Me At All

Leaves in the fall
Nothing can harm me at all
Going to tear down your walls
None of those storms will make landfall

I feel you nearby
And never have to ask you why
The sun comes out at night
My darkness turns to light

Your inner circle says
"She's no good for you"
But what do they see?
It's not the real me
The neighborhood, will never set us free
You tell me, what's it going to be?
The choice rests with you
To see me through

Nothing can harm me at all
My problems & worries are so very small
For each night I beg and pray
That you'll be with me for a million days

The Price Was Loaded From The Start

Jools and Jim walking on the first day of spring
He takes her hand and says, you and me, how 'bout it?
She laughs and says why ruin a good thing...
You really surprised me, I must admit

Jim says, it's all good no worries
Jools stops and pulls back
Why make the lines so blurry
We're good as is, lets not go down that track

Jim, the price was loaded from the start
The secret is to know when to stop
Don't tell me I exploded into your heart
And please don't go out on a limb
It's just that the time's not now, Jim

We came from different places
Have run different races
Dreams can be so cruel
Especially when they're never gonna come true

He says you can fall for someone prettier
Someone who can talk a good game and who's a lot wittier
But I'll be there when the deal is done
When he leaves because he wasn't having fun

I can't promise you everything
But I'll be there through thick and thin
There's a place for us beyond the stars
No, Jim, it's not sink or swim
And it's just that the time's not now, Jim

I can't sing like the guy on the radio
And sometimes my thoughts are too slow
But I promise I'd give all of you my everything
Heads over heels in love with you is what I'd bring
Things will never be the same between us
Jim, we can't go back to an easier time
For in you I do trust
To string you along would be a crime

Jim, the price was loaded from the start
The secret is to know when to stop
Don't tell me I exploded into your heart
And please don't go out on a limb
It's just that the time's not now, Jim

He's Walking Through The Clouds

Well, he's walking through the clouds
He was too good to hang around this place
Rode out with the wind
On the way to outer space

Digital black epilogue
The sun rises at the funeral at dawn
He never did anything halfway
The preacher says "for his soul, I thee pray"
Heavenly baby
Baby baby please
Just one more time, your hand I'd love to squeeze

Well, he's walking through the clouds
He was too good to hang around this place
Around him the sun came out at night
Too soon gone was his plight

Console myself knowing deep down
He knew how I felt
He ran until there was nothing left
Until the end, forever my friend